MATHEMATICAL METHODS
IN SMALL GROUP PROCESSES

Contributors

Alan R. Anderson · Richard C. Atkinson · Kurt W. Back
C. J. Burke · Robert R. Bush · E. C. Carterette
Bernard P. Cohen · James S. Coleman · Joan H. Criswell
W. K. Estes · Claude Flament · Uriel G. Foa · Robert L. Hall
Georg Karlsson · Bernhardt Lieberman · Irving Lorge
Omar K. Moore · Frank Restle · Thornton B. Roby
Seymour Rosenberg · Madeleine Schlag-Rey
Maynard W. Shelly · William H. Smoke · Herbert Solomon
Patrick Suppes · M. J. Wyman · Robert B. Zajonc

Stanford Mathematical Studies in the Social Sciences, VIII
Editors: Kenneth J. Arrow, Samuel Karlin, and Patrick Suppes

MATHEMATICAL METHODS IN SMALL GROUP PROCESSES

Edited by

JOAN H. CRISWELL
HERBERT SOLOMON
PATRICK SUPPES

STANFORD UNIVERSITY PRESS · STANFORD, CALIFORNIA · 1962

Stanford University Press
Stanford, California
© 1962 by the Board of Trustees of the
Leland Stanford Junior University

Preface

The Symposium on Mathematical Methods in Small Group Processes was held at Stanford University, June 20–23, 1961. It was sponsored by the Institute for Mathematical Studies in the Social Sciences and the Applied Mathematics and Statistics Laboratories of Stanford University, and the Office of Naval Research. The Symposium had its beginnings in the spring of 1960, when discussions which led to its inception first took place. At that time, the two Stanford co-editors presented to Dr. Joan Criswell, who was then with the Group Psychology Branch of the Office of Naval Research, the problem of bringing into focus the developments in mathematical methods in small group research. It was felt that much work had been done, but that the results either were scattered in the literature or had not yet been published. One vehicle for demonstrating a scholarly area to workers in the field is a symposium on the topic followed by publication of the proceedings. It was agreed that the three who are now the editors of this volume would serve as the organizers of the symposium.

The Symposium was intended to set forth current developments in psychological research in small groups, with the limitation that mathematical methods and new experimentation suggested by mathematical developments would be featured. A large body of literature exists on small group research, and so it was in this rather restricted framework that we planned the Symposium.

The papers presented fall into several major categories, but these have not been given names or separated by sections in the volume. It was thought best to present the papers in alphabetical order by author. The Introduction summarizes and relates the content of the 22 papers.

There is a wide variety in the papers that follow, and it is hoped that their appearance in one volume will serve to give some representation of the state of the field as of the summer of 1961 and, in addition, will serve as a point of departure. In fact, in the short time that has passed some of the work presented here is already outdated in the sense that more results have been obtained by several of the authors.

To achieve a measure of stylistic uniformity, a moderate amount of editing has been done on certain papers. Some of the papers have appeared in their original form elsewhere (chapter 1 by Anderson in *Ratio*, and chapter 16 by Moore and Anderson in *The Review of Metaphysics*, 1962, **15**, 409–33). The editors take the responsibility for such minor changes as have been made in the versions of the papers that appear here.

The editors wish to thank the contributors for their cooperation in preparing the papers and in getting them into final form for publication. The generous financial support of the Office of Naval Research and the general helpfulness and encouragement of Dr. Luigi Petrullo of the Group Psychology Branch are gratefully acknowledged. We also wish to record that the Symposium had the official sponsorship of the Division of Logic, Methodology and Philosophy of Science, International Union of History and Philosophy of Science.

THE EDITORS

Washington, D.C.
Stanford, California
May 1962

Contents

MATHEMATICAL METHODS
IN SMALL GROUP PROCESSES

Introduction

Joan H. Criswell, *Department of
Health, Education, and Welfare*

A familiar problem of research methodology is the need to find effective means of introducing mathematical concepts into the collection and analysis of data on interpersonal relations. One attempted solution has been to bring together mathematicians and social scientists in the hope that their interaction would generate the desired mathematical applications. Perhaps more effective than this simple confrontation has been the actual acquisition of social-research knowledge by mathematicians and of mathematical techniques by social scientists. The present symposium brings together a group of such investigators, who combine talent in both areas but exhibit a wide variety of orientations toward the use of mathematics in social research.

In spite of differences of viewpoint, all these contributors have at least one concern in common: an interest in the process analysis of interpersonal relations. Thus their approach contrasts with that of another strong mathematical tendency in social science, the trait-measurement approach typified by a long line of investigators from McDougall with his "sentiments" [7] to Cattell with his "ergs" and "engrams" [1].

In contrast to trait methods, the analysis of interpersonal processes is basically concerned with situational referents of behavior and dynamic patterns of response. The growth of mathematical applications in this area has therefore been associated with the attempt to specify precisely systems of situational and adjustmental elements.

Lewin [6], in his exposition of field theory, was one of the earliest and strongest proponents of the process as contrasted to the trait approach and showed keen awareness of the mathematical implications of this type of treatment. Although his topological methods were unsuccessful, he provided a useful setting for quantitative analysis through his concept of the social space that characterized the stimulus to problem-solving behavior and provided possible pathways to the task goal.

The Lewinian emphasis has become of increasing importance as a part of the growth of interest in social process, since the presentation of the

---

The views expressed are those of the author and are not to be construed as necessarily reflecting those of the Office of Vocational Rehabilitation.

1

stimulus to the subject or subjects is a crucial act in the experimenter-subject pattern of group interaction.

1. Mathematical Analysis of Stimulus Characteristics

In experimental investigations, the stimulus is not something that just happens to the subject. It is prepared, or at least chosen, by the experimenter. Even in field experiments, stimuli are devised in the form of questionnaires, interviews, or adaptations of naturally occurring situations. The situational setting in which the stimulus proper occurs is, or should be, also deliberately chosen, since it has analyzable effects on the subject. This complex of formally defined stimulus against a selected background has come to be called the stimulus situation by those who are interested in the analysis of the stimulus-in-context.

The stimulus situation can be considered very broadly as including all the environmental and background factors impinging on the experimental subject, even including those which may be of very slight influence such as (in most experiments) the weather, the illumination in the room, type of pencil and paper used, etc. In the present discussion, however, the stimulus situation is limited to those factors which are critical to the subject's behavior.

Although some stimulus requirements are more formally job duties than are others, all experimental situations can be considered as essentially problem-solving tasks, even those which elicit a predominantly emotional response. Thus the experimental situation is usually a social encounter in which the subject receives a communication directly or indirectly offering him two kinds of information: certain requirements which he will be rewarded for meeting or punished for not meeting, and certain resources for fulfilling the requirements.

These requirement–reward structures, with some information on means of reaching the specified goal, partially define pathways to the terminating act or acts. In solving the problem so presented, the subject also attempts to satisfy his own personal requirements or needs and to utilize his own personal resources or his repertoire of goal-relevant knowledges and skills.

The study of stimulus-situation structure, then, helps to interpret findings by clarifying the action-generating elements in the experimental setting. In addition, such analysis can lead to the construction of improved experimental treatments which make stimulus elements explicit in some desired way. A comprehensive analysis of such elements would make it possible to set up a classification of treatments indicating the points at which investigations have been adequate and the gaps where new developments are needed. Such a study could lead to construction of new types of experiments. Bush (chapter 5) has pointed out the urgent need for advances of this sort in the mathematical study of group interaction.

The preceding discussion indicates that mathematical methods can be used to analyze the task selected in order to illuminate its intellectual or social demands, the utility of these demands for the subject, and the presence of informational resources which may be correct or incorrect guides to problem solution.

In at least one area already mentioned, that of classifying elements in stimulus material, factor-analytic approaches become relevant to problems of process analysis. Studies such as those of Guilford [2] and Guttman [3] have identified elements of mental-test stimulus content which lead to the discovery of certain relationships between the responses generated.

Facet theory, as employed by Guttman [4], [5] and Foa, goes further in developing a method of ordering stimulus variables according to their content in the form of demands on the subject. This procedure provides a means for determining the pattern of elements composing the universe of data from which a given set of test items is derived. When this underlying semantic structure has been properly established for a group of tests or items, it serves as the basis for predicting their statistical structure or pattern of intercorrelations.

Foa's theoretical framework employs a facet approach in determining the structure of person perceptions in husband–wife pairs (chapter 11). Analysis of the facets of dyadic behavior in such pairs produces eight types of relationship in an identifiable order. This analysis serves as a basis for the construction of multiple-choice interview questions whose structure of intercorrelations is then predicted from the order of the eight relationships. A circumplex is the result. If in this case interview questions are viewed as requirements on the subject to describe certain relationships, such as the husband's emotional acceptance of the wife, then facet theory becomes a method of deriving meaningfully related stimuli from their subuniverses of behavioral content.

Another analysis of task requirements is provided by Restle's "waiting-time model" of group problem solving (chapter 17). Based on times needed for solution by different subjects, this model reveals the number of stages of solution required by a problem. This aspect of stimulus structure has been shown by Restle, and in particular by Lorge and Solomon (chapter 15), to be an important element in the prediction of group problem-solving efficiency.

The above approaches relate most commonly to the intellectual requirements placed on the subject by experimental instructions or test items; these requirements lead to the discriminations, judgments, or reasoning tasks that he is asked to perform. Another kind of demand is imposed by social norms implicit in task instructions or developed by the experimental group, for example, prescriptions of the roles expected of an experimental subject or standards operating in small group interaction. This kind of requirement leads the subject into behavior involving the application of rules, behavior which Moore and Anderson (chapter 16) distinguish as typically social. The formulation of "ought" elements in the stimulus situation requires as a first step the formal analysis of the logic of norm imposition. In chapter 1 Anderson discusses the derivation of a logic for the application of a rule by an individual as a part of social-role behavior.

Closely related to the requirements, intellectual or social, imposed by the task is the reward or punishment for carrying out the assigned actions. This aspect may sometimes be overlooked in research. Thus the power of the experimenter over the subject or of one subject over another may be ignored or wrongly estimated. A number of our symposium papers are concerned with the effects of reward on behavior. Karlsson's chapter (13), however, is the only one providing a mathematical characterization of the reward or punishment potential of the stimulus.

Karlsson sees power as an attribute of an individul in a given group, a characteristic existing at all times even when not being exercised. Thus we can construe it as a part of the stimulus value of a person, a part which indicates the punishment imposition or reward withdrawal which one individual can visit upon another. In his formulas Karlsson effectively uses linear utility functions to express how much one person can punish another.

Besides making demands on the subject, the stimulus situation provides some resources for meeting these requirements. Treatménts of such informational inputs have been contributed to this symposium by Roby, Shelly, and Flament. Through investigation of information available on task characteristics, the optimal structure of required problem-solving actions can be determined. Roby's paper (chapter 18) offers a means of deriving optimal solutions of team tasks from the analysis of task information.

In computing the coordination requirements of different subtasks in a series, Roby uses information theory and expresses in bits the structuring information in each subtask of the total group activity. In this case all information provided is considered correct. Incorrect or obscure information can, however, be included. Shelly (chapter 20) handles this problem in terms of measures of distinguishability of stimuli and uncertainty, using a topological analysis of relationships of "closeness" and a definition of a scale such that the concept of uncertainty between measures is included. He points out that his method can be used to study the function of the information made available to the experimental subject.

If the structure of the experimental situation includes serial presentation of stimuli, feedback, and resultant learning, probability methods of defining the stimulus situation can be used. Serial stimulus structure is successfully conceptualized in the sampling model of the stimulus employed by theorists of statistical learning. Flament (chapter 10) approaches the serially presented stimulus and accompanying reinforcements from the point of view of their informational value for the subject. In considering the Asch experiment on social influence, he discusses the elements that help the subject to develop an estimate of the probability that a given stimulus has occurred. Such a task would seem to require the use of a Bayesian procedure for arriving at judgments about the stimulus, and Flament offers evidence that partial conformity to such a model is present. Roby also, in characterizing the stimulus information which tells a team member the optimal moment for performance of his part of a group task, shows how the Bayes theorem can be used in arriving at this judgment. As in the rest of Roby's task analysis, experimental work could be carried out to determine whether team members actually follow such an optimal path to problem solution.

From stimulus-situation analysis can come novel experimental treatments such as Rosenberg's application of tracking techniques to social interaction (chapter 19). His method of presentation of stimuli for a dyadic tracking task makes it possible to define clearly contrasting reward structures and the associated goal paths possible to interacting pairs. Through these techniques, longitudinal studies of social interaction can be made in terms of principles of individual behavior already available.

The task developed by Rosenberg can be considered to fall toward one end of a continuum expressing a fundamental characteristic of the stimulus-situation structure: the degree to which the subject is permitted to program his own problem solution on the basis of his ability resources and his personal needs. This attribute, which might be called stimulus permissiveness, seems to be a function of comprehensibility of task demands, number and predictability of possible alternative solutions, and need-satisfying characteristics of permitted solutions.

In fact a "model" can be constructed for our remaining symposium papers which concentrate on response rather than stimuli. If stimulus situations leading to the responses to be studied are arranged along a roughly defined continuum from strong control by the experimenter at one end to considerable permitted ingression of subject requirements and skill repertoire at the other, the papers fall all along the way, from those of the learning theorists at one extreme to Moore and Anderson's autotelic models and Back's communication processes at the opposite one. The papers concerned with responses can be discussed by reference to such a continuum, starting with the least "permissive" end of the distribution.

2. Mathematical Analysis of Response Characteristics

In the process approach to social behavior, the analysis of stimulus situations leads to the discovery of specific patterns of elements which elicit predictable response sequences. The resultant "programming" of responses has offered tempting possibilities for the control of behavior through training and has, because of its rigor, proved particularly amenable to precise mathematical treatment. Although such experiments have been classified rather narrowly under learning theory, their increasing recognition of social incentives seems to be leading to provision for problem-solving elements. Thus our group of papers on mathematical learning shows the underlying theory to be in a far from static condition.

Several papers, for example, introduce perceptual elements often ignored in this type of experiment. Carterette and Wyman (chapter 6) employ a combination of psychophysical and learning approaches to investigate perceptual factors in conformity experiments. The stimulus-sampling concept is found to be applicable to psychophysical processes, but the findings raise difficult problems for both signal detection and statistical learning theory.

The authors point out the need to try out a variety of models in order to analyze the perceptual elements on which the observer is basing his response.

Suppes and Schlag-Rey's treatment (chapter 22) of the Asch conformity experiment determines the effect of perception on response to social pressure under conditions of hard and easy discrimination, social reinforcement before and after the discrimination, and correct and incorrect reinforcement. Predictions from eight stimulus parameters are tested against obtained behavioral data and thus lead to identification of the stimulus elements most important in producing conforming responses.

Also related to this analysis of the perceptual response is Flament's work, already mentioned, on the subjective probability of existence of stimulus elements. Although Flament does not consider his concepts to be incompatible with those of statistical learning models, he is able to incorporate the utilization of a rational procedure by the subject.

The remaining contributors in the area of learning are more concerned with motivational effects of social stimuli. For it is apparent that introduction of another subject has tended to reduce the "inhumanness" of the learning situation employed. Of the symposium participants, the most pessimistic about the consequences of social inclusion is Bush, who takes the position that new kinds of experiments may have to be developed before adequate models for two-person learning can be constructed. He refers to the somewhat alarming difficulties raised by the presence of two interacting stochastic processes and mentions in particular the behavioral complexities (for example, the use of a plan or strategy) which conditioning theory would encounter in the treatment of two-person binary prediction experiments.

Burke is inclined to search for appropriate models of experimental settings such as are currently in use. His discussion of learning experiments that can be extended to two-person interaction offers evidence of the social applicability of experiments involving non-reinforced trials and those involving paired associate learning. For the latter type of experiment he suggests Estes' model, which includes a guessing state in addition to conditioned states.

Hall poses more urgently the need for a change in theory to meet current intractable problems (chapter 12). His experimental conditions encouraged departure from probability matching of responses to fixation on the "correct" action; however, incorrect responses did not entirely extinguish. He considers, but rejects until more work can be done, the temptation to "patch up" the old theory by introducing new assumptions.

Other contributors do attempt modifications of the old model. Atkinson, chiefly concerned with motivational complications produced by monetary reward, finds prediction from current learning theory to be defective, subjects behaving more rationally than expected. He is able to adapt theory by assuming a new factor of strength of conditioning. Estes, in explaining behavior in two-person interactions with varying payoffs, differs from Atkinson in preferring not to alter learning axioms. In his situations, behavior is also more rational than the probability learning model would predict. He therefore modifies the "response rule" and introduces a "scanning model" that incorporates a decision process leading to choice of the response expected to be most rewarding.

In general, the mathematical-learning theorists seem to be expanding their theory and experiment to let a little light into the cognitively dim area in which their subjects have previously been penned. As we move away from these workers into the area of interest to Cohen (chapter 7), we find still more freedom for the subject, who can now express preference for reference groups within the framework of the Asch experiment. The operation of standards of a majority group, originally treated less formally by Asch and by Sherif, is introduced in mathematical form and provides an approach to the study of preferences of potential importance to the chooser.

Lieberman's discussion of game situations occupies a position intermediate between the preceding strictly controlled experiments and studies of group problem-solving (chapter 14). His three types of game demonstrate how different formulations of the experimental task can lead to different degrees of rationality and need-oriented behavior. He shows how subjects presented with a payoff matrix which they do not fully understand revert toward probability-matching behavior. He also demonstrates the introduction of personal requirements by subjects when the problem does not force a single rational solution.

At this point on our continuum of stimulus permissiveness, the emphasis of the contributors shifts considerably toward experiments in which the subject or group has greater opportunity for self-programming of responses. In these experiments, the freedom of the subject consists chiefly in employment of his resources, since he is encouraged to deploy in a specific problem the relevant contents of his repertoire of knowledges and skills.

Smoke and Zajonc (chapter 21) consider from a theoretical point of view the problems raised by a task in which group members must reach a common decision and in which all members have an equal probability of being correct. They determine the relative efficiency of different ways of reaching this shared decision, including such structures as dictatorship, oligarchy, unanimity, and quorum. Group-behavior models of this type can provide baselines against which to evaluate experimental results such as are obtained by Lorge and Solomon and by Restle.

Both the Lorge–Solomon and Restle papers are concerned with models for deriving efficiency of solution in groups of different size. The Lorge–Solomon probability model was constructed for predicting group behavior from individual problem-solving success. After initial development on Eureka-type problems, the model is now applied to data on verbal recall. Discrepancies in the fit of the model seem to derive from interfering effects of social interaction, although Solomon has not yet tested for this.

Restle also uses the Lorge–Solomon model, adapted for stages in problem solving. His "waiting-time model," yielding the number of stages of solution required by a problem, has already been mentioned. His results include cases where the interaction efficiency is reduced by the group's handling of subjects offering incorrect solutions. Thus, as in Solomon's results, the necessity to include measurement of social needs seems to be present.

In the previous experiments, the emphasis on intellectual efficiency caused non-intellectual elements to appear only as deviations from optimal paths. In contrast, Coleman (chapter 8) concerns himself centrally with the effects of members' requirements upon group interactions. He focusses on two types of reward patterns developed by groups: mutual reward in which group members' actions are contributing to each other's goals and mutual punishment in which members' achievements reduce each other's goal efforts. Unlike Karlsson, he is interested not so much in the formalization of the reward pattern as in the derivation of the equilibrium distributions of group actions which will result from the two different types of structure.

Coleman points out that his treatment falls far short of his goal of integrating in one model a number of different activities and including reward–punishment consequences other than distribution of effort. In his characterization of "ambitious goals" and the current "modest results," he reflects the increasingly complex demands made by social data on the mathematical methods available. The three papers falling at the farthest extreme of our continuum are chiefly concerned with this problem. Because of their dissatisfaction with the current mathematical attempts at rigorous treatment of social data, these authors all veer toward use of the more permissive experimental situation.

Back's position is that elegantly executed experiments such as those of the learning theorists may be using a mathematics suitable for things but not for people. The fact that these methods stem from the methodology of physical science increases the probability that they may be not entirely suited to treatment of that "organism" which the learning theorist so often mentions. In order to deal better with living people, Back recommends more studies of all sorts of the social-communication aspects of experiments as a preliminary to the development of more appropriate mathematical treatments.

Dissatisfaction with current approaches is also evident in Shelly's paper, in which he seeks through a topological treatment to get as near as possible to social phenomena as they are. Unlike Lewin, Shelly is successful in developing a topological analysis, starting in his present paper with the derivation of an expression for "closeness."

Moore and Anderson's criticism of mathematical methodology follows a line of reasoning supporting that of Back. They distinguish between puzzle stimuli in which the opponent is not really human and game situations in which the subject cannot maximize his own utility without taking a human opponent into account. They recommend the development of experimental and mathematical treatments based on a human or autotelic model rather than a mechanistic model of problem-solving behavior. Moore's experimental method is of particular interest in that it incorporates operant conditioning procedures into a setting in which the subject develops his own reward structure and at times may even control the experimenter's behavior.

3. Mathematics and Social Science

Our discussion has indicated that mathematicians and social scientists cooperate well when conceptualizations of experimental data take a dynamic rather than a static form and behavior is expressed in terms of complex directed patterns of specific acts. For this purpose, the stimulus situation which in part shapes the acts must be well understood and deliberately structured after logical analysis. Mathematical models can also be used to express the ways in which the subject utilizes the stimulus presentation and his own repertoire in adjusting to the environmental demands made upon him.

The contributions reflect encouraging progress in the years since Lewin's pioneer formulations of social interaction. Through formal logical analysis, matrix methods, and probability theory, the structure of the stimulus situation is revealed in its character of guide to a charting of possible response sequences. Methods are provided for determining optimal problem solutions or solutions based on the use of certain concepts by the subject. The latter type of analysis, testing the occurrence of hypothesized perceptions, judgments, or feelings, is especially promising in providing a rigorous approach to the study of cognition and motivation.

At the same time, progress has been made in understanding the problems raised by mathematical analysis. The demands of the data for new methods are shown to increase with added variables, starting with the mere presence of another person and progressing to group structures associated with goals or requirements of individual members. The necessary increase in complexity of mathematics seems to be greater than the corresponding change in the data. The question which arises is whether mathematics might not need to be so much more complex, if it could be different. Mathematical or proto-mathematical concepts derived from topology, formal logic, and biology are contributed for the clarification of these problems.

The chapters which follow thus provide illustrations of how mathematics can enter at every stage of the study of small group processes. Previous experimental intuitions are formalized in models leading toward both the shaping of theory and exploration of novel methodology.

References

[1] Cattell, R. B., The dynamic calculus: concepts and crucial experiments, in *Nebraska Symposium on Motivation*, M. R. Jones, ed., Lincoln, Nebraska: University of Nebraska Press, 1959.

[2] Guilford, J. P., Three faces of intellect, *Am. Psychol.*, 1959, **14**, 469-79.

[3] Guttman, L., A new approach to factor analysis: the radex, chap. 6 in *Mathematical Thinking in the Social Sciences*, P. F. Lazarsfeld, ed., Glencoe, Ill.: The Free Press, 1954.

[4] GUTTMAN, L., What lies ahead for factor analysis?, *Educ. and Psychol. Meas.*, 1958, **18**, 497–515.
[5] GUTTMAN, L., A structural theory for intergroup beliefs and action, *Amer. Sociol. Rev.*, 1959, **24**, 318–28.
[6] LEWIN, K., *Field Theory in Social Science, Selected Theoretical Papers*, D. Cartwright, ed., New York: Harper, 1951.
[7] MCDOUGALL, W., *Introduction to Social Psychology*, London: Methuen, 1908.

1

Logic, Norms, and Roles

Alan R. Anderson, *Yale University*

Our principal concern in this paper will be to use some elementary tools from formal logic to clarify such sociological concepts as *rights*, *duties*, and *powers*, etc., especially from the point of view of W. N. Hohfeld [6]. The relevance of these notions to sociological studies seems obvious; they all play a part in the more general notion of a *norm*. We proceed as follows: section 1 offers some background material designed to motivate the considerations to follow. In section 2 we point to some existing logical systems that seem to be of relevance to sociological matters; and in section 3 we offer an example analysis of some notions that are central to the sociological concept of a *role*.

1. Roles

In two previous papers ([1] and chapter 16 of this volume), Moore and I have considered a question that may be put as follows: What sense can be made of the prevalence of rule-directed play among societies? What *good* does it do to sit around playing bridge, or hearing operas, or playing the string games of the Eskimo? One could understand why children play so much, since they are not able to do much else, but why are adults interested in teaching games to children? Why not simply let them engage in the sort of unorganized play characteristic of one-year-olds? And why do adults themselves play games? Our answer is roughly this: that in playing games of strategy, working puzzles, and enjoying aesthetic objects, the adult is practicing at, and playing at, the more serious concerns of everyday life. The fact that the game of bridge and submarine warfare are both models of the theory of strategy might lead us to believe that bridge is a *folk-model* that we use to help us understand some of life's problems. Actually, however, we are acting *autotelically*, i.e., we are playing the game for its own sake and with relatively few consequences.

Among the autotelic folk-models is the drama, in a broad sense that includes Greek drama, the miracle and morality plays, opera, and the contemporary theater (even motion pictures and television). While drama is perhaps no more effective as a vehicle for moral instruction than, say,

11

novels or short stories, it is especially important from our point of view in that it has given us the concept of *acting a role*.

Indeed in the informal (nonmathematical) terminology of sociology, the dramaturgical metaphor of a role has been of enormous importance. Aside from the generality of its usage, one finds evidence of the usefulness of *role* and other dramaturgical metaphors in Goffman [4]. The concept of a role does not have the transparency that we might like, but it does seem clear that some insights into social behavior can be gotten from its application.

Sociologists and social psychologists have from time to time made attempts to define what they mean by a "social role"—frequently with results as devastatingly unhappy as those of social anthropologists when they try to explain what they mean by "culture." In the case of "role," what one frequently comes up with is something which, while vague and not terribly helpful, at least clearly points in the right direction: "a collection of rights and duties." My first point in this paper is that the notion of a social right or duty makes no sense apart from the notion of a *social rule*. And here we have a concept whose logical character has only recently come under investigation.

2. The Logic of Norms

The term "Deontik Logik" goes back to Ernst Mally [9], but it was only with the publication of G. H. von Wright's essay "Deontic Logic" [12] that any general interest was created in the topic. Since this article appeared, a number of logicians (see Castañeda [2], Hintikka [5], Lemmon [7], Prior [10], Rescher [11], and others; see also references in Anderson and Moore [1]) have proposed a variety of systems of formal logic designed to clarify the way we reason from sets of rules to certain consequences of these rules—a practice that we follow not only in the case of sets of rules for games, but also in the law. My principal object in this paper is not to discuss systems of deontic logic, but rather to make some general comments on these systems and to indicate some ways of extending them, especially in the law.

By common consent, the current situation as regards deontic logic is not altogether satisfactory. The sources of dissatisfaction are at least two, which I should like to distinguish rather sharply.

(1) There are a number of systems in the literature, each differing from the others in rather subtle, but significant, respects. The variety of systems in the literature has led some people to conclude that this suggests that we have not been able to capture formally our intuitions, concerning reasonings from sets of rules, in a satisfactory way. The present situation in deontic logic might be compared (at least by those of us who are optimistic) with the theory of "fluxions" as originated by Newton and Leibnitz: it seemed in the nineteenth century perfectly clear that the existing treatments of the calculus were not altogether satisfactory, but it

seemed equally clear that there was something of importance there to get clear about. Similarly in the case of deontic logic, it seems to me at least that though we have not yet been able to characterize the logic of rules in a completely satisfactory way, there is something there to be studied.

(2) A second, and to my mind less happy, reaction to the present instability in studies of deontic logic has been to regard it as evidence that there is no stable subject matter there to be studied. The argument runs more or less as follows. "Our reasonings in legal matters, or in matters of morality, or indeed in anything involving rules, are much too vague, imprecise, and amorphous to admit of any kind of careful, formal study. Compare the situation with the theory of effectively computable functions. Here we have four different, or at least quite different-looking, characterizations of effectively computable functions, all of which are very plausible from an intuitive point of view. And then they all turn out to be equivalent. *That's* when you know you have hold of something. But these deontic systems are not only non-equivalent, but demonstrably so—which we may take as evidence, not that the formalisms are fuzzy, but that the subject itself is. There is nothing stable there to look at."

As regards the second or "hard-headed" reaction, I should like to make two points. In the first place, there are indeed cases where our reasonings from sets of rules are every bit as solid, straightforward, and objective as the most hard-headed of extensional logicians could ask. For example, no chess manual ever states that it is forbidden for White to open with P–KR6. It nevertheless *follows* from the rules of any satisfactory chess manual that White cannot open with P–KR6. If the situation were as the hard-headed critics envision it, there ought to be endless squabbling as to whether P–KR6 is permissible as an opening move by White; but there isn't, as can be verified by going to any chess club. This is simply an empirical fact. Secondly, it seems clear that none of the usual extensional systems of logic can be used to account for the way we reason from sets of rules to conclusions. (I say "it seems clear" because, although I have no proof that it can't be done, I know of no attempts that have been even remotely successful.) It was presumably some such considerations as these that motivated von Wright to make his first attack on the problem of characterizing formally the kinds of reasonings we use in arguing from sets of rules to conclusions about what kinds of behavior the rules permit or forbid.

A system of deontic logic (minimally) has as its parts the following:

(a) variables p, q, r, etc., ranging over propositions or states-of-affairs;

(b) the ordinary Boolean operations over such propositions, to wit, conjunction "&," disjunction "v," and negation "∼";

(c) an operator "O" such that "Op" means "It ought to be the case that p"; and an operator "P" such that "Pp" means "It is permitted to be the case that p";

(d) as axioms or theorems such formulae as

$$Op \rightarrow Pp ,$$
$$O(p \mathbin{\&} q) \leftrightarrow Op \mathbin{\&} Oq ,$$
$$P(p \vee q) \leftrightarrow Pp \vee Pq ,$$

together with their consequences (by such rules as the system may have). And perhaps other theorems.

For the purpose of this paper one may take as the underlying deontic logic any of the systems we have mentioned. Our principal concern will be with the finer analysis of the propositions p on which the deontic operators act.

3. Hohfeld's Analyses of Elements of the "Role"

If one thinks of chess as an example of a set of rules, it seems fairly clear that one can abstract from a *move* three quite easily distinguishable parts or aspects. For instance, when as his fourteenth move White chooses Kt-QB4, we can distinguish (1) the player White who (as we shall say) *acted*, i.e., produced a new state-of-affairs; (2) the player Black, who was affected by the act (in older philosophical terminology, the player Black was *patient* to an act by the *agent* White); and (3) the situation, or state-of-affairs, brought about by White's action.

If we let the variables $x, y, z, \cdots$ range over persons (agents and patients), and variables $p, q, r, \cdots$ range over states-of-affairs, or propositions, then the *move* in a game might be represented as a three-termed relation $M(x, p, y)$. That is, when x executes what is regarded as an *action* (say, moving Kt-QB4), this creates a new situation or state-of-affairs p on the board, and y is the recipient or patient of the action executed by x (say, y's queen is now threatened).

This analysis may be more general than is required for chess. What is interesting is that it is closely in line with an analysis of legal reasoning which originated with Hohfeld [6] and also is very close to Hohfeld's way of viewing legal relations. Our general point, of course (as readers of earlier papers by Moore and myself will see immediately), is to substantiate the view that there is an important *formal* similarity between games of strategy and other sorts of social interaction.

But first I would like to anticipate one important and widespread misunderstanding of what constitutes an *action*. Much of the literature on sociology assumes that it is immediately clear, from an observational or causal standpoint, when one has *done* something. Such an attitude neglects the fact that *actions* are social matters, and that though the connection between causation and execution of an action is close, they certainly cannot be considered identical. When one asks, for example, "Who left the door open?" it is obviously inappropriate to answer "Everybody," even though it is true that nobody closed the door. The person or persons who are regarded (socially) as having left the door open are identified by certain social conventions which are largely (in the case of closing doors) arbitrary. Lacking any further guide, we may want to say that the last person through the door was the one who left it open; on the other hand, if a certain person had as a part of his duties the job of seeing to it that the door was closed after each entry, we might want to say that he (rather than the last person through) was the one who "left the door open."

A more interesting example is provided by a recent application of the Felony Murder Doctrine, in Anglo-American law, which states roughly that if a homicide results from the activities initiated by a felon in the course of committing a felony (e.g., when a policeman, while attempting to prevent a felony, accidentally kills a bystander), the felon may be charged with first-degree murder, the required malice aforethought being supplied by the felon's intent to commit the felony. In a recent case this doctrine was extended to cover a situation in which the following were the pertinent agreed facts:

> Defendant and one Henry Jackson, Jr., entered the grocery store of one Cecchini and ordered him to open the cash drawer. Jackson was armed with a revolver which he displayed to Cecchini. The defendant removed the money, and he and Jackson ran from the store, Jackson running one way and the defendant the other. Cecchini secured his own pistol and chased Jackson. In the exchange of shots Cecchini killed Jackson. Defendant escaped, but was later apprehended. [Commonwealth of Pennsylvania vs. Thomas; *Atlantic Reporter*, 2nd series, vol. 117, p. 204.]

At the first trial, Thomas, the defendant, was acquitted of the charge of first-degree murder, but the State appealed the case, and in the appeal Thomas lost; in a subsequent appeal by Thomas, judgment was again reversed, and a new trial ordered.

The case is of interest not only because it shows the importance of decision-making in borderline cases (i.e., in cases where policy is not clear), but also because it is clear that, putting aside questions about the wisdom of the doctrine, other ways of assigning responsibility for the event might reasonably be adopted. Jackson might be regarded as responsible for his own death, for example, or Cecchini might have been held responsible, with the proviso that the circumstances justified his act. (Note incidentally that Thomas, convicted of first-degree murder, was not even armed.)

The chief point of the foregoing remarks is to indicate that we cannot think of a system of rules as consisting *simply* of a collection of assertions of obligations and prohibitions. We require also that it include policies concerning the imputation of responsibilities, and these policies are not necessarily invariant from system to system.

We have raised this issue, however, only to dodge it. We will assume that problems associated with the ascriptions of responsibilities have been solved, and consider in abstraction from these difficulties the three-termed relation $M(x, p, y)$ defined above. In particular we shall seek to connect the notion of x *doing p to* (or *for*) y with the Hohfeldian analysis of legal concepts.

Writers of the Hohfeldian school have stressed as central to their analysis of "legal relations" the view that such relations must be construed as *two*-termed relations between persons: "... in each case one plaintiff, one defendant, one issue; one privilege or one right is all that needs examination: the one relation between these two people." (See Llewellyn [8, p. 86].) But it is clear from the examples they discuss that the relations under consideration are in fact at least three-termed, i.e., relations holding (say) among two litigants and some state-of-affairs in dispute. When discussing examples, Hohfeld implicitly recognizes the three-termed character of the relations in question: "if *X* has a right against *Y that he shall stay off the former's land*, [then] *Y* is under a duty toward *X that he stay off the place*," and "*X* has the power *to transfer his interest* to *Y*" [6, p. 38]. The point is that rights, powers, duties, etc., are not only rights (powers, duties) *toward* some person or persons, but also rights (powers, duties) *that* something-or-other be the case.[1]

Thus conceiving of Hohfeld's relations as being three-termed, involving two persons *x* and *y* and state-of-affairs *p*, we can exhibit Hohfeld's first group of relations in a table as follows:

x has a *demand-right* over *y* that *p*	*y* has a *duty* toward *x* that *p*
x has *no demand-right* over *y* that *p*	*y* has a *privilege* toward *x* that *p*

,

where propositions in the same row are "jural correlatives" and propositions in the same column are "jural opposites" (the terms are Hohfeld's). We will consider these relations under four headings: (1) Demand-right and its *correlative*, Duty; (2) No-Demand-right and its *correlative*, Privilege; (3) Duty, and its *opposite*, Privilege; (4) Demand-right and its *opposite*, No-Demand-right.

(1) To say that *x* has a demand-right (or *claim* or sometimes simply *right*) over *y* that *p*, is to say that *x* has a "legal expectation" that *y* shall bring about *p* on *x*'s behalf; equivalently we may say that *x* deserves *p* from *y*, in the sense that the law (or "justice" say) requires that *y* do *p* for *x*. Using the notation considered above, together with some deontic calculus, we may express the notion that *x* has a demand-right over *y* as $OM(y, p, x)$. That is, "It ought to be the case that *y* does *p* to (or for) *x*."

To say that *y* has a duty to *x* to do *p* is similarly to say that it ought to be the case that *y* does *p* to (or for) *x*, or in our notation $OM[y, p, x]$. And Hohfeld's assertion that the two are equivalent[2] is immediate.

---

[1] We do not wish to suggest that this oversight in logical form by itself vitiates the work of Hohfeld or his followers. Indeed, it is sometimes explicitly recognized that there are three entities involved, as when Llewellyn writes "one defendant, one issue."

[2] We interpret his "correlative" to mean "equivalent," which has a better-established usage in the literature on logic. (Hohfeld's "demand-right" might be more reasonably interpreted as "$O\tilde{M}(x, p, y)$," where $\tilde{M}$ is the appropriate "converse" of M, but such points will not be relevant to our subsequent discussion.)

This construction seems fairly close to that of Hohfeld, save for the following proviso. It seems to be assumed tacitly by Hohfeld and his followers that if, for example, x has a demand-right over y that p, then p is some situation which, were it actually the case, would be beneficial in some way or other to x. Thus one could say that x has a demand-right over y that y repay a loan of money that y borrowed from x, but apparently one could not say that x has a demand-right over y that y slit x's throat. The only way in which we here (intentionally) depart from Hohfeld—if indeed we do depart—is in allowing for the *possibility* that x may have a demand-right over y that y bring about some state-of-affairs p injurious to x. (Our hesitation stems from the facts (a) that the tone of Hohfeld's discussion of demand-rights suggests that if x has a demand-right over y that p, then p is beneficial to x, but (b) that in discussing liability Hohfeld says expressly that if x is under a liability from y that p, then it still may be that p would be beneficial to x. Our intention is merely to get clear about the matter, rather than to defend any particular interpretation of Hohfeld.)

(2) Hohfeld calls *no-demand-right* the "opposite" of demand-right, and we might plausibly interpret this to mean the negation of a demand-right, taking "x has no demand-right over y that p" to be expressed by $\sim OM(y, p, x)$. To say that y has a privilege over x that p may be construed as saying that it is permitted that y do p to (for) x, or in our notation $PM(y, p, x)$. But now it becomes apparent that there is a certain confusion in Hohfeld's original statement of the equivalence relation between *privilege* and *no-demand-right*. Hohfeld's table suggests that there ought to be a parallel of some sort between the relationship between the latter two relations on the one hand, and the relationship between *demand-right* and *duty* on the other. But confusion about the role of negation leads to the following mis-statement:

> Thus, the correlative of x's right [i.e., demand-right] that y shall not enter on the land is y's duty not to enter; but the correlative of x's privilege of entering himself is manifestly y's "no-right" that x shall not enter. [6, p. 39.]

We claim that the first part of the quotation accurately reflects the trivial equivalence between $OM(y, p, x)$ and $OM(y, p, x)$. It is at any rate clear that the logical relations thus expressed are distinct from those of the second case because the second comes to saying that x has a privilege over y to do p, if and only if y has no demand-right over x that x do *not-p*, or formally

$$PM(x, p, y) \leftrightarrow \sim OM(x, \sim p, y) .$$

Now it is true that, under reasonable assumptions about M, *if* x has a privilege over y to do p, *then* y has a no-demand-right over x that not-p, or

$$PM(x, p, y) \rightarrow \sim OM(x, \sim p, y) .$$

But the converse (which would be required to support Hohfeld's equivalence statement above) is not provable. Nor should it be, as can be seen by the following considerations. Let us consider the consequent in the equivalent form

(a) $$P \sim M(x, \sim p, y) \ .$$

To see that (a) does not entail

(b) $$PM(x, p, y) \ ,$$

it will suffice to give an example where (a) might be true and (b) false. To this end consider the following: Surely it is permitted in this society that Jones *not* see to it that Smith's lawn is not mowed (conceived as a situation affecting Smith), or

(a') $$P \sim M(\text{Jones, Smith's lawn is } not \text{ mowed, Smith}) \ .$$

It is even obligatory, in general, that Jones refrain from interfering with Smith's lawn-mowing, from which it follows that it is permitted, i.e., (a'); but it does not follow that it is permitted for Jones to case Smith's lawn to be mowed, or

(b') $$PM(\text{Jones, Smith's lawn is mowed, Smith}) \ .$$

In general, it is not permitted for Jones to meddle at all with Smith's lawn, either causing it to be mowed or causing it not to be mowed. And it cannot therefore follow that if Jones is permitted *not* to see that it is *not* mowed, then he *is* permitted to see that it *is* mowed.

The foregoing example may illustrate how easy it is to be misled by the ordinary English grammar of "not" (and by the plausibility of the example of trespass). Owing to a superficial similarity with the principle that two negatives make a positive, it is easy to confuse "Jones is *permitted not* to see that the lawn is *not* mowed" with "Jones *is* permitted to see that the lawn *is* mowed," and even with "Jones is *not permitted* to see that the lawn is *not* mowed."

(3) The confusion regarding negation makes it difficult to reconstruct accurately Hohfeld's notion of "opposition" as among legal relations. That this relation is not simply negation is recognized by Hohfeld:

> In the example last put, whereas x has a *right* or *claim* that y, the other man, should stay off the land, he himself has the *privilege* of entering on the land; or, in equivalent words, x does not have a duty to stay off. The privilege of entering is the negation of a duty to stay off. As indicated by this case, some caution is necessary at this point; for, always, when it is said that a given privilege is the mere negation of a *duty*, what is meant, of course, is a duty having a content or tenór precisely *opposite* to that of the privilege in question. (*ibid.*)

Again the wording ("The privilege of entering is the negation of a duty to stay off") suggests that

$$PM(x, p, y) \leftrightarrow \sim OM(x, \sim p, y)$$

should be a theorem, but this is equivalent to the assertion discussed and rejected under (2) above. We propose that Hohfeld has here been misled by his example. (It may also be the case that the confusion arose from a failure to distinguish $\sim M(x, p, y)$, "It is not the case that x does p to (for) y," from $M(x, \sim p, y)$, "x does *not-p* to (for) y." The latter implies the former, but not conversely. In any event, the example chosen has a special feature, namely, it is reasonable to suppose that at any time, x is either on y's land or is not on y's land and that whichever is the case, x is responsible for the fact. That is, the situation p (entering on y's land), is so chosen that the following is true:

$$M(x, p, y) \vee M(x, \sim p, y) .$$

Under these special circumstances, it is true that "the privilege of entering is the negation of a duty to stay off"; that is, we have as a theorem

$$[M(x, p, y) \vee M(x, \sim p, y)] \rightarrow [PM(x, p, y) \leftrightarrow \sim OM(x, \sim p, y)] .$$

But in the general case when x and p may be so chosen that the antecedent fails, Hohfeld's alleged equivalence also fails.

(4) Similarly, it is difficult to construe the "opposition" between demand-right and no-demand-right. The wording initially suggests that if we are correct in taking $OM(y, p, x)$ as asserting that x has a demand-right over y that p, then the no-demand-right should be construed as $\sim OM(y, p, x)$. The assertion that x has a right over y that p if and only if x does not have a no-right over y that p, becomes

$$OM(y, p, x) \leftrightarrow \sim\sim OM(y, p, x) ,$$

a trivial theorem of the two-valued calculus of propositions.

However, this interpretation destroys the apparently intended parallelism between duty and privilege on the one hand, and demand-right and no-demand-right on the other, and in any event conflicts with what was said under (2), where the assertion that x has no-demand-right over y that p was taken to mean $\sim OM(y, p, x)$, namely that x is lawfully exposed to p from y. Thus (on the analogy of the preceding example) we may formulate the assertion "the right of x over y that y stay off x's land is the negation of x's exposure (no-right) to y's entering" as

$$OM(x, p, y) \leftrightarrow \sim PM(x, \sim p, y) .$$

But again (and for reasons similar to those discussed under (2), which we will not repeat), this equivalence is too strong, only the weaker assertion,

$$OM(x, p, y) \rightarrow \sim PM(x, \sim p, y) ,$$

being provable.

A similar formal treatment could be obtained for Hohfeld's second set of legal relations. As an example we select the concept of a *legal power*. Introducing his conception of a *power*, Hohfeld writes:

> A change in a given legal relation may result (1) from some super-added fact or group of facts not under the volitional control of a human being (or human beings); or (2) from some superadded fact or

group of facts which are under the volitional control of one or more human beings. As regards the second class of cases, the person (or persons) whose volitional control is paramount may be said to have the (legal) power to effect the particular change of legal relations that is involved in the problem. [6, pp. 51–2.]

In order to handle the general notion of a "legal relation," we now introduce the letter D as a variable, ranging over the deontic operators O and P, so that in particular Dp will say of p that it is either obligatory or permitted, i.e., Dp is a statement ascribing some deontic status to p. The statement that x changes the legal status of the proposition p (making p obligatory, or permitted, etc.), relative to y can be rendered

$$M(x, Dp, y) \, ,$$

i.e., x changes one of his legal or normative relations with y. The latter we propose to regard as embodying the notion of *exercising* a power, in Hohfeld's sense, and the statement that x *has* the power we take as

$$\Diamond M(x, Dp, y) \, ;$$

i.e., it is possible ($\Diamond$) for x to change his legal relations with y.

To take an example from Hohfeld, let us suppose that y, as a contractor, has sent a bid for some construction to x. Then x has a power over y in the sense that x can, by accepting the bid, make it therefore obligatory for y to carry out the terms of the contract. Letting p describe the situation which consists of y's fulfilling the terms of the contract, we express x's power over y thus:

$$\Diamond M(x, OM(y, p, x), y) \, .$$

That is, it is possible for x to make it the case that y ought to carry out the contract for x, a situation which would affect y as a patient.

We have had two purposes in discussing Hohfeld's classification of legal relations at such length:

First, Hohfeld's analyses, while never enjoying universal acceptance among lawyers, have been thought to have considerable interest as an attempt to codify the vastly heterogeneous collection of concepts used in the law. One may therefore regard it as a *desideratum* of a formal system that it be able to cope with Hohfeld's relations, since these relations are, at least to some extent, relevant to the general character of normative systems. Our discussion has shown that the formal analysis proposed here can embody some of the Hohfeldian ideas.

But more important, the proposed formalism brings to light some (from a logical point of view) elementary blunders in Hohfeld's writing.[3] Hohfeld

---

[3] One could wish to soften this. We do *not* intend to suggest that Hohfeld's work enjoys an undeservedly high estimation. Quite to the contrary, it strikes me as being remarkable that Hohfeld should have brought as much as he did to the chaos of legal terminology. In calling the errors "elementary" we mean not that they should have been spotted by Hohfeld himself, but that they are easy to apprehend when once pointed out.

writes, in effect, that x is privileged to do p if and only if x has no duty to do *not-p*. In the course of trying to prove this assertion, we are led to find first that it is unprovable, and that it is not true: I have no duty to see to it that your lawn is not mowed, but it does not follow that I am privileged to mow your lawn. Moreover, we are led to see that Hohfeld's concept of "opposition" actually concerns two quite distinct logical relations when applied to his two groups of legal relations. We hope thus to have offered some slight vindication of the usefulnes of formal logic in uncovering ambiguities and *non sequiturs*, and to have offered some evidence in favor of Church's remark that

> ...the value of logic to philosophy [and, we might add, to other fields as well] is not that it supports a particular system, but that the process of logical organization of any system (empiricist or otherwise) serves to test its internal consistency, to verify its logical adequacy to its declared purpose, and to isolate and clarify the assumptions on which it rests. [3, p. 55.]

Of course, we would not claim that analysis by methods of modern formal logic is the *only* way of seeing clearly that some of Hohfeld's reasonings are fallacious; we *do* claim that using formal methods is the only way of uncovering such fallacies in such a way as to exhibit the source of the error and the underlying assumptions thereof.

There is not space here for a full description of the systems of formal logic in which the foregoing analysis can be carried out;[4] our purpose here was rather to show by an example how the formalism may be applied to a problem which is not altogether trival. We do hope to have made it clear that it is possible to treat some of the concepts involved in the notion of a social role in a way that is precise and rigorous.

REFERENCES

[1] ANDERSON, A. R., and O. K. MOORE, "Autotelic Folk-models," Office of Naval Research, Group Psychology, Technical Report No. 8, Contract SAR/Nonr-609(16), New Haven, Conn., 1959. (Reprinted in *Sociol. Quart.*, 1960, **1**(4), 203-16.)

[2] CASTAÑEDA, H. N., The logic of obligation, *Philosoph. Studies*, 1959, **10**, 17-22.

[3] CHURCH, A., *Introduction to Mathematical Logic*, vol. 1, Princeton, N. J.: Princeton Univ. Press, 1956.

[4] GOFFMAN, H., *The Presentation of Self in Everyday Life*, Edinburgh: Social Science Research Center, 1956.

[5] HINTIKKA, K. K. J., Quantifiers in deontic logic, *Soc. Scient. Fennica: Commentat. hum. litt.*, 1957, **23**, 3-23.

[6] HOHFELD, W. N., *Fundamental Legal Conceptions as Applied in Judicial Reasoning and Other Essays*, Walter Wheeler Cook, ed., New Haven: Yale Univ. Press, 1919. (An expanded edition containing additional essays was published by Yale Univ. Press in 1923.)

---

[4] A detailed elaboration of some of these systems is in preparation, under ONR Contract No. SAR/Nonr-609(16), Group Psychology Branch, Office of Naval Research.

[7] LEMMON, E. J., New foundations for Lewis modal systems, *J. Symbol. Log.*, 1957, **22**(2), 176–86.

[8] LLEWELLYN, K. N., *The Bramble Bush*: *Lectures on Law and its Study*, New York: Oceana Publications, 1951.

[9] MALLY, E., *Grundgesetze des Sollens*, Graz, Austria: Leuschner & Lubensky, 1926.

[10] PRIOR, A. N., Escapism, the logical basis of ethics, chap. 5 in *Essays in Moral Philosophy*, A. I. Melden, ed., Seattle: Univ. of Washington Press, 1958.

[11] RESCHER, N., An axiom system for deontic logic, *Philosoph. Studies*, 1958, **9**, 24–30.

[12] VON WRIGHT, G. H., Deontic logic, *Mind*, 1951, **60**(237) 1–15.

2

Choice Behavior and Monetary Payoff: Strong and Weak Conditioning

Richard C. Atkinson, *Stanford University*

1. Introduction

In *Markov Learning Models for Multiperson Interactions* [11], Suppes and I analyze a series of small group experiments in terms of stimulus-sampling theory [5]. These experiments deal with multiperson interaction situations involving social conformity, communication, bargaining, and various von Neumann-type games. The essential feature of many of these experiments is that they involve a series of discrete trials, and on all trials either a win or a loss is recorded for each subject. Further, the outcome of the trial for a given subject is determined by his response and by the response of the other subjects in his group (collaborators or antagonists as the case may be). Except for a few specific developments, the research in [11] deals only with situations where each subject is instructed to maximize the number of trials on which he wins; otherwise, there is no reward in the sense of any exchange of money or goods among the participants. For many of our experimental situations, however, the introduction of monetary payoff has a marked influence on behavior, and a theoretical treatment of these effects accordingly requires a more general formulation of stimulus-sampling notions than the one given in [11].

The purpose of this paper is to examine a modification of stimulus-sampling concepts that provides a framework within which such variables as reward magnitude and motivation can be analyzed as determiners of behavior. The assumptions differ from the original formulation only with regard to the definition of the conditioning process. We still postulate all-or-none conditioning in that a given stimulus is conditioned to one and only one response. However, a *weak* state and a *strong* state of conditioning are also defined: extinction of a response proceeds more quickly if the stimulus is in a weak conditioning state than if it is in a strong state. This variation of our original notions provides a more general analysis of reinforcement variables, and in special cases is equivalent to the axioms presented in [11].

This work was supported by the Office of Naval Research under Task NR 170-282.

As the model is developed it will become evident that the distinction between strong and weak conditioning has properties in common with the concept of permanent and temporary memory storage and related notions that have played a role in some of the recent work on simulation of behavioral processes. Also relevant is a discussion by Matalon [9] in which he compares the work of Bush and Mosteller [3] with that of Jonckheere [8] and proposes a distinction between *temps faible* and *temps fort*. The former process would take into account the total number of past reinforcing events (independent of order); the latter would be restricted to the most recent events, but the order of these events would be crucial. Matalon's suggestion of a dual system of this type is similar to our notion of weak and strong states of conditioning.

2. Basic Notions and Axioms

We begin by stating the axioms for a situation where on each trial there are r mutually exclusive and exhaustive responses available to the subject $(A_1, A_2, \cdots, A_r)$. Several applications will then be examined to illustrate certain properties of models derived from these axioms. For simplicity, the examples will be limited to simple learning problems involving varying amounts of monetary payoff. However, as will be evident later an extension of these ideas to discrimination learning and multiperson interactions is straightforward.

STIMULUS AXIOM. *The stimulus situation associated with the onset of each trial is represented by a set of N stimuli. On each trial exactly one stimulus is randomly sampled from this set.*

CONDITIONING-STATE AXIOM. *On every trial each stimulus is conditioned to exactly one response; further, the stimulus is either strongly or weakly conditioned to that response. (The strong conditioning state for the A_i response is denoted by C_i, the weak state by c_i.)*

RESPONSE AXIOM. *If the sampled stimulus is conditioned to the A_i response (either weakly or strongly), then that response will occur with probability 1.*

CONDITIONING AXIOMS.

(1) *If a stimulus is sampled on a trial and is strongly conditioned to the A_i response, then (a) the stimulus remains strongly conditioned to the A_i response if that response is reinforced, and (b) with probability α the stimulus becomes weakly conditioned to the A_i response if some other response is reinforced.*

(2) *If a stimulus is sampled on a trial and is weakly conditioned to the A_i response, then (a) with probability β the stimulus becomes strongly conditioned to the A_i response if that response is reinforced, and (b) with probability θ the stimulus becomes weakly conditioned to the A_j $(i \neq j)$ response if the A_j is reinforced.*

3. Contingent and Noncontingent Reinforcement Schedules for the Two-Response Case

We define E_i as the event representing the reinforcement of the A_i response. Then a contingent reinforcement schedule for the two-response case is defined by the probabilities π_1 and π_2. The parameter π_i specifies the likelihood of an E_1 event on trial n given that an A_i response occurred on that trial; specifically,

$$\text{(1)} \qquad \begin{aligned} \pi_i &= P(E_{1,n} \mid A_{i,n}) , \\ 1 - \pi_i &= P(E_{2,n} \mid A_{i,n}) , \end{aligned} \qquad (i = 1, 2) .$$

Now consider those trials in a contingent reinforcement experiment on which the kth stimulus is sampled from the set of N stimuli; we denote this subsequence of trials as $\omega^{(k)}$. We may define a random variable associated with the kth stimulus which takes the conditioning states $C_1, c_1, c_2,$ and C_2 as its values. From our axioms, it can be shown that over the subsequence $\omega^{(k)}$ of trials this random variable is a Markov chain with the following transition matrix:

$$\text{(2)} \qquad \begin{array}{c} \\ C_1 \\ c_1 \\ c_2 \\ C_2 \end{array} \begin{array}{cccc} C_1 & c_1 & c_2 & C_2 \\ \left[\begin{array}{cccc} 1 - \alpha(1 - \pi_1) & \alpha(1 - \pi_1) & 0 & 0 \\ \beta\pi_1 & 1 - \beta\pi_1 - \theta(1 - \pi_1) & \theta(1 - \pi_1) & 0 \\ 0 & \theta\pi_2 & 1 - \theta\pi_2 - \beta(1 - \pi_2) & \beta(1 - \pi_2) \\ 0 & 0 & \alpha\pi_2 & 1 - \alpha\pi_2 \end{array}\right] \end{array}.$$

For simplicity, these states will be numbered as follows: $1 = C_1$, $2 = c_1$, $3 = c_2$, and $4 = C_2$. We next define $p_{ij}^{(m)}$ as the probability of being in state j on the $(m + 1)$th trial of the subsequence $\omega^{(k)}$ given that on trial 1 of the subsequence $\omega^{(k)}$ we were in state i. Moreover, if the appropriate limit exists and is independent of i, we set

$$\text{(3)} \qquad u_j = \lim_{m \to \infty} p_{ij}^{(m)} .$$

The Markov chain defined by (2) is irreducible and aperiodic; for such a finite-state chain it is well known that the limiting quantities u_j exist (see Feller [6]). For our case,

$$\text{(4)} \qquad u_j = \frac{D_j}{D_1 + D_2 + D_3 + D_4} ,$$

where

$$\text{(5)} \qquad \begin{aligned} D_1 &= \pi_1\pi_2^2 , & D_3 &= (1 - \pi_1)^2\pi_2\alpha/\beta , \\ D_2 &= (1 - \pi_1)\pi_2^2\alpha/\beta , & D_4 &= (1 - \pi_2)(1 - \pi_1)^2 . \end{aligned}$$

We next define a random variable $X_{i,n}$ $(i = 1, 2, 3, 4)$ which denotes the number of elements in state i on trial n of an experiment; of course, $X_{1,n} + X_{2,n} + X_{3,n} + X_{4,n} = N$. Then, by our Response Axiom, we have

$$\text{(6)} \quad P(A_{1,n}) = \sum_{x_1, x_2, x_3, x_4} P(X_{1,n} = x_1, X_{2,n} = x_2, X_{3,n} = x_3, X_{4,n} = x_4)\frac{x_1 + x_2}{N} .$$

The u_i's given in (4) are defined for a subsequence of trials on which a particular stimulus is sampled. However, in terms of these quantities, we can obtain an expression for $P(X_{1,n} = x_1, X_{2,n} = x_2, X_{3,n} = x_3, X_{4,n} = x_4)$ as the number of trials becomes large; namely,

(7)
$$\lim_{n \to \infty} P(X_{1,n} = x_1, X_{2,n} = x_2, X_{3,n} = x_3, X_{4,n} = x_4)$$
$$= \frac{N!}{x_1! \, x_2! \, x_3! \, x_4!} u_1^{x_1} u_2^{x_2} u_3^{x_3} u_4^{x_4} \, .$$

Therefore, from (6) it follows that

(8)
$$\lim_{n \to \infty} P(A_{1,n}) = u_1 + u_2$$
$$= \frac{\pi_1 \pi_2^2 + (1 - \pi_1)\pi_2^2 \varphi}{\pi_1 \pi_2^2 + (1 - \pi_2)(1 - \pi_1)^2 + [(1 - \pi_1)\pi_2^2 + (1 - \pi_1)^2 \pi_2]\varphi} \, ,$$

where $\varphi = \alpha/\beta$. Note that the asymptote is independent of both θ and the number N of stimuli. Henceforth, to simplify notation, the trial subscript will be omitted to indicate asymptotic expressions; i.e.,

$$\lim_{n \to \infty} P(A_{1,n}) = P(A_1) \, .$$

A noncontingent reinforcement schedule is defined when the E_i event on a trial is independent of the response; i.e., when $\pi_1 = \pi_2 = \pi$. Under these conditions, (8) simplifies to

(9)
$$P(A_1) = \frac{\pi^3 + \pi^2(1 - \pi)\varphi}{\pi^3 + (1 - \pi)^3 + \pi(1 - \pi)\varphi} \, .$$

Other results for the model will be examined later, but we now turn to some data relevant to the asymptotic predictions. In the analysis of these data we shall not be concerned with a statistical evaluation of the agreement between observed and theoretical values or with a detailed treatment of data from individual subjects. Thus, these analyses are not to be regarded as tests of the axioms, but are included merely to illustrate some of the quantitative properties of the model.

Siegel and Abelson's Study. Siegel [10, p. 733] reports an unpublished study conducted with Abelson in which a noncontingent procedure was employed. On each trial the subject either won or lost five cents depending on whether his response was correct ($A_1 - E_1$ or $A_2 - E_2$) or incorrect ($A_1 - E_2$ or $A_2 - E_1$).

TABLE 1

PREDICTED AND OBSERVED ASYMPTOTES FOR THE
SIEGEL AND ABELSON EXPERIMENT

π value	Predicted $P(A_1)$	Observed $P(A_1)$
.75	.905	.929
.70	.850	.850
.65	.781	.753

TABLE 2

PREDICTED AND OBSERVED ASYMPTOTES FOR A
CONTINGENT REINFORCEMENT EXPERIMENT

π_1 value	Predicted $P(A_1)$	Observed $P(A_1)$	s_p^2
.60	.592	.601	.017
.70	.704	.685	.019
.80	.831	.832	.009

Three groups of subjects were run, each for a total of 300 trials. The independent variable was the value of π (.65, .70, and .75). The final block of 20 trials was used to estimate asymptotic responding. The observed values for $P(A_1)$ are given in table 1. If we use the observed asymptote for the .70 group to estimate φ via (9), we obtain $\varphi = .90$. The predictions for $P(A_1)$ given in table 1 were computed using this value of φ. Siegel does not report observed variances, but in view of the variability generally reported for studies of this type, the correspondence displayed in table 1 is fairly good.

Taub and Myers' Study. Taub and Myers [12] report a similar study in which the subject won or lost one cent on each trial; for one group $\pi = .6$, and for another $\pi = .8$.[1] The observed asymptotic proportion of A_1 responses was .644 for the .6 group and .869 for the .8 group. Using the observed asymptote for the .8 group, we estimate φ to be 5.44. If we take this value of φ, the prediction for $P(A_1)$ is .630 for the .6 group and .869 for the .8 group. The agreement here is extremely good.

Contingent Reinforcement Study. In an unpublished study by the author, subjects were run for 340 trials employing the experimental procedure described in [11, sec. 10.2]. On each trial a subject won or lost five cents depending on whether his response was correct or incorrect. Three groups were run on a contingent schedule with 20 subjects per group. The groups differed with respect to π_1, which took the values of .6, .7, and .8; for all groups $\pi_2 = .5$. Table 2 presents the observed proportion of A_1 responses over the last 80 trials and the associated variances. The observed proportion of A_1's was fairly stable over the last 100 or so trials, and consequently the proportions presented in the table may be regarded as estimates of $P(A_1)$.

The parameter φ was estimated for this experiment by selecting that φ which minimizes the squared differences between the predicted and observed values of $P(A_1)$ summed over the three groups. The obtained value of φ

---

[1] Taub and Myers report other experiments in which differential amounts of payoff occur following an A_1 response versus a fixed payoff following an A_2 response. These experiments are not treated here but have a natural interpretation in this model if we assume that different sets of conditioning parameters are associated with an E_1 and an E_2 reinforcement (see, for example, Atkinson and Sommer [2]).

was 2.1, and the predictions in table 2 are based on this estimate. Once again, the correspondence between theory and observation is quite good.[2]

4. Noncontingent Reinforcement for the Three-Response Case

We now apply the axioms to a three-response experiment conducted by both Gardner [7] and Cotton and Rechtschaffen [4]. The observed asymptotes reported in these studies are particularly interesting in that they fail to support the "combining of response classes condition" which characterized many of the earlier models of learning.[3]

In the Gardner situation, three responses (A_1, A_2, A_3) are available to the subject and three reinforcing events (E_1, E_2, E_3) are employed. One of the reinforcing events occurs on each trial, and the probability that event E_i occurs on trial n of the experiment is simply γ_i where $\gamma_1 + \gamma_2 + \gamma_3 = 1$.

Again, consider the subsequence of trials on which the kth stimulus is sampled. We define a random variable associated with the kth stimulus which takes the conditioning states C_1, C_2, C_3, c_1, c_2, and c_3 as its values. It may be shown that over the subsequence of trials on which the kth stimulus is sampled, this random variable is a Markov chain. The appropriate transition matrix is as follows:

(10)

$$
\begin{array}{c}
\\ C_1 \\ C_2 \\ C_3 \\ c_1 \\ c_2 \\ c_3
\end{array}
\begin{array}{cccccc}
C_1 & C_2 & C_3 & c_1 & c_2 & c_3 \\
\left[\begin{array}{cccccc}
1 - \alpha(1 - \gamma_1) & 0 & 0 & \alpha(1 - \gamma_1) & 0 & 0 \\
0 & 1 - \alpha(1 - \gamma_2) & 0 & 0 & \alpha(1 - \gamma_2) & 0 \\
0 & 0 & 1 - \alpha(1 - \gamma_3) & 0 & 0 & \alpha(1 - \gamma_3) \\
\beta\gamma_1 & 0 & 0 & 1 - \beta\gamma_1 - \theta(1 - \gamma_1) & \theta\gamma_2 & \theta\gamma_3 \\
0 & \beta\gamma_2 & 0 & \theta\gamma_1 & 1 - \beta\gamma_2 - \theta(1 - \gamma_2) & \theta\gamma_3 \\
0 & 0 & \beta\gamma_3 & \theta\gamma_1 & \theta\gamma_2 & 1 - \beta\gamma_3 - \theta(1 - \gamma_3)
\end{array}\right].
\end{array}
$$

The states will be numbered in the order given by the matrix, $1 = C_1$, etc. Then u_j, as defined by (3), is simply

(11)
$$ u_j = \frac{D_j}{D_1 + D_2 + D_3 + D_4 + D_5 + D_6}, $$

where

(12)
$$
\begin{aligned}
D_1 &= \gamma_1^2(1 - \gamma_2)(1 - \gamma_3), & D_4 &= \gamma_1(1 - \gamma_1)(1 - \gamma_2)(1 - \gamma_3)\varphi, \\
D_2 &= \gamma_2^2(1 - \gamma_1)(1 - \gamma_3), & D_5 &= \gamma_2(1 - \gamma_1)(1 - \gamma_2)(1 - \gamma_3)\varphi, \\
D_3 &= \gamma_3^2(1 - \gamma_1)(1 - \gamma_2), & D_6 &= \gamma_3(1 - \gamma_1)(1 - \gamma_2)(1 - \gamma_3)\varphi,
\end{aligned}
$$

and, again, $\varphi = \alpha/\beta$.

---

[2] The above group analysis of data implies that φ is constant for all subjects. This is obviously not the case, and a more detailed test of the model would require an estimate of φ for each subject. Granted that we expect intersubject variablity in φ; nevertheless, theoretically φ should not depend on the particular reinforcement schedule. Therefore, no difference in the mean values of φ is predicted between the three groups. To test this hypothesis, a value of φ was computed for each subject by equating his observed proportion of A_1 responses over the last block of 80 trials with $P(A_1)$ defined by (8). An F test was computed for these three samples of φ's, and the obtained value was 1.83 (df = 2, 57), which does not approach significance.

[3] See Bush and Mosteller [3] for a discussion of this condition.

By an argument similar to the one given in the preceding section an expression for $\lim_{n\to\infty} P(A_{i,n}) = P(A_i)$ may be obtained in terms of the u_j's; namely,

$$(13) \qquad P(A_1) = u_1 + u_4, \qquad P(A_2) = u_2 + u_5, \qquad P(A_3) = u_3 + u_6.$$

As before, these expressions do not depend on θ and N.

Gardner [7] conducted several studies, but we shall consider only a replication of one of his experiments that was reported by Cotton and Rechtschaffen [4]. The results of the Gardner study and the Cotton-Rechtschaffen replication are in excellent agreement; we use the latter because more subjects were employed in it. Of the six groups run, four involved three responses; they were denoted (70–15–15), (70–20–10), (60–20–20), and (60–30–10), the numbers indicating the value of r_1, r_2, and r_3, respectively. Asymptotic predictions for these groups are given by (13). For purposes of comparison, two additional noncontingent groups were run using the same equipment but with only two responses available to the subject. These groups were denoted (70–30) and (60–40), the numbers indicating the value of π and $1-\pi$, respectively. Asymptotic predictions for these two groups are given by (9). The observed values for $P(A_1)$ over trials 286–450 and the related variances (s_p^2) as reported by Cotton and Rechtschaffen are given in table 3.

Predictions for $P(A_1)$ are a function of φ, and for a well-specified experimental procedure, one would want this parameter to be invariant with regard to the number of responses and the particular reinforcement schedule. We have therefore obtained an over-all estimate of the parameter by selecting that φ which minimizes the sum of the squared differences between the predicted values of $P(A_1)$ and the six observed values given in table 3. The estimated value for φ equals 3.7; the predicted asymptotes for this value of φ are given in table 3. Considering that a single parameter has been estimated, the agreement between theory and observation is fairly good. The average absolute difference between observed and predicted values is less than .014, which is not large in view of the observed variances.

There are several comments to be made about these predictions. Note that the predicted value of $P(A_1)$ in the (70–30) group is less than the predicted value of $P(A_1)$ for groups (70–15–15) and (70–20–10), and similarly, that the predicted value of $P(A_1)$ for the (60–40) group is less than $P(A_1)$

TABLE 3

PREDICTED AND OBSERVED ASYMPTOTES FOR THE
COTTON AND RECHTSCHAFFEN EXPERIMENT

Condition	Predicted $P(A_1)$	Observed $P(A_1)$	s_p^2
60–40	.641	.641	.0139
60–30–10	.658	.658	.0149
60–20–20	.671	.660	.0093
70–30	.773	.741	.0098
70–20–10	.783	.801	.0188
70–15–15	.784	.805	.0082

for groups (60–20–20) and (60–30–10). This result holds in general for the noncontingent reinforcement model: if the A_1 response is reinforced with probability greater than $\frac{1}{2}$, then for a fixed value of φ the prediction for $P(A_1)$ increases as a function of the number of alternative responses.

Another result can be established for the three-response noncontingent model. Let $\gamma_1 > \frac{1}{2}$ and define $\delta = \gamma_2 - \gamma_3$; then, for fixed values of γ_1 and φ, the asymptote $P(A_1)$ increases as δ approaches 0.

5. Sequential Predictions for the Two-Response Noncontingent Case

In this section we examine some sequential data reported in [11, ch. 10] for a two-response noncontingent experiment involving varying amounts of monetary payoff.[4] The sequential statistics to be analyzed are the first-order dependencies reported in [11, table 10.6]; in particular,

$$(14) \qquad \lim_{n \to \infty} P(A_{i,n+1} \mid E_{j,n} A_{k,n})$$

for $i, j, k = 1, 2$. To simplify notation, the trial subscripts will be omitted to indicate the asymptotic expression; i.e.,

$$\lim_{n \to \infty} P(A_{i,n+1} \mid E_{j,n} A_{k,n}) = P(A_i \mid E_j A_k) \, .$$

The expressions for these sequential probabilities are as follows:

$$P(A_1 \mid E_1 A_1) = \frac{N-1}{N}(u_1 + u_2) + \frac{1}{N} \, ,$$

$$P(A_1 \mid E_1 A_2) = \frac{N-1}{N}(u_1 + u_2) + \frac{1}{N}\left(\frac{u_3 \theta}{u_3 + u_4}\right),$$

(15)

$$P(A_1 \mid E_2 A_1) = \frac{N-1}{N}(u_1 + u_2) + \frac{1}{N}\left[\frac{u_1 + u_2(1 - \theta)}{u_1 + u_2}\right],$$

$$P(A_1 \mid E_2 A_2) = \frac{N-1}{N}(u_1 + u_2) \, ,$$

where u_i is defined by (4). The derivation of these equations is not difficult but is too lengthy to reproduce here. Note that these first-order predictions depend only on φ, θ, and N.

The experiment involved a noncontingent schedule where $\pi = .6$. Three groups were run, with the independent variable being the amount of money won or lost on each trial when the subject was correct ($A_1 - E_1$ or $A_2 - E_2$) or incorrect ($A_1 - E_2$ or $A_2 - E_1$). For subjects in Group Z, no money was won or lost; for Group F, five cents was won when the subject was correct or lost when he was incorrect; for Group T, ten cents was won or lost. The obtained proportions of A_1 responses at asymptote (trials 141–240) were .593 (Group Z), .644 (Group F), and .690 (Group T). The predicted asymptote is given by (9) and depends on φ; thus, as monetary payoff increases, the value of φ decreases, approaching 0 in the limit.

---

[4] Subjects were run in pairs and were instructed that they were competing in a two-person game; in actual fact, however, each subject was run on a separate, noncontingent schedule.

By inspection of (9), note that $P(A_1)$ must be greater than π for $\pi > \frac{1}{2}$. Therefore, for Group Z we assume that the asymptote is in fact $\pi = .6$. Given this asymptote, necessarily $\beta = 0$ and then our model reduces asymptotically to the multi-element stimulus-sampling model presented in [11, sec. 10.6]; that is, with $\beta = 0$, the system absorbs into the set of conditioning states c_1 and c_2. Therefore, asymptotic predictions for this case depend only on π, θ, and N. The values of θ and N have been estimated for Group Z [11, sec. 10.6] by a pseudomaximum likelihood method and are as follows: $\theta = .594$, $N = 3.42$. Using these estimates and $\pi = .6$, predictions for $P(A_i \mid E_j A_k)$ are obtained by means of (15). The predicted and observed quantities are given in table 4.

If we assume that θ and N do not change as monetary payoff is varied, then to predict $P(A_i \mid E_j A_k)$ for Groups F and T we need estimate only the single parameter φ for each group. This can be done by equating (9) with the observed values of $P(A_1)$ given above. The obtained estimates of φ for Groups F and T are 3.38 and 1.06, respectively. Using these values of φ and the original estimates of θ and N, predictions for all of the sequential data in table 4 may be computed. In view of the fact that only four parameters have been estimated to predict the entire array of numbers in the table, the correspondence between theory and observation is quite good.[5]

TABLE 4

PREDICTED AND OBSERVED VALUES FOR $P(A_1 \mid E_i A_j)$

Observed values are given in parentheses.

Group	$P(A_1 \mid E_1 A_1)$	$P(A_1 \mid E_1 A_2)$	$P(A_1 \mid E_2 A_1)$	$P(A_1 \mid E_2 A_2)$
Z	.72	.60	.54	.43
	(.69)	(.60)	(.54)	(.43)
F	.75	.60	.63	.46
	(.79)	(.62)	(.60)	(.39)
T	.78	.59	.71	.49
	(.86)	(.65)	(.68)	(.32)

Of interest is the predicted and observed inversion in the relation between $P(A_1 \mid E_1 A_2)$ and $P(A_1 \mid E_2 A_1)$ as monetary payoff increases: i.e., the fact that the prediction for $P(A_1 \mid E_1 A_2) - P(A_1 \mid E_2 A_1)$ takes on the values $+.06$, $-.03$, and $-.11$ as we go from Group Z to Group T. Apparently, increasing the magnitude of payoff leads to a situation where the emitted response is slightly more self-reinforcing than the objective reinforcement. (For a discussion of this interesting empirical effect, see [11, sec. 10.5].)

6. Absorbing Behavior

Some subjects, when placed on reinforcement schedules of the type described in this paper, will respond probabilistically for varying periods of

---

[5] A statistical evaluation of these results may be made by the methods described in [11, ch. 2].

time and then absorb on a single response, making that response throughout the remainder of the experiment. Currently, several studies with rats are being conducted to determine some of the variables affecting such absorption behavior.

This form of behavior has a natural interpretation in the present model if one assumes that $\alpha = 0$, or at least that α approaches 0 as the number of learning trials becomes large. In order to examine some of the implications of variations of this sort, consider a one-element model for a two-response noncontingent experiment where $\alpha = 0$. When $N = 1$, the single stimulus is sampled on all trials and the transition matrix in the states C_1, c_1, c_2, and C_2 is simply

$$(16) \quad \begin{array}{c} \\ C_1 \\ c_1 \\ c_2 \\ C_2 \end{array} \begin{array}{cccc} C_1 & c_2 & c_2 & C_2 \\ \left[\begin{matrix} 1 & 0 & 0 & 0 \\ \beta\pi & 1 - \beta\pi - \theta(1 - \pi) & \theta(1 - \pi) & 0 \\ 0 & \theta\pi & 1 - \beta(1 - \pi) - \theta\pi & \beta(1 - \pi) \\ 0 & 0 & 0 & 1 \end{matrix} \right] \end{array}.$$

If x_i denotes the probability of absorption in state C_1 given that the subject initially is in state c_i, then

$$x_1 = \beta\pi + [1 - \beta\pi - \theta(1 - \pi)]x_1 + \theta(1 - \pi)x_2 ,$$
$$x_2 = \theta\pi x_1 + [1 - \beta(1 - \pi) + \theta\pi]x_2 .$$

Solving for x_i, we obtain

$$(17) \quad \begin{aligned} x_1 &= \frac{\pi^2 + \pi(1 - \pi)\xi}{\pi^2 + (1 - \pi)^2 + \pi(1 - \pi)\xi} , \\ x_2 &= \frac{\pi}{\pi + (1 - \pi)\xi} x_1 , \end{aligned}$$

where $\xi = \beta/\theta$. If we assume that the subject starts in either c_1 or c_2 and that the probability of starting in c_1 is η, then the probability $\mathscr{A}_1$ of absorption on the A_1 response is

$$(18) \quad \begin{aligned} \mathscr{A}_1 &= \eta x_1 + (1 - \eta)x_2 , \\ &= x_1 \left[\eta + (1 - \eta)\frac{\pi}{\pi + (1 - \pi)\xi} \right]. \end{aligned}$$

If one postulates that β is very small with regard to θ (i.e., $\xi \to 0$), then for an individual subject's response protocol (i.e., a single realization of the experiment) the probability of an A_1 response could well appear to stabilize at π for a period of time and then switch to 1 or 0, the probability of absorption at A_1 being

$$(19) \quad \lim_{\xi \to 0} \mathscr{A}_1 = \frac{\pi^2}{\pi^2 + (1 - \pi)^2} .$$

Thus, if $\pi = .85$, the probability of absorbing on A_1 would be .95; for $\pi = .9$, .99; and so forth.

In the present analysis the upper bound on $\mathscr{A}_1$ is given by (19). However, this bound can be increased and be as close to 1 as desired (for $\pi > \frac{1}{2}$) by postulating intermediate states of conditioning between C_i and c_i. A discussion of such a formulation is given in [1]. The upper bound also can be increased by assuming that $\alpha \neq 0$ initially, but that $\alpha \to 0$ during the course of the experiment.

7. Comments

The foregoing discussion has illustrated some of the properties of the axioms of section 2 when applied to simple decision-making problems involving varying amounts of monetary payoff. Although the analysis has been confined primarily to asymptotic results, it should be pointed out that the theory yields interesting predictions concerning the effect of overlearning on subsequent extinction and also offers a tractable framework within which to formulate a model of response-time measures.

In principle, the axioms can be applied directly to small group situations in which the outcome of a given member's response is determined both by his response and by those of the other members of the group. Unfortunately, the phrase "in principle" is all-important since such applications lead to mathematical processes for which the practical difficulties of computing predictions are awesome. As an example, consider the simplest two-person game treated in *Markov Learning Models for Multiperson Interactions* [11, ch. 3]. Each of the players (i.e., subjects) has two available responses and the outcome of a trial is a function defined on the four possible response pairs. If we assume that the stimulus set for each subject has a single element available for sampling, then application of the axioms to this game yields a 16-state Markov chain. A one-element assumption, however, leads to certain unrealistic predictions regarding sequential effects, and to avoid this difficulty it is necessary to postulate at least two stimuli for each subject. Unhappily, if we assume that the stimulus set for each player has two elements, we obtain a 100-state chain; with three elements per player, a 400-state chain; and so forth. The most discouraging feature about this large number of states is that there are no obvious principles of continuity that would permit us to convert the theory into a continuous one and apply more powerful mathematical methods of analysis.

REFERENCES

[1] ATKINSON, R. C., A generalization of stimulus sampling theory, *Psychometrika*, 1961, **26**, 281–90.

[2] ATKINSON, R. C., and G. R. SOMMER, Decision making by children as a function of amount of reinforcement, *Psychol. Rept.*, 1960, **6**, 299–306.

[3] BUSH, R. R., and F. MOSTELLER, *Stochastic Models for Learning*, New York: Wiley, 1955.

[4] COTTON, J. W., and A. RECHTSCHAFFEN, Replication report: Two and three choice verbal conditioning phenomena, *J. Exptl. Psychol.*, 1958, **56**, 96.

[5] ESTES, W. K., and P. SUPPES, "Foundations of statistical learning theory, II: the stimulus sampling model for simple learning," Technical Report No. 26, Institute for Mathematical Studies in the Social Sciences, Stanford University, 1959.

[6] FELLER, W., *An Introduction to Probability Theory and Its Applications*, 2d ed., New York: Wiley, 1957.

[7] GARDNER, R. A., Probability-learning with two and three choices, *Amer. J. Psychol.*, 1957, **70**, 174-85.

[8] JONCKHEERE, A., Models for learning, in *Apprentissage, logique et probabilité* (Etudes Epist. Génét., VIII), Paris: Presses Universitaires de France, 1959.

[9] MATALON, B., Note sur les modèles d'apprentissage, in *Apprentissage, logique et probabilité* (Etudes Epist. Génét., VIII), Paris: Presses Universitaires de France, 1959.

[10] SIEGEL, S., Decision making and learning under varying conditions of reinforcement, *Ann. New York Acad. Sci.*, 1961, **89**, 766-83.

[11] SUPPES, P., and R. C. ATKINSON, *Markov Learning Models for Multiperson Interactions*, Stanford: Stanford Univ. Press, 1960.

[12] TAUB, H. A., and J. L. MYERS, Differential monetary gains in a two-choice situation, *J. Exptl. Psychol.*, 1961, **61**, 157-62.

3

Can Subjects Be Humans and Humans Be Subjects?

Kurt W. Back, *Duke University*

1. Introduction

The social psychologist is a human being who can reason or speculate, like or dislike, construct theories or conduct experiments, jump to conclusions or make commitments. The subject with whom he deals often seems to him to be a different creature, a sort of mechanism that has been designed to fit a particular theory and is supposed to ignore everything else. This fiction has been useful in isolating variables and establishing simple relationships. But it is, after all, a fiction. We shall attempt in this paper to state some of the problems faced by the social psychologist when he modifies this approach and admits that he is not the only man on earth. We shall consider especially how this approach to social psychology can be reconciled with formal mathematical reasoning.

The method of this paper might be called proto-mathematical. That is, we shall try to state, mainly from empirical considerations, some of the concepts that are needed in experimental studies and mathematical systems if we are to deal with individuals who are recognizable as human beings. In an earlier paper [1] we have shown that mathematical systems which have been designed to simulate biological systems can be adapted to represent quite complex social-psychological concepts.

In several recent symposia a variety of approaches to simulating complex biological processes have been explored [3, 11, 16]. These models show that there is a sufficient flexibility in potential mathematical techniques to treat any models that might be developed, although at present we need an extremely complex apparatus to arrive at comparatively trivial results. We can avoid the temptation, however, to adapt problems in social psychology to existing mathematical methods. Rather, we shall concentrate on developing the specifications of the concepts and relationships which will have to be taken into account in dealing with humans. This will establish the

Preparation of this paper was supported by a grant from the Office of Naval Research, Group Psychology Branch, under Contract Nonr 1181(11), Project NR 177-470. Reproduction in whole or in part is permitted for any use of the United States Government.

35

limits of the quantitative and human approaches and will show whether or not there is a fundamental conflict between the two.

2. Stimuli and Communication

One of the fundamental characteristics of the human being is his capacity to accept and interpret messages. Nonhuman mechanisms do this too, to a certain degree, but in an essentially different way. A detailed consideration of different types of interaction, the different kinds of "languages" with which an organism is able to deal, will be a fruitful way to design a method to deal with humans as humans.

When I hear a sound, I can recognize its loudness, its pitch, the direction from which it comes, and the meaning it mediates; the proper response will be forthcoming to the sound as a stimulus. When I hear a sentence, it also has stimulus value, and its meaning makes its semantic content. In addition, I interpret the meaning according to the speaker: I can take the meaning as referring to some objective situation or some characteristic of the speaker, e.g., his belief or his intentions. The meaning is further modified by the speaker's relationship to me and by the context of the situation. My reaction will depend on all these factors. In the first case I respond to a stimulus, in the second to communication.

This example indicates that there is some structure in common between stimuli and communication, but it also demonstrates some fundamental differences between them. Both communication and stimuli form a bridge between the outer world and the organism through the use of certain well-defined, continuous or discrete, quantitative dimensions. Thus each can be described as a set of measurable events adding up to a reality that interacts with the organism. This reality is called the stimulus object or the referent. In both cases the response to the world can be analyzed into the reactions to the different units that stimulate the organism. The organism can be said to react to the reality represented by the stimuli, but this reality is represented to him as a function of sets of stimuli or communication units.

There is, however, an important difference between communication and stimuli. The former comes from human sources, i.e., from organisms the recipient considers to be equivalent to himself. Whereas a stimulus is a message representing an objective state of affairs, a communication represents this state of affairs as content and in addition describes the originator of the message. The reality mediated by communication is thus twofold: the physical situation in the content of the message and the social situation implied by some additional cues. People do, then, make a distinction between people and other objects.

In terms of information theory, the transmitting source (or encoding system) itself is an important source of information that affects the contents of the message. This formulation shows the difficulty of applying information theory to social situations. The encoding system is a person, just as the recipient or the user of the system is, and he is perceived as such. Insofar as a person considers himself to be different and distinct from the surrounding world, he is likely to endow the communicator with the same identity. This kind of procedure is called anthropomorphism; it can also, of course, be applied to inanimate objects or to animals. In the normal communication situation, however, we are dealing with another person, and we may speak here of the *anthropomorphism of the other person*.

In accepting this anthropomorphism of the other person, we accept an intuitive distinction between two types of interaction, and this causes difficulty in the application of mathematical models. A consequence of the use of a mathematical language is the reduction of all observations to a single set of concepts which we can call the common currency, from the example of economic theory. Economists have translated different objects into cash value or utility, producing scales based on considerations important in this science. This has made possible precise mathematical theories but has limited the applicability of economic theory where other considerations or motives are important. Breakthroughs in constructing mathematical models occur if theorists find common currencies of this kind, i.e., common features among disparate objects. Behavior theory and information theory have their start in assigning a common measure to a variety of a person's perceptions, to his reactions, and to the information he receives. The measures selected are also assumed to fit a mathematical calculus and to follow its law [4]. This procedure severely restricts the kinds of phenomena that can be handled, since the type of measure selected already implies a theoretical position. Thus the introduction of a basic qualitative distinction, such as the one implied in the anthropomorphic treatment, raises trouble for mathematical analysis. In fact, that is why anthropomorphism is so often considered the opposite of scientific method. But can we dispense with it altogether in the study of man?

When dealing with the world transmitted by stimuli, reduction to common currencies has worked admirably—for example, in constructing manageable theories leading to the stringent mathematical theories of physics. Piaget has shown how the change from qualitative to quantitative differences occurs in the process of individual maturation: the child comes to construct a physical world that is dominated by the relations more and less. It is significant, however, that Piaget has never written of the child's construction of the social world. Is there a different process operating? The child's construction of physical reality can be said to be a process of learning about relations between things that are not like himself, things that are simply "things." This process does not necessarily culminate in reaching the conclusion that nothing is like himself, that everything is a question of common quantitative currency.

3. From Stimulus to Communication

3.1 Stochastic and Equilibrium Models.

The two most common types of theories have tried to deal in different ways with the language and messages to which people are exposed. Stochastic theories have explicitly tried to ignore the differences between stimuli and communication by reducing all communication to stimuli. Equilibrium theories have dealt with interrelations of or interactions with the organism, giving the organism an active role in arranging an optimal design. The definition of optimal is assumed to be given to the organism and to be an equilibrium condition, although there may be choices between different types of equilibria.

Stochastic theories are, in effect, attempts to explain the sort of human behavior that would occur if the human being were solely a physical object. Behavior is derived from antecedent stimulation, social and physical stimulation being treated as essentially identical. The individual person is treated as a unit on which certain units of events impinge, each event having a probability of causing a certain output of the system. These theories, commonly using the tools of learning theory, conditioning, game theory, and strictly mathematical information theory, can collectively be called stochastic theories.[1] They derive a change in behavior as a probability function of discrete preceding events. Since human individuals do obey the laws of physics and are limited in their further capacities by the physical properties of all events impinging on them, these theories can at least set the limiting conditions of human behavior.

Equilibrium theories differ in their approach to the organism's relation to the physical and social world. Some theorists, like Newcomb and Heider, talk separately about the orientation to persons and the orientation to things; others, like Festinger, regard all these relations as different cognitions. All these theories, however, admit concepts that refer directly to relations between people, such as liking and disliking. In general, they admit the kinds of description the human subject gives of himself, although they do not analyze the differences in his relationships with different kinds of environment.

Although equilibrium theories draw hardly any distinction between people and objects and thus between communication and stimuli, a comparison of these theories with stochastic theories will explicate the differences in construction between the physical and the interpersonal world. Galanter and Miller [6] have shown that the stochastic models are based on psychological theories that conceive of psychological processes as a function of the reflex arc, i.e., as a rather simple mechanical system. They try to remedy this by proposing a more sophisticated mechanical model based on feedback and control mechanisms. Even this difference could show, by contrast, some important features and limitations of the stochastic model. The following distinctions between the stochastic and equilibrium approaches will show the strengths and limitations of each.

(a) Stochastic models are in keeping with the cosmological point of view, that is, the attempt to apply a uniform set of models to all phenomena. The models follow the Galileian-Newtonian principles that have been applied successfully in studying physical phenomena. Moore and Anderson's paper

---

[1] This terminology follows that of Galanter and Miller [6] in describing theories based on these assumptions. As purely computational techniques, stochastic methods may be used with any theory.

in this volume (chapter 16) describes certain other implications of the Newtonian model in the social sciences. We know how Galileo's position produced a revolution in physics and was of immeasurable aid to progress in the field and to the general understanding of scientific method [9]. By contrast, Aristotelian theory in mechanics depended on the doubtful distinction between natural and forced action. Aristotle advanced this theory as a biologist, applying biological concepts to physical phenomena [14]; the appeal of his approach stemmed from the fact that he was closer to personal experience, projecting from biology and psychology to physics. Stochastic theories using the opposite approach project physical models on human experience, using in this case not an appeal to experience but an appeal to the prestige of the success of physical sciences. It is true that heavy objects do not find a naturally low place and that light objects do not rise naturally; this is anthropomorphism for physical objects. However, this fact does not rule out the assumption of equilibrium theories that there is a normal state in human experience.

(b) The difference between the two theories is reflected in the experimental situations in which they are tested, and especially in the controls used to make the situation conform to the theory. Experiments in the stochastic tradition restrict verbal interaction severely, usually to uniquely defined signals. Preferably, subjects do not have any contact with each other or do not even know that another subject is present. Equilibrium theories, by contrast, distinguish carefully between stimulus and communication. Typical studies contrast objective facts or evaluations of things with interpersonal communications and influences. Their principal restriction is directed against any carry-over from outside that might affect the experimentally created situation to which the subject responds.

(c) Stochastic models relate sets of variables which reduce the individual to a sort of random apparatus that applies the proper probability relationships between stimuli and responses. Equilibrium theories start out with a state of being that a person prefers or rather a number of states that he tries to avoid, dissonance, inconsistency, etc. This leaves the organism two autonomous functions: he decides what is consistent and what is not, and he finds different ways to achieve this consistency. This freedom gives the individual at least the possibility of distinguishing between people and things by his categorization and by his different reactions to discrepancies.

(d) The equilibrium theories offer the possibility of viewing the experimental subject as a person, just as the experimenter or theorist is a person. However, even in this compromise solution we can see the difficulty that the mere possibility of qualitative differences creates for strict mathematical formulation. Stochastic theories can accept mathematical concepts and their full implications in a mathematical calculus: as in the physical sciences, once the concepts are coordinated to empirical facts, they can be used purely as mathematical concepts and only the results need be related back to the empirical situation [4]. Equilibrium theories know little of this convenient separation of mathematical theory and empirical generalization. Even the mathematical approach most closely adapted to equilibrium models, namely directed graph theory, often must hark back to the empirical meaning of the terms [7]. In the main, however, equilibrium theories proceed by relating concepts that are derived from empirical generalization instead of by applying a complete logical or mathematical calculus [4]. It can be said that they use scientific reasoning but not mathematical analysis.

(e) In the return translation from the mathematical model to empirical fact, both types of theory deal with small, isolated aspects of behavior. For two reasons equilibrium theories are generally more applicable to actual performances, even in the laboratory: (1) they accept integrative behavior and individual decisions of the organism in their framework, and (2) they predict only ordinal differences. Weakness in mathematical formulation therefore becomes strength in empirical application.

3.2 Content Analysis. Neither of the experimental models deals with the measurement of communication. Each tries to restrict communication within the experimental situation in order to make it represent a predetermined measure. In this way communications are measured as pure stimuli whose dimensions are well known and accurately measured. Information theory measures communications in the same way, and, in its application to social science, has been more useful in handling stimulus data than in treating interpersonal communication.

Content analysis of communication data, on the other hand, has been developed in many ways. In fact, its main drawback has been its very multiplicity, a new scheme being developed for every purpose. However, each method has taken communication between humans as its central problem and has tried to adapt to this purpose. The lack of a theoretical base and the multiplicity of dimensions have made the construction of mathematical models of content analysis difficult, the tendency being to return to a complete stimulus analysis. For this reason advanced content-analysis methods have rarely found their way into group experiments. In another paper in this volume (see chapter 18) Roby discusses the need for techniques for analyzing communication data within experiments and suggests many applications.

Content analysts have developed some techniques that would make the transition between stimulus and communication easier. Among them are measurements of amount of semantic information, as in the cloze technique [12], measurements of emotionality in a message, analysis of style, or measurements of categories of what is revealed. This partial listing shows that the techniques are available for using actual communication in experimental contexts. In addition, the variables that are used in content analysis suggest the variable that we must concentrate on in analyzing communication processes as opposed to stimulus effects. Three variables stand out in this regard: knowledge of the communicator, knowledge of group structure, and self-evaluation of the subject.

4. Aspect of the Universe of Communication

4.1 Secondary Information. Let us start with a purely cognitive problem. Can a distinction be drawn between communication as transmission of general information and as transmission of information about the communicator? We can label the two types of information primary and secondary information. Each message can transmit both kinds of information. A plausible hypothesis about their relation is that the two are inversely proportional. If a message carries no information in the usual sense at all, e.g., if it is a complete repetition of a previous message, at least we know that the transmission was reliable or that the communicator is dependable. The more primary the information that is transmitted, the less the recipient need worry about the state of the source itself. If the story is taken at face value, we learn little about the storyteller. These dilemmas are familiar in interviewing practice, in which definite attempts are made to obtain secondary information. The problem in such cases then is to determine how much time should be devoted to obtaining secondary information, what the indications are that an item is primary or secondary, and whether or not the two can be combined into one measure of information. The question of the apportionment of primary and secondary information also arises in situations that are not devoted purely to information transmission, for instance, in questions of first-impression formation, social perception, and impression management [8]—in short, this is an important aspect of social interaction.

In terms of information theory we can differentiate the message into the signal input and the parameters of the system. In relating the signal to the message it is important to know something about the nature of the system. But information about the parameters comes to the recipient in the same way as the message content—as a part of the message. Thus, the problem is to assign a message either to the system itself or to the information source. If this can be done, we can then, within a mathematical system, distinguish people from stimulus objects: the latter are represented in the signal and the person by the parameter. For instance, a communicated system that includes a large random-noise source would represent an indiscriminate liar while a noise source that systematically changes messages to a message favorable to the recipient can represent a flatterer.

Let us first sketch a content analysis system capable of distinguishing primary and secondary information within a message. Certainly statements referring specifically to the speaker himself are secondary information. Further, there are many qualifying expressions that are actually part of the primary information, e.g., words like "perhaps," "too much," or evaluative statements. With the latter we reach an area where the distinction between primary and secondary information must be made arbitrarily. For instance, if A says that B is obnoxious, this can be considered either an item of information about B, or secondary information about A's feelings. The decision will depend in general on previous knowledge of both A and B. Another set of items depends even more on previous information. In this category fall questions of internal consistency, patterning (such as acquiescence), and deviation from expected behavior (e.g., confessions are usually more believable than denials). This category conforms neatly to the hypothesis that primary and secondary information are inversely related. If any item of this kind is taken as information, it can tell nothing about the respondent, and vice versa.

This listing has shown that it may be possible in specific cases to expand information theory in this way to include the human respondent. However, it has also shown that in general this classification cannot be made within the system. Some initial information about the parameters, or some independent knowledge of the data to be transmitted, is needed to evaluate the borderline cases. Even more important is the relationship between the people in the system, since this determines what proportion the recipient expects to obtain between information about the situation and information about the speaker himself. The analysis proposed here is therefore most fruitful where the relation between the people involved is clearly determined by the communication situation itself, that is, in a type of interviewing situation. In most cases the social structure must be included as an additional variable. We shall turn now to a formalization of group structure that can be used in connection with a communication system.

4.2 Group Structure and Empathy. Many approaches have been made to the problem of categorizing social structure. We shall proceed by typing the reaction to another person's behavior. Person A, confronted with a certain feeling in person B, can react positively in any of three different ways: he can have an immediate reaction and feel and act the same way as B does; he can understand B's feelings and be able to talk to him about them or give a correct description of them; or he can know what is needed and do it. Each of these reactions has at various times been called empathy; we can call them, respectively, emotional, intellectual, and active empathy. The cohesion of the group may depend on any or all of these factors, and we may say that extreme low cohesion is reached when all three are low. At the high end, however, the situation is more complicated. An attempt is being made to study the relationship of the three variables and the conditions for the existence of different types of empathy.[2]

From the point of view of communication, the important distinction is the one between intellectual and emotional empathy. What kind of communication is needed to produce emotional identification as compared to simple understanding of what the other person thinks? It should be noted in passing that the difference here corresponds to the difference between perceiving the other as a person, from inside as it were, as part of one's world, and perceiving him as one would an object, through pure stimuli, as part of one's environment. A person can identify only with what he accepts to be equivalent to himself, at least in some respects.

[2] Experiments to this end have been conducted at Duke University under Contract Nonr 1181(11), NR 177–470, with the Office of Naval Research, by David M. Shaw, Mary L. Brehm, and the author.

It can be seen that this classification does not exactly agree with either the general notion of cohesiveness of small groups or with the usual typology of societies (mechanical–organic, sacred–profane, etc.). We would expect a high amount of group cohesion or integration under conditions in which each member feels intuitively what the other feels and also is able to express the other's views. It seems, however, that this occurs only under special circumstances. Under many conditions emotional empathy can actually inhibit communication. This can easily be seen in complementary relationships, e.g., teaching and punishing. If A feels like B, he feels as ignorant or as self-justified as B, and he cannot teach B what B needs to know or correct B's behavior. On the other hand, in order to interact with another person in such situations a certain distance is required.

Emotional empathy is a base for group structure that can occur practically without verbal communication, but is felt like immediate perception. It may be thought that it is the strongest base for group cohesion, but actually some evidence suggests that ambivalent relationships are likely to lead to emotional empathy. Intellectual empathy, on the other hand, needs a more detached, stable relationship in which information about the ideas, attitudes, and feelings can be exchanged.

Our experiments have shown that it is possible to distinguish the two types of empathy as a base for group structure. This was done by identifying a reaction of an observer that was identical to the reaction that the person observed would have had, usually the remembering of incompleted tasks (the so-called Zeigarnik effect). The ratio of incompleted to completed tasks could be compared with the actual communication between the two persons with the knowledge they had about each other. The relationship between the two types of empathy turned out to be rather complex. If the group was over a minimum size, emotional empathy occurred where the two partners agreed on the topic under discussion in the presence of a hostile audience, where they were of opposite sex, and where little communication had occurred. In small groups of three persons, the person who took the lead in discussion also showed the most empathy.

It therefore seems that emotional empathy will result from certain subtle aspects of the communication pattern rather than from the quantity of interaction as measured by length or number of words. These subtle aspects do not carry information; they have no content, either about some outside event or about the person himself, but they nonetheless define the situation. Frequently these aspects are nonverbal or practically subliminal. Thus they are difficult to measure and are best inferred from the situation itself rather than from an analysis of items of communication. In short, the study of empathy reveals an aspect of interpersonal reactions that stands beyond the analysis of communication content. It corresponds to a direct perceptual effect that is an immediate function of the relationships, independent of the actual, measurable communication processes.

4.3 Attitudes and Influence. A third aspect of interpersonal reactions is the individual attitude or stance taken by a person and by the other persons with whom he is dealing. This will manifest itself especially in such effects of interaction as influence. We can take as our example the standard experimental influence situation popularized in the experiments of Asch, Crutchfield, and others. In this situation a person is confronted by physical stimuli to which he is supposed to give the correct response, and by stimuli or communications from other persons that contradict the message given by the physical stimulus. (This situation is also the basis for some stochastic models.) The subject in the experiment can look at the messages from the other members of the group in either of two ways. Either he can take them as stimuli (i.e., regard them as additional clues to the correct response), in which case he is doing what amounts to copying from his neighbor's test paper. Or, he can look at the messages as communications (i.e., as an expression of opinion from people with whom he wants to have some relationship), in which case his reaction may be colored by many factors, e.g., his relation to the other people, how important he thinks the particular issue or choice is to them, what kind of impression he wants to make, and what relation he feels should obtain between members of the group. The first alternative, the individual or cheating reaction, is close to the stochastic theories, the second, the group or conformity reaction, is close to the equilibrium theories.

What concerns us here, however, is not whether one or the other kind of theory is more nearly correct, but that either can be correct depending on the subject's feelings. Experimental controls are usually designed to force the subject into feeling either one way or the other. The usual requirement that the subjects should not know each other beforehand prevents any carryover of actual strong relationships and orientations toward other people. On the other hand, running this experiment with a close-knit group, we found that the social desirability orientation (i.e., the desire to keep up a good face) was important for conformity if the subject had a close friend in the group [2]. Proceeding from the supposition that the subject could look at the social stimuli as cheating opportunities, as cues from friends, or in some other way, we are trying to study the consequences of conformity for the individual with each point of view. As a measure of the stress of different solutions on the individual, physiological measures of tension have been useful.[3] This has enabled us to show that if a group orientation is paramount, conformity is accompanied by a release in tension; if the problems are seen as individual tasks, conformity (i.e., using other people's solutions) tends to increase the tension.

This last research approach has shown another aspect of communication beyond manifest content, personal expression, and group structure, namely,

[3] These experiments have been conducted under Contract Nonr 1181(11), NR 177–470, with the Office of Naval Research and the Health Team Project of the Center for Research on Aging at Duke University by Morton Bogdonoff, David M. Shaw, Mary L. Brehm, Thomas Hood, and the author.

the individual stance taken by the persons involved. This factor, which is primarily a function of individual disposition and previous experience, will give an appropriate kind of meaning to the information transmitted.

5. The Circle of Interaction

Let us now compare the approaches we have considered. Do they show the possibility of making a distinction between human and nonhuman that admits of a quantitative approach? In reviewing all the kinds of interaction discussed, we can extract two dimensions. One dimension can be called the degree of immediacy. It ranges from a signal impinging directly on the organism to the rigid symbolism that can only be understood through a coding scheme. The second dimension relies on a fundamental orientation of the individual. It corresponds closely to the terms *Umwelt* and *Mitwelt* of existential analysis, and we may borrow the terms cognition and encounter for the corresponding modes of interaction [10]. Cognition means here the mere apperception of the natural environment, while encounter represents the human interaction with the world. A series of examples will make this distinction clearer (see also figure 1).

As our starting point let us take a pure stimulus; for instance, the orange so dear to authors of psychology textbooks. The perception of the orange gives a picture of the actual orange, a stimulus pattern that is directly given to the organism. Here we have an example of direct, perceptual

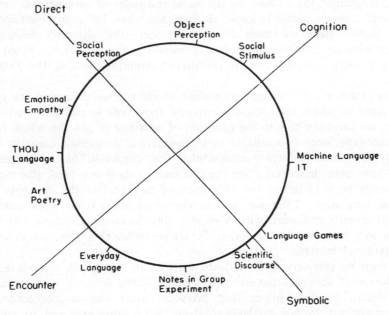

FIG. 1. The Circle of Interaction

transmission. Slightly more symbolic is the social reinforcement of stochastic theories. If words or other symbols are to define the object, we leave the realm of direct transmission. Staying with informational transmission, we turn to languages that are like stimuli. The purest examples are the computer languages, in which each term represents exactly one stimulus or a well-defined set of stimuli. It is probably no coincidence that one of the oldest of these is called IT language, since it is a language to communicate with things [13]. We turn next to languages that are less purely informational, and find them better adapted to human interaction. The first step could be said to be Wittgenstein's language games, which are built of things that can be pointed to or actions that can be rigidly described [15]. Almost equivalent to them is the most theoretically pure scientific discourse, the language of pointer readings and functional relationships. Here we have reached the point of experimental messages and the instructions in social perception experiments that provide secondary information. Messages designed to persuade or group situations designed for this purpose resemble more closely an encounter. Going further to languages of encounter, we reach everyday languages, with their mixture of information transmission and establishment of interpersonal relationships. As the example of advertising shows, languages may be more effective with direct stimuli where no symbolic coding is needed, although many would call this a pseudo-encounter. In a more real way, works of art have a direct personal effect: this stimulus, at the opposite pole from the IT language, we may call the "THOU-language" [5]. Thus, we arrive at the point of interpersonal empathy, where a person seems to know, through his whole behavior, what another person feels. Here we reach direct encounter: the situation determines empathy without the intermediacy of symbolic communication. From this point it is only one step back to the direct stimulus, i.e., to the familiar orange.

If this is a workable though somewhat crude representation of the range of messages to which the human is exposed from both human and nonhuman sources, we can turn now to the question of whether or not the whole range of human experience is amenable to mathematical methods. Clearly, these methods have been eminently successful in the "cognition" half of the circle. As we have seen, however, when the encounter side is involved, the method has usually been to ignore the difference or to translate the concepts into stimulus language. Thus we hear of communication from work partners as social stimuli and work with a rigidly limited communication which filters out any human communication. Only referents that generate emotions are considered human.

One step in conceiving of subjects as human beings is, therefore, the construction of schemes that allow for the use of the languages of encounter and a definition of situations that produce direct human interaction. It seems important to find methods to study these situations and to analyze them without being tied down in advance to any calculus. Mathematical methods have been developed to deal with biological data and can and have been adapted to these purposes. Similarly, it is possible to adapt into schemes of this kind analyses of the form of languages and of all the features that do not fit into straight information-theory set-up. The development of mathematical systems of nerve-nets, artificial neurons, and other analogs seems promising, but, as we have seen, this development is still in the stage of using an extremely complex mechanism for simplified results which have for the most part only demonstration value [3], [11], [16]. For this reason, we have concentrated on reviewing empirical approaches that may lead to a unified theory of interpersonal behavior rather than attempting to develop a mathematical system capable of handling the data of today's experiments. Concepts such as those discussed will have to be developed as building blocks for any mathematical theory of the behavior of persons who are just as human as the theorist himself.

REFERENCES

[1] BACK, K. W., Power, influence, and pattern of communication, chap. 9 in *Leadership and Interpersonal Behavior*, L. Petrullo and B. Bass, eds.; New York: Holt, Rinehart, and Winston, 1961.

[2] BACK, K. W., and K. E. DAVIS, "The Generality of Conformity," paper presented at 1961 American Sociological Association Convention, St. Louis, September 1961.

[3] "Bionics Symposium," WADD Technical Report 60-600, Wright Air Development Division, Wright-Patterson Air Force Base, Ohio, 1960.

[4] BRAITHWAITE, R. B., *Scientific Explanation*, Cambridge: Cambridge Univ. Press., 1953.

[5] BUBER, M., *I and Thou*, New York: Scribner, 1958.

[6] GALANTER, E., and G. A. MILLER, Some comments on stochastic models and psychological theories, chap. 19 in *Mathematical Methods in the Social Sciences 1959*, K. Arrow, S. Karlin, and P. Suppes, eds., Stanford Calif.: Stanford Univ. Press,, 1960.

[7] HARARY, F., and R. Z. NORMAN, *Graph Theory as a Mathematical Model in Social Science* (Research Center for Group Dynamics Monograph Series No. 2), Ann Arbor: Univ. of Michigan, 1953.

[8] JONES, E. E., K. E. DAVIS, and K. J. GERGEN, Role-playing variations and their informational values for person perception, *J. Abnorm. Soc. Psychol.*, 1961, **57**, 302-7.

[9] LEWIN, K., *A Dynamic Theory of Personality*, New York: McGraw-Hill, 1935.

[10] MAY, R., E. ANGEL, and H. F. ELLENBERGER, eds., *Existence*, New York: Basic Books, 1958.

[11] NATIONAL PHYSICAL LABORATORY, *Mechanization of Thought Processes*, London: H. M. Stationery Office, 1959.

[12] OSGOOD, C. E., The representational model and relevant research methods, chap. 2 in *Trends in Content Analysis*, I. de S. Pool, ed., Urbana: Univ. of Illinois Press, 1959.

[13] PERLIS, A. J., J. W. SMITH, and H. R. VAN ZOEREN, *Internal Translator (IT)*, *A Compiler for the 650*, Ann Arbor: Univ. of Michigan, Statistical Research Laboratory, 1957.

[14] TOULMIN, S., and J. GOODFIELD, *The Fabric of the Heavens*, London: Hutchinson, 1961.

[15] WITTGENSTEIN, L., *Philosophical Investigations*, New York: Macmillan, 1953.

[16] YOVITZ, M., and S. CAMERON, eds., *Self-Organizing Systems*, New York: Pergamon Press, 1960.

4

Two-Person Interactive Learning:
A Progress Report

C. J. Burke, *Indiana University*

This paper reports investigations carried out in my laboratory for two-person interactive learning at Indiana University. It is not a single, simple treatment of a self-contained topic but falls into two major parts. The first is an informal report on several experimental investigations, the second poses and discusses several theoretical problems that occur when the linear model of statistical learning theory is applied to the two-person interactive situation.

It is perhaps worth noting at the outset that none of the experimental investigations is, strictly speaking, an investigation of two-person interaction. However, there are intimate connections between two-person interactive learning and the learning of an individual. For certain types of individual learning, there are corresponding two-person interactive situations. One such type is the simple prediction experiment (Humphrey's verbal conditioning type), which has been widely used for investigations of both individual learning and two-person interactive learning. The simple prediction experiment has certain features that make it rather easy to adapt for two-person interactive situations. A question now arises: "What other kinds of learning experiments can be so related?" During the past few years, Bower [4] and Estes [9], [10] have successfully applied to paired-associate learning simple Markov models embodying a guessing state in addition to conditioned states. The classical paradigm in paired-associate learning does not lend itself readily to extension to the two-person case. However, I shall discuss a bit further the possibilities of modifying the paired-associate paradigm in order to permit extension to the two-person case.

Most of the investigations of two-person interactive learning in the verbal conditioning or simple prediction experiment have been cases of determinate reinforcement. In other words, for each subject of the interacting pair, there have been two responses and two reinforcements, one reinforcement

The studies reported in the present paper were carried out under U. S. Public Health Service Grant No. M3939 Cl.

being associated with each response. The experimental routines have involved a precise reinforcement of each response on each trial; never in the course of the experiment have there been nonreinforced trials, i.e., trials on which neither response is reinforced.

Prediction experiments that do involve nonreinforced trials have been of interest to a number of investigators of simple learning and have the properties that permit extension to the two-person case. There is a line of experimentation beginning with Detambel [8] and Neimark [14], continuing through papers by Anderson and Grant [1] and Atkinson [2]. The simple learning situation involving nonreinforced trials introduces interesting theoretical problems when interpreted in terms of the linear model of statistical learning theory and has, furthermore, the properties that permit extension to the two-person case. For this reason, I shall comment on an experiment involving a case of simple learning that is especially easy to handle from the theoretical viewpoint, looking forward to an extension of the case involving nonreinforced trials to two-person interactive learning.

Before describing specifically the paired-associate experiment and the prediction experiment involving nonreinforced trials, I shall first set out paradigms for the simple learning experiment and the two-person interactive learning experiment, in order to point out the features of simple learning experiments that must be present in order to provide a basis for the step to two-person interactive learning.

The discussion of mathematical topics that constitutes the second portion of the paper is clear and straightforward. In previous research, I have dealt in detail with the predicted mean learning curves for two subjects in a two-person interaction. Solutions can be obtained in the straightforward way by the simplest techniques of linear difference equations, provided that an experimental restriction is placed on reinforcement probabilities. This restriction, called the diagonal-sums restriction, has been discussed in considerable detail in previous work and will be presented later in this paper. It will be shown that its mathematical significance lies quite deep in the structure of the linear model of statistical learning theory, going in fact far beyond the obtaining of solutions for the mean learning curves. Specifically, it will be shown that when the diagonal-sums restriction is maintained, one can obtain important moments for the probabilities of response which characterize the learning process; but that when it is not maintained, the recursions can only be solved by approximative techniques. In other words, without the diagonal-sums restriction, one does not obtain simple closed solutions to the recursions that describe the learning process. The structure of this aspect of two-person interaction theory is much like the mathematical structure of the unequal-alpha case discussed by Bush and Mosteller [7].

A second section of the mathematical portion of the paper is concerned with the issue of absorption in certain special two-person interactions. Atkinson and Suppes [3], [16] have represented two-person interactive learning by a simple Markov model with four states. For certain choices of reinforcement parameters, the Atkinson–Suppes Markov model predicts absorption of the process in one or two so-called absorbing states. The Markov model represents learning as occurring by abrupt transitions of the process from one to another of the four states on a given trial. The linear model, on the other hand, represents the learning process as a gradual wandering. In a previous paper [6], I argued that for cases of absorption in the Markov model, the linear model should also lead to the prediction of absorption, but I did not give an unimpeachable proof. In fact, what was shown is that if the process does get to one or another of two absorbing points, it must remain there. What was not shown is that the process must go to one or another of the absorbing points. Hence, the two models may differ. One could lead to definite predictions of absorption; the other could possibly predict a failure of absorption, with certain choices of experimental parameters. I shall prove that this is not, in fact, the case and, therefore, that there is no question of absorption *vs.* nonabsorption between the Markov model and the linear model.

1. Paradigms for Simple Learning and Two-Person Interactive Learning

Social behavior has been described from various viewpoints. Recent successes in systematic learning theory have led to systematic research by a number of investigators whose aim is to represent and predict two-person interactions on the basis of the results of learning experiments. In this enterprise, social behavior is described in terms of the concepts and categories of the behavioral psychologist. The descriptions of two-person interactions are mediated, therefore, by the psychological concepts of stimulus (S), response (R), and reinforcing event (E). In terms of the symbols representing these concepts, a trial of an individual learning experiment is represented by paradigm (P1).

Trial Paradigm for Individual Learning

(P1) $$S \to R \to E$$

The trial begins with the presentation of a stimulus. After the stimulus is presented, the subject in the experiment may make a response, and after his response a reinforcing event which terminates the trial is presented by the experimenter. The symbols S, R, and E refer not to single, unique objects, but to classes of objects. In a discrimination experiment, there is a set of stimulus objects, and some subset is presented on each trial. The subset is not uniform over all trials. Similarly, a learning experiment may involve response differentiation. When it does, the response is a set of response alternatives, and some subset occurs on each trial. Finally, in an experiment involving variable reinforcement, the set of reinforcing events has a number of members, and presentation of the reinforcing events is not uniform over the trials of the experiment.

In an experimental context, from the point of view of the behavioral psychologist, the learning process is envisioned as occurring over a sequence of trials. Each trial begins with the presentation of a stimulus or set of stimuli. The kinds of behavior available to the subject organism are assigned to response classes. The particular classification appropriate to any experiment depends on the interest of the experimenter, as well as the kinds of behavior available to the subject. Response classes are usually defined so as to be exhaustive and mutually exclusive. Following the occurrence of a member of any response class, the experimenter presents a reinforcing event. Reinforcing events also are defined so as to be described by a set of exhaustive and mutually exclusive classes. In a simple conditioning experiment, the stimulation is frequently uniform over all trials. The response classes are often simply two subclasses corresponding to the occurrence or non-occurrence of some simple response defined in terms of its environmental consequences, and the class of reinforcing events frequently has a single member which occurs uniformly over the trials. The simple paradigm (P1), however, can also represent experiments of great complexity. If there is more than one reinforcing event, the particular reinforcing event to be delivered on a single trial can be made deterministically or probabilistically contingent on the responses which the subject has made on one or more previous trials. Furthermore, when the stimulus is a class from which subsets are to be presented on any trial, the particular subset which is presented on a given trial may also depend on the responses made by the subject over one or more of the preceding trials.

A two-person interaction is the simplest instance of a social interaction. In a two-person interaction, each member of the pair of subjects makes responses that can affect the reinforcements of his partner. Sidowski, Tabory, and Wyckoff [15] have named a social situation in which the only effect of one participant on the others is the mediation of reinforcing events via the responses of the subject, a *minimal* social situation. Also, in a two-person interaction, the responses of one subject may serve to either stimulate the partner or affect his stimulation. I shall call a social situation in which the responses of one participant affect the stimulation, as well as the reinforcements, of the other participants, an *extended minimal* social situation. Paradigm (P2) represents an extended minimal social situation for the two-person case.

Two-Trial Paradigm for Two-Person Interactive Learning

(P2)
$$S \to R \to E \qquad S \to R \to E$$
$$S' \to R' \to E' \qquad S' \to R' \to E'$$

The paradigm shows two trials of an interactive learning experiment involving two subjects. The paradigm for either subject on a single trial is simply paradigm (P1). For one of the subjects, the symbols are unprimed; for his partner, the symbols are primed. The broken arrows show interactive effects across the pair of subjects. The short-dashed arrows represent dependence of reinforcing events for one subject upon the responses of his partner. The long-dashed arrows represent the effects on the stimulation for either subject of his partner's response on the previous trial.

Examination of paradigm (P2) shows what sort of learning experiments can be extended to two-person interactions. The learning experiments must have the following simple properties. (1) There must be either variability in the reinforcing event from trial to trial or variability in the stimulation from trial to trial. If there is variability in the reinforcing event and not in the stimulation, extension can be made to a minimal social situation. If there is variability in the stimulation, with or without variability in the reinforcing event, extension can be made to the extended minimal social situation. (2) The effects of both the reinforcing events and the stimuli, with their attendant variabilities, must be understood for the individual learning experiment. If such effects can be handled precisely by theoretical means in the individual learning experiment, it is possible to extend the theoretical treatment to cover two-person interactive learning.

2. The Prediction Experiment as a Two-Person Interaction

The prediction experiment has often been described as either an individual learning experiment or a two-person interaction [5], [11], [16]. The trial paradigm for the prediction experiment is given in (P3).

Trial Paradigm for Prediction Experiment (Individual Learning)

$$(P3) \qquad S \left\langle \begin{array}{l} A_1 \left\langle \begin{array}{l} E_1 \\ E_2 \end{array} \right. \\ A_2 \left\langle \begin{array}{l} E_1 \\ E_2 \end{array} \right. \end{array} \right.$$

Each trial begins with the presentation of a signal or stimulus. Following the signal, the subject makes a response which is restricted to two alternatives, A_1 (a prediction of the subsequent occurrence of E_1) or A_2 (a prediction of the subsequent occurrence of E_2). Finally, either E_1 or E_2 is presented, and the trial is terminated. When the experimenter has set down rules for presenting the events E_1 and E_2, an experiment can be run off. The presentation of E_1 or E_2 is sometimes independent of the response of the subject, in which case the experiment is called noncontingent. However, the presentation of E_1 or E_2 can be made to depend upon the response of the subject, in which case the experiment is called contingent. Typically, the rules of the experimenter are a set of probabilities for the delivery of the E_1 or E_2 event on each trial. In most experiments, the probabilities of the E_1 and E_2 events are constant over trials, although this need not be the case. Since the reinforcing events E_1 and E_2 are exhaustive and mutually exclusive, it suffices to specify the probability of E_1. In cases where the reinforcement probabilities are constant over all trials, they may be specified by a simple reinforcement array like (A1), giving the probability of the E_1 event when an A_1 response is made and when an A_2 response is made.

Probability of E_1

$$(A1) \qquad \begin{array}{ll} A_1 & \pi_1 \\ A_2 & \pi_2 \end{array}$$

We let π_1 be the probability of the E_1 event following the A_1 response and π_2 its probability following the A_2 response. If π_1 equals π_2, the situation is noncontingent.

The trial paradigm for the prediction experiment involving two-person interactive learning has been given in detail elsewhere [6]. It involves a fairly detailed tree and will not be presented here. Essentially, it is paradigm (P3) complicated so as to take into account two subjects designated by primed and unprimed symbols. Each subject has two response alternatives, so that four combinations, $A_1 A_1'$, $A_1 A_2'$, $A_2 A_1'$, and $A_2 A_2'$ can occur. Each subject has two reinforcing events, so that four similar combinations, $E_1 E_1'$, $E_1 E_2'$, $E_2 E_1'$, and $E_2 E_2'$ are possible. There must be a reinforcement array for each of the subjects, and each reinforcement array must have four cells corresponding to the four response combinations. Reinforcement arrays for two-person interactive learning in the prediction experiment are given in (A2).

	Probability of E_1		Probability of E_1'	
	A_1'	A_2'	A_1'	A_2'
A_1	π_{11}	π_{12}	π_{11}'	π_{21}'
A_2	π_{21}	π_{22}	π_{12}'	π_{22}'

(A2)

If E_{1n} and E_{1n}' represent the occurrences, respectively, of the reinforcing events E_1 and E_1' on trial n and, further, if A_{jn} and A_{kn}' represent the occurrences of responses A_j and A_k' on trial n, the π_{jk} and π_{kj}' values given in reinforcing array (A2) may be defined by

$$\pi_{jk} = \Pr\{E_{1n} \mid A_{jn} A_{kn}'\},$$
$$\pi_{kj}' = \Pr\{E_{1n}' \mid A_{jn} A_{kn}'\}.$$

(1)

A complication of paradigm (P3) together with the reinforcement arrays (A2) defines a two-person interactive learning situation for the prediction experiment. Many such experiments have been run. The dependent variables of the experiment are the proportions of responses A_1, A_2, A_1', A_2', and of combinations of pairs of responses, as well as other measures such as response latency, which may be associated with the responses. There have been fairly extensive comparisons of two types of theoretical models with the data from the experiments. It might be noted that occasionally experiments of this type have been run with differential payoffs for various response combinations. Difficulties that arise in the interpretation of differential payoffs are discussed in this volume by Estes (chapter 9).

The theoretical discussion that forms the later part of this paper will be based on the two-person interaction we have just described. Before taking it up, however, we digress to consider two other learning experiments that might be extended to two-person interactions.

3. Two-Person Interactions Based on Indeterminate Reinforcement and on Paired-Associate Learning

3.1 Indeterminate Reinforcement.

A fair number of two-person interaction experiments have been based on the prediction situation. In general, these interactive learning experiments have involved determinate reinforcement; that is, no nonreinforced trials have been included. The trial paradigm for a simple learning experiment involving nonreinforced trials is given below.

Paradigm for a Prediction Experiment with Nonreinforced Trials

(P4)

$$S \overset{\nearrow}{\underset{\searrow}{}} \begin{matrix} A_1 \overset{\nearrow E_1}{\underset{\searrow E_0}{\rightarrow E_2}} \\ A_2 \overset{\nearrow E_1}{\underset{\searrow E_0}{\rightarrow E_2}} \end{matrix}$$

The paradigm indicates a single stimulus uniformly presented over the trials. There are two responses, A_1 and A_2, such as depressing one or another of two telegraph keys; and three reinforcing events: E_1, a reinforcement of response alternative A_1, E_2, a reinforcement of response alternative A_2, and E_0, neither E_1 nor E_2. The three reinforcing events are readily seen to be a set of exhaustive and mutually exclusive events. In general, the application of the linear model associated with statistical learning theory leads to particular kinds of mathematical difficulties when the E_0 events are included.

In the linear model, operators are introduced to represent the effects of reinforcement. If E_1 occurs on trial n, the probability of A_1 on trial $n + 1$ will be a specific linear function of the probability on trial n. If E_2 occurs on trial n, then a different linear function is used to calculate the probability on trial $n + 1$. The probabilities of the A_2 response are treated symmetrically and need not be considered, since, in view of the exhaustive and mutually exclusive character of the two response alternatives, the probabilities of the two must always sum to one. The simplest way to introduce the E_0 event into the theory is to assume that no change in probability occurs from trial n to trial $n + 1$ whenever an E_0 event occurs. In other words, one assumes an identity operator on the probability of the A_1 response or the probability of the A_2 response in going from one trial to the next, when an E_0 event occurs. The difference equations representing the process become complicated, and it is difficult to find a solution in closed form for the general case. Solutions are readily obtained in the particular case where, although the probabilities of the E_1 and E_2 events are contingent upon the response made on the trial, the probability of the E_0 event is not so contingent. This case is sufficiently complex to permit investigations of the learning phenomenon with nonreinforced trials, yet mathematically simple, so that learning curves and other statistics associated with the data can be computed. The experiment involving nonreinforced trials, on which I shall comment briefly, is of this nature. More specifically, the experimental routine is described by the trial paradigm and by the specification of the conditional probabilities of the E_k reinforcing events ($k = 0, 1, 2$) contingent upon the A_j responses ($j = 1, 2$). We can then write the probability π_{jk} to represent the probability of reinforcing event E_k

following response A_j. The experimental routine can then be described in terms of the array of reinforcement probabilities (A3).

	E_1	E_2	E_0
(A3) A_1	π_{11}	π_{12}	π_{10}
A_2	π_{21}	π_{22}	π_{20}

Whenever the experimenter has chosen specific numerical values for the six values of π_{jk}, he has established a set of rules by which he can run his experiment. In general, only four of the probabilities may be freely chosen, since, whatever the value of j, the set of reinforcing events constitutes an exhaustive and exclusive class of events so that the following restrictions must obtain:

$$(2) \qquad \pi_{11} + \pi_{12} + \pi_{10} = 1 , \qquad \pi_{21} + \pi_{22} + \pi_{20} = 1 .$$

As was pointed out above, imposition of a further restriction,

$$(3) \qquad \pi_{10} = \pi_{20} ,$$

leads to a case of learning which, from the point of view of the linear operator model, is simple and easily dealt with theoretically. In the experiment reported here, two values were chosen for the proportion of blank trials, π_{10} and π_{20}: for two groups, .50; for the other two groups, .25. Orthogonal to the proportion of blank trials was a classification according to the relative frequency of E_1 events on the reinforced trials, so that four experimental groups resulted. In each group, subjects were run for about twelve hundred trials in three daily sessions of forty to fifty minutes each. Data have been analyzed from two aspects. The first aspect is with respect to the mean learning curve. All four groups overshoot the theoretical asymptote predicted by the linear model of probability learning theory on the second and third days, but three of the four groups are fitted very closely by the mean learning curve predicted from that theory with a learning-rate parameter estimated at 0.15 to 0.20. The second analysis concerned the probability that various response-reinforcing events would occur. One can calculate from the model the mean probabilities over the entire sequence of trials of getting an A_i response on the nth trial, an E_j reinforcing event on the nth and an A_k response on the $(n + 1)$th for $i = 1, 2, j = 0,$ 1, 2, and $k = 1, 2$. These probabilities can be compared. The linear model of statistical learning theory makes certain a priori predictions of which of these probabilities shall exceed others; these predictions were tested over the groups and the probabilities estimated from the observed proportions in the actual data. There are thirty-four possible comparisons; only one inversion from theoretical prediction occurs. However, the learning-rate parameter estimated from the proportions has a value in the vicinity of .20, ten to fifteen times as large as the value needed to fit the mean learning curve. This is really an interesting situation. The linear model works well on data representing the mean learning curve and also on data that are intimately associated with changes in probability of response from one trial to the next. Separately, the model represents the two aspects of the data excellently, but the parameter value to be used in looking at one aspect of the data differs markedly from the parameter value to be used in looking at the other. From a theoretical point of view, this is an interesting situation for the linear model of statistical learning theory. In spite of this puzzle, results in the simple learning experiment seem to be orderly and regular and indicate that there might be real interest in the results of a two-person interaction embodying the same types of reinforcement conditions.

3.2 Paired-Associate Learning. Paired-associate learning is described by paradigm (P5).

$$
\begin{aligned}
S_1 &\to R_1 \\
S_2 &\to R_2 \\
&\;\;\vdots \\
S_m &\to R_m
\end{aligned}
$$

(P5)

There is a set of perfectly discriminable stimuli. Corresponding to each stimulus is a unique response. The learning task is the association of the appropriate response with each of the stimuli. A single trial in the paired-associate learning experiment is the presentation of each of the stimuli and the occurrence of some response, appropriate or not, followed by a reinforcing event that indicates which response was appropriate on that trial. As the paradigm stands, there is no opportunity for a two-person analog. Since, for each stimulus–response pair, the stimulus is unique and uniform over all trials, the reinforcement in the simple paired-associate learning experiment is also uniform for each stimulus–response pair over the trials. In order to construct a two-person analog the paired-associate experiment must be complicated in some way. A simple technique is to disturb the uniformity of the stimuli over all trials. During the past few months, an experiment has been carried out which follows the paired-associate paradigm except for uniformity of stimulation. Each stimulus consists of two components. The first component is uniform over all trials. The second is a "noise" stimulus which varies at random from one trial of the experiment to the next. Several experimental groups were run. For the different groups, the weight of the noise component of the stimulus was varied as compared with the weight of the uniform component. The data are presently undergoing detailed analysis. As of the present, it can be said that results are in qualitative agreement with theoretical expectations. Learning curves seem fairly regular, and the rate of learning decreases as the relative weight of the noise component increases for each group. The paradigm for paired-associate learning with noise is given in (P6).

$$
\begin{aligned}
S_1 + N &\to R_1 \\
S_2 + N &\to R_2 \\
&\;\;\vdots \\
S_m + N &\to R_m
\end{aligned}
$$

(P6)

The reason for interest in the paired-associate learning with noise is easy to explain. Understanding two-person interactive experiments in terms of simple learning proceeds most readily when the individual learning experiment involved is amenable to easy theoretical treatment. Estes (see [9] and chapter 9 of this volume) and Bower [4] have recently obtained beautiful and precise accounts of paired-associate learning by applying simple Markov models with two states, a guessing state and a state in which the stimulus is conditioned to the appropriate response. Their models reproduce details of even the fine structure of the data in certain simple experiments with surprising accuracy. If the data from the paired-associate experiment with noise can be handled adequately by simple complications of the Estes–Bower model, then it should be possible to extend the theoretical treatment to an asymmetric two-person interaction where the introduction of noise for one member of the pair depends upon the correctness or incorrectness of the response of his partner.

4. Two Models for the Two-Person Interactive Prediction Experiment

Two models which will be described below have been used as mathematical representations of the simple interactive prediction experiment. The first is a Markov model introduced and used extensively by Atkinson and Suppes. The second is the linear model of statistical learning theory. The models have been described in great detail elsewhere by Estes and Suppes [12], [13], by Suppes and Atkinson [3], [16], and by Burke [5], [6]. Therefore only a brief review of the models will be given here.

The models are both probability models defined over an underlying space. The underlying space is common to the two models and can be described as follows. On each trial of the experiment there are four response combinations for each of the two subjects and four combinations of reinforcing events. In general, any of the response combinations can occur with any of the reinforcing-event combinations so that the learning process beginning with the first trial could be described by a tree which has 16 branchings at each point. At trial 1, there would be 16 distinguishable occurrences of response combinations paired with reinforcing-event combinations. Through the first two trials there are 16 times 16 or 256 distinguishable combinations, and so on. The sample space Ω is the space of all sequences of distinguishable reinforcing-event–response combinations over all (that is, infinitely many) trials. Each sequence of infinite length is a point ω of the sample space.

Various events of interest can be defined over this sample space. For example, the event A_{jn} defined for a fixed j and a fixed n is the set of all sample points which have the occurrence of response A_j on trial n. Similarly, the event E'_{kn} is defined for a fixed k and a fixed n and is the set of all sample points that have the reinforcing event E'_k for the subject denoted by primes on trial n. Thus, for a fixed n, the events A_{1n}, A_{2n}, A'_{1n}, A'_{2n}, E_{1n}, E_{2n}, E'_{1n}, E'_{2n} can all be easily defined. Other important events are cylinder events. The cylinder event $\omega(n)$ consists of all sequences which coincide with a fixed sample point ω through the first n trials. It should be noted that in applying the model all events of interest can be constructed readily from the cylinder events by elementary set operations, such as taking unions and intersections.

Over the sample space, a learning theory must provide two things. First, it must provide rules for calculating various response probabilities as random variables over the sample space. Second, it must provide techniques by which events of interest, such as cylinder events, the events A_{jn}, A'_{jn}, can be assigned unique weights or probabilities. The Markov model and the linear model are alternative methods for doing these two things.

4.1 The Markov Model. The Markov model is easily described. A function is defined on the stimulus for each subject, according as the stimulus is considered to be conditioned to response A_1 or to response A_2. On any trial of the experiment, the stimulus S must be conditioned to either A_1 or A_2, never to both. A similar statement holds for the other subject— the stimulus S' is conditioned on each trial to the response A'_1 or to the response A'_2. U_n and U'_n are random variables that represent the conditioned status, respectively, of S and S' according to

(4)
$$U_n = \begin{cases} 1 & \text{if } S \text{ is conditioned to } A_1, \\ 0 & \text{if } S \text{ is conditioned to } A_2, \end{cases}$$
$$U'_n = \begin{cases} 1 & \text{if } S' \text{ is conditioned to } A'_1, \\ 0 & \text{if } S' \text{ is conditioned to } A'. \end{cases}$$

Changes in the values of U_n and U'_n depend on the reinforcing events on the particular trial and occur according to the following conditioning axioms.

1. If $U_n = 0$, and reinforcing event E_2 occurs on the trial, then $U_{n+1} = 0$. Correspondingly, if $U_n = 1$, and E_1 occurs on the trial, then $U_{n+1} = 1$.
2. If $U_n = 0$, and reinforcing event E_1 occurs on the trial, then U_{n+1} goes to the value 1 with probability c and remains at the value 0 with probability $1 - c$. Correspondingly, if $U_n = 1$, and reinforcing event E_2 occurs on the trial, then $U_{n+1} = 0$ with probability c and remains at 1 with probability $1 - c$.

A similar set of statements using the parameter c' holds for the random variable U'_n with respect to the reinforcing events E'_1 and E'_2. The probability of the A_1 response depends upon the value U_n, according to the following response-evocation axiom: If $U_n = 1$, response A_1 occurs on trial n. If $U_n = 0$, response A_2 occurs on trial n. Similarly, if $U'_n = 1$, response A'_1 occurs, and if $U'_n = 0$, response A'_2 occurs. The information we have given defines a learning theory that can be applied to the data from an experiment. On each trial, we are in a position to calculate changes in response probabilities across the trial first by calculating changes in the values of U_n and U'_n, according to the conditioning axioms, and then by determining the probability of occurrence of a given response according to the response-evocation axiom.

The process that results can be easily described as a Markov process. We define four states corresponding to the four values of U_n and U'_n. The states, therefore, are 1, 1; 1, 0; 0, 1; and 0, 0. From the conditioning axiom it is easy to calculate a matrix of transitional probabilities for going from one state to another on any given trial. The transitional probabilities will depend on the values of the conditioning parameters for the two subjects, c and c', as well as on the reinforcement probabilities given in the reinforcement arrays. It is easy to see, therefore, that a simple Markov process results from this definition of the states and from the conditioning axioms. The probabilities of the A_1, A_2, A_1', A_2' responses are 1 or 0, depending on which state the pair of subjects is in, so that response probabilities for either subject are easily calculated as functions on the states.

4.2 The Linear Model. The linear model of statistical learning theory is somewhat more complex mathematically than the Markov model. It too provides rules for the calculation of changes in probability as determined by the reinforcing event that occurs on a given trial. Furthermore, it permits calculation of response probabilities in the course of a learning experiment.

Response probabilities, which are the dependent variables of the theory, occur in the linear model as sequences of random variables on the underlying space. That is, the probability on the first trial is a random variable on the underlying space, as is the probability on the second trial and the probability, in general, on the nth trial. If we consider the set of probabilities over the first n trials, this is a finite sequence of random variables. In the linear model we define the sequence recursively. That is, the model has rules for operating on the probabilities on trial n to obtain those on trial $(n + 1)$. In general, the probability on trial n will depend on the particular point ω of the sample space which we examine. But its probability on the next trial, the $(n + 1)$th, will depend also on the particular reinforcing event which occurs on trial n. Thus we write the following recursions for the probabilities on trial $(n + 1)$ in terms of the probabilities on trial n for a fixed point ω of the sample space.

$$
\begin{aligned}
p_{n+1}(\omega \mid E_{1n}) &= (1 - \theta)p_n(\omega) + \theta , & 0 < \theta < 1 ; \\
p_{n+1}(\omega \mid E_{2n}) &= (1 - \theta)p_n(\omega) , & \\
p_{n+1}'(\omega \mid E_{1n}') &= (1 - \theta')p_n'(\omega) + \theta' , & 0 < \theta' < 1 . \\
p_{n+1}'(\omega \mid E_{2n}') &= (1 - \theta')p_n'(\omega) , &
\end{aligned}
$$

(5)

The symbols p_n and p_n' refer, respectively, to the probabilities of the A_1 response for the two subjects. The symbols θ and θ' are so-called learning-rate parameters and are restricted to the open interval from 0 to 1. The essential problem of applying the theory is the problem of going from the recursions given in equations (5) to the sequence of random variables that gives the probability of response A_1 and A_1' on each trial. For some applications we may be interested in something more than this. We may want not the probabilities for individual subjects as a pair of random variables, but rather the probability for a given response combination across the pair of subjects as a single sequence of random variables.

Mathematically speaking, application of the Markov model is straight-forward, but the linear model can become exceedingly complex. The concern of the theoretical portion of this paper is to examine certain mathematical problems that arise in connection with the linear model.

5. Some Properties of the Linear Model

In the present section of the paper, we shall extend results previously obtained with respect only to the mean learning curve to expected values of other random variables that are of considerable interest. We begin by writing the recursions for the operators in somewhat more detail, and always with explicit reference to the probability $q_n(\omega)$ and $q_n'(\omega)$ of the A_2 responses. We shall make frequent use of Kronecker's delta, which is written δ_{jk} and which is equal to unity or zero according as j is equal to or not equal to k. From the operators (5) and the restrictions

$$(6) \qquad p_n(\omega) + q_n(\omega) = 1 , \qquad p_n'(\omega) + q_n'(\omega) = 1 ,$$

we obtain general conditional expectations for the quantities $p_n - q_n$ and $p_n' - q_n'$:

$$(7) \qquad \begin{aligned} [p_{n+1}(\omega) - q_{n+1}(\omega) \mid E_j] &= (1 - \theta)[p_n(\omega) - q_n(\omega)] + (\delta_{1j} - \delta_{2j})\theta , \\ [p_{n+1}'(\omega) - q_{n+1}'(\omega) \mid E_{kn}] &= (1 - \theta')[p_n'(\omega) - q_n'(\omega)] + (\delta_{1k} - \delta_{2k})\theta' . \end{aligned}$$

Since a simultaneous occurrence of E_j and E_k' on a trial n is simply the intersection of E_j on trial n and E_k on trial n, one can rewrite the recursions (7) in the following form:

$$(8) \qquad \begin{aligned} [p_{n+1}(\omega) - q_{n+1}(\omega) \mid E_{jn} \cap E_{kn}'] &= (1 - \theta)[p_n(\omega) - q_n(\omega)] + (\delta_{1j} - \delta_{2j})\theta , \\ [p_{n+1}'(\omega) - q_{n+1}'(\omega) \mid E_{jn} \cap E_{kn}'] &= (1 - \theta')[p_n'(\omega) - q_n'(\omega)] + (\delta_{1k} - \delta_{2k})\theta' . \end{aligned}$$

The form (8) is useful because both functions $p_n - q_n$ and $p_n' - q_n'$ are written as conditional expectations over the same event, namely the intersection of E_{jn} and E_{kn}'. By squaring both sides of equations (8) and by multiplying, respectively, the right sides and the left sides of the two members of equations (8), one easily gets recursions for the squared differences $(p_n - q_n)^2$ and $(p_n' - q_n')^2$, as well as for the cross product of the two differences:

$$(9) \qquad \begin{aligned} &\{[p_{n+1}(\omega) - q_{n+1}(\omega)]^2 \mid E_{jn} \cap E_{kn}'\} \\ &\quad = (1 - \theta)^2[p_n(\omega) - q_n(\omega)]^2 + 2(\delta_{1j} - \delta_{2j})\theta(1 - \theta)[p_n(\omega) - q_n(\omega)] + \theta^2 , \\ &\{[p_{n+1}'(\omega) - q_{n+1}'(\omega)]^2 \mid E_{jn} \cap E_{kn}'\} \\ &\quad = (1 - \theta')^2[p_n'(\omega) - q_n'(\omega)]^2 + 2(\delta_{1k} - \delta_{2k})\theta'(1 - \theta')[p_n'(\omega) - q_n'(\omega)] + \theta'^2 , \\ &\{[p_{n+1}(\omega) - q_{n+1}(\omega)][p_{n+1}'(\omega) - q_{n+1}'(\omega)] \mid E_{jn} \cap E_{kn}'\} \\ &\quad = (1 - \theta)(1 - \theta')[p_n(\omega) - q_n(\omega)][p_n'(\omega) - q_n'(\omega)] \\ &\qquad + (\delta_{1k} - \delta_{2k})\theta'(1 - \theta)[p_n(\omega) - q_n(\omega)] \\ &\qquad + (\delta_{1j} - \delta_{2j})\theta(1 - \theta')[p_n'(\omega) - q_n'(\omega)] + (2\delta_{jk} - 1)\theta\theta' . \end{aligned}$$

We shall be concerned in the sequel with the five functions whose recursions are given by equations (8) and (9).

In order to obtain expectations of the random variables of interest, we must be able to calculate the weights associated with intersections of each E_{jn} and E'_{kn}—in other words, with the probability on trial n that the reinforcing event for the first subject will be an E_j and for the second subject an E_k. Obviously, these probabilities must depend on the sequence ω, since the probability of an A_1 response and the probability of an A'_1 response depend on the sequence, and since the reinforcement probabilities associated with the E_1 and E'_1 events depend in turn on the response probabilities. The result of somewhat tedious calculations is summarized in equation (10):

(10) $\quad \Pr\{E_{jn} \cap E_{kn} \mid \omega\} \equiv P_{jkn}(\omega)$

$$= \sum_{\alpha=1}^{2} \sum_{\beta=1}^{2} [\delta_{j1}\pi_{\alpha\beta} + \delta_{j2}(1 - \pi_{\alpha\beta})][\delta_{k1}\pi'_{\beta\alpha} + \delta_{k2}(1 - \pi'_{\beta\alpha})]$$

$$\cdot [\delta_{\alpha1}p_n(\omega) + \delta_{\alpha2}q_n(\omega)][\delta_{\beta1}p'_n(\omega) + \delta_{\beta2}q'_n(\omega)] .$$

The weight given in equation (10) is to be applied to the recursions given by equations (8) and (9) in order to attempt to calculate expectations of the sequences of random variables defined by the expressions in equations (8) and (9).

5.1 The Diagonal-Sums Restrictions and Solutions of the Recursions. For the purpose of dealing with expectations, we shall define $\mu_{\alpha\beta}$ as the expectation of the product of $p_n(\omega) - q_n(\omega)$ to the αth power by $p'_n(\omega) - q'_n(\omega)$ to the βth power, as follows:

(11) $\qquad \mu_{\alpha\beta n} = E \sum_{j=1}^{2} \sum_{k=1}^{2} P_{jkn}(\omega)[p_n(\omega) - q_n(\omega)]^{\alpha} [p'_n(\omega) - q'_n(\omega)]^{\beta} .$

Expectations are taken over the points ω of the space. The substance of a fundamental theorem in elementary probability theory relates the expectation of a random variable to the expectation of its conditional expectations where the hypotheses of the conditional expectations form a partition of the space. If $X_n(\omega)$ represents any of the random variables of equations (8) or (9), we can calculate the expectation of $X_{n+1}(\omega)$ occurring on the left sides of the recursions in equations (9) according to equation (12):

(12) $\qquad E[X_{n+1}(\omega)] = E \sum_{j=1}^{2} \sum_{k=1}^{2} [X_{n+1}(\omega) \mid E_{jn} \cap E'_{kn}]P_{jkn}(\omega) ,$

where again the expectations are taken over the points of the sample space. If equations (11) and (12) are applied to the fundamental recursions (8) and (9) with substitution of the expression in equation (10) for the weights, the result of the calculation is a recursion on the appropriate moments of the distribution of the particular random variables dealt with. The coefficients in the recursions are rather complicated functions of the reinforcement parameters π_{jk} and π'_{jk}. A clear picture of the underlying mathematical structure of the relations can best be obtained by introducing abbreviations for the particular functions of the reinforcement parameters which occur in the equations, as follows:

$$2a_{11} = \pi_{11} - \pi_{12} - \pi_{21} + \pi_{22} , \qquad 2a'_{11} = \pi'_{11} - \pi'_{12} - \pi'_{21} + \pi'_{22} ,$$
$$2a_{10} = \pi_{11} + \pi_{12} - \pi_{21} - \pi_{22} , \qquad 2a'_{10} = \pi'_{11} + \pi'_{12} - \pi'_{21} - \pi'_{22} ,$$
$$2a_{01} = \pi_{11} - \pi_{12} + \pi_{21} - \pi_{22} , \qquad 2a'_{01} = \pi'_{11} - \pi'_{12} + \pi'_{21} - \pi'_{22} ,$$
$$2a_{00} = \pi_{11} + \pi_{12} + \pi_{21} + \pi_{22} - 2 , \qquad 2a'_{00} = \pi'_{11} + \pi'_{12} + \pi'_{21} + \pi'_{22} - 2 ,$$

(13) $\quad f_{jk} = \pi_{jk}\pi'_{kj} - (1 - \pi_{jk})(1 - \pi'_{kj}) \qquad (j = 1, 2; \quad k = 1, 2) ;$

$$2b_{11} = f_{11} - f_{12} - f_{21} + f_{22} ,$$
$$2b_{10} = f_{11} + f_{12} - f_{21} - f_{22} ,$$
$$2b_{01} = f_{11} - f_{12} + f_{21} - f_{22} ,$$
$$2b_{00} = f_{11} + f_{12} + f_{21} + f_{22} - 2 .$$

Then, if expectations are taken on the two sides of the recursions (8) and (9), according to the theorems (11) and (12), and the abbreviations (13) are used, the basic recursions (14) and (15) result:

(14)
$$\mu_{10n+1} = [1 - \theta(1 - a_{10})]\mu_{10n} + \theta a_{01}\mu_{01n} + \theta a_{11}\mu_{11n} + \theta a_{00} ,$$
$$\mu_{01n+1} = \theta' a'_{01}\mu_{10n} + [1 - \theta'(1 - a'_{10})]\mu_{01n} + \theta' a'_{11}\mu_{11n} + \theta' a'_{00} .$$

$$\mu_{20n+1} = [(1 - \theta)^2 + 2\theta(1 - \theta)a_{10}]\mu_{20n} + 2\theta(1 - \theta)[a_{00}\mu_{10n} + a_{01}\mu_{11n} + a_{11}\mu_{21n}] ,$$
$$\mu_{02n+1} = [(1 - \theta')^2 + 2\theta'(1 - \theta')a'_{10}]\mu_{02n}$$
$$+ 2\theta'(1 - \theta')[a'_{00}\mu_{01n} + a'_{01}\mu_{11n} + a'_{11}\mu_{12n}] ;$$

and

(15)
$$\mu_{11n+1} = [(1 - \theta)(1 - \theta') + \theta\theta'b_{11} + \theta'(1 - \theta)a'_{10} + \theta(1 - \theta')a_{10}]\mu_{11n}$$
$$+ \theta'(1 - \theta)[a'_{11}\mu_{21n} + a'_{01}\mu_{20n} + a'_{00}\mu_{10n}]$$
$$+ \theta(1 - \theta')[a_{11}\mu_{12n} + a_{01}\mu_{02n} + a_{00}\mu_{01n}]$$
$$+ \theta\theta'[b_{10}\mu_{10n} + b_{01}\mu_{01n} + b_{00}] .$$

Previous theoretical discussions on the application of the linear model to the two-person interaction have been restricted to the recursions of equations (14). These are the recursions of importance in obtaining mean learning curves. In other words, these are the equations whose solutions lead to the mean probability over all sequences of the A_1 and A'_1 responses as functions of trials. It has been pointed out by Atkinson and Suppes [3] and by Burke [5] that the recursions are not easy to solve in the general case because of the intrusion of the cross-product function μ_{11n} into the recursions. In dealing with asymptotic results, Atkinson and Suppes solved the two recursions simultaneously to eliminate μ_{11n} and then tested theoretical predictions against the data on the basis of the resulting linear relationship between the probability of an A_1 and an A'_1 response at asymptote. Burke, on the other hand, imposed the diagonal-sums restriction which, in present notation, can be written as

(16) $$a_{11} = a'_{11} = 0 .$$

In terms of the reinforcement arrays, equation (16) states that the sum of the upper left and lower right diagonal entries in either reinforcement array equals the sum of the lower left and upper right entries, so that the reinforcement array can be written as follows.

	Probability of E_1			Probability of E_1'	
	A_1'	A_2'		A_1'	A_2'
A_1	$k - \pi_2$	$k - \pi_1$	A_1	$k' - \pi_2'$	π_1'
A_2	π_1	π_2	A_2	$k' - \pi_1'$	π_2'

When the diagonal-sums restriction (16) is imposed, recursions (14) simplify to the form given by

$$\text{(17)} \quad \begin{aligned} \mu_{10n+1} &= [1 - \theta(1 - a_{10})]\mu_{10n} + \theta a_{01}\mu_{01n} + \theta a_{00}, \\ \mu_{01n+1} &= \theta' a_{01}'\mu_{10n} + [1 - \theta'(1 - a_{10}')]\mu_{01n} + \theta' a_{00}'. \end{aligned}$$

Equations (17) represent simultaneous difference equations in two variables and are readily solved by elementary methods. The solutions have been discussed extensively by Burke [5], [6].

The diagonal-sums restriction is a restriction on experimental parameters that are chosen by the experimenter. Therefore, the experimenter can select reinforcement situations that satisfy the diagonal-sums restriction and carry out tests of his theory in the restricted situations. The restriction was originally imposed simply to define a set of experiments for which the mean learning curves of the two subjects of an interacting pair could be readily obtained from the theory. In the present discussion, however, it can be seen that its significance is much deeper than merely the obtaining of mean learning curves by simple methods. In fact, if we examine equations (14) and (15), we see that attempts to solve for the means μ_{10} and μ_{01} result, as shown in equations (14), in the intrusion of μ_{11} into the system. If we examine the third member of equation (15), namely the recursion on μ_{11} which must necessarily be introduced if we are to solve even for μ_{10} and μ_{01}, we see that the expectations μ_{20} and μ_{02} intrude. Furthermore, we cannot solve the system of the five functions μ_{10}, μ_{01}, μ_{20}, μ_{02}, and μ_{11} because of the presence of the functions μ_{12n} and μ_{21n}, with coefficients a_{11} and a_{11}'. It is readily seen from the appearance of these equations and the structure of the argument leading to them that one can never write recursions for any fixed subset of expectations arising from the underlying variables $p_n(\omega)$ and $p_n'(\omega)$. For in trying to deal with the five recursions that have been introduced above, two new functions enter on the right-hand sides. If one tries to write recursions for these new functions, in order to complete the solutions, additional functions will enter. Therefore, so long as the diagonal-sums restriction is not satisfied, one cannot, by simple direct methods associated with the solution of difference equations, obtain any sequential representations of the functions describing the learning process. When the diagonal-sums restriction is imposed, however, things become much better. We have seen how equations (13) are simplified to equations (17) when the diagonal-sums restriction is imposed. Similarly, equations (15) become

$$\mu_{20n+1} = [(1 - \theta)^2 + 2\theta(1 - \theta)a_{10}]\mu_{20n} + 2\theta(1 - \theta)[a_{00}\mu_{10n} + a_{01}\mu_{11n}] \,,$$

$$\mu_{02n+1} = [(1 - \theta')^2 + 2\theta'(1 - \theta')a'_{10}]\mu_{02n} + 2\theta'(1 - \theta')[a'_{00}\mu_{01n} + a'_{01}\mu_{11n}] \,,$$

(18) $\quad \mu_{11n+1} = [(1 - \theta)(1 - \theta') + \theta\theta'b_{11} + \theta'(1 - \theta)a'_{10} + \theta(1 - \theta')a_{10}]\mu_{11n}$

$$+ \theta'(1 - \theta)[a'_{01}\mu_{20n} + a'_{00}\mu_{10n}]$$

$$+ \theta(1 - \theta')[a_{01}\mu_{02n} + a_{00}\mu_{01n}] + \theta\theta'[b_{10}\mu_{10n} + b_{01}\mu_{01n} + b_{00}] \,.$$

Equations (18) are readily solved by elementary methods.

5.2 A Case of Absorption in the Linear Model. It is easy to show that the reinforcement probabilities given in array (A5) lead to absorption in the Markov model. The question to be answered here is whether they lead also to absorption in the linear model.

		Probability of E_1		Probability of E'_1	
		A'_1	A'_2	A'_1	A'_2
(A5)	A_1	1	$1 - \pi$	1	π'
	A_2	π	0	$1 - \pi'$	0

For the reinforcement array (A5), the coefficients of the solutions take on the simple values given in equations (19):

(19)
$$a_{11} = a_{00} = 0 \,, \qquad a'_{11} = a'_{00} = 0 \,,$$
$$a_{01} = 1 - a_{10} = \pi; \qquad a'_{01} = 1 - a'_{10} = \pi' \,;$$
$$b_{11} = 1 - b_{00} = \pi\pi' + (1 - \pi)(1 - \pi') \,,$$
$$b_{01} = b_{10} = 0.$$

The recursions for the mean learning curve take on the special forms

(20)
$$\mu_{10n+1} = (1 - \theta\pi)\mu_{10n} + \theta\pi\mu_{01n} \,,$$
$$\mu_{01n+1} = \theta'\pi'\mu_{10n} + (1 - \theta'\pi')\mu_{01n} \,.$$

These recursions are easily solved. The solutions have been given in detail in [6]. The equations for the second moments and the cross-product function are

(21)
$$\mu_{20n+1} = [1 - \theta^2 - 2\theta(1 - \theta)\pi]\mu_{20n} + 2\theta(1 - \theta)\pi\mu_{11n} + \theta^2 \,,$$
$$\mu_{02n+1} = [1 - \theta'^2 - 2\theta'(1 - \theta')\pi']\mu_{02n} + 2\theta'(1 - \theta')\pi'\mu_{11n} + \theta'^2 \,,$$
$$\mu_{11n+1} = [(1 - \theta\pi)(1 - \theta'\pi') + \theta\theta'\pi\pi']\mu_{11n}$$
$$+ \theta'(1 - \theta)\pi'\mu_{20n} + \theta(1 - \theta')\pi\mu_{02n} + \theta\theta'(\pi + \pi' - 2\pi\pi') \,.$$

The recursions for these three functions depend, in this special case, only on the three functions. No outside functions enter, and the recursions can always be solved in detail. Our major concern is the issue of absorption: for this issue we wish to calculate the asymptotic values of the three functions. The results of the calculations are most easily seen if we write the recursion in matrix form. Accordingly, we define the matrix R as follows:

$$(22) \quad R = \begin{bmatrix} 1 - \theta^2 - 2\theta(1-\theta)\pi & 0 & 2\theta(1-\theta)\pi & \theta^2 \\ 0 & 1 - \theta'^2 - 2\theta'(1-\theta')\pi' & 2\theta'(1-\theta')\pi' & \theta'^2 \\ \theta'(1-\theta)\pi' & \theta(1-\theta')\pi & (1-\theta\pi)(1-\theta'\pi') + \theta\theta'\pi\pi' & \theta\theta'(\pi+\pi'-2\pi\pi') \\ 0 & 0 & 0 & 1 \end{bmatrix}$$

The first three rows of this matrix are the coefficients of equation (21). The first column has the coefficients of μ_{20n}, the second column the coefficients of μ_{02n}, the third column the coefficients of μ_{11n}, and the fourth column the constant terms of the equations. It is easy to show that the entries in the matrix are all between 0 and 1 for all possible values of the parameters θ, θ', π, and π'. Further, it is immediately evident that the row sums are unity. Hence R is a stochastic matrix. Using the matrix R, the recursions of equation (21) can be written in the form

$$(23) \qquad [\mu_{20n+1}\mu_{02n+1}\mu_{11n+1}1] = [\mu_{20n}\mu_{02n}\mu_{11n}1]R' ;$$

where R' is the transpose of R. Hence, the recursions are governed by a matrix which is the transpose of a stochastic matrix. Important properties of the process represented by equation (23) can be obtained by considering the integral powers of the stochastic matrix R. From the extensive theory of stochastic matrices, it is easy to see that R has two important properties. First, it represents a Markov chain with an absorbing state. The absorbing state is the state associated with the last row which is, of course, the state associated with the constant term in the recursion (23). Also, all other states of the chain represented by R must be transient states provided that θ and θ' differ from 0, as they must. It is finally readily apparent that the matrix R can never be written in any canonical form corresponding to a Markov chain with an undamped oscillation.

From the foregoing description of the chain related to the matrix R, we see, first, that the process (23) will have a fixed point; second, that the fixed point will be unique; and third, that the fixed point will always be approached. It is immediate that the vector $[1\,1\,1\,1]$ is a fixed point of the process (23) as shown in

$$(24) \qquad [1\,1\,1\,1] = [1\,1\,1\,1]R' .$$

This means that the solution for the asymptote of the set of recursions (21) or (23) is the limiting value of 1 for each of the three functions of interest:

$$(25) \qquad \lim_{n} \mu_{20n} = \lim_{n} \mu_{02n} = \lim_{n} \mu_{11n} = 1.$$

Returning to the definitions of the equations and recalling that $p_n(\omega)$ and $q_n(\omega)$ are always both bounded between 0 and 1, we see that (25) can be satisfied if, and only if, for all sample points ω,

(26)
$$\lim_n [p_n(w) - q_n(\omega)] = \lim_n [p_n'(\omega) - q_n'(\omega)] = 1 , \quad \text{or}$$
$$\lim_n [p_n(\omega) - q_n(\omega)] = \lim_n [p_n'(\omega) - q_n'(\omega)] = -1 .$$

But the satisfaction of equations (26) implies, in turn, absorption at either of the two pairs of points given by

(27)
$$\lim_n p_n(\omega) = \lim_n p_n'(\omega) = 1 \quad \text{and} \quad \lim_n q_n(\omega) = \lim_n q_n'(\omega) = 0 , \quad \text{or}$$
$$\lim_n p_n(\omega) = \lim_n p_n'(\omega) = 0 \quad \text{and} \quad \lim_n q_n(\omega) = \lim_n q_n'(\omega) = 1 .$$

Thus, under the reinforcement conditions of array (A5), the linear model predicts absorption. Furthermore, the absorbing points of the linear model coincide with the absorbing states which have been found for the Markov model. The two models, therefore, cannot be distinguished on the issue of the occurrence or non-occurrence of absorption for the array (A5). The possibility still remains that they can be differentiated in terms of the rate of absorption.

REFERENCES

[1] ANDERSON, N. H., and D. A. GRANT, A test of a statistical learning theory model for two choice behavior with double stimulus events, *J. Exptl. Psychol.*, 1957, **54**, 305–16.

[2] ATKINSON, R. C., An analysis of the effect of non-reinforced trials in terms of statistical learning theory, *J. Exptl. Psychol.*, 1956, **52**, 28–32.

[3] ATKINSON, R. C., and P. SUPPES, An analysis of two-person game situations in terms of statistical learning theory, *J. Exptl. Pyschol.*, 1958, **55**, 369–78.

[4] BOWER, G. H., Application of a model to paired associate learning, *Psychometrika*, 1961, **26**, 255–80.

[5] BURKE, C. J., Applications of a linear model to two-person interactions, chap. 9 in *Studies in Mathematical Learning Theory*, R. R. Bush and W. K. Estes, eds., Stanford Calif.: Stanford Univ. Press, 1959.

[6] BURKE, C. J., Some two-person interactions, chap. 16 in *Mathematical Methods in the Social Sciences*, K. J. Arrow, S. Karlin, and P. Suppes, eds., Stanford, Calif.: Stanford Univ. Press, 1960.

[7] BUSH, R. R., and F. MOSTELLER, *Stochastic Models for Learning*, New York: Wiley, 1955.

[8] DETAMBEL, M. H., A test for multiple choice behavior, *J. Exptl. Psychol.*, 1955, **49**, 97–104.

[9] ESTES, W. K., Learning theory and the new "mental chemistry," *Psychol. Rev.*, 1960, **67**, 207–23.

[10] ESTES, W. K., B. L. HOPKINS, and E. J. CROTHERS, All-or-none and conservation effects in the learning and retention of paired-associates, *J. Exptl. Psychol.*, 1960, **60**, 329–39.

[11] ESTES, W. K., and J. H. STRAUGHAN, Analysis of a verbal conditioning situation in terms of statistical learning theory, *J. Exptl. Psychol.*, 1954, **47**, 225–34.

[12] ESTES, W. K., and P. SUPPES, Foundations of linear models, chap. 8 in *Studies in Mathematical Learning Theory*, R. R. Bush and W. K. Estes, eds., Stanford, Calif.: Stanford Univ. Press, 1959.

[13] ESTES, W. K., and P. SUPPES, "Foundations for statistical learning theory, II: The stimulus sampling model for simple learning," Technical Report No. 26, Contract Nonr-225(17), Institute for Mathematical Studies in the Social Sciences, Stanford University, Stanford, Calif., 1959.

[14] NEIMARK, E. D., Effects of type of non-reinforcement and number of alternative responses in two verbal conditioning situations, *J. Exptl. Psychol.*, 1956, **52**, 115-19.

[15] SIDOWSKI, J. B., L. B. WYCKOFF, and L. TABORY, The influence of reinforcement and punishment in a minimal social situation, *J. Abnorm. Soc. Psychol.*, 1956, **52**, 115-19.

[16] SUPPES, P., and R. C. ATKINSON, *Markov Learning Models for Multiperson Interactions*, Stanford, Calif.: Stanford Univ. Press, 1960.

5

The Application of Learning Models
to Interactive Behavior

Robert R. Bush, *University of Pennsylvania*

The past successes and current popularity of stochastic models for describing individual behavior have led many of us from time to time to attempts at extending the range of application of those models to small group behavior (see [2], [5], and [9]). I first became interested in experimental studies of learning and in models for such experiments in 1949. To me, the striking feature of this branch of psychology was the vast amount of quantitative data in the literature and the lack of anything more than routine analyses of the data. The existing theories were verbal and non-quantitative. What greater challenge could an ex-physicist hope to find?

In 1951, with the extension of the hydrogen atom model to the helium atom still fresh in my mind, I began thinking about linear operator models for two-person interactions. In decided contrast to my earlier experience in the field of learning, I found no experiments and no data on two-person interactions, although I did discover an appreciable literature about two-person phenomena. Parsons and other sociologists viewed two people as the simplest social system. Many psychologists wrote at length about parent–child relations, parent–therapist interactions, marital conflict, and so on. But no one did experiments. I therefore spent a year with two research assistants trying to design and carry out experiments on two-person interactions. We wanted them to be both psychologically interesting and mathematically analyzable. We failed and the work was never published. A few years later, David Hays did a doctoral dissertation under my direction on models and experiments for two- and three-person interactions, but time has now shown that this was not a very fruitful avenue of research.

Ten years have now passed, and in my opinion the situation has not materially changed. During that time a fair number of papers and at least one book have appeared on the subject of stochastic models for two-person interactions. The mathematical analyses presented are interesting, and an occasional experiment has been reported. But by and large we are just where we were in 1951. We still do not have a substantial body of data and experimental paradigms on which we can focus our model-building efforts; we are not even in agreement on what questions should be asked.

Science progresses in devious ways, so the picture may not be as black as I have painted it. In the field of learning, the experiments and concepts came first, the models later. Perhaps in the field of small group behavior the reverse will be true. Perhaps the current interest in two-person models will lead to a body of empirical facts that will have real substantive interest to psychologists and sociologists. If so, then logical analysis of possible classes of two-person experiments (from the point of view of stochastic models) may be more than intellectual masturbation. It is with this hope that the present paper was written.

Most stochastic learning models are concerned with a large class of experiments that can be characterized in the following way. We begin with a sequence of trials. We have a set S of stimulus situations, a set R of possible responses, and a set O of possible outcomes. On each trial an element of S is presented to the subject, he chooses an element of R, and an element of O occurs. A period of time elapses and the next trial begins. In the various models we impose measure functions on the set R—either probability measures or response strength measures such as Luce's v [6, pp. 22-5]. We next introduce a set of operators that modify the measures on R. In general, we have an operator for each element of $S \times R \times O$, and so the models imply branching processes.

In simple learning experiments the set S has only a single element. This is not a stimulus element in the sense that Estes has introduced the term. An element of S as used here is an entire stimulus situation presented to the subject and characterizes an experimental procedure, not an organism's perception. In simple learning experiments, the same stimulus situation is presented on every trial, while in a more complicated class of experiments, the set S has two elements. These have been classically called "discrimination experiments" by learning theorists. Recently, Luce, Galanter, and I have tried to unify the terminology in learning and psychophysics by calling them "identification experiments." I will use the term here without presenting our rationale for it.

In an identification experiment one or the other element of S is presented on each trial. The order of the two elements s_1 and s_2 is determined in advance by the experimenter and is usually "random"; e.g., s_1 may involve a black card at the choice point and s_2 may involve a white card. In general, the pay-off schedules (the outcome programs) are different for s_1 trials than for s_2 trials. The subject's task is to learn the most appropriate response for each type of trial.

In models for identification experiments, we need two measures on the set R. For example, we might need conditional probabilities $\Pr\{r_i \mid s_j\}$ for $j = 1, 2$, and where $r_i \in R$. We could introduce a single measure on $S \times R$, but it must be recalled that the set S is programmed by the experimenter— the sequence of occurrence of its elements is not part of the behavior being studied. Models for such experiments become complicated because of the phenomena of stimulus generalization; what happens on an s_1 trial will alter the probabilities $\Pr\{r_i \mid s_2\}$ as well as $\Pr\{r_i \mid s_1\}$, and what happens on an s_2 trial will change $\Pr\{r_i \mid s_1\}$. It is easy to formulate such models but very hard to analyze them in full detail.

I have sketched the basic structure of two classes of learning experiments and the models for them because I now wish to show that they are strikingly similar, in a formal sense, to some possible two-person experiments and models. We need to introduce a set A of actors that will have two elements in the present discussion. To simplify matters, the set S will be suppressed; I will restrict my remarks to experiments in which the same stimulus situation is presented on each trial. Thus, we have a set A of actors, a set R of responses, and a set O of outcomes.

The general experimental paradigm is as follows. On each trial, one of the two (or more) actors chooses one of the possible responses; one of the possible outcomes then occurs. (Later I will discuss the modification in which both actors act on a single trial.) Two possible experimental procedures now emerge: either the set A is programmed or it is not; i.e., the experimenter can specify which actor is to respond on each trial or he can leave this up to the two subjects and let whoever responds be part of his data. Consider this latter possibility first. On each trial, an element of $A \times R$ will occur.[1]

In the models we would introduce a measure on the set $A \times R$ and a set of operators corresponding to the elements of $A \times R \times O$. In the simplest possible case R would have a single element, and so $A \times R$ would have only two elements. If O had two elements and symmetry assumptions were made (e.g., equal θ's), we would have one of the now well-known two-operator models. Even without symmetry assumptions, we would have at worst a four-operator model such as those used for analyzing T-maze experiments. The data would constitute a binary sequence corresponding to whichever actor responded on each trial. The models are completely developed and estimation schemes are available. All that we need are data.

With two response alternatives available to the two subjects (and A not programmed), we are led to models with probability vectors having four elements and with as many as eight stochastic operators, assuming that there are two possible outcomes. This is not so easy. Such models have not been analyzed in detail and estimation schemes have not been developed, although the research program is straightforward. Again, data are needed.

Now consider the procedure of programming the set A. The experimenter decides which of the two elements a_1 and a_2 shall occur on each trial, i.e., whose turn it is to respond. As in the models for identification experiments, we will need two sets of conditional probabilities, $\Pr\{r_i \mid a_1\}$ and $\Pr\{r_i \mid a_2\}$, and we will want to build in a generalization effect which we will call "interaction," i.e., what happens on an a_1 trial will change $\Pr\{r_i \mid a_2\}$, and vice versa. This formal equivalence of identification experiments on

---

[1] As pointed out to me by Eugene Galanter, this paradigm is formally identical to that for a simple learning experiment with twice the number of response alternatives.

single subjects and actor-programmed two-person experiments is worth noting. (A similar but different comparison of two-person models and identification models was made by Restle [8].) Model developments for one type of experiment will contribute to research on the other type. In both types of experiments the main difficulty is that two interacting stochastic processes are not trivial to study. Furthermore, data are needed. The 1952 experiment of Schwartz on imitation [3, p. 259] and Suppes' recent experiment on conformity[2] fit this general paradigm: A is programmed so that the actors alternate, but the situation is intentionally unsymmetric.

In the preceding paradigms for two-person experiments only one actor responded on each trial. Suppose both actors respond on each trial, as in a simple 2×2 game such as the "prisoner's dilemma." Restrict attention to two possible responses for each subject so that the two-person group has four possible responses. Stochastic models designed for experiments on single subjects and four-response alternatives may then be used, although we would most likely want to introduce an independence assumption. Let p_i be the probability that a_i makes response $r_1 (i = 1, 2)$. Then let the probability that both actors make r_1 be $p_1 p_2$, and so on. Many people have done experiments of this type, but few have reported their data in detail or carried out learning model analyses, the notable exception being Suppes and Atkinson [9]. The reason for this apparently cavalier approach is not clear. Such experiments and models appear more promising and interesting than do most others in the two-person field.

I shall conclude with some general comments on possible areas of application of two-person learning models. Although one-person learning models have been most successful in describing animal data, most of the applications to human experiments have been confined to binary prediction and verbal learning. The models for the verbal data have been quite good (e.g., [1], [3], [7]), but it is not obvious from them how one may conduct two-person verbal learning experiments. The work described by H. Solomon[3] was concerned with group-learning of words, not with responses of individual participants, so that his experiment does not fit any of the paradigms discussed here.

In my opinion, models for individual learning have suffered their greatest defeat in attempting to describe binary prediction data. They have generated reasonable group-learning curves and have predicted group asymptotes which sometimes agree with data. But detailed analyses of binary prediction data [4] have shown that no path-independent conditioning axiom is even close to the truth. It appears that these data must be described by models that involve strategies or "plans." If a conditioning mechanism operates, it must be at a complex level and not at the level of individual predictions.

The extension of binary prediction experiments to two-person situations looks inviting and has occurred in more than one research program. The

---

[2] See chapter 22.

[3] See chapter 15.

experiments may be enlightening, but it does not appear to me that the stochastic models have the slightest prayer of a chance at describing the data in any detail. If binary prediction is an important psychological phenomenon, we should tread lightly in developing adequate descriptive models for one-person experiments before we march into the two-person field.

What direction should we take in our research on two-person interactions? My advice is to find an interesting phenomenon and a clean experimental paradigm first, then to collect data, and finally to develop models for describing the data. We must first develop a set of experimental techniques comparable to those in individual psychology (e.g., classical conditioning, instrumental conditioning, avoidance training, discrimination, detection, rote memory, and concept formation). One of the very few comparable methods in the whole of social psychology is the Asch-Cohen conformity paradigm. A few more such experimental designs, and model building would follow at a rapid rate. It took individual psychology a century to provide the applied mathematicians with material to work with. It may take social psychology even longer.

REFERENCES

[1] BOWER, G. H., Application of a model to paired-associate learning, *Psychometrika*, 1961, **26**, 255-80.

[2] BURKE, C. J., Applications of a linear model to two-person interactions, chap. 9 in *Studies in Mathematical Learning Theory*, R. R. Bush and W. K. Estes, eds., Stanford: Stanford Univ. Press, 1959.

[3] BUSH, R. R., and F. MOSTELLER, *Stochastic Models for Learning*, New York: Wiley, 1955.

[4] DERKS, P. L., *Human Binary Prediction and the Generality of the "Conditioning Axiom" under Temporal, Incentive, Contingency, and Experimental Variations*, Ph.D. Thesis, Univ. of Penn., 1960.

[5] HAYS, D. G., and R. R. BUSH, A study of group action, *Amer. Soc. Rev.*, 1954, **19**, 693-701.

[6] LUCE, R. D., *Individual Choice Behavior*, New York: Wiley, 1959.

[7] MILLER, G. A., and W. J. MCGILL, A statistical description of verbal learning, *Psychometrika*, 1952, **17**, 369-96.

[8] RESTLE, F., A survey and classification of learning models, chap. 20 in *Studies in Mathematical Learning Theory*, R. R. Bush and W. K. Estes, eds., Stanford: Stanford Univ. Press, 1959.

[9] SUPPES, P., and R. C. ATKINSON, *Markov Learning Models for Multiperson Interactions*, Stanford: Stanford Univ. Press, 1960.

6

Application of a Markov Learning Model to a Simple Detection Situation Involving Social Pressure

E. C. Carterette and M. J. Wyman,
University of California, Los Angeles

There appears to be considerable work in social psychology, especially in that area called "small groups," that is amenable to being put into the framework of a standard discrimination experiment. It is important to verify this because, if it is true, social situations could be considered as complex learning and discrimination behavior. Hardly anyone will deny that social interaction could then be investigated somewhat more rigorously than it is now. At the same time, the relation between the laboratory and real life would become less tenuous.

It will be seen also that the experiments to be described have important implications for psychophysics and perception. If the model adequately describes the sequential and asymptotic responses of our subjects, the influence of the experimenter's behavior on the observer's responses will be better understood. Some experimenters suspect that fluctuations in perception and response–response dependencies may be described by models designed for the description of learning. Our experiments are aimed in part at clarifying this problem.

Now we want it to be perfectly clear that our experiments were designed to show the anatomy of social pressure in its most rudimentary form, the Yes–No detection or threshold experiment. For if effects of social pressure *alias* experimenter-controlled events are like those found in the vastly more complex social-pressure studies of the literature on small groups, then our experiments and their quantitative descriptions articulate at once with important studies in social psychology. If clearly different effects are found, one has to discover the class of experiments linking our simple analog to the classical experiments. But more than that, those like Suppes and Krasne [12], who regard the theory of social behavior "as a highly important case of the general theory of individual behavior," may be less serene in their position.

In the present context the experimenter takes on the role played by the

This research was supported by the Group Psychology Branch of the Office of Naval Research.

"stooge" in such classical social-pressure experiments as those of Asch [1] and Sherif [8], [9]. In most psychophysical work the experimenter gives true information after each response or block of trials or even gives continuous feedback. The experiments reported here treat social pressure as the amount of correct information given the observer. We assume that at least two of the following three kinds of reinforcing events are at work: (1) social support, (2) muscular movements (e.g., subvocal responses), and (3) tangible rewards, such as money or praise, which we know influence performance. On the grounds that (3) remains constant throughout a session or belongs in some sense to (1), we will deal, theoretically, with the first two classes.

The first group of experiments is closely related to the study of Suppes and Krasne [12]. They presented subjects with pairs of lines, one of which was longer than the other. The task was to say which of the two lines was the longer. There were two degrees of task difficulty, easy and hard, with probabilities of correct responding estimated from first trials of .92 and .72, respectively. Following the subject's response, the experimenter gave the "correct" response, the concordance between it and the true state of affairs being a parameter.

1. The Experiment and the Theory

On each of a sequence of trials an observation interval was defined during which either a stimulus masked by random noise, S_1, occurred, or noise alone, S_2, occurred. Following the observation interval the observer indicated whether the observation interval contained the stimulus plus the noise or the noise alone. The observer's response was followed by the experimenter's response, which ostensibly said what event the observation interval contained. The experimenter's response was correct only on a randomly chosen subset of the trials. For ease in comparing these experiments with those of Suppes and Krasne, the following description and notation is essentially identical with theirs.

S_1: Event of presenting an observation interval of one second in a band-limited Gaussian noise, the interval containing a pulsed sinusoid (1000 c/s), 100 msec in duration.

S_2: Event of presenting an observation interval of 1 second in a band-limited Gaussian noise that does *not* contain the sinusoid of S_1.

A_1: Response of observer pressing a key labelled "signal."

A_2: Response of observer pressing a key labelled "no signal."

E_1: Reinforcing event of experimenter lighting a jewelled lamp above the "signal" key.

E_2: Reinforcing event of experimenter lighting a jewelled lamp above the "no signal" key.

Ω_i: Reinforcement (unobserved) of the A_i response ($i = 1, 2$).

ρ_i: $P(E_j \mid S_i)$ $(i, j = 1, 2)$.

r: $P(S_1)$.

δ_i: Probability that an observer makes a correct discrimination of S_i in a sequence of trials where no information is given him by the *experimenter* about the correctness of his response ($i, j = 1, 2$; $0 < \delta_i \leq 1$).

The outcomes of interest will be the various conditional probabilities of a response as a function of $P_1, P_2, \gamma, \delta_1$, and δ_2.

Any trial generates a sequence $C \to S \to A \to \Omega \to E \to C'$, where C and C' refer to the state of conditioning before and after the trial. Two stimulus elements s_1 and s_2 are assumed to exist. As a trial begins, each s_1 and s_2 is conditioned to either A_1 or A_2. Since S_2 trials cannot reasonably be separated, when an S_1 trial occurs, s_1 is sampled with probability δ_1 and s_2 with probability $1 - \delta_1$; and on an S_2 trial, s_2 is sampled with probability δ_2 and s_1 with probability $1 - \delta_2$.[1] The conditioned response occurs, followed by the pair of reinforcing events $\Omega_i = I_{i,n}$ (self-reinforcement) and $\Omega_i' = G_{i,n}$ (social reinforcement) leading to a possible change in the state of conditioning at the start of the next trial. The four possible states of conditioning may be given as the set of stimulus elements conditioned to A_1. They are $\{s_1, s_2\}, \{s_1\}, \{s_2\}$, and 0.

It is assumed that on any trial, independently of the observer's response, there are one of three possible outcomes: (1) the self-reinforcement Ω_1 is effective with probability θ_i; (2) the social reinforcement Ω_2 is effective with probability θ_g; or (3) neither is effective with probability $1 - \theta_i - \theta_g$. The above assumptions give rise to a 4×4 matrix of transition probabilities, the rows derived from four trees, three in addition to the one shown as figure 1, which is for state $\{s_2\}$.

For completeness, we give the set of 16 transition probabilities as follows, where p_{ij} is the probability of moving from conditioning state i on trial n to conditioning state j on trial $n + 1$ ($i, j = 1, 2, 3, 4$; 1: $\{s_1, s_2\}$, 2: $\{s_1\}$, 3: $\{s_2\}$, 4: 0):

(1)
$$p_{11} = P(\{s_1, s_2\} \mid \{s_1, s_2\}) = 1 - \theta_i[\gamma(1 - \delta_1) + \delta_2(1 - \gamma)]$$
$$- \theta_g[(1 - \gamma)\rho_2 + \gamma(1 - \rho_1)],$$

$$p_{12} = P(\{s_1\} \mid \{s_1, s_2\}) = \gamma(1 - \delta_1)[\theta_i + \theta_g(1 - \rho_1)] + (1 - \delta)\delta_2[\theta_i + \theta_g\rho_2],$$

$$p_{13} = P(\{s_2\} \mid \{s_1, s_2\}) = \gamma\delta_1(1 - \rho_1)\theta_g + (1 - \gamma)(1 - \delta_2)\rho_2\theta_g,$$

$$p_{14} = P(0 \mid \{s_1, s_2\}) = 0;$$

$$p_{21} = P(\{s_1, s_2\} \mid \{s_1\}) = \gamma(1 - \delta_1)\rho_1\theta_g + (1 - \gamma)\delta_2(1 - \rho_2)\theta_g,$$

$$p_{22} = P(\{s_1\} \mid \{s_1\}) = 1 - \gamma\theta_g[\delta_1 + \rho_1 - 2\rho_1\delta_1]$$
$$- (1 - \gamma)\theta_g[\delta_2 + \rho_2 - 2\rho_2\delta_2],$$

$$p_{23} = P(\{s_2\} \mid \{s_1\}) = 0,$$

$$p_{24} = P(0 \mid \{s_1\}) = \gamma\delta_1(1 - \rho_1)\theta_g + (1 - \gamma)(1 - \delta_2)\rho_2\theta_g;$$

---

[1] Note that there are two discrimination parameters δ_1 and δ_2. In the Suppes and Krasne experiment, only a single discrimination parameter occurs because S_1 and S_2 are arbitrary names for the two aspects of a single event, line 1 being longer than line 2. The converse event (line 2 being longer than line 1) is symmetrical; as their data show, $P(A_1 \mid S_1) = P(A_2 \mid S_2)$. However, the events "tone in noise" (S_1) and "noise alone" (S_2) are not symmetrical, for $P(A_2 \mid S_2) \cong .80$ when $P(A_1 \mid S_1) \cong .50$.

$$p_{31} = P(\{s_1, s_2\} \mid \{s_2\}) \quad = r\delta_1[\theta_i + \theta_g\rho_1] + (1-r)(1-\delta_2)[\theta_i + \theta_g(1-\rho_2)] \,,$$

$$p_{32} = P(\{s_1\} \mid \{s_2\}) \quad = 0 \,,$$

$$p_{33} = P(\{s_2\} \mid \{s_2\}) \quad = 1 - \theta_i - \theta_g r[\delta_1\rho_1 + (1-\delta_1)(1-\rho_1)]$$
$$- \theta_g(1-r)[\delta_2\rho_2 + (1-\delta_2)(1-\rho_2)] \,,$$

$$p_{34} = P(0 \mid \{s_2\}) \quad = r(1-\delta_1)[\theta_i + \theta_g(1-\rho_1)] + (1-r)\delta_2[\theta_i + \rho_2\theta_g] \,;$$

$$p_{41} = P(\{s_1, s_2\} \mid 0) \quad = 0 \,,$$

$$p_{42} = P(\{s_1\} \mid 0) \quad = r\delta_1(\theta_i + \theta_g\rho_1) + (1-r)(1-\delta_2)[\theta_i + \theta_g(1-\rho_2)] \,,$$

$$p_{43} = P(\{s_2\} \mid 0) \quad = r(1-\delta_1)\rho_1\theta_g + (1-r)\delta_2(1-\rho_2)\theta_g \,,$$

$$p_{44} = P(0 \mid 0) \quad = 1 - \theta_g[r\rho_1 + (1-r)(1-\rho_2)]$$
$$- \theta_i[r\delta_1 + (1-r)(1-\delta_2)] \,.$$

These transition probabilities are essentially the same as those given in Suppes and Atkinson [11, p. 261], differing only in having two psychophysical parameters δ_i. If $\delta_1 = \delta_2 = \delta$, our equations reduce to theirs. If discrimination were assumed perfect as well, the model reduces to that used by Suppes

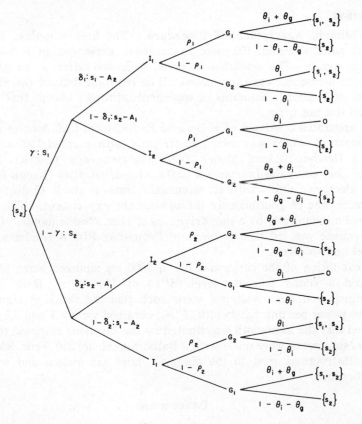

FIG. 1. The tree for state $\{s_2\}$. The trees for the other three states are analogous in form.

and Krasne, in which the S_1 and S_2 processes are treated as independent, which is a nice simplification.

By standard methods the asymptotic probability of being in one of the four states $\mu_{[i]}$ ($i = \{s_1, s_2\}, \{s_1\}, \{s_2\}, 0$) may be obtained in terms of the p_{ij}. The observed asymptotic probabilities of responding may be shown to be

$$P_\infty(A_1 \mid S_1) = \mu_{[s_1 s_2]} + \mu_{[s_1]}\delta_1 + \mu_{[s_2]}(1 - \delta_1) ,$$
(2)
$$P_\infty(A_2 \mid S_2) = \mu_{[0]} + \mu_{[s_2]}\delta_2 + \mu_{[s_1]}(1 - \delta_2) ;$$

in general they depend on the experimenter-determined γ, ρ_1, ρ_2, and the observer-determined $\theta_i, \theta_g, \delta_1$, and δ_2. (Actually, only three parameters need be estimated since equations may be written as functions of the *ratio* $\theta_i/\theta_g = \theta$, δ_1, and δ_2.) The special case $\rho_1 = \rho_2 = 1$, where the stooge always agrees with the stimulus, corresponds to the classical psychophysical situation in which the observer is given correct information about the stimulus after each trial.

2. Method

2.1 **Stimuli, Apparatus, and Procedure.** The first stimulus, S_1, was a 1000 c/s gated sinusoid, 100 msec in duration, presented in a band-limited Gaussian noise. The stimulus occurred $\frac{1}{2}$ second after a red panel light, 1.2 cm in diameter, was illuminated. The red light defined the observation interval of 1 second. Stimulus S_2 was identical to S_1, except that the gated sinusoid did not occur.

The apparatus consisted of a General Radio Model 1390-A noise generator, the output of which was mixed electrically with a gated 1000 c/s sinusoid from a Hewlett-Packard Model 202-A low-frequency function generator. The sinusoid was passed through a 1000 c/s bandpass filter (Krohn-Hite Model 330-M electronic filter) with an attenuation rate of about 18 db per octave. The noise was on continuously throughout the experiment. The tone was switched mechanically by a cam driven by a synchronous motor. The output of the mixer was led to two binaural Permoflux PDR-8 headsets wired in parallel and in phase.

An excitation of the earphones by a 1000 c/s sinusoid wave at one volt produced a sound pressure level (SPL) of 110 db re .0002 dynes/cm². The signal and noise voltages were such that the ratios of signal energy to noise power per unit bandwidth (E/N_0) obtained were 2.5 and 5.5 db. It is assumed that the bandwidth was limited by the earphone response to 6000 c/s. All measurements were made with a Ballantine Model 320 True RMS Meter.

The instructions read to the observer pairs are quoted and will clarify the procedure:

Instructions

This is an experiment to see how well you can detect a tone that is masked by noise. In front of you is a pair of earphones through which you will hear the noise and the tone. The tone is very brief. If you will put on the earphones, I will demonstrate how the tone sounds both in and out of the noise. The noise will be present continuously throughout the experiment.

Now, this is the task. That light [indicate] will go on for one second. About one-half second after it lights up, on some trials the tone may be heard. On some trials it will not be presented. Your job is to decide quickly whether the tone was there or not during the time that the light was on. You can show me your decision by pressing one of the two keys in front of you labelled "signal" or "no signal." Be sure to respond quickly, for you must make your choice within two seconds after the warning light goes out. If you made the correct choice, that key will light up shortly afterward. If you made the wrong choice the other key will light up. For example if you press the "signal" key and there was a tone, the light over the "signal" key will go on; if there was no tone, the "no-signal" key will light up instead. And so on.

There will be quite a few trials. Listen carefully and try to be as accurate as possible. Things will move quickly and often the tone will be difficult to hear. Keep alert and try to respond as rapidly as possible after the panel light goes out.

Any questions?

OK. Let's review the procedure. The panel light comes on. Listen carefully for the tone and press the appropriate key quickly after the panel light goes out. One of the keys will light up to tell you whether your response was correct or incorrect

Are you ready?

The observer indicated whether or not the tone was present during the observation interval by pressing one of the two noiseless push-button switches labelled "signal" or "no signal." The social response (E_j) was the illumination of a green jewelled panel light below the response button, 1.2 cm in diameter and 2 seconds in duration.

A trial lasted 6 seconds with the sequence of events as shown in figure 2.

Five hundred trials were run in a single session of 50 minutes. The sequences of S_i and E_j events was randomized within blocks of 100. For each condition (see table 1) two different random sequences of 500 trials were used. Presentation was controlled by a punched-tape reader. Observers' responses operated holding relays; following each trial the $S_i E_j A_k$ triplet was punched into a final tape.

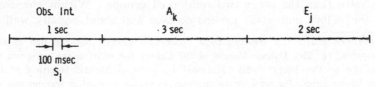

FIG. 2

TABLE 1

THE VALUES OF THE EXPERIMENTER-CONTROLLED
PARAMETERS USED IN THE TWO EXPERIMENTS

Group	Hard Discrimination			Easy Discrimination		
	Number of Observers	π^*	γ	Number of Observers	π^*	γ
$\pi(100)$	15	1.0	.50	16	1.0	.50
$\pi(75)$	15	.75	.50	13	.75	.50
$\pi(50)$	15	.50	.50	17	.50	.50
No E_j events	10	—	.50	10	—	.50

* $\rho_1 = \rho_2 = \pi$, throughout, that is to say, $P(E_1 \mid S_1) = P(E_2 \mid S_2)$

The observers were all males who received some course credit for their service. No test of hearing was made. The data for two observers was discarded because of apparatus failure, for three observers because they made fewer than 25 "signal" responses in the entire 500 trials, for one subject because he removed the earphones after about 450 trials ("to smoke a cigarette").

We should mention that most observers, especially those in the "hard-discrimination" groups, remarked that the task was very difficult and tiring.

The data were obtained automatically on paper tape as a coded sequence of 500 trials, each of which was one of the eight possible $S_i E_j A_k$ triplets. The coded sequences were transferred to IBM cards, in a form suitable for data analysis by a high-speed computer.[2]

3. Results

Our main interest is in the influence of the experimenter's responses on the detection rates $P(A_1 \mid S_1)$ and the false-alarm rates $P(A_1 \mid S_2)$ of the observers. Table 2 and figures 3 and 4 show these rates over blocks of trials for the two signal energies. The most striking result is the relationship between the "no E_j events" groups and the social-pressure groups. When the task is difficult, the addition of a reinforcing event, even when randomly related to the stimulus, *increases* the detection rate by about 15 per cent and *decreases* the false-alarm rate by about 8 per cent. But when the task is easier, the addition of a reinforcing event *decreases* the detection rate by about 12 per cent and *increases* the false-alarm rate by about 6 per cent. Within the hard-task groups the $\pi(100)$ group performs slightly better on both rates than the other two reinforced groups. Within the easy-task groups the $\pi(100)$ and $\pi(75)$ groups do best and about equally well on the

[2] We are indebted to the Western Data Processing Center for the use of the IBM 7090 computer; to Mr. Daniel Morris of the Center for writing the program to solve equations (2); to Dr. Peter Neely, National Institute of Mental Health Post Doctoral Fellow in Biostatistics, for writing the program to obtain transition frequencies and test their Markov properties; and to Mr. Edwin Kusick, IBM Corporation, Santa Monica, for arranging the tape-to-card conversion.

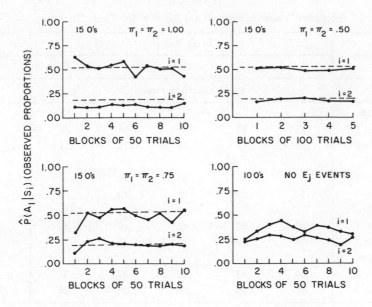

FIG. 3. The observed proportions $P(A_1 \mid S_i)$ for blocks of 50 and 100 trials, hard discrimination. Asymptotes predicted from equations (2) are shown as dashed lines.

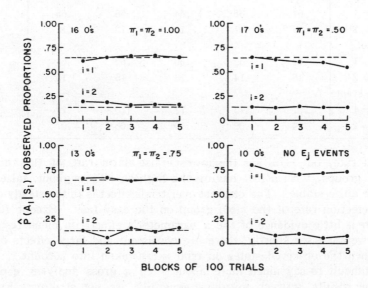

FIG. 4. The observed proportions $P(A_1 \mid S_i)$ for blocks of 100 trials, easy discrimination. Asymptotes predicted from equations (2) are shown as dashed lines.

TABLE 2

OBSERVED PROPORTIONS $\hat{P}(A_1 \mid S_i)$ FOR 100-TRIAL BLOCKS

Condition	Trial Block					Mean
	1	2	3	4	5	
Hard Discrimination						
$\pi = 1.00$						
$i = 1$	.61	.55	.50	.52	.48	.53
$i = 2$	.15	.14	.14	.12	.11	.13
$\pi = .75$						
$i = 1$	.45	.53	.53	.50	.49	.50
$i = 2$	.17	.23	.21	.20	.20	.20
$\pi = .50$						
$i = 1$	.51	.52	.48	.49	.51	.50
$i = 2$	.17	.19	.21	.17	.17	.18
No E_j events						
$i = 1$	.30	.43	.35	.37	.31	.35
$i = 2$	.25	.29	.26	.25	.23	.26
Easy Discrimination						
$\pi = 1.00$						
$i = 1$	.61	.65	.67	.67	.67	.65
$i = 2$	.19	.19	.16	.17	.17	.18
$\pi = .75$						
$i = 1$	.67	.68	.64	.66	.66	.66
$i = 2$	.15	.07	.15	.13	.16	.13
$\pi = .50$						
$i = 1$	.64	.62	.60	.59	.54	.60
$i = 2$	.15	.14	.16	.15	.15	.15
No E_j events						
$i = 1$	.81	.73	.72	.73	.74	.75
$i = 2$	.14	.09	.10	.06	.07	.09

detection rate, but $\pi(75)$ has the lowest false-alarm rate of the three re-inforced groups, with $\pi(100)$ having the highest. Throughout, false-alarm rates are quite stable. The clearest over-trials effect is in the steady decline of the detection rate of the $\pi(50)$ group on the easy task. Except for this case there is little evidence of the π parameter's effects on mean responses. Yet, as we shall see shortly, there are consistent and large effects on trial $n + 1$ when the observed states on trial n are taken into account.

It is difficult to say much more about such a gross analysis, especially when the results between π-groups generally are not striking. Even so, one remark is in order. Signal-detection theory says that for a fixed signal-to-noise ratio there cannot be an increase in detection rate without a corresponding increase in false-alarm rate. Our results offer substantial problems for this view, as the previous paragraph will have made clear. (In a separate paper we expect to discuss the relationship of these results to some expectations based on the Tanner–Swets signal-detection model of perception [14] and a recent threshold model of Luce [6].)

We shall want to make three basic tests of these data for Markov properties.[3] First, is the process stationary; i.e., are the transition probabilities independent of the trial number? Second, may we reject the null hypothesis that our Markov process is zero-order (that trial outcomes are independent), the alternative being that the process is a first-order Markov chain? Third, are the subjects equivalent in the sense that their responses form a set of samples from a first- or higher-order Markov chain? The results of these last tests will not be ready for this paper. These tests are discussed in [11], and by Billingsley [3], [4].

3.1 Stationarity and Learning Curves. The rows of the transition matrices for the first and second 250-trial blocks were analyzed by a χ^2 test of homogeneity. The outcomes form table 3. The null hypothesis tested is that the transition probabilities p_{ij} in blocks 1 and 2 are not different from the p_{ij} in the transition matrix based on the entire 500 trials. Note that there are four *observable* "states" (rows) in the $\pi(100)$ and the *no-information* (no E_j-event) groups, but eight observable states in the $\pi(75)$ and $\pi(50)$ groups, since in the latter groups there are two independent outcomes for each one of the S_i, E_j, and $A_k (i, j, k = 1, 2)$. When $\pi = 1.00$, the experimenter's response (E_j) always agrees with the stimulus (S_i), so that $i \neq j$ cannot occur. There is no E_j event for the no-information group. Each row may be tested separately and then summed to obtain a value of χ^2 for all rows. Only the no-information group is stable in each row and for all rows combined.

The classical psychophysicist was very little concerned with learning effects. Hopefully, he cast off this problem by using practised subjects or by looking only at asymptotic effects. The naive, variable, irresponsible subject has stigmata to be viewed only when their range is of interest. But our naive subject is also docile. The failure to find stationarity for many of the rows is due to the substantial changes that occur between the two blocks of 250 trials. The different schedules of experimenter events are not so apparent when comparing the blocks entire. However, in tables 4 and 5, it may be seen that substantial changes in detection and false-alarm rates occur between the two blocks of trials for various states.

In the $\pi(100)$ group the process is stationary after A_1 responses but not after A_2 responses. That is, the observer is settled in his way of responding on the next trial after he has said, rightly or wrongly, that a signal was present. This generalization holds up in the $\pi(75)$ group, except for those trials on which he falsely said a signal was present. The $\pi(50)$ group is approaching stability in most of its rows (if we are willing to work at

---

[3] The data for the easy-discrimination group were collected after the Symposium, and it has not been possible to include any finer analysis of those data than is given in table 1 and figure 4.

TABLE 3

RESULTS OF THE χ^2 TEST OF HOMOGENEITY FOR STATIONARITY OF THE STATES
(ROWS) OF THE TRANSITION MATRICES BROKEN DOWN INTO BLOCKS

(Hard Discrimination Only)

State on Trial n	First Block*	Second Block*	Total	df	Level
		$\pi = 1.00$			
$S_1E_1A_1$	2.38	2.74	5.12	3	.25
$S_1E_1A_2$	6.34	9.60	15.94	3	.005†
$S_2E_2A_1$	1.03	4.38	5.41	3	.25
$S_2E_2A_2$	8.60	7.65	16.22	3	.005†
			Total: 42.69	12	.001†
		$\pi = .75$			
$S_1E_1A_1$	4.23	3.82	8.05	7	.50
$S_1E_1A_2$	11.06	11.24	22.30	7	.005†
$S_1E_2A_2$	10.55	12.40	22.95	7	.005†
$S_1E_2A_1$	3.36	4.52	7.85	7	.50
$S_1E_1A_1$	3.25	5.26	8.51	7	.50
$S_2E_1A_2$	10.90	9.66	20.56	7	.01†
$S_2E_2A_1$	14.37	12.32	26.69	7	.001†
$S_2E_2A_2$	27.38	26.30	53.68	7	.001†
			Total: 170.62	56	.001†
		$\pi = .50$			
$S_1E_1A_1$	7.06	7.45	14.50	7	.05
$S_1E_1A_2$	6.94	3.73	10.66	7	.10
$S_1E_2A_2$	1.10	3.37	4.47	7	.50
$S_1E_2A_1$	2.38	4.56	6.94	7	.50
$S_2E_1A_1$	5.13	7.69	12.82	7	.05
$S_2E_1A_2$	5.57	5.46	11.13	7	.10
$S_2E_2A_1$	1.29	1.49	2.78	7	.90
$S_2E_2A_2$	13.79	8.51	22.30	7	.01†
			Total: 84.60	56	.005†
		No E_j Events			
$S_1 - A_1$	2.95	3.23	6.18	3	.25 > P > .10
$S_1 - A_2$	.48	.51	.99	3	.90 > P > .75
$S_2 - A_1$	1.84	2.28	4.12	3	.25 > P > .10
$S_2 - A_2$	2.54	1.22	4.76	3	.25 > P > .10
			Total: 16.05	12	.25 > P > .10

* First block is trials 2-250, second block is trials 251-500, except for the case of "no E_j events," where estimates are over the blocks of trials 101-300 and 301-499.

† Significance levels given are the probabilities that the value of χ^2 for the degrees of freedom (df) indicated equals or exceeds the calculated value shown in the "Total" column.

ERRATA

Page

133　For University of Michigan read Indiana University

181　Delete (see equation 7), last line

182　Equation (1) should read: $p_{n+1} = p_n + \theta(\overline{p_n p_n'} - 2p_n + 1)$

　　　Line 7, should read: for A' are p_{n+1}', p_n', $\overline{p_n p_n'}$, and θ', respectively

　　　Line 21, add and E_1' after E_1

　　　Line 32, add for before Condition I

184　Delete equals sign, center of equation (I)

187　Line 6, the interval should read $1\frac{1}{2}$-sec

　　　Table 3, next-to-last box heading should read $\overset{Obt.}{\pi'}$

189　Line 17, for fix read fixate

　　　Line 28, for σ_p read σ_p'

　　　Line 40, end of line, read second subject's response

190　Line 11, delete for

　　　Line 20, for the Markov learning model read one Markov learning model

Criswell, Solomon, and Suppes, eds.,
Mathematical Methods in Small Group
Processes

$\alpha = .01$), except following those trials on which there is no signal, the observer says there is no signal, and the experimenter agrees with him. This change is due to a decreased detection rate; the false-alarm rate stays about the same. There appears to be little learning in the sense that there is some kind of negatively accelerated learning curve. This holds for both $P(A_1 \mid S_1)$ and $P(A_1 \mid S_2)$—observers are very near asymptote from the outset and show only minor variations thereafter. Suppes and Krasne's results are in agreement with ours for the most nearly analogous condition that they report, $\pi_1 = .7$ and $\pi_2 = .6$, and $\delta = .72$.

If we rearrange the data in table 5, it is possible to consider $P(A_1 \mid S_i)$ on trial $n + 1$ following those states on trial n in which we aggregate the data to consider only the S_i, E_j, A_k states on trial n (table 6). There is given as well the same conditional probabilities on trial $n + 1$ following those trials on which the experimenter's response was in agreement or disagreement with the observer's response. In all cases only the last blocks of 250 or 200 trials were analyzed. The clearest result follows A_1 trials, where for all three reinforcement groups both detection rates and false-alarm rates are considerably higher than those following A_2 trials. The effect is greatest for $\pi = 1.00$. The reverse is true for the no-information group. The differences noted following A_1 responses are palely present following E_1 trials; following S_1 trials, the two rates are about the same for all groups. The last two rows of table 6 partition the data according to whether the experimenter agreed or disagreed with the observer's response on trial n. It seems clear that both rates are proportional to the

TABLE 4

THE CONDITIONAL PROBABILITIES $\hat{P}(A_1 \mid S_i)$ ON TRIAL $n + 1$
FOR TWO BLOCKS OF TRIALS

Condition	Conditional Probability				Number of Observers
	First Block		Second Block		
	$\hat{P}(A_1 \mid S_i)$	$\hat{P}(A_1 \mid S_i)$	$\hat{P}(A_1 \mid S_i)$	$\hat{P}(A_1 \mid S_i)$	
Hard Discrimination					
$\pi = 1.00$	.516	.155	.536	.126	15
$\pi = .75$	.515	.219	.513	.194	15
$\pi = .50$	.526	.207	.487	.189	15
No E_j events	.361	.264	.338	.252	10
Easy Discrimination					
$\pi = 1.00$	.660	.175	.660	.170	16
$\pi = .75$	.660	.110	.660	.145	13
$\pi = .50$	.610	.150	.565	.150	17
No E_j events	.770	.095	.735	.065	10

$\pi_1 = \pi_2 = P(E_1 \mid S_1)$ and $P(E_2 \mid S_2)$, respectively.

TABLE 5

CONDITIONAL PROBABILITIES $P(A_1 \mid S_i)$ ON TRIAL $n+1$ FOR THE VARIOUS STATES $S_i E_j A_k$ ON TRIAL n

(Hard Discrimination Only)

| Trial Block | State on Trial n | Conditional Probability | | | | | | No E_j Events | |
| | | $\pi = 1.00$ | | $\pi = .75$ | | $\pi = .50$ | | | |
		$\hat{P}(A_1 \mid S_1)$	$\hat{P}(A_1 \mid S_2)$	$\hat{P}(A_1 \mid S_1)$	$\hat{P}(A_1 \mid S_2)$	$\hat{P}(A_1 \mid S_1)$	$\hat{P}(A_1 \mid S_2)$	$\hat{P}(A_1 \mid S_1)$	$\hat{P}(A_1 \mid S_2)$
First 250*	$S_1E_1A_1$	.69	.21	.68	.28	.65	.25	.52	.33
	$S_2E_2A_1$	.50	.13	.43	.22	.51	.23	.48	.42
	$S_1E_2A_1$			.48	.20	.57	.18		
	$S_2E_1A_1$			.65	.27	.68	.41		
	$S_2E_2A_2$	.48	.14	.47	.18	.52	.16	.38	.21
	$S_1E_1A_2$	.40	.33	.45	.21	.47	.19	.29	.26
	$S_2E_1A_2$			.51	.13	.52	.20		
	$S_1E_2A_2$			.49	.26	.36	.20		
Second 250*	$S_1E_1A_1$	.74	.18	.65	.19	.69	.23	.42	.30
	$S_2E_2A_1$	.62	.14	.52	.28	.54	.28	.38	.34
	$S_1E_2A_1$			.46	.24	.56	.19		
	$S_2E_1A_1$			.50	.40	.57	.32		
	$S_2E_2A_2$	.51	.12	.51	.13	.44	.15	.30	.22
	$S_1E_1A_2$	.33	.07	.46	.20	.43	.21	.30	.21
	$S_2E_1A_2$			.50	.14	.44	.16		
	$S_1E_2A_2$			.38	.19	.36	.16		

* Except in case of no E_j events, where estimates are over the blocks of trial 101-300 and 301-499.

TABLE 6

CONDITIONAL PROBABILITIES $\hat{P}(A_1 | S_i)$ ON TRIAL $n + 1$ FOR A_k, E_j AND S_i STATES ON TRIAL n

$\sum_{E_j S_i} A_k$ has the meaning that detection and false-alarm rates are based on the rows of table 5 collapsed over stimulus conditions (S_i) and experimenter responses (E_j) for the second block of 250 trials (200 in the case of "no E_j" condition). The last two rows partition the data according to whether the experimenter agreed or disagreed with the observer's response on trial n. The proportion of consonance and dissonance states on trial n is shown in parentheses.

State on Trial n	Conditional Probability							
	$\pi = 1.00$		$\pi = .75$		$\pi = .50$		No E_j Events	
	$\hat{P}(A_1 \mid S_1)$	$\hat{P}(A_1 \mid S_2)$	$\hat{P}(A_1 \mid S_1)$	$\hat{P}(A_1 \mid S_2)$	$\hat{P}(A_1 \mid S_1)$	$\hat{P}(A_1 \mid S_2)$	$\hat{P}(A_1 \mid S_1)$	$\hat{P}(A_1 \mid S_2)$
$\sum_{E_j S_i} A_1$	.72	.17	.58	.27	.63	.24	.40	.32
$\sum_{E_j S_i} A_2$	.44	.11	.48	.16	.42	.16	.51	.51
$\sum_{A_k S_i} E_1$	.55	.13	.54	.22	.51	.24		
$\sum_{A_k S_i} E_2$	.52	.12	.49	.17	.46	.18		
$\sum_{S_i} E_j A_k \; j \neq k$	.38 (.31)	.09	.48 (.42)	.20	.52 (.50)	.19		
$\sum_{S_i} E_j A_k \; j = k$	.60 (.69)	.14	.54 (.58)	.19	.46 (.50)	.19		

number of consonance or dissonance trials. Thus the rates are higher following consonance than following dissonance trials for $\pi(100)$, where about 70 per cent of the time the experimenter and observer are in disagreement. In the $\pi(75)$ and $\pi(50)$ groups, the rates following the different types of trials approach equality.

3.2 Order. The process is not zero-order, that is, it is not true that trial outcomes are statistically independent. This is shown clearly by the following χ^2 tests, made on the data of the hard discrimination group.

Group	χ^2	df	α-Level
1.00	286.24	9	.001
.75	303.05	49	.001
.50	275.87	49	.001
No E_j	86.47	9	.001

We have not tested yet the obvious and important null hypothesis that the process is a first-order chain against the alternative hypothesis that it is a second-order chain. If one could reject this null hypothesis, it would mean that response probabilities on trial $n + 1$ could be predicted better by looking at the responses on both trials n and $n - 1$. There is some relevant evidence that at least a second-order process is involved, especially at low values of the stimulus energy. Verplanck, Collier, and Cotton [15] found that the successive responses of a subject given in measurements of his visual threshold are far from being statistically independent of one another. In fact they found significant serial correlations of time-ordered sequences of responses out to about lag 11. However, as signal energy increases, the responses on successive trials tend to become independent of the preceding response. Speeth and Mathews [10] forced subjects to report in which of four successive intervals a tone in noise appeared. The probability of repeating the previous response was at chance for signal values at which the probability of a correct response approached 40 per cent. The correct interval was reported to the subject as soon as he responded, a procedure analogous to our $\pi = 1.00$ situation. They found response dependency on the previously indicated correct interval, and this effect disappeared with increasing signal energy. Such a tendency is present in our data for the $\pi(100)$ group, comparing hard and easy tasks.

We mention that, using the magnitude of χ^2 as a criterion, one may suspect that at our level of signal energy increasing correct information to the observer will increase the order of the Markov process, which is to say that social pressure in this form may perhaps be measured by the order of the chain.

4. Predictions from the Model

Explicit solutions of equations (2) are quite difficult in general but may be obtained for the case $\gamma = .50$, $\rho_1 = \rho_2 = .50$ in the simple form

$$P_\infty(A_1 \mid S_1) = \frac{1/2 + \delta_1\theta_1}{1 + \theta},$$

(3) $$P_\infty(A_2 \mid S_2) = \frac{1/2 + (1 - \delta_2)\theta}{1 + \theta},$$

$$P_\infty(C) = \frac{1 + \theta(1 + \delta_1 - \delta_2)}{2(1 + \theta)},$$

where $P_\infty(C)$ is the mean of the first two equations and is the absolute probability of a correct response. The last function exists for $0 \leq \theta < \infty$ and $0 \leq (1 + \delta_1 - \delta_2) \leq 1$. $P_\infty(A_1 \mid S_1)$ is bounded by 1/2 and δ_1 for $\theta = 0$ and ∞, respectively; $P_\infty(A_2 \mid S_2)$ is bounded by 1/2 and $(1 - \delta_2)$ for $\theta = 0$ and ∞, respectively.

Now Suppes and Krasne [12] used first-trial data to obtain an estimate of δ by means of which they predict response asymptotes with good success. However, it did not seem reasonable to us that stable estimates of δ_1 and δ_2 could be obtained in this way and we preferred to use separate groups which received no information about their performance. For the hard-discrimination group $\hat{\delta}_1 \cong .35$ and $\hat{\delta}_2 \cong .75$, and for the easy-discrimination group $\hat{\delta}_1 \cong .75$ and $\hat{\delta}_2 \cong .93$. We get from the above equations the tabulation below.

	Hard Discrimination			Easy Discrimination		
	$\theta \to 0$	$\theta \to \infty$	Observed	$\theta \to 0$	$\theta \to \infty$	Observed
$P_\infty(A_1 \mid S_1)$	.50	.35	.487	.50	.75	.564
$P_\infty(A_2 \mid S_2)$	.50	.25	.811	.50	.07	.853

Note that the observed values are not even within the predicted bounds in two of the four cases. Note also that if δ_2 rather than $(1 - \delta_2)$ were the parameter in equation (3), the predictions would be within the bounds and much better for $P_\infty(A_2 \mid S_2)$.

Elegant though it is, the estimation of δ_1 and δ_2 from separate groups must be abandoned. We now describe another method that does not use much of the information in the data but leads to rather good asymptotic predictions. We minimized

(4) $$\sum_{i=1}^{3} \{ \mid P_1^{(\pi_i)} - \hat{P}_1^{(\pi_i)} \mid + \mid P_2^{(\pi_i)} - \hat{P}_2^{(\pi_i)} \mid \},$$

where $\hat{P}_1^{(\pi_i)} = P_\infty(A_1 \mid S_1)$ and $\hat{P}_2^{(\pi_i)} = P_\infty(A_2 \mid S_2)$. Summation is over the three π groups. A minimum exists and the values of θ, δ_1, and δ_2 which minimized the function were used to predict various asymptotic quantities from equations (2) and (3). The results are given in table 7.

As may be seen by inspection, the individual predictions are reasonably close to the data. In both the hard and easy discriminations, function (4) has a minimum in the neighborhood of $\theta = 15$ and for the values of δ_i shown. When $\theta = 5$ the model's predictions and the data diverge widely, at least for $P_\infty(A_2 \mid S_2)$. Certain obvious points of difference in our estimates of

TABLE 7

OBSERVED VALUES OF $P_\infty(A_i \mid S_i)$ COMPARED WITH THOSE
PREDICTED FROM EQUATIONS (3)

Comparison is for several ratios of θ, and for three π conditions. The estimates θ, δ_1, and δ_2 were found by minimizing equation (4). In both the hard- and easy-discrimination tasks, the minimum occurred for $\theta = 15$.

			Predicted								
	Observed		$\hat\theta = 20$		$\hat\theta = 15$		$\hat\theta = 5$		$\hat\theta = 1$		$\hat\theta = .10$	
π Condition			$\hat\delta_1 =$ .512	$\hat\delta_2 =$ .164	$\hat\delta_1 =$ .512	$\hat\delta_2 =$ .164	$\hat\delta_1 =$ .51	$\hat\delta_2 =$ .10	$\hat\delta_1 =$ .45	$\hat\delta_2 =$ .075	$\hat\delta_1 =$ 1.0	$\hat\delta_2 =$ .10
	$i = 1$	2	1	2	1	2	1	2	1	2	1	2
Hard Discrimination												
1.00	.536	.874	.514	.801	.515	.803	.524	.786	.541	.543	.569	.943
.75	.513	.806	.531	.805	.513	.809	.516	.810	.508	.628	.557	.740
.50	.487	.811	.511	.806	.511	.815	.508	.833	.475	.713	.546	.536
Easy Discrimination												
			$\hat\delta_1 =$ .65	$\hat\delta_2 =$ .125	$\hat\delta_1 =$ .65	$\hat\delta_2 =$ .125	$\hat\delta_1 =$ .65	$\hat\delta_2 =$ .025	—*		—*	
1.00	.659	.829	.645	.848	.643	.839	.639	.826	....	....	....	....
.75	.663	.857	.644	.852	.642	.845	.632	.861	....	....	....	....
.50	.564	.853	.643	.857	.641	.852	.625	.896	....	....	....	....

* Values for $\theta = 1$ and $\theta = .10$ were not computed in this series, since first approximation grids showed rapid divergence for $P_\infty(A_2 \mid S_2)$.

$\hat\theta$ and those found by Suppes and Krasne should be mentioned. They found by maximum-likelihood estimates that for fixed symmetry (i.e., fixed values of π_1 and π_2) θ decreased from easy to hard discrimination. Furthermore, for a similar parameter range their estimate is $\theta = .77$, much smaller than 15.

A generalization that may be made from our minimization procedure is that $P_\infty(A_1 \mid S_1) = P_\infty(A_2 \mid S_2)$ independently of π, whenever $\delta_1 + \delta_2 = 1$. We should also mention that the best estimates of δ_2 tend to be close to the observed false-alarm rate; $1 - P_\infty(A_2 \mid S_2) = P_\infty(A_1 \mid S_2)$, rather than $P_\infty(A_2 \mid S_2)$.

In one sense asymptotic predictions from the model are not too bad. In another sense, the parameter that carried the interpretation of both a learning-rate parameter and a measure of social pressure shows no change between a hard and easy condition. That is, the effect of changing π from .50 to 1.00 is small where θ is large. We have perhaps strained the model in the simple Yes–No detection situation. A more appropriate experiment is the forced-choice test, where the stimulus occurs on every trial but randomly in the first or second half of an observation interval. The sym-

metry here would offer a more propitious setting for the theory. We intend
to do these experiments next.

5. Application of a Generalized Conditioning Model

It is of considerable interest to illustrate the application of the generalized
conditioning models (GCM), discussed in some detail by Suppes and Atkinson
in [11]. The GCM is a consequence of a generalized conditioning axiom,

AXIOM C2.' *If a stimulus element is sampled on a trial, and if response
A_i is made and then followed by reinforcement E_j, there is a probability C_{ij}
that the stimulus is conditioned to A_1.*

They point out what is very clear in our experimental result, namely that
experimenter-defined events E_j may not necessarily reinforce as intended.
Unobservable (subjective) reinforcing events E_j may operate. Stimulus
conditioning on trial $n + 1$ may depend more heavily on the relationship
between the response A_k on trial n than on the reinforcing event E_j on
trial n. Because the details of the conditioning process are shadowy, it
would be very useful to have a model that makes allowance for the change
of conditioning parameters over trials, approaching a long-term stability
which reflects both observer variables and the reinforcing schedule. One
of the most important implications to us is that stimulus-sampling theory
may be applied to psychophysical processes ordinarily dealt with only at
asymptote and usually in highly practiced subjects. The changes in C_{ij} as
stability is approached may throw considerable light on how subjects arrive
at stable response modes—if, indeed, they do. Many other advantages
accrue, not the least of which is the growing analytic power of statistical
inferences about Markov chains. As we show below, even if practically
every model tried is a poor fit, comparing different models having the same
number of degrees of freedom allows us to converge on the major conditioning events.

Before we apply the several GCM's to our data, consider a fundamental
arrangement of the data, the transition numbers or transition frequencies;
that is, how many times in a large number of trials do we observe that
state j is entered from state i. The observed state on trial n is one of
the eight possible events $S_iE_jA_k$ $(i, j, k, = 1, 2)$ and on trial $n + 1$ it is
possible to enter any one of these states. Thus the transition frequencies
take the form of the 8×8 matrix shown as table 8 for the data of group
$\pi(75)$, based on the aggregated frequencies of 15 observers for the last 250
trials. The rate of false alarms and correct detections on trial $n + 1$ for
each of the states on trial n have been discussed already.

In applying the GCM, the most obvious question to ask is how does the
response $A_{1,n+1}$ depend on certain preceding events, e.g., the stimulus pair
$(S_{i,n}; S_{i,n+1})$. We proceed to test five different GCM models of this and
other dependencies as shown in table 9.

Here as before the $S_iE_jA_k$ triplet represents stimulus, reinforcing event
(experimenter's response), and observer's response, C_r refers to an event
on trial n such that in the pair $(A_{k,n}E_{j,n})$, $r = 1$ when $k = j$, and $r = 2$

TABLE 8

OBSERVED TRANSITION FREQUENCIES FOR LAST 250 TRIALS OF GROUP $\pi(75)$

(Values are based on aggregated scores of 15 observers.)

Trial n \ Trial $n+1$	$S_1E_1A_1$	$S_1E_1A_2$	$S_1E_2A_2$	$S_1E_2A_1$	$S_2E_1A_1$	$S_2E_1A_2$	$S_2E_2A_1$	$S_2E_2A_2$	N_i
$S_1E_1A_1$	168	102	23	68	28	94	59	167	709
$S_1E_1A_2$	138	163	32	29	17	84	48	171	682
$S_1E_2A_2$	23	48	12	14	7	22	15	70	211
$S_1E_2A_1$	39	44	14	11	5	20	27	80	240
$S_2E_1A_1$	21	12	7	5	7	9	12	27	100
$S_2E_1A_2$	63	60	24	22	12	70	19	110	380
$S_2E_2A_1$	53	48	19	20	3	13	36	87	279
$S_2E_2A_2$	197	207	76	73	13	68	68	446	1148

when $k \neq j$—that is $r = 1$ when the reinforcement agrees with the observer's response and $r = 2$ when the reinforcement and the observer's response disagree.

The problem is to estimate the various C_{ij}'s from the transition frequencies, and then to test how well these C_{ij}'s describe the dependency of $A_{1,n+1}$ on the preceding events. For this we use the transition matrix (5).

(5)

Trial n \ Trial $n+1$	$S_{1,n+1}, A_{1,n+1}$	$S_{1,n+1}, A_{2,n+1}$	$S_{2,n+1}, A_{1,n+1}$	$S_{2,n+1}, A_{2,n+1}$
$S_{1,n+1}, A_{1,n}$	$C_{11}\pi$	$C_{11}(1-\pi)$	$(1-C_{11})\pi$	$(1-C_{11})(1-\pi)$
$S_{1,n+1}, A_{2,n}$	$C_{12}\pi$	$C_{12}(1-\pi)$	$(1-C_{12})\pi$	$(1-C_{12})(1-\pi)$
$S_{2,n+1}, A_{1,n}$	$C_{21}(1-\pi)$	$C_{21}\pi$	$C_{21}(1-\pi)$	$(1-C_{21})\pi$
$S_{2,n+1}, A_{2,n}$	$C_{22}(1-\pi)$	$C_{22}\pi$	$C_{22}(1-\pi)$	$(1-C_{22})\pi$

Matrix (5) is derived from trees like those shown in figure 5 for $\langle S_{i,n+1}, A_{k,n} \rangle$ and $\langle S_{2,n+1}, A_{k,n} \rangle$. There are four such trees because $i = 1, 2$, independently. The trees for the other models are similar except that when $\pi = 1.00$, the bottom tree branches disappear for the $\langle S_{1,n+1} \rangle$ states, while the top two branches disappear for the $\langle S_{2,n+1} \rangle$ states. This of course results from the fact that the experimenter's response (E_j) always agrees with the stimulus event (S_i). This reduces the number of branches to eight.

The coefficients of conditioning C_{ijk} may be estimated by maximum-likelihood methods discussed in detail in [11], in Bartlett [2], and more recently by Billingsley [3], [4]. In the present case, these estimates are functions only of the transition numbers n_{ij}. The several estimates depend of course on which model of the conditioning process is used. Furthermore, under certain assumptions these estimated conditioning parameters may be

TABLE 9

RESPONSE DEPENDENCE OF FIVE GCM MODELS

Model	Relationship of Conditioning Parameters C to Preceding Events
I	$C_{ig} = P(A_{1,n+1} \mid S_{i,n+1}, S_{g,n}) \quad i, g = 1, 2$
II	$C_{ij} = P(A_{1,n+1} \mid S_{i,n+1}, E_{j,n}) \quad i, j = 1, 2$
III	$C_{ik} = P(A_{1,n+1} \mid S_{i,n+1}, A_{k,n}) \quad i, k = 1, 2$
IV	$C_{ir} = P(A_{1,n+1} \mid S_{i,n+1}, C_{r,n}) \quad i, r = 1, 2$
V	$C_{ijk} = P(A_{1,n+1} \mid S_{i,n+1}, E_{j,n} A_{k,n}) \quad i, j, k = 1, 2$

used in a χ^2 goodness-of-fit test, provided the number of degrees of freedom is reduced by the number of parameters estimated. These assumptions further imply that the maximum-likelihood estimate of the probability of reinforcement is γ. This assumption is met very closely by the restricted randomization of the $S_i E_j$ sequences.

An illustration may be helpful. Consider the transition numbers for the last 250 trials of the $\pi(75)$ group (table 8). We obtain the maximum-likelihood estimates of the C_{ij} for Model III in the theoretical form, for $A_{1,n+1}$, as follows:

$$C_{11} = .588$$
$$C_{12} = .475$$
$$C_{21} = .262$$
$$C_{22} = .158$$

For $A_{2,n+1}$, the values are $1 - C_{11}$, and so on.

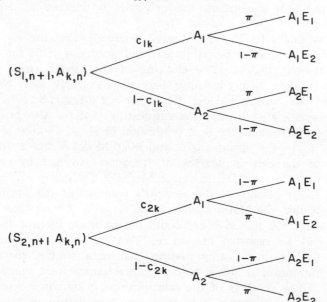

FIG. 5. The trees for the two states of Model III (see table 9).

These estimates may be computed from the transition numbers for Model III ($\pi = .25$), which were obtained by combining the appropriate cells of the 8×8 matrix of the observed transition numbers shown in table 8, giving the following result.

	$A_{1,n+1}, E_{1,n+1}$	$A_{1,n+1}, E_{2,n+1}$	$A_{2,n+1}, E_{1,n+1}$	$A_{2,n+1}, E_{2,n+1}$
$S_{1,n+1}, A_{1,n}$	n_{11} (281)	n_{12} (104)	n_{13} (206)	n_{14} (63)
$S_{1,n+1}, A_{2,n}$	n_{21} (423)	n_{22} (138)	n_{23} (478)	n_{24} (144)
$S_{2,n+1}, A_{1,n}$	n_{31} (43)	n_{32} (134)	n_{33} (136)	n_{34} (361)
$S_{2,n+1}, A_{2,n}$	n_{41} (49)	n_{42} (150)	n_{43} (264)	n_{44} (797)

These maximum-likelihood estimates of the C_{ij} may be shown by standard methods to depend, in this simple present case, only on C_{ij}, and are given by

$$\hat{C}_{11} = \frac{n_{11} + n_{12}}{\sum_j n_{1j}}, \qquad \hat{C}_{21} = \frac{n_{31} + n_{32}}{\sum_j n_{3j}},$$

$$\hat{C}_{12} = \frac{n_{21} + n_{22}}{\sum_j n_{2j}}, \qquad \hat{C}_{22} = \frac{n_{41} + n_{42}}{\sum_j n_{4j}},$$

where $j = 1, \cdots, 4$. Thus, e.g.,

$$\hat{C}_{11} = \frac{281 + 104}{281 + 104 + 206 + 63} = .588 .$$

On estimating four quantities, the original 16 degrees of freedom are reduced to 12.

In this way tables 10, 11, and 12 were produced, showing the conditioning parameters, transition probabilities, and goodness of fit for the generalized conditioning models. The clothing of the model hangs loosely on the frame of the data, as any learning theorist will clearly see. Nonetheless, of the first four models, Model III, $\langle C_{ij} \rangle = P\{A_{1,n+1}, S_{in}, A_{in}\}$, has by all odds the smallest χ^2, a condition suggesting that for the price of only four degrees of freedom the best prediction of $A_{1,n+1}$ is knowledge of the pair $(S_{i,n+1}, A_{i,n})$. For groups $\pi(75)$ and $\pi(50)$ Model V fits a little better even at twice the cost in degrees of freedom. (In fact by conventional standards we might even fail to reject Model V for group $\pi(75)$.)

The most likely reason for the generally poor fits of the various models to the data is that the Markov chain is of an order higher than one. The test of first against second order could not be made in time for inclusion here, but will be reported elsewhere. We have aleady mentioned the Verplanck, Collier, and Cotton finding that in a simple visual-detection experiment significant response–response correlations were found out to at least lag 11. Close scrutiny of the relationships in our own experiment for trials $n - 1$ and $n - 2$ should help in seeing the nature of the conditioning dependencies. Even if the process were first-order, the experiments and their analysis have shown the complexity of what is considered to be

TABLE 10

CONDITIONING PARAMETERS, TRANSITION PROBABILITIES, AND GOODNESS OF FIT
OF FOUR GENERALIZED CONDITIONING MODELS

$(\pi = 1.00)$

n	$n+1$	A_1 Obs.	Model				N
			I*	II*	III	IV	
$S_1E_1A_1$	S_1	.741	.547	.547	.721	.603	515
$S_1E_1A_1$	S_2	.177	.128	.128	.169	.140	469
$S_1E_1A_2$	S_1	.327	.547	.547	.442	.384	455
$S_1E_1A_2$	S_2	.073	.128	.128	.106	.089	409
$S_2E_2A_1$	S_1	.528	.523	.523	.721	.384	108
$S_2E_2A_1$	S_2	.138	.123	.123	.169	.089	130
$S_2E_2A_2$	S_1	.509	.523	.523	.442	.603	769
$S_2E_2A_2$	S_2	.120	.123	.123	.106	.140	879
		χ^2	189.19	189.19	53.46	114.67	
		df	4	4	4	4	
		α	$< .001$	$< .001$	$< .001$	$< .001$	

* Models I and II are identical for $\pi = 1.00$, since $A_1, S_{i,n+1}, S_{g,n} = PA_{i,n+1}, E_{j,n}$; that is, the experimenter's response always agrees with the stimulus.

one of the simplest of psychophysical situations, the Yes–No detection experiment.

One additional remark about the fit of the generalized conditioning models ought to be made. Suppes and Schlag-Rey (chapter 22) report a series of experiments similar to ours and to the earlier Suppes and Krasne study on social pressure. Briefly, an observer reported which of two lights, S_1 or S_2, was extinguished first. The social information was ostensibly his knowledge about which response a co-observer had made. In one of two variants, the social information came before the observer's response, in the other (as in our situation) the social information came after the observer's response. In neither case was the social information contingent on what the observer did. Suppes and Schlag-Rey obtain remarkably good fits of a large number of general conditioning models. Now there are two points to be made here. First, if several models fit about equally well, as they do in the Suppes and Schlag-Rey experiment, it does not afford much insight into details of the conditioning process. Secondly, there is a crucial difference in the meaning of the S_1 and S_2 involved. In Suppes and Schlag-Rey's experiments (chapter 22) S_1 and S_2 was the arbitrary designation of each of a pair of identical lights. A_i was the observer's statement that the ith light was extinguished first. In one condition the lights were always extinguished simultaneously. Presumably the E_j event operated on a response bias of the observer. Thus the complexity introduced by having a physically meaningful distinction between two stimulus events is avoided nicely.

TABLE 11

CONDITIONING PARAMETERS, TRANSITION PROBABILITY, AND GOODNESS OF FIT
OF FIVE GENERALIZED CONDITIONING MODELS

$(\pi = 1.00)$

n	$n+1$	A_1 Obs.	Model					N
			I	II	III	IV	V	
$S_1E_1A_1$	S_1	.559	.528	.544	.588	.539	.645	361
$S_1E_1A_1$	S_2	.250	.225	.229	.262	.188	.263	348
$S_1E_1A_2$	S_1	.461	.528	.544	.475	.481	.474	362
$S_1E_1A_2$	S_2	.203	.225	.229	.158	.208	.181	320
$S_1E_2A_2$	S_1	.381	.528	.485	.475	.539	.472	97
$S_1E_2A_2$	S_2	.193	.225	.165	.158	.188	.445	114
$S_1E_2A_1$	S_1	.463	.528	.485	.588	.481	.495	108
$S_1E_2A_1$	S_2	.242	.225	.165	.262	.208	.262	132
$S_2E_1A_1$	S_1	.577	.503	.544	.588	.539	.645	45
$S_2E_1A_1$	S_2	.345	.167	.229	.262	.188	.263	55
$S_2E_1A_2$	S_1	.503	.503	.534	.475	.481	.474	169
$S_2E_1A_2$	S_2	.145	.167	.229	.158	.208	.181	211
$S_2E_2A_1$	S_1	.521	.503	.485	.588	.481	.495	140
$S_2E_2A_1$	S_2	.281	.167	.165	.262	.208	.262	139
$S_2E_2A_2$	S_1	.488	.503	.485	.475	.539	.472	553
$S_2E_2A_2$	S_2	.136	.167	.165	.158	.188	.145	595
		χ^2	71.63	62.44	33.34	69.56	14.44	
		df	12	12	12	12	8	
		α	$<.001$	$<.001$	$<.001$	$<.001$	$<.10$	

6. The Fundamental Detection Problem and the Concept of Likelihood Ratio[4]

The paper on a new theory of visual detection by Tanner and Swets [14] was the first of many concerned with applying the theory of signal detectability and statistical decision theory to psychophysics. (See also Peterson, Birdsall, and Fox [7].) We sketch the theory, which is clearly intended as an alternative to the threshold theory, in extremely brief form. The heart of the matter is the criterion problem—the definition of the observer's criterion for making a positive response. This is the fundamental detection problem: In an observation interval an observer is instructed to watch or listen to some event, ordinarily under control of the experimenter, and to make a report following the observation interval. The theory assumes that this report is both variable and underlaid by a process of single dimension—at least the sensory response may be described as a unidimensional variable. It is also assumed that the observer knows the probability of a response when the stimulus occurs in the continuously present background

---

[4] For an excellent general account see Swets [13]. Green's longer paper [5] deals with the technical details as well as the theory.

TABLE 12

CONDITIONING PARAMETERS, TRANSITION PROBABILITIES, AND GOODNESS OF FIT
OF FIVE GENERALIZED CONDITIONING MODELS

$(\pi = .50)$

n	$n+1$	A_1 Obs.	Model					N
			I	II	III	IV	V	
$S_1E_1A_1$	S_1	.687	.513	.513	.612	.505	.660	262
$S_1E_1A_1$	S_2	.233	.188	.182	.230	.190	.278	215
$S_1E_1A_2$	S_1	.425	.513	.513	.424	.468	.433	247
$S_1E_1A_2$	S_2	.179	.188	.182	.162	.186	.206	235
$S_1E_2A_2$	S_1	.364	.513	.457	.424	.505	.415	209
$S_1E_2A_2$	S_2	.162	.188	.175	.162	.190	.154	228
$S_1E_2A_1$	S_1	.557	.513	.457	.612	.468	.550	183
$S_1E_2A_1$	S_2	.185	.188	.175	.230	.186	.259	214
$S_2E_1A_1$	S_1	.571	.460	.513	.612	.505	.660	77
$S_2E_1A_1$	S_2	.367	.188	.182	.230	.190	.278	79
$S_2E_1A_2$	S_1	.438	.460	.513	.424	.468	.433	376
$S_2E_1A_2$	S_2	.164	.188	.182	.162	.186	.206	329
$S_2E_2A_1$	S_1	.535	.460	.457	.612	.468	.550	84
$S_2E_2A_1$	S_2	.280	.188	.175	.230	.186	.214	100
$S_2E_2A_2$	S_1	.443	.460	.457	.424	.505	.415	388
$S_2E_2A_2$	S_2	.150	.188	.175	.162	.190	.154	406
		χ^2	99.06	103.16	28.61	100.26	22.08	
		df	12	12	12	12	8	
		α	$<.001$	$<.001$	$<.005$	$<.001$	$<.005$	

noise, $P(R \mid S + N)$ (part of which may be sensory noise), as well as the
probability of a response when the noise alone is present, $P(R \mid N)$. He bases
his response on the ratio of these two quantities, which is a likelihood ratio,
$l(X)$. He reports a stimulus value when $l(X) \geqq K$, the criterion. Clearly
$l(X)$ is real and positive.

The likelihood-ratio criterion is established by the observer but depends
on several variables, such as goals, the probability of a stimulus, the value
of a hit, the cost of a false-alarm and feedback. A simple Yes-No form
of the detection experiment yields a stimulus-response $(S-R)$ matrix on
each of a series of trials t, as follows:

$$S_i(t)$$

$R_i(t)$		$S + N$	N
	Yes	OK	False Alarm
	No	False Rejection	OK

The similarity to simple statistical hypothesis-testing is obvious. What is important is that a probability matrix of this form provides two independent measures: (1) an index of sensitivity, i.e., the probability of a correct detection, and (2) an index of criterion, the false-alarm rate. This pair of numbers $P(\text{Yes} \mid S + N)$ and $P(\text{Yes} \mid N)$, plotted for all possible values, is called a receiver-operating characteristic or simply an ROC curve. It has the property that $P(\text{Yes} \mid N)$ is a nondecreasing function of $P(\text{Yes} \mid S + N)$ and for a fixed ratio of signal energy (E) to noise power per unit bandwidth (N_0), the quantity

$$d' = \left(\frac{2E}{N_0} \right)^{\frac{1}{2}} = \frac{\mu_{S+N} - \mu_N}{\sigma_N} ,$$

where μ_{SN} and μ_N are the means of the $S + N$ and N distributions respectively and σ_N is the standard deviation of μ_N. Also, $dp(\text{Yes} \mid S + N)/ dp(\text{Yes} \mid N)$ at any point is equal to the value of the likelihood ratio that produces that point.

The (experimental) interpretation is that for fixed d' it is impossible for an optimal observer to increase sensitivity without a corresponding increase in false-alarm rate; the best and worst performance of an observer is bounded by the area between the ROC curve of an optimal detector (the d' curve) and its reflection across the 45-degree axis. The quantity d' is fundamental and has been shown to be relatively invariant in various experimental conditions under changes in criterion and different procedures such as the Yes–No and the forced-choice. Thus predictions may be made about performance in a Yes–No situation from data obtained in a forced-choice experiment and conversely. Useful extensions by analogy have been made to complex recognition experiments. It should be pointed out that nothing in the theory restricts it to sinusoids in noise. The distributions may be of any kind.

Those who favor signal-detection theory as an alternative to the threshold model have had to specify an explicit threshold theory. It is their reasonable claim that this threshold model as they have defined it does not handle several classes of data; it does not explain, for example, the apparently nonlinear relationship between $P(\text{Yes} \mid S + N)$ and $P(\text{Yes} \mid N)$. Neither does it account for data taken from the same observer under the same signal-to-noise conditions but using a different design, say a forced-choice experiment.

But it is possible to define a threshold model which leads to predictions very much like those of the signal-detection models. Luce has done this.[5] He postulates two unobservable states assumed by the subject, D (a detection) and $\bar{D}$ (no detection). On the presentation of a stimulus-plus-noise, or noise alone, one of these two states is entered. The entry process has a random character whose probabilities are fixed for a given observer in a given situation. These probabilities may be manipulated by means of, e.g., the instructions, payoff matrix, or a priori probability of the occurrence of

---

[5] Personal communication.

a signal. Luce's model leads to a relationship between $P(\text{Yes} \mid S)$ and $P(\text{Yes} \mid N)$ which takes the form of a two-branched linear function. The basic detection model is generalized to the forced-choice case. A very important feature is Luce's treatment of the detection paradigm in conjunction with a linear-operator learning model. Asymptotic response probabilities and associated statistics are derived, which is of course a great advantage over the Tanner–Swets signal-detection theory. A disadvantage is the apparent impossibility of determining the energy corresponding to threshold. Luce's model seems to do about as well as the signal-detection model in fitting the data of visual and auditory Yes–No detection experiments.

Let us look at these two theories in relationship to one of our important outcomes. Recall that in the low-signal-energy task considerable improvement in $P(\text{Yes} \mid S)$ and $P(\text{Yes} \mid N)$ over the no-information group followed upon the introduction of a reinforcing event. At a higher signal level the opposite was true. (Naturally, since observers were different in the various groups, we must assume that our observers were a random sample from the same population.) Signal-detection theory says nothing about asymptotic rates or the process of attaining them, but the apparent departure of the data from a curvilinear ROC curve for which $P(\text{Yes} \mid N)$ is a nondecreasing function of $P(\text{Yes} \mid S)$ would be explained as follows. If in a series of trials an observer vacillates between two criteria, the resulting point on his operating characteristic curve will be a straight line connecting the points corresponding to the two criteria; this average point falls below the curve on which the two criteria are located. [13, p. 172.] Using averaged data from the second block of trials, extreme criteria for all four hard-task groups do indeed give an (unweighted) mean that agrees closely with the overall mean criterion for these groups. However, we still have the problem of accounting for the increased or decreased performance under conditions of reinforcement. The extreme criteria of the no-information group give us no clues because they are clearly points on a different ROC curve than the ones of the π-groups.

Luce, in the learning analysis of his threshold theory for simple detection says, "It also suggests that information feedback need not always be beneficial in inducing subjects to yield up the desired information, as has often been assumed by modern psychophysicists." In a less formal analysis he argues as follows. Subjects with no information report what they detect, e.g., in the easy discrimination $P(\text{Yes} \mid S) = .73$, $P(\text{Yes} \mid N) = .09$. When there is feedback, the subject is driven away from this point, either on the upper limb or lower limb. We do not know which way a given subject will go. Suppose that half go one way and half the other. Those on the upper limb will have a much higher value of $P(\text{Yes} \mid N)$ than .09 and only a slightly higher value $P(\text{Yes} \mid S)$ than .73. Those on the lower limb will have $P(\text{Yes} \mid N)$ near .09 with $P(\text{Yes} \mid S)$ much less than .73. For the group mean $P(\text{Yes} \mid S)$ will be less than .73 and $P(\text{Yes} \mid N)$ greater than .09. The argument is of course essentially that of Swets although the result derives from reinforcement theory.

However, the data on individual subjects do not in general bear Luce out.

But it does not seem to us that Luce's predictions are properly tested in this way, for the measures taken in the no-information task ought to come from the same subjects as in the feedback task. He himself suggests that such data are crucial to establish the validity of this prediction.

ACKNOWLEDGMENTS

We are most grateful to Professor R. C. Atkinson for his aid and comfort during the conduct of these studies and for some illuminating remarks; to Professor R. D. Luce for letting us see the manuscript of an unpublished paper and for his informal account of certain predictions from his model; and to Professor P. Suppes for his editorial acumen.

REFERENCES

[1] ASCH, S. E., Studies of independence and conformity: I. A minority of one against a unanimous majority, *Psychol. Monog.*, 1956, **70**(9) (whole no. 416).

[2] BARTLETT, M. S., *An Introduction to Stochastic Processes*, Cambridge: Cambridge Univ. Press, 1955.

[3] BILLINGSLEY, P., *Statistical Inference for Markov Processes*, Chicago: Univ. Chicago Press, 1961.

[4] BILLINGSLEY, P., Statistical methods in Markov chains, *Ann. Math. Stat.*, 1961, **32**, 12-40.

[5] GREEN, D. M., Psychoacoustics and detection theory, *J. Acoust. Soc. Amer.*, 1960, **32**, 1189-1203.

[6] LUCE, R. D., A threshold theory of simple detection and recognition experiments, 1961 (in press).

[7] PETERSON, W. W., T. O. BIRDSALL, and W. C. FOX, The theory of signal detectability, *I.R.E. Trans. on Inform. Theory*, 1954, **IT-4**, 171-212.

[8] SHERIF, M., A study of some social factors in perception, *Arch. Psychol.*, 1935, **27**, 187.

[9] SHERIF, M., and O. J. HARVEY, A study in ego functioning: elimination of stable anchorages in individual and group situations, *Sociometry*, 1952, **15**, 272-305.

[10] SPEETH, S. D., and M. V. MATHEWS, Sequential effects in the signal-detection situation, *J. Acoust. Soc. Amer.*, 1960, **32**, 932.

[11] SUPPES, P., and R. C. ATKINSON, *Markov Learning Models for Multiperson Interactions*, Stanford, Calif.: Stanford Univ. Press, 1960.

[12] SUPPES, P., and F. KRASNE, Application of stimulus sampling theory to situations involving social pressure, *Psychol. Rev.*, 1961, **68**, 46-59.

[13] SWETS, J. A., Is there a sensory threshold? *Science*, 1961, **134**, 168-77.

[14] TANNER, W. P., Jr., and J. A. SWETS, A decision making theory of visual detection, *Psychol. Rev.*, 1954, **61**, 401-09.

[15] VERPLANCK, W. S., G. H. COLLIER, and J. W. COTTON, Nonindependence of successive responses in measurements of the visual threshold, *J. Exptl. Psychol.*, 1952, **44**, 273-82.

7

The Process of Choosing a Reference Group

Bernard P. Cohen, *Stanford University*

1. Introduction

The objective of this paper is to present an extension of the author's probability model for conformity behavior [6] which is appropriate to the study of reference group phenomena. We believe that the model to be discussed here is tied directly to substantive issues in current conceptions of reference group behavior and will provide a basis for the experimental study of some of these questions. It is our view that with this model and the experimental framework we will outline, it will be possible to develop and test propositions which could be incorporated into a theory of reference-group behavior.

It should be clear at the outset that this model is in no sense a formalization of reference group theory. What is termed "reference group theory" in the sociological literature is not sufficiently spelled out to be amenable to formal treatment. It seems to us that previous work on reference groups has attempted to isolate a phenomenon and argue for its importance as an object of research. Although research of this type is an important precursor to the construction of a theory, it lacks the concentration of focus which theoretical development requires. Thus we find ourselves in a situation in which it is premature to expect that an attempt to construct *formal* theory would be fruitful. In examining the literature one finds too many diverse ideas, which are too often unanalyzed, and too little marshaling of evidence for one to even consider the task of codification. Merton [11], for example, lists 26 properties of groups which he feels should be taken into account in work on reference groups. In light of the wide range of factors that could serve as the basis for many alternative theories, it appears to us that it would be prudent to provide conceptual and empirical apparatus for selecting among these factors rather than to formulate a theory based on some arbitrary selection among them.

This research is part of a project on "Probability Models for Conformity Behavior" under Grant No. 9030 from the National Science Foundation. The support of the National Science Foundation is gratefully acknowledged. The author also wishes to express his appreciation to Mr. Thomas Mayer, Mr. Jack Yellott, Mr. Bruce Bushing, and Mrs. Mary Comstock for their assistance in the course of this research.

The present model is a representational model in the sense that Berger, Cohen, Snell, and Zelditch [4] have used the term. It is an attempt to incorporate what we believe are key elements of the phenomenon and so to develop descriptive tools for the analysis of experiments. Berger *et al.* have pointed out that a major function of this type of model is that it "provides a means for systematically studying experimental variations in the basic situation." The implications in the present context are clear. If we succeed in capturing the core of the phenomenon in our model and in the experimental situation, then the model will enable us to evaluate how the introduction of some of Merton's factors affects the basic process. An illustration of how this can be accomplished must wait until we have described our basic tools. But, as will be evident later, the model and its interpretation suggest several lines of research.

We believe that applications of this model can serve to bring together two important traditions of social psychological research. One tradition, with which we associate the names of Asch, Festinger, and Sherif, is the experimental study of social influence. The second, which may be termed "the survey analysis of cross-pressure phenomena," is exemplified in the works of Lazarsfeld and Merton. The concept of reference group is central to the integration of these two traditions, but there are problems that arise with this concept. Since we hope to accomplish more than an integration by verbal fiat, we hope to show (1) that our model can be a vehicle for clarifying the concept of reference group and (2) that in terms of the model the experimental situations of Asch and Sherif have direct bearing on the problems that Lazarsfeld and Merton raise. To accomplish this, we will concentrate on one aspect of the phenomenon: the problem of the individual's choice of a group as a reference group.

Our discussion will proceed in the following way: first, we will examine the concept of reference group and the related idea of cross-pressures to indicate some of their key features and how they have been used. In the course of this analysis, we intend to point out some of the difficulties with both of these notions, but our primary purpose is to consider some of the important research questions that have been raised concerning reference group phenomena. These questions suggest the general outline of an experimental situation that will be analyzed in section 3. Section 4 will present our model, describe its features, derive some of its properties, and provide a substantive interpretation for the model. In this connection, we will examine the substantive assumptions built into the model and the restrictions which these assumptions impose. Finally, section 5 will return to the experimental situation to suggest the ways in which it could be used to investigate some attributes of groups which affect the individual's choice of a reference group. In this section, we will also point out how the model enters into the analysis of these experiments.

2. Reference Groups and Cross-Pressures

To the investigator concerned with social phenomena, the concept of reference group is intuitively compelling. In some metaphorical form, the idea has a long history. Our concern, however, is not with historical review nor with an exhaustive consideration of contemporary applications of these notions. Since Merton can be regarded as one of the most prominent students of this phenomenon, we will focus on some of his work. Merton and Rossi write, "In general, then, reference group theory aims to systematize the determinants and consequences of those processes of evaluation and self-appraisal in which the individual takes the values or standards of other individuals and groups as a comparative frame of reference." [12, p. 234.] In this statement we can see several foci of concern. We will restrict ourselves to "determinants" rather than "consequences" and thus concentrate on the individual confronted with group influences. Furthermore, taking a "comparative frame of reference" can involve several types of behavior. For example, consider the questions, "What should I do?" and "How rich am I?" To capture this distinction, Merton distinguishes two main types of reference groups: "...the first is the 'normative type' which sets and maintains standards for the individual and the second is the 'comparison type' which provides a frame of comparison relative to which the individual evaluates himself and others." [11, p. 283.] Although we believe that processes of self-evaluation and other-evaluation are involved in both "normative" and "comparison" reference groups, at present the primary interest of this work is in the determinants of choice of normative reference groups.

Now the idea that groups of which an individual is a member provide standards for him arose before the advent of reference group theory, but the distinctive character of reference group theory is that it extends the "long established conception of group determination of behavior" to those groups of which the individual is not a member. Merton and Rossi write:

> That men act in a social frame of reference yielded by the groups of which they are a part is a notion undoubtedly ancient and probably sound. Were this alone the concern of reference group theory, it would merely be a new term for an old focus in sociology, which has always centered on the group determination of behavior. There is, however, the further fact that men frequently orient themselves to groups *other than their own* in shaping their behavior and evaluations, and it is problems centered about this fact of orientation to nonmembership groups that constitute the distinctive concern of reference group theory. Ultimately, of course, the theory must be generalized to the point where it can account for *both* membership and nonmembership group orientations, but immediately its major task is to search out the processes through which individuals relate themselves to groups to which they do not belong. [12, p. 234.]

This view of reference group theory opens Pandora's box. One need only consider how reference group concepts are used for the problem to become apparent. Typically, reference group ideas are applied as *post hoc* interpretive concepts. In discussing the use (in *The American Soldier* [15]) of the concept of relative deprivation, one of many reference group notions, Merton and Rossi write, "We may thus tag the major function of the concept of relative deprivation as that of a provisional after-the-fact interpretive concept which is intended to explain the variations in attitudes expressed by soldiers of differing social status." [12, p. 230.]   The *post hoc* employment of the concept in itself is not an issue, but when one considers the complete lack of constraints on how the concept is applied, one can question the utility of this type of analysis.   The problem is serious enough when we restrict ourselves to membership groups as reference groups, since an individual belongs to many groups which can be invoked as the purpose suits us.   Allowing nonmembership groups and social categories to serve as comparative frames of reference removes what few constraints there might be.   It is this lack of constraint that has led to the waggish comment, "Your reference group is a group that you behave like, and you behave like them because they're your reference group." (See [5], for example.)

The difficulties posed by this type of *post hoc* analysis are widely recognized, but discussions of the way to resolve them with respect to reference group theory usually omit a significant alternative.   It should be clear that we do not wish to abandon the concept nor do we wish to restrict it to membership groups.[1]   Furthermore, we do not believe that the only way out is to make the concept operational in the sense usually meant.[2]   Since the problem arises as a result of the complete freedom of the analyst, it may be met by imposing limitations on the interpretive use of the concept of reference group.   Regarding reference groups as intervening variables in survey analysis is perfectly consistent with imposing such limitations, provided that there is a set of general theoretical principles that serve as rules for the application of reference group ideas.

Using such a set of rules would require an *a priori* conceptualization of the alternative frames of reference "available" to the individual.[3]   Presumably the theory would contain propositions such as: Given alternative frames of reference, $F_1, F_2, \cdots, F_n$, individuals with characteristics C_i will refer their judgments to F_j.[4]   Then if we observe an individual conforming to the standard of F_j and if that standard is unique, we can account for this behavior by invoking the reference group ideas in propositions such as our example.   What is needed, then, is a set of general principles of this form. Our own particular interest is in developing propositions dealing with choice

---

[1] Nonmembership groups must be included on many grounds including empirical demonstration of their importance (see Siegel and Siegel [14]).   Social categories, such as high-status people, as comparative frames of reference raise problems that are outside the scope of the present analysis, since these categories are not groups in the ordinary sense of the word.

[2] This would require us *in every instance* to observe the fact of orientation to a given group before invoking this group as a reference group in our explanation.   In interviewing street cleaners, then, we must inquire whether or not they respect the opinions of other street cleaners, garbage men, road workers, and on and on.   The absurdity of this example dramatizes some of the practical difficulties of this approach.

[3] This immediately suggests one line of development for reference group theory, namely the formulation and testing of propositions concerning how the size and composition of the set of alternatives varies with, for example, characteristics of the individual.

[4] The example is stated in deterministic form for the sake of simple exposition.   Other variables such as characteristics of the decision confronting the individual are omitted for the same reason.

among reference groups as a function of the attributes of the groups in the set of available alternatives. Merton and Rossi make a start in this direction by advancing (albeit in a footnote) the following proposition [12, p. 247]: "When primary environment of opinion and secondary environment operate at cross purposes, it appears that the primary environment does take some measure of precedence."

In general, there has been a notable lack of research aimed at developing such propositions. The work of Ruth Hartley [10] is an exception. She has tested a large number of hypotheses dealing with the acceptance of new reference groups. Her concern was primarily with individual characteristics as they relate to the acceptance of college in one study and the Navy in a second study. Her focus is somewhat different from the one we want to emphasize here, namely that of a choice between alternative reference groups. One of her findings may bear out this difference. She reports that "Relative acceptance of a new group as a reference group is positively correlated with the number of group memberships and negatively correlated with the importance of these memberships to the individual." [10, p. 17.] But for the fact that her correlations are low (about .4), though significant, this result would be extremely puzzling to us. We are puzzled because it is not clear what makes the choice of college as a reference group problematic. One must examine the attributes of these other group memberships to determine what other groups are predisposing or antagonistic to the acceptance of college as a reference group. In so far as individuals belong to groups predisposing to the acceptance of college, we would expect positive correlations *both* with number of other group memberships and with the importance of these other groups. For those individuals who belong to some favoring and some antagonistic groups, we would want to examine those attributes that affect selection of the standard to which the individual would conform. In the way we look at the problem, acceptance of college as a reference group itself becomes a standard of the other reference groups to which the individual may or may not orient himself.

Our interest, then, is in those attributes of groups which affect the selection of a group as a reference group when that selection is problematic. We believe that an experimental program is necessary to investigate these attributes because of some inherent limitations of the survey approach with respect to this problem. Among these limitations are two of major concern: (1) the fact that groups in nature are bundles of heterogeneous attributes, so that it is difficult and expensive to isolate those attributes one wishes to study; and (2) in dealing with groups in nature there is a tendency to focus on specific historical attributes signified by everyday labels such as Catholic, Protestant, Democrat, etc., rather than to concentrate on more abstract conceptions of group properties, as for example, "specific-task" groups or "diffuse value-setting" groups.

Of course, there are limitations to an experimental program as well, but we believe that such a program is strategic for the development of the general principles we have briefly mentioned. One of the limitations is that at present we are restricted to considering choice among two alternative possible reference groups. However, there is much to be done even in this narrow context.

Before turning to the details of this experimental program, we should like to examine the concept of cross-pressures, since it is definitely related to the experimental paradigm we hope to develop. In their study of voting in Elmira, N.Y., Berelson, Lazarsfeld, and McPhee defined cross-pressures as "combinations of characteristics, which, in a given context, would tend to lead an individual to vote on both sides of a contest." [3, p. 283.] In its application to survey materials, this concept has some of the same difficulties as the concept of reference group. For example, it is argued that in an election a high-status Catholic is subject to cross-pressures because most Catholics vote one way and most high-status people vote another. In other words, a high-status Catholic potentially has two conflicting frames of reference that give rise to cross-pressures on him. Here again we do not have any rules by which to decide whether or not the concept of cross-pressures is applicable; consider, for example, the possibility that *any* individual possesses at least two attributes that lead to diverse voting intentions.[5] The importance of imposing constraints on the analyst's interpretation is once again evident.

Despite the difficulties with the *post hoc* interpretive usage of the idea of cross-pressures, two principles emerge from this type of analysis which are important here. The first is that an individual who is subject to cross-pressures is likely to make his decision late, while the second is that such an individual is likely to switch back and forth between alternatives. Both of these principles suggest an emphasis on a temporal process of responding to cross-pressures. To us, then, choosing among alternative reference groups is a dynamic process involving conflict and its resolution. It is not enough to examine an individual's behavior at a point in time to determine his reference group unless that point in time represents an equilibrium state; in so far as an individual is switching back and forth we would not want to argue that he has selected or rejected a given reference group. A key feature of our experimental situation is that it enables us to detect equilibrium states.

3. The Basic Experimental Situation

The central feature of the experimental situation is that an individual is forced to make a sequence of choices between two mutually exclusive

---

[5] In survey research, the analysis often proceeds as follows: An individual is characterized by attributes X and Y; the analyst examines all the respondents to the survey who have attribute X. He finds that this category has a high probability of voting Democratic, and then he examines all respondents who have attribute Y and finds this category has a low probability of voting Democratic. Hence he asserts that the individual is subject to two conflicting frames of reference. The present view is that a given individual can be characterized by at least one X and at least one Y attribute; of course, these attributes differ from individual to individual. Thus, for example, we believe high-status Protestants, a non-cross-pressure category, would be considered subject to cross-pressure if other attributes of these high-status Protestants were examined.

behavioral alternatives. The connection between each of these behavioral alternatives and a given frame of reference is established in advance. For example, if a high-status reference group offered one frame of reference, it could do so by always choosing one of the two alternatives. Since we require a sequence of choices, we would not infer the selection of this high-status reference group from a single response which conforms to its standard; we would require consistent conformity to that group's standard.

In examining the possibilities offered by this basic situation, two factors require attention: (1) the individual's initial predisposition for one or the other behavioral choice, and (2) the presence of one or more group standards providing frames of reference for that choice.

Case I. If there is no predisposition favoring one of the alternatives and there are no group standards evident to the subject, we assume that his choices will be random. The results of a pilot study support this view. The subject was told that his task was to determine whether or not one of two lines was equal in length to a standard line. After seeing a sample stimulus which clearly defined the task, he was informed that we were interested in subliminal perception and that he would be asked to judge slides he could not consciously see. The experimenter urged the subject to respond quickly so as not to "censor his first unconscious impression." In fact, the subject made a sequence of judgments of blank slides with the projector set to simulate rapid exposure of the stimulus. As we had hoped, the data closely resembled the independence process of coin tossing.

Case II. If there are no group standards evident to the subject and he has an initial predisposition favoring one of the alternatives, then his choice will reflect his initial predisposition. For example, Asch's control groups show that where one of the alternatives represents a veridical judgment and no confederates are involved, subjects choose the correct answer. [2, p. 9.]

Case III. If the individual has no predispositions favoring one of the alternatives but he is aware of a single group with one of the alternatives as its uniform standard, then his referring his choice to that group is *not* problematic. Sherif's work on the auto-kinetic phenomenon supports this contention [13].

There are two ways in which choosing a given group as a reference group and conforming to the standard of that group become problematic.

Case IV. If the individual has an initial predisposition to choose one alternative and is aware of a group that takes the other alternative as its standard, then his selection or rejection of the reference group is determined in part by the attributes of that group and by his relation to the group. This case has been studied extensively by Asch and by others using the Asch situation. Here we find that we can increase or decrease the probability of selecting the experimenter's confederates as a reference group by manipulating their attributes. For example, Cohen, Mayer, Schulman, and Terry [8] compared subjects facing a group who were "more competent perceivers" than the subject, with subjects confronting a group of "less competent perceivers." When the confederates were more competent, the subjects were about twice as likely to conform to the group standard.

Case V. If the individual has no initial bases for choice but is aware of two groups each of which takes one of the alternatives as its standard, we assume that attributes of the respective groups, including those which affect the individual's relation to each group, are the sole determinants of his choice. To our knowledge, there has not been any research to date dealing with this case.

Although this classification is not intended to be exhaustive, there is another case which should be mentioned to illustrate a problem.

Case VI. If the individual has an initial predisposition for one of the alternatives and also is aware of two groups, one of which chooses as its standard the alternative to which the individual is predisposed, while the other chooses the opposite alternative, we have a complicated case where one of the possibilities is that both groups are irrelevant to the individual's choice. Another interesting possibility is that the opposing group is rejected but the supporting group is not selected. This possibility calls attention to what could be two completely independent processes, that of selection and that of rejection, which could be present in other cases as well.

We will not discuss this case further except to indicate that Asch's experiments, in which he provided the naive subject with a partner who supported the subject's choice of the correct answer, bear directly on this case [1, ch. 16.] The fact that the partner's presence drastically reduced the amount of yielding to the incorrect majority suggests to us that this is an instance of rejection of the majority without selection of the partner. Since such an overwhelming effect occurred without regard to the attributes of the partner, we believe that it is unlikely that the subject bases his decision on the partner's choices. This could be tested by having the partner switched to a third alternative after a number of trials in which he supported the subject. If our interpretation is correct, the subject should continue to give the correct response.

Cases IV, V, and VI may be distinguished from Cases I, II, and III by the presence of conflicting bases of choice. These cases appear to have the essential ingredients of a cross-pressure phenomenon; hence they are of most interest to us. Cases I, II, and III represent appropriate control groups for the type of experiments we have in mind. Since Case IV has been extensively studied and Case VI depends on an understanding of Case V, we will focus on Case V and discuss the model in terms of that case.

Case V contains what we regard as the basic process involved in the selection of a reference group, i.e., the process of conflict resolution. The model we will present is an effort to represent the core elements of this process and, for that reason, we have termed it "the conflict model."

4. The Conflict Model

A special case of this model was originally developed to describe Asch-type experiments; we are now in a position to present a more general model

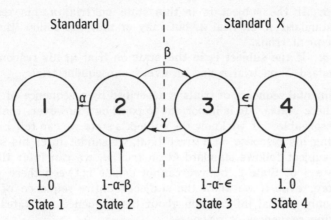

FIG. 1. Schematic diagram of the conflict model (Case V). Arrows indicate allowable transitions, which are labeled with their probabilities. The states are defined in the text.

which we believe will apply to all six cases. Each case will require its own coordinating definitions and slight modifications in the interpretation of the model, but the general form should hold for each case we have analyzed.

At the time the original model was developed, it was not worthwhile to consider its generalization because of difficulties in estimating the model's four parameters. The form we are about to discuss adds a fifth parameter, but it has become possible to estimate these parameters in a straightforward manner.[6]

We will describe the general model and some of its properties and then consider its interpretation. Figure 1 summarizes the elements of the model and should aid in following our description.

We assume two standards, O and X; the trial-to-trial changes in the individual's behavior with respect to these two standards is described by a four-state Markov chain.[7] On a given trial, an individual can be in any one of the four states; on the next trial, he can move to another state with specified probability. The states are the numbered circles in figure 1 and are defined as follows:

State 1: If the subject is in this state on trial n, his response will follow standard O on trial n and on every subsequent trial.

State 2: If the subject is in this state on trial n, his response will follow standard O on trial n, but may or may not follow that standard on subsequent trials.

---

[6] We are indebted to Dr. E. Gilbert for the analysis of the distributions of "run-lengths" and to Dr. R. Hamming for his suggestions about a computer technique which approximates "least-squares" fitting of these distributions. These suggestions have provided us with a direct estimation method.

[7] We deal with standards rather than with responses R_1 and R_2 to allow for the possibility that on some trials conformity to standard O requires R_1 and on other trials conformity to the same standard requires response R_2.

State 3: If the subject is in this state on trial n, his response will follow standard X on trial n, but may or may not follow that standard on subsequent trials.

State 4: If the subject is in this state on trial n, his response will follow standard X on trial n and on every subsequent trial.

An experimental sequence of trials is described by a sequence of movements between these states. It is important to point out, however, that the states are not observable. If we know the subject's state we can tell his response, but knowing his response on a given trial, we cannot infer his state. That is, if the subject follows standard O on trial n, we can infer that he is in either State 1 or State 2, but we cannot decide between these two states. Furthermore, even if we know the subject's entire sequence of responses, we have only partial information about his sequence of states. Consider the following sequences of responses:

(a) $\qquad\qquad$ $OXOXOXOOOOOOOOO \cdots\cdots\cdots O$,

and

(b) $\qquad\qquad$ $OOOOOOO \cdots\cdots\cdots\cdots\cdots\cdots O$.

For sequence (a), we have complete information for the first seven trials, but we know only that the subject is not in State 3 or State 4 for the remainder of the sequence. From the definitions of the states, (a) could result from any sequence of states of the following form:

$$2323232 \underbrace{\cdots\cdots\cdots 21}_{i+1} \qquad i = 0, 1, 2, \cdots, n \ .$$

Similarly (b) could be generated by any sequence of states of the form:

$$2 \underbrace{\cdots\cdots\cdots 21}_{i+1} \cdots\cdots \qquad i = 0, 1, 2, \cdots, n \ .$$

The fact that the states are not observable gives rise to some practical difficulties in estimating parameters, but is also a source of some of the model's power.[8]

As figure 1 indicates, not all transitions between states are allowed. (The arrows show the allowable transitions from trial n to trial $n + 1$ and the labels stand for the probability of each transition.) The rationale for assuming that certain transitions do not occur has been discussed previously [7]; here we should merely point out that assuming no transitions out of States 1 and 4 helps to capture the distinction made above between a relatively permanent and a transitory following of a standard.

If we let $p_i(n)$ be the probability of being in state i on trial n, we have the following set of transition equations:

(1) $\qquad\qquad$ $p_1(n + 1) = p_1(n) + \alpha p_2(n) \ ,$

$\qquad\qquad$ $p_2(n + 1) = (1 - \alpha - \beta)p_2(n) + \gamma p_3(n) \ ,$

---

[8] See Berger *et al.* [4] for a discussion of this point.

$$p_3(n + 1) = (1 - \gamma - \varepsilon)p_3(n) + \beta p_2(n),$$
$$p_4(n + 1) = p_4(n) + \varepsilon p_3(n).$$

The transition probabilities, α, β, γ, and ε are parameters to be estimated from the data. If we knew the distribution on trial 0 before the start of the experiment—that is, $p_i(0)$—and the values of the transition probabilities, we would have complete information about the process involved in the experiment. For example, let $P_0(n)$ be the probability of following standard O on trial n; then,

(2) $$P_0(n) = p_1(n) + p_2(n).$$

Unfortunately we cannot write an explicit expression for $P_0(n)$ for all n except for two special cases ($\alpha = \beta = \gamma = \varepsilon$ and $\alpha = \varepsilon, \beta = \gamma$). Repeated numerical substitution in (1) and (2), however, yields a theoretical curve of P_0 which can be compared with the observed proportion of responses following standard O. As we will soon show, the transition probabilities can be estimated without reference to $p_i(0)$. But many other properties depend on this initial distribution; hence we require one further assumption:

(3) $$p_1(0) = 0, \qquad p_2(0) = \mu, \qquad p_3(0) = 1 - \mu, \qquad p_4(0) = 0.$$

Our assumption that no one is initially in States 1 or 4 is based on the belief that no one is impervious to the conflict created by the presence of alternative frames of reference. For some of the cases discussed above, we want to assume a value for μ; thus, for example, in the model for the Asch experiments (Case IV) we assumed $\mu = 1.0$. In general, however, μ is a fifth parameter to be estimated from the data.

Since the major concern of this paper is to show the utility of our model for investigating propositions dealing with the choice of reference group, we will consider only those properties of the model that are immediately relevant to this objective. Detailed presentation of formal results and examination of questions of "goodness of fit" must await another context.[9]

We regard the transition probabilities as a basic set of dependent variables that summarize the experimental data and that can be used to relate behavior in the experiment to external variables. Our first concern, then, is with estimating these parameters. The state of the Markov chain can be inferred from the response whenever the response changes: OX implies State 3 and XO implies State 2. This suggests using the distribution of runs of O's and X's to estimate the parameters. Our notation is

$$O^K = O, O, \cdots, O \qquad (K \text{ responses following standard } O),$$
$$X^K = X, X, \cdots, X \qquad (K \text{ responses following standard } X).$$

Consider responses following standard O. The probability that a run of

---

[9] These matters will be considered in a forthcoming technical report on the research on probability models for conformity behavior, currently being conducted at Stanford.

O's is exactly length K (K finite) is

(4) $$\Pr(XO^K X \mid XO) = (1 - \alpha - \beta)^{K-1}\beta \ .$$

The probability that a run of O's continues forever, that is, that the subject moves to State 1 during the run, is

(5) $$\Pr(XO \mid XO) = \frac{\alpha}{\alpha + \beta} \ .$$

By summing (4) from K to infinity and adding (5), we obtain the probability that a run (finite or infinite) has K *or more* O's,

(6) $$\Pr(XO^K \mid XO) = \frac{\alpha + \beta(1 - \alpha - \beta)^{K-1}}{\alpha + \beta}$$

$$= 1 + \frac{\beta}{\alpha + \beta}[(1 - \alpha - \beta)^{K-1} - 1] \ .$$

Given experimental data on runs of O's, we can fit the fraction of runs of length K or greater by a curve of the form $1 - c_1(1 - c_2^{K-1})$. Then we obtain

(7) $$\beta = c_1(1 - c_2) \ , \qquad \alpha = (1 - c_1)(1 - c_2) \ .$$

Similarly, data on runs of X's yield estimates of γ and ε.

The fitting of the curve is accomplished by an approximation to a "least-squares" technique. (Least-squares estimates of both c_1 and c_2 yield an expression which would be extremely tedious to evaluate numerically even on a high-speed computer.) The procedure is as follows:

We obtain from the data the proportion of runs of length K or more for several values of K up to K_1; let us call these proportions n_K. By repeated iteration with chosen values of c_2, we attempt to minimize the sum of squares of deviations, S, where

(8) $$S = \sum_{K=2}^{K_1}\left\{1 - n_K - (1 - c_2^{K-1})\left[\frac{\sum_{K=2}^{K_1}(1 - n_K)(1 - c_2^{K-1})}{\sum_{K=2}^{K_1}(1 - c_2^{K-1})^2}\right]\right\}^2 \ .$$

The summations run from $K = 2$, since the proportion of runs of length 1 or greater is 1.0. (The bracketed fraction at the right is simply a least-squares estimate of c_1.)

Values of c_2 between 0 and 1 are chosen in a systematic fashion to bracket the interval containing the minimum S. To begin with, we evaluate (8) for four values of c_2: 0, .33, .67, and 1.0, dividing the range under consideration into thirds. If the smallest S occurs at an end point of the range (here, for example, at 0 or 1), we choose as our new c_2's those values that divide the interval between the end point and the nearest adjacent c_2 into thirds. In the case of 0, we would choose .11 and .22, dividing the interval 0 to .33. If the smallest S occurs at an interior point, we would consider that point as the mid-point of a new interval and choose as new c_2's those values that divide this interval into thirds. Thus, if the smallest S occurs at .33, our new interval is 0 to .67, and the c_2's for the next iteration are .22 and .44. Values for successive iterations are chosen in the same manner.

This procedure has been programmed for the Burroughs 220 computer, which can accomplish 24 iterations in less than a minute of computer time. This yields three-digit estimates of our parameters. For a single set of parameters, particularly where two-digit estimates are satisfactory, a desk calculator would be adequate. Since the computer is programmed to consider only the jth iteration in choosing values for the $(j + 1)$th, it is possible that the procedure would require fewer iterations on a desk calculator.

The estimation procedure does not depend on the initial distribution among the states nor indeed on knowing in which state a given subject is on trial 0. All runs of whatever length *before the first observed change of response* are discarded in calculating the conditional distribution of run-lengths. Furthermore, there is also a question about measuring the length of the last run in each subject's response sequence. These final runs cannot just be ignored, because they include all of the infinite runs. One solution is to conduct the experiment with an optional stopping rule: Each subject should be continued until a run of prescribed length appears (say K_1 O-responses or K_2 X-responses) and then be terminated. This will allow us to classify uniquely each run as having one or more of the K_1 lengths and to apply the curve-fitting process in the range $1 \le K \le K_1$. When it is desirable to expose all subjects to the same number of experimental trials, another procedure is necessary. Here we discard all runs that begin at points closer to ¦the end of the experiment than K_1 digits. If we did not discard these runs we would be disproportionately loading some cells of the conditional distribution. Thus if we counted a run of, for example, length 3 ($K_1 > 3$), which began three trials from the end of the experiment, we would be ignoring the fact that this might be a longer run arbitrarily cut off by the experimenter. Furthermore, as we approach the end of the experiment, the only runs that begin become shorter and shorter, so that a counting procedure without discarding will overestimate the conditional proportion of short runs. The discarding procedure permits all the run-lengths that we intend to classify to occur and thus gives a better representation of the conditional distributions.

Once we have obtained values for the transition probabilities, it is possible to estimate μ. The asymptotic probability of an O response, $P_0(\infty)$, is a convenient quantity to use:

(9)
$$P_0(\infty) = \frac{\alpha(\mu\varepsilon + \gamma)}{\alpha\gamma + \alpha\varepsilon + \beta\varepsilon} .$$

We have considered the basic quantities of the model and have shown a procedure for estimating these quantities. We turn now to a substantive interpretation of the model and its parameters in order to indicate its relationship to the problem of choosing a reference group. Since Case V is of most interest to us at present, we will consider only the interpretation of the model for this case. Case V, it will be remembered, involves two groups, each of which takes one of the alternatives as its standard, and an individual with no initial predisposition with respect to the alternatives.

As the name "conflict model" implies, the basis for interpretation is a two-pole conflict situation generated by the cross-pressures arising from the two groups. States 2 and 3 are conflict states; although the subject at the moment is responding according to one group standard, he is still subject to the influence of the other group. States 1 and 4 are resolution states; once the individual has entered one of these states, he has resolved the conflict by selecting one group and rejecting the other. As we unwind the process, all subjects will end in either State 1 or State 4. (Thus the model captures our point that all individuals subject to cross-pressures will eventually reduce the pressure by selecting or rejecting one source of influence.)

Earlier in the discussion we made a distinction between selection of one reference group and rejection of another. In Case V selection of Group O implies rejection of Group X, but this is not generally the case; for example, Case VI requires a somewhat different interpretation. At this point we want to introduce another distinction: that between influence and acceptance.[10] In Case V, we regard influence as a temporary phenomenon while acceptance is permanent and requires rejection of the other frame of reference. In terms of the model, movement between States 2 and 3 is interpreted as acceding to influence, whereas movement to States 1 or 4 is interpreted as rejection. (We use rejection rather than acceptance to be consistent with other cases and also to be able to make use of other research results.) We view the transition probabilities α and ε, then, as the probability of rejecting Group X and the probability of rejecting Group O, respectively. These quantities may also be considered "rejection rates" for each of the two groups. Similarly, β and γ are the probabilities of acceding to influence from the respective groups, or the "influence rates" of Group X and Group O, respectively. The rejection and influence rates for each of the groups are regarded as independently variable.[11]

The model is coordinated to Case V specifically by assuming that

$$(10) \qquad\qquad \mu = 1 - \mu = \tfrac{1}{2} .$$

If the individual has no initial preference for either alternative, he is equally

---

[10] This distinction provides one means of restricting the concept of reference group. We would limit the concept to those phenomena in which the individual accepts the group as an appropriate frame of reference. We would not use the concept to refer to temporary influence phenomena.

[11] Considering influence and rejection to be independent processes is very similar to the distinction which Festinger makes in his work on informal social communication [9]. For example, he offers two propositions in which the force to reject the other members of the group and the force to change in the direction of the group are regarded as separate entities.

likely to be in State 2 or State 3 prior to the start of the experimental sequence. The model can be fitted to the data with this assumption or μ can be estimated from the data as a check that the situation meets the initial conditions of Case V.

Before turning to some specific suggestions for experiments, we should briefly mention some of the highly restrictive assumptions which the model incorporates. The substantive implications of these assumptions affect the kinds of experimental situations to which the model might be applied. The model assumes: (1) the state on trial $n + 1$ depends only on the state on trial n and the transition probabilities; (2) the same transition probabilities apply to all individuals; (3) the transition probabilities are constant through time; and (4) the transition probabilities are independent of the state in which the individual starts the process.

We can evaluate assumptions (1) and (2) against alternative models. Assumption (2), for example, assumes that it is not necessary to invoke *a priori* individual differences to describe the experimental process; although this assumption fits the Asch situation, it is clear that individuals could differentially evaluate the attributes of two opposing groups. Then it would not be surprising to find varying rejection rates. If this differential evaluation is related to an *a priori* means of classifying individuals, we could estimate the parameters separately for each class so generated. The classification rule would then lead to an alternative model.

In order for assumption (3) to apply, the experimental situation must meet at least two conditions. Since we consider the transition probabilities to be a function of the attributes of the respective groups, it is important that these attributes do not change during the course of the experiment. Thus, for example, we would not want the individual to continue to gain information about the group as the experiment progresses. Secondly, it is necessary to hold constant the relation of each group to judgments involved in the experiment. If, for example, the relevant attribute of Group O was competence in a particular task, each judgment in the experimental sequence should involve this competence; we would not expect the model to apply to an experiment that involved some trials requiring veridical judgments and some requiring esthetic preferences.

In our interpretation of the model, assumption (4) means that the influence process and the rejection process do not depend on the individual's initial position. This is reasonable in those instances where the attributes of Groups O and X are unrelated to the alternatives they choose as standards. The subliminal experiment mentioned above appears to meet this requirement. On the other hand, the assumption is not tenable in a situation where the attributes change according to whether or not the group supports the individual's initial position. In some circumstances, we can test whether or not the starting state affects the transition probabilities. If we know each individual's initial position, we could estimate the parameters separately for those starting in State 2 and those starting in State 3, and compare the results with those obtained in the present model.

5. Suggested Experiments on Choice of Reference Group

We have indicated some of the conditions that a basic experimental situation must fulfill. Pilot studies are now under way in an effort to develop a test situation that will have general applicability and that can be used to test a variety of propositions dealing with the choice of reference group. In these pilot studies, the alternative frames of reference are taken as given: two sets of confederates role-play Group O and Group X. Assuming that these pilot studies will be successful, we can illustrate how the test situation and the model will be employed.

Our interest is in propositions relating attributes of a group to its "influence rate" and "rejection rate." Of course, these rates are relative to the available alternative group and its attributes. Consider the following proposition: If two groups are equivalent in their relevant attributes, then their rejection and influence rates are equivalent. Providing the individual subjects with no information about the two sets of confederates and randomizing the assignment of confederates to Group O and X should approximate the desired conditions. In this experiment, we would expect to find $\alpha = \varepsilon$ and $\beta = \gamma$. If such is the case, the model indicates an interesting property of the data: $P_O(n)$ should be a straight line at .5. As a corollary, at asymptote half the subjects will have rejected Group X, some of whom initially chose the standard of Group X, i.e., were in State 3. This proposition is of interest since it focuses on what might be considered the strongest cross-pressure situation. In addition, it points to a base-line against which to evaluate experiments in which the two groups are not equivalent.[12]

In section 3, we quoted a proposition to the effect that primary environment of opinion takes precedence over secondary environment. If we coordinate primary environment to a physically present group of confederates in face-to-face interaction with the subject and secondary environment to a physically absent group, perhaps simulated by a tape recorder, we can test and extend this proposition. Let Group O be the physically present and Group X the physically absent group. If these groups were equivalent in all respects but "physical presence," we believe Merton's hypothesis would hold; in terms of the model, we would expect α to be greater than ε. We feel that there are more immediate psychological consequences to rejecting those with whom the subject is in face-to-face interaction so that it would be more difficult to reject Group O than Group X. Physical presence probably also affects the influence rates in the same direction; that is, $\gamma > \beta$, but this is not necessary to the hypothesis.

Casting Merton's hypothesis in terms of our model raises an intriguing question: Suppose we could create a situation in which $\beta > \gamma$; would the proposition still hold? In other words, if the secondary group's influence

---

[12] There are a number of propositions that could be examined in the situation of two equivalent groups. For example, the time (number of trials) to equilibrium is a function of the ratio of β to α; we would hypothesize that the greater the status discrepancy between the individual and the two groups, the smaller this ratio.

rate were higher, would this affect its rejection rate? If our reasoning about the difficulty of rejection in a face-to-face situation is correct, simply altering the influence rates of the two groups should not change the ratio of α to ε. Experimentally, we might achieve $\beta > \gamma$ by making Group X "experts" at the task while Group O are peers of the subject. Then we should observe more temporary conformity to the standard of Group X early in the experiment, but more consistent conformity to Group O's standard at asymptote.

The last example illustrates but one of the possible contrasts that can be studied within the framework we have developed. There is a wide range of attributes that can be ascribed experimentally to Groups O and X; some of these attributes should affect both influence and rejection rates, while some should affect one rate but not the other. A program employing this framework should provide us with a set of group attributes that are clearly related to the selection of reference groups.

6. Summary

This paper has been concerned with a new approach to the development of reference group theory, an approach based on the generalization of a probability model and an experimental situation. We were critical of the lack of constraints on the application of reference group concepts as *post hoc* interpretive devices, but we believe that the development of general principles to govern the use of these ideas would contribute to their utility as interpretive concepts.

The problem for which theoretical development is most needed is that of choice of reference group, which up to the present has received little experimental attention. To us, this is an unfortunate oversight, since we regard experimentation as most strategic for the development of the general principles required.

Section 3 analyzed the core elements of a basic experimental situation into six cases, three of which are germane to the problem of choice of reference group. The cases were generated by considering two factors: the individual's initial predisposition and the presence of one or more group standards.

The distinction between being influenced by a group and selecting that group as a reference group was made in terms of temporary versus long-term conformity. This distinction formed the basis of a probability model which we believe will describe behavior in our experiments.

In discussing the model, we emphasized its focus on the process of resolving cross-pressures, a process which we regard as central to the selection of reference groups. In addition, we presented key properties of the model, noting that the parameters were appropriate quantities for comparing variations in the basic experiment.

The final section offered a few examples of how the model and the experimental situation could be applied to some theoretical problems in reference group research.

It is our contention that the model and the experimental situation provide an apparatus for generating and testing propositions about those group attributes that affect the selection of reference groups. When a sufficient number of these propositions have been codified, we will be able to speak about a theory of reference group behavior.

REFERENCES

[1] ASCH, S. E., *Social Psychology*, Englewood Cliffs, N.J.: Prentice-Hall, 1952.

[2] ASCH, S. E., Studies of independence and conformity: I. A minority of one against a unanimous majority, *Psychol. Monog.*, 1956, **70**(9) (whole no. 416).

[3] BERELSON, B. R., P. F. LAZARSFELD, and W. N. McPHEE, *Voting*, Chicago: Univ. of Chicago Press, 1954.

[4] BERGER, J., B. P. COHEN, J. L. SNELL, and M. ZELDITCH, *Types of Formalization in Small Group Research*, Boston: Houghton Mifflin Co., 1962.

[5] BORGATTA, E. F., Sidesteps toward a non-special theory, *Psychol. Rev.*, 1954, **61**(5), 343-52.

[6] COHEN, B. P., A probability model for conformity, *Sociometry*, 1958, **21**(1), 69-81.

[7] COHEN, B. P., Conflict and conformity: A probability model and its application, Cambridge, Mass.: The Technology Press (in press).

[8] COHEN, B. P., T. MAYER, G. SCHULMAN, and C. TERRY, "Relative Competence and Conformity," inforn al report prepared under National Science Foundation Grant No. G9030, Depar' ent of Sociology, Stanford University, 1961.

[9] FESTINGER, L., Informal social communication, *Psychol. Rev.*, 1950, **57**, 271-92.

[10] HARTLEY, R. E., "The Acceptance of New Reference Groups," final report, Contract Nonr-1597(01), Group Psychology Branch, Office of Naval Research, N.Y.: Department of Psychology, The City College, 1958.

[11] MERTON, R. K., Continuities in the theory of reference groups and social structure, chap. 9 in *Social Theory and Social Structure*, rev. ed., Glencoe, Ill.: The Free Press, 1957.

[12] MERTON, R. K., and A. S. ROSSI, Contributions to the theory of reference group behavior, chap. 8 in *Social Theory and Social Structure*, rev. ed., Glencoe, Ill.: The Free Press, 1957.

[13] SHERIF, M., *The Psychology of Social Norms*, New York: Harper, 1936.

[14] SIEGEL, A. E., and S. SIEGEL, Reference groups, membership groups and attitude change, *J. Abnorm. Soc. Psychol.*, 1957, **55**(3), 360-64.

[15] STOUFFER, S. A., *et al.*, *The American Soldier: Adjustment During Army Life*, Princeton, N.J.: Princeton Univ. Press, 1949.

8

Reward Structures and the Allocation of Effort

James S. Coleman, *Johns Hopkins University*

In society just as in the laboratory, men work to gain rewards and escape punishments. In society, however, there is no experimenter to establish the reward schedule. Instead, social systems, whether they be large or small, establish their own structures of reward and punishment to motivate their members. Of course, these structures of reward are ordinarily not imposed by an omnipotent "society," nor do they occur purely capriciously.

It is, in fact, the peculiar character of social systems that the various members are, for one another, the purveyors of rewards and punishments. One person's reward or punishment occurs through the actions of another member of the system. For example, in a team activity, one member's accomplishments bring rewards for the other team members. Or in a race, the winner's accomplishments constitute a punishment for the others, who automatically become losers. Or whenever a group establishes a set of norms, the norms act to punish those members who violate them, or reward those who live up to them. In a delinquent gang, the members reward one another for one set of activities; in a women's bridge club, the members reward one another for a totally different set of activities.

It is my purpose in this paper to begin to examine how the structure of rewards in a group affects the effort expended in the rewarded (or punished) activity. The motivation to do this came from a number of observations, some casual, some systematic, about the distribution of activities in groups. Some examples will indicate what I mean.

(a) In gangs, boys will carry out delinquent acts together that they would never initiate alone. Systematic observation of this behavior indicates that it depends for its sustenance upon the rewards provided by other gang members.

(b) In a high school, there are usually norms holding down scholastic effort; on the other hand, norms about athletics encourage unlimited effort. Research has indicated that this is because scholastic achievements on the part of one student in effect reduce the rewards accruing to others, while athletic achievements in interscholastic games benefit all students of the school.

(c) Best track times are generally recorded in competitive races, rather than in races against time. Concurrently, however, casual observation suggests that the poorest runners in a race run more slowly, even to the point of dropping out, than they do in races against time.

(d) In team activity, where the efforts of each aid the team, there is ordinarily more expenditure of effort than in individual activity. And in small group experiments testing ability to withstand electric shock, persons will subject themselves to a stronger shock in a social situation than when alone.

Thus my intent is wholly substantive here: to establish some ways of characterizing reward structures that can first explain, then make more precise and explicit, their effects on allocation of effort.

In particular, there are two kinds of reward structures that I want to focus on:

(1) Situations where one person's achievement contributes to another's goals, and where, in turn, the other person encourages the efforts leading to such achievement. An example is an athletic contest between two high schools: The achievements of one school's athletes contribute to the goals of all members of that school, who in turn cheer their team on, accord the athletes high status, and give them numerous other rewards.

(2) Situations in which one person's achievement takes away from another's success, and in turn the other person discourages efforts leading to such achievement. For example, in scholastic activity in a high school, one person's extra efforts force others to work harder simply to maintain the same relative position, and as a consequence the others discourage such unlimited efforts.

There is a special case of these two structures, of particular interest because of its frequent occurrence: the case where the activities are *alike* among performers and rewarders, so that each performer is a rewarder (or punisher), and each rewarder is a performer.

The problem, then, is to examine the allocation of group members' efforts between two or more activities under these two different reward structures: when one member's efforts help bring success to others who are engaging in that activity, and when his efforts subtract from their success. Depending on the particular situation found in nature or experiment, different mathematical models are appropriate. One very general situation, however, might be modelled this way: Each individual, alone, vacillates between two activities, allocating his effort to one or the other. Diagrammatically, we can characterize him as being in one of two states, A or B, with the possibility of movement from each to the other (figure 1). If the probability of his movement from A to B in a very small period of time is independent of the length of time he has been in A (and similarly for the reverse movement), then the system

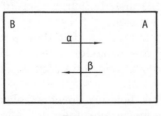

FIG. 1.

is a continuous-time Markov process governed by the following equation:

$$\frac{dP_A}{dt} = -\beta P_A + \alpha P_B ,$$

(1)

where P_A is the probability of being in state A, α is the transition rate from B to A, independent of time ($0 \leq \beta < \infty$), β is the transition rate from A to B, independent of time ($0 \leq \beta < \infty$), and $P_B = 1 - P_A$. (Since P_A is a function of t, the correct notation is $P_A(t)$; however, the notation is shortened for convenience.)

That is, as an individual, each member of the group has "tendencies" α and β toward states A and B, respectively. If there were no encouragement or discouragement from others, then his probability of being in each state at any time τ after initially being observed in one of the two states could be calculated. Similarly, the relative amounts of time he would spend in each state at stochastic equilibrium could easily be found by setting equation (1) equal to zero. This gives

(2)
$$\frac{P_A}{P_B} = \frac{\alpha}{\beta} ,$$

or

(3)
$$P_A = \frac{\alpha}{\alpha + \beta} .$$

If a group of N members consisted merely of N persons governed independently by this process, then what distribution of activities would we expect to find in the group? Obviously, we would expect to find a proportion P_A engaging in activity A, and P_B engaging in activity B. And since each person acts independently of each of the others, we have, in effect, a binomial process, so that if we observed this group a number of times, we would expect to find a binomial distribution,

(4)
$$p_i = \binom{N}{i} P_A^i P_B^{N-i} ,$$

where p_i is the probability that i persons will be carrying out activity A, given N persons in the group, and P_A is the probability that each will carry out A (will be in state A).

1. Structures with Mutual Reward

Suppose, however, that the activities are interrelated so that a member's efforts can help others when they are engaged in the same activity, and he is consequently encouraged to join in this activity by those engaging in it. One way this effect may occur is through an added transition rate γ toward an activity from every person engaging in the activity.[1] If there are i per-

---

[1] This is not the only way that such effects may occur. Part of the difficulty in deciding between alternative forms of effect resides in the very concept of reward. This problem is discussed briefly toward the end of the paper.

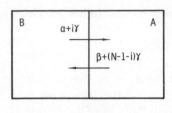

sons in activity A, and he is in B, then his transition rate to A will be $\alpha + i\gamma$; the remainder of the $N-1$ persons, $N-1-i$, are in activity B, so that if he finds himself in A, the transition rate to B will be $\beta + (N-1-i)\gamma$ (see figure 2).

If all other members of the group were fixed in their choice of A or B (as in the Asch experiments, where all members of the group but one were accomplices of the experimenter), then the variable individual, governed by the process pictured in figure 2, would be found in A and B with probabilities as follows:[2]

(5)
$$P_A = \frac{\alpha + i\gamma}{\alpha + \beta + (N-1)\gamma} ,$$

(6)
$$P_B = \frac{\beta + (N-1-i)\gamma}{\alpha + \beta + (N-1)\gamma} .$$

However, the interesting systemic problem arises when we let all N-group members be variable. What division of activities would we then expect to find among the N members, and what distribution would we expect to find around this number if we observed the group a number of times? The answer to this will tell something different from the answers given by equations (5) and (6), which show how the individual's behavior is influenced by others in his group under a particular assumption about individuals' effects on one another. These latter questions ask how the *group's* behavior is affected by this reward structure.

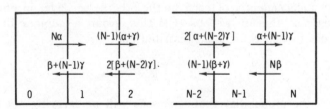

FIG. 3

It is useful, in answering these questions, to diagram, as in figure 3, the states of the group in the stochastic process that characterizes the group's behavior. The transition rates for this stochastic process consist simply of the sum of the transition rates for every member who could, by his change, move the group across the given boundary. For example, when the group is in state 2, this means that two persons are carrying out activity A, each of them characterized by a transition rate to B of $\beta + (N-2)\gamma$. Thus

---

[2] It is evident from Asch's data that the subjects in his experiments did not behave in accordance with equations (5) and (6). However, there are a number of factors that make Asch's experiments differ from those necessary to test the above model.

the group transition rate to state 1 is simply the sum of these two (for if either transition occurred, the group would move into state 1), i.e., $2[\beta + (N-2)\gamma]$. The expected distribution of groups at stochastic equilibrium in the case of independence was simply a binomial distribution. In this case, the distribution may be found from the fact that at equilibrium, the "flow" across each boundary must be equal in the two directions.

By setting up a set of N simultaneous equations (one for each boundary), then expressing each p_i in terms of p_0, we obtain equations of the following sort:

$$\text{(7)} \qquad \frac{p_0}{p_0} = 1 \text{ ,}$$

$$\text{(8)} \qquad \frac{p_1}{p_0} = \frac{N\alpha}{\beta + (N-1)\gamma} \text{ ,}$$

$$\text{(9)} \qquad \frac{p_2}{p_0} = \frac{N(N-1)\alpha^2}{2[\beta + (N-1)\gamma][\beta + (N-2)\gamma]} \text{ .}$$

By using the fact that the sum of p_i is 1, it is possible to solve for p_0 and then get a general expression for p_i (first letting $\alpha/(\alpha + \beta) = a$, and letting $\gamma/(\alpha + \beta) = c$):[3]

$$\text{(10)} \qquad p_i = \frac{\binom{N}{i} \prod_{j=0}^{i-1}(a + jc) \prod_{j=0}^{N-i-1}(1 - a + jc)}{\prod_{j=0}^{N-1}(1 + jc)} \text{ .}$$

This distribution is analogous to the binomial distribution, but under the condition that there is a particular kind of interdependence, i.e., that a reward structure of the sort shown in figures 2 and 3 exists. The distribution may be thought of as a kind of "contagious binomial," for the rewards act so as to induce more and more of the group into the activity that most people are doing. The parameters a and c may be estimated by using the mean and variance of i, which are estimated as follows:

$$\text{(11)} \qquad \mu = \sum i p_i \text{ ,}$$

and

$$\text{(12)} \qquad \sigma^2 = \sum i^2 p_i - \mu^2 \text{ .}$$

Then

$$\text{(13)} \qquad a = \frac{\mu}{N} \text{ ,}$$

and

$$\text{(14)} \qquad c = \frac{\sigma^2 N - \mu(N - \mu)}{N\mu(N - \mu) - \sigma^2 N} \text{ .}$$

Curiously (or so it seemed to me when I first discovered it), the equilibrium distribution obtained from this process is the same as a Pólya distribution derived from a somewhat different physical model: N balls are drawn from

---

[3] The terms under the first product sign of the numerator vanish for p_0, and those under the second product term vanish for p_N. The same convention holds for equation (17).

an urn containing α "A" balls and β "B" balls. Every time an A ball is drawn, c other A's are added to the urn when it is replaced; every time a B ball is drawn, c other B's are added when the B is replaced. Such an experiment produces as an expected distribution equation (10) above (see [2, p. 128]). This identity with the Pólya distribution is of merely incidental interest, however, for the process we are concerned with is one mirrored by the group stochastic process illustrated in figure 3.

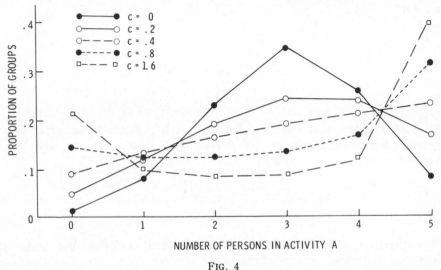

NUMBER OF PERSONS IN ACTIVITY A

FIG. 4

An indication of the way in which this distribution relates to the binomial distribution is shown in figure 4, by giving a set of distributions with varying c's for $N = 5$ and $a = .6$. Note where the difference between this distribution and the unrewarded, independent activities of the binomial distribution lies. The difference is not at all in the *average* allocation of effort in the group: it remains divided proportionally to the individual tendencies α and β. The difference lies in the group's *stability* around this average. If the reward coefficient γ is large relative to α and β, the group is highly unstable near its mean and finds stability only at one or the other extreme, when *all* are engaging in A or all in B. Thus the behavior of this social system as a system differs sharply from that of the aggregate of independent persons.

After a discussion of the other model, examination of empirical data will be carried out.

2. Structures with Mutual Punishments

In structures of activity where each member's achievements reduce the success of others in that activity, the interdependence is of a very different sort (e.g., if several boys are competing for the attention of two girls, each boy will attempt to discourage the others from trying for the same girl he is trying for). If $N-1$ of the group members are fixed, and i are in A, while $N-1-i$ are in B, then the one variable member might be characterized by the process shown in figure 5, where θ is the transition rate brought about by each member's punishment.[4] In this model, the i other persons carrying out activity A act to force this variable member *out*

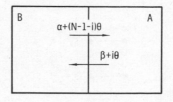

Fig. 5

of A if he is there, while previously they acted to induce him *into* A, if he was in B. In this case, the equilibrium probabilities of an individual's being found in A and B are

$$(15) \qquad P_A = \frac{\alpha + (N-1-i)\theta}{\alpha + \beta + (N-1)\theta},$$

and

$$(16) \qquad P_B = \frac{\beta + i\theta}{a + \beta + (N-1)\theta}.$$

But as in the previous case, our interest is not in the behavior of the individual but rather in the behavior of the *group*, under this structure of punishments. A diagram for the group stochastic process is given in figure 6. By a procedure similar to that carried out for the reward model, it is possible to find the expected distribution of groups that would be found at equilibrium:

$$(17) \qquad p_i = \frac{\binom{N}{i} \prod_{j=N-i}^{N-1} (a+js) \prod_{j=i}^{N-1} (1-a+js)}{\prod_{j=N-1}^{2N-2} (1+js)},$$

where $s = \theta/(\alpha+\beta)$. The mean and variance of i are related to the parameters a and s as follows:

$$(18) \qquad \mu = \frac{N[a+(N-1)s]}{1+2(N-1)s},$$

$$(19) \qquad \sigma^2 = \mu\left[1 + \frac{(N-1)[a+(N-2)s]}{1+(2N-3)s}\right] - \mu^2.$$

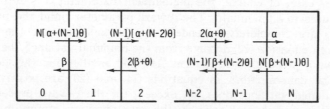

Fig. 6

----

[4] Again, this is not the only form for a punishment mechanism, as later discussion will indicate.

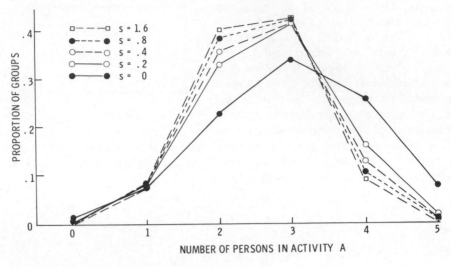

NUMBER OF PERSONS IN ACTIVITY A

FIG. 7

The two parameters of the distribution, a and s, may be estimated by first estimating the mean and variance from equations (11) and (12).   Then

$$(20) \qquad s = \frac{\mu(N - \mu) - \sigma^2 N}{\sigma^2 N(2N - 3) - \mu(N - 2)(N - \mu)} ,$$

$$(21) \qquad a = \frac{\mu}{N} + \left(\frac{2\mu - N}{N}\right)(N-1)s .$$

It is interesting to compare the parameters of this "punishment" distribution with those of the "reward" distribution as given in equations (13)
and (14).   In that case, the individualistic tendency a toward activity A
was directly reflected by the mean number of people carrying out activity
A, as is true also for the binomial.   In this case, the individualistic tendencies described by a are not directly reflected by the mean.   The punishment
distorts the mean in the direction of $N/2$, as equation (18) and figure 7 indicate.   The mean mirrors a only under special circumstances: if the mean
of i is equal to $N/2$ [so that $2\mu - N = 0$ in equation (21)], or if the variance
equals the binomial variance [so that $\mu(N - \mu) - \sigma^2 N = 0$ in equation (21)].
In the latter case, of course, the punishment parameter s is zero, and the
process reduces to a binomial.   The reward parameter c and the punishment
parameter s are completely dependent on the amount that the estimated
variance from equation (12) departs from the binomial variance, being larger
for the reward process [see equation (14)] and smaller for the punishment
process.   The denominators in equations (14) and (20) are positive so long
as the estimated variance does not exceed, for the reward process, or fall
below, for the punishment process, the maximum or minimum variances
consistent with the model, i.e., when $\gamma \to \infty$ or $\theta \to \infty$.
The relation of this punishment distribution to the independent binomial

distribution is shown in figure 7 by the set of distributions having $N = 5$ and $a = .6$ as before, with varying values of s. The effect of this punishment structure is to hold the group far closer to an equal number of persons engaging in each activity than would be found if people were behaving independently.

3. Empirical Examination

Suppose I am now confronted with a sceptic who says: "So what? These are nice intellectual exercises, but what relation do they have to the real world? And, in fact, just how do you mean them to be used in relation to experiments or observations in groups?" The sceptic's intuitions would be precisely right, because serious problems do arise in the application of models such as these. I will state several possible ways the models might be used in relation to data, and let the sceptic indicate the objections he might find in each.

(1) In controlled experiments, the model can test the mathematical form taken by the effect of rewards and punishments in a group. That is, the effects shown by figures 4 and 7 are only single possibilities out of a wide range. Since different forms of effect will give different equilibrium distributions of effort in groups, the empirical distributions could be used to test the form of the effect.

"But," says the sceptic, "such testing is obviously inefficient, for it is possible in most cases to test the form of the effect by holding constant all the group except one member. This allows testing at the individual level, a far stronger test than the group-level test. Obviously, if we're interested in the form of psychological mechanisms, it is best to test them without letting the group vary without control."

(2) Suppose, however, that the rewards provided by group members for one another are so fragile and difficult to control that we cannot easily "hold the group constant" as implied in paragraph (1) above. In this case, it seems to be clearly necessary to turn to the systemic consequences rather than to the consequences for a single "dependent" individual.

"This is a valid use of these models," says the sceptic. "Nevertheless, it should be remembered that the equilibrium distribution is merely one deduction that can be tested. Even if the group is not 'held constant,' separate individuals can be observed over time, thus providing stronger tests than that of the single distribution."

(3) But suppose now we *know* that the individual mechanisms are as implied in these models. Then clearly the models provide a useful calculating device to predict the allocation of effort in groups when we know the parameters a and c or a and s.

"To be sure," says the sceptic. "But we are a long way from such knowledge. At best, we know when a process fulfills the assumption of independent Bernoulli trials, and thus gives rise to the binomial distribution, a degenerate case of both of these models."

(4) The models may be used in connection with observed data from nat-

urally occurring groups, to "explain" these data. (An example of such a use will be given below.)

"Clearly, this is one frequent use of models of this sort," says the sceptic. "Nevertheless, one must remain fully aware that the data might be equally well explained by a number of other models, proceeding from different assumptions. Such a use of the model can hardly be considered a 'test.' Rather, it seems that this use of the model is to reduce a distribution to a pair of parameters, whose interpretation is open to argument."

(5) Even without our knowing the precise form of the effect of reward and punishment, these models, and elaborations of them, can be used to deduce the systemic consequences of a particular structure of activities. Because the form of the effect would differ only in detail from that postulated, it is likely that the systemic deductions would be wrong only in detail, if at all. This is important to a sociologist, who is interested in the behavior of the system. If the psychologists are not going to give him the form of individual-level processes, he must assume some form in order to get on to the things that concern him.

"Ah, now," says the sceptic, "I begin to understand what you are doing. You're really interested in developing a theory to relate two variables at the level of the group itself—in this case, reward structures as the independent variable, and distribution of effort in various activities as the dependent one. Your only concern with the form of the individual-level process is as a necessary evil, which must be used in order to link these two variables together. In that case, the data you need to test your theory consist of group data in which *both* variables are explicitly measured: the reward structure along with the distribution of effort."

But now I must reply to the sceptic that he is still not absolutely clear about my intentions. If the psychologists had done their job well, so that I could have confidence in the form of effect that reward and punishment take, there would be no question of "testing" the group-level deductions, any more than there is a question of testing the binomial distribution when we have N independent trials, each with the same probability of success. In such a case, the model in effect tells you the systemic or aggregate consequences of this individual-level process. Thus the sociologist's interest in such model-building lies not so much in testing separate processes as in synthesizing so as to examine systemic consequences.

But it is here that I must point to an extreme weakness of these models in synthesis. They constitute a far lesser accomplishment than is desirable, and fall far short of the goal I have in mind. I hope, for example, to consider a model with a number of activities, each with its own reward structure, and then to generate the equilibrium distribution of activities in the various activities. Such a model would be far more appropriate to any naturally occurring system than those above, for in social systems, different activities have different reward structures. In schools, for example, where my interest is greatest, athletic and scholastic activity have quite different reward structures, as I indicated earlier. One of my major aims is to derive the expected distribution of effort in these activities, given these reward structures.

Furthermore, since reward and punishment structures have consequences other than channeling of effort, I hope to examine some of these other consequences. For example, rewards received from an experimenter or a fellow group member cause the performer to associate pleasure with the rewarder, and to be attracted toward him; punishments cause the performer to associate discomfort with the punisher, and to be repelled from him. Such effects are as evident in rats in the laboratory as they are in human subjects. But suppose that the rewarder or punisher is not merely an experimenter but is himself a performer, and suppose that the reward or punishment schedule is established by the structure of activities in the group. Then it becomes possible to conceive of a model in which the dependent variable is not the distribution of effort but rather the consequent attraction or repulsion that members feel for one another.

These are some of the directions in which I hope models of this sort may be carried in the future. Because of the discrepancy between these ambitious goals and the modest results so far produced, I must present these results somewhat hesitantly. I do so partly to indicate the direction in which I hope to proceed and partly to point out a way that I hope some others may follow.

3.1 A Use of the Reward Model to Explain Naturally Occurring Data. In making a choice between two activities that are mutually supportive, or in lending one's allegiance to one of two candidates in an election, the conditions exist in which one would expect the reward structure to operate. For the election situation, voting data is sometimes recorded for groups. The largest collection of such data of which I am aware consists of voting data in union elections among typographers in small printshops. Voting records by size of shop for shops from 2 to 8 men in size are shown in table 1. Men's votes are obviously not distributed randomly relative to these groups, for there are far too many groups whose votes are near the extremes. For

TABLE 1

NUMBER OF SHOPS OF SIZE N IN NEW YORK TYPOGRAPHICAL UNION IN WHICH
i MEN VOTED FOR THE WINNING CANDIDATE (CANDIDATE A)

N \ i	0	1	2	3	4	5	6	7	8
2	3	2	11						
3	32	15	30	52					
4	22	13	20	26	62				
5	16	7	15	13	20	24			
6	9	8	19	14	17	18	21		
7	4	7	13	14	12	12	13	20	
8	5	4	2	6	8	9	6	9	16

TABLE 2

VALUES OF a AND c FROM EQUATIONS (13) AND (14) APPLIED TO
DATA OF TABLE 1

N	a	c
2	.75	2.00
3	.60	1.08
4	.66	0.95
5	.65	0.86
6	.58	0.42
7	.60	0.40
8	.63	0.56

each size of shop, values of a (the individual tendency toward candidate A) and c (the reward parameter) have been calculated separately, and from these values the theoretical distributions have been regenerated, as shown in figures 8 and 9. In table 2, the values of a and c are listed for each size of group. Of some interest is the value of c for different-sized groups, since (according to the model) c measures the reward provided by each member for each other member. Obviously, from table 2, c decreases as group size increases. But to answer the question of how c decreases with increase in group size, and what accounts for this decrease, requires further data for larger groups, which cannot be presented here. (A more complete examination of data is given in [1].)

This empirical application of the reward model is an example of paragraph (4) above in the discussion of uses. The full value of such a use occurs

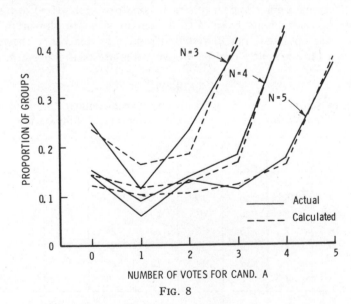

FIG. 8

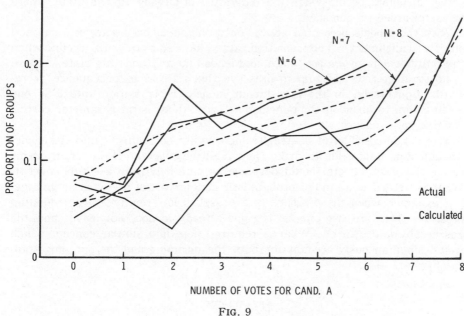

FIG. 9

when the variation of a parameter with some group attribute (such as the variation of c with group size) is studied. But it should be reiterated that the last-described use of these models [see paragraph (5)] is probably the most valuable from the sociologist's viewpoint.

I would like to have a similarly illustrative set of data for the punishment model, either from naturally occurring situations or from experiments. It would be simple to set up experiments in which each member, by carrying out an activity, provided punishment for all others who were in the same activity. Unfortunately, however, I know of no systematic data that can illustrate the application of this model.

4. A Note About the Effect of Rewards and Punishments

In Thorndike's early discussion of the "law of effect," he defined a satisfying state of affairs (that resulting from reward) and an annoying state of affairs (that resulting from punishment) as follows: "By a satisfying state of affairs is meant one which the animal does nothing to avoid, often doing such things as attain and preserve it. By a discomforting or annoying state of affairs is meant one which the animal commonly avoids and abandons." [3, p. 241.]

This statement of the effect of rewards and punishments implies that each has *two* effects. Reward induces the subject to both *attain* and *preserve* the state which brings reward. Punishment leads him to *avoid* and *abandon* the state which brings punishment. The first pair of these effects (attain, avoid) occurs when the individual is in another state; the second pair (preserve, abandon) occurs when the individual is already in the state where he is rewarded or punished.

With the models presented above, only one effect occurs for reward, and one for punishment. The transition rate γ, induced by reward, occurs when the individual is in *another* state, and leads him to *attain* this state. There is no parameter to lead him to preserve this state as a consequence of reward. Conversely, in the punishment model, the transition rate θ is one leading him to abandon the punished activity; there is no parameter corresponding to avoidance.

It is not impossible, of course, to incorporate both effects into the model (though it is impossible to make them additive effects). However, it seems to me that such effects should derive simultaneously from a single concept. What is needed is a kind of probabilistic counterpart of pressure or voltage. For example, when the pressure in a vessel is low relative to surrounding pressure, there are two effects: the gas already in does not leave; and the gas nearby is drawn in. What is required here is a similar concept which would simultaneously account for both the incoming and the outgoing transition rates.

REFERENCES

[1] COLEMAN, JAMES S., *Elements of Mathematical Sociology*, Glencoe, Ill.: The Free Press (in press).
[2] FELLER, WILLIAM, *An Introduction to Probability Theory and Its Applications*, New York: Wiley, 1950.
[3] THORNDIKE, E. L., *Animal Intelligence*, New York: MacMillan, 1911.

9

Theoretical Treatments of Differential Reward in Multiple-Choice Learning and Two-Person Interactions

W. K. Estes, *University of Michigan*

Mathematical theories for human learning in two-choice situations have been developed primarily in relation to simple verbal conditioning experiments in which reinforcing events are simply informational signals indicating to the subject whether his response was correct or incorrect on each trial [7]. Thus when interest arose in extending learning theory to the treatment of two-person interactions, it was natural to use essentially the same experimental conditions, except that the reinforcing signals for each of two interacting subjects should be made contingent upon the other's responses. With experimental situations so contrived, a considerable quantity of research has been accomplished during the past five years, and on the whole, applications of statistical learning theory have yielded satisfactory accounts of long-term response proportions [2], [4], [12].[1] Although there is reason to doubt that comparable success in theoretical interpretation can readily be attained, an equally interesting problem is that of a two-person interaction in which the amount of reward associated with each response for each subject, rather than the probability of being right or wrong, depends jointly upon his own response and the response of the other subject. This varying payoff situation is closer to those dealt with explicitly by game theory, but it poses greater difficulty for learning theory, for little work has been done on the basic problem of reward as a parameter of the learning process for a single human subject. Only one stratagem has occurred to me that might enable us to bypass this difficulty without major theoretical effort; it will be discussed in connection with an exploratory study now to be described.

Preparation of this paper was supported by Contract Nonr-908(16) between the Office of Naval Research and Indiana University, and Contract Nonr-225(17) between the Office of Naval Research and Stanford University.

[1] In some instances, detailed statistics of learning data for interacting subjects have been treated [12], but in this paper attention will be confined to the prediction of asymptotic choice probabilities.

1. Experimental Comparison of Game Theory and Statistical Learning Theory

In this section we shall first summarize an experiment designed to explore the course and limits of learning in an experiment concerning two-person interactions with varying payoffs. Terminal response proportions for both players in each of two experimental games will be compared, first with the response probabilities specified by game theory (as we interpret the theory in this situation), and then with predictions generated by an extension of the statistical learning model that has been successfully applied to simpler experimental games not involving varying payoffs.

1.1 Design and Procedure of the Exploratory Experiment. This experiment was conducted by Michael Cole, Alfred Bruner, Jane Bond, and Suchoon Mo as a project in my advanced laboratory psychology course at Indiana University in the fall, 1959–60 semester. The initial interest of the group was partly in developing an experimental situation suitable for evaluating the degree to which human subjects competing in simple games of strategy approximate the strategies prescribed by von Neumann and Morgenstern's theory of games.

During an experimental session, two subjects confronted each other across a table. On each subject's side of the table, out of sight of the other, were two response keys. In the center of the table top, visible to both subjects, was a double row of windows. When any pair of windows was illuminated, numerals became visible, indicating the payoff, in "points," to each subject on the given trial. A pair of signal lamps on each subject's side of the table top was so wired that after both subjects had operated their response keys on a trial, the lights indicated to each subject the choice made by the other.

The subjects, Indiana University undergraduates who were serving to fulfill part of a course requirement, were told that they were participating in a "reasoning game" and that the object of the game was to score as many points as possible on each play of the game (i.e., on each trial). Each trial began with the sounding of a signal buzzer; then, during a $2\frac{1}{2}$-sec response interval, each subject operated one of his response keys; finally, during the $3\frac{1}{2}$-sec information interval, the response lamp and the payoff windows were illuminated. Each pair of subjects was run for 200 of these trials in a continuous session with no communication permitted between them except for that mediated by the apparatus.

Two payoff conditions were investigated, each with 20 pairs of subjects; one (Game 1) represented a strictly determined game in the sense of game theory, and the other (Game 2) a nondetermined game requiring mixed strategies. The payoff matrices for the two games were as follows: For Game 1,

$$
\begin{array}{cc}
 & B_1 \quad\ B_2 \\
\begin{array}{c} A_1 \\ A_2 \end{array} &
\begin{bmatrix} 0,\ 4 & 2,\ 2 \\ 1,\ 3 & 4,\ 0 \end{bmatrix},
\end{array}
$$

and for Game 2,

$$A_1 \quad \begin{matrix} B_1 & B_2 \\ \begin{bmatrix} 1,\ 3 & 3,\ 1 \\ 2,\ 2 & 0,\ 4 \end{bmatrix} \end{matrix},$$

where A and B, with appropriate subscripts, represent the choices available to the row and column players, respectively, and the pair of numbers in cell ij represents the payoffs to the row and column player, respectively, when their combination of choices on a given trial is A_iB_j.

It will be seen that the matrix for Game 1 has a saddle point at A_2B_1, whereas the matrix for Game 2 has no saddle point and its game-theoretic solution requires the row player to choose A_1 with probability .50 and the column player to choose B_1 with probability .75.

1.2 Comparison of Experimental Results with Game-Theoretic Strategies. Proportions of A_1 and B_1 choices during the final 20 trials of the experiment for each group are compared with the values prescribed by game theory in table 1.

TABLE 1

PROPORTION OF A_1 AND B_1 CHOICES DURING THE FINAL 20 TRIALS FOR EACH
GROUP COMPARED WITH VALUES PRESCRIBED BY GAME THEORY AND
BOUNDS PREDICTED BY A LINEAR LEARNING MODEL

	Observed Proportions	Game Theory	Bounds
Game 1			
Row player (A_1)	.13	0	.38–.50
Column player (B_1)	.92	1	.75–.88
Game 2			
Row player (A_1)	.50	.50	.54–.62
Column player (B_1)	.69	.75	.46–.64

In contrast to the results reported for the type of game with right–wrong payoffs [4], [12], all four groups in this experiment clearly tended to approach terminal response probabilities corresponding to the appropriate game-theoretic strategies. A considerable proportion of the subject pairs in Game 1 were following the minimax strategy $(0, 1)$ during the last part of the experiment, and it seems not unlikely that nearly all would have arrived at this state if the series had continued long enough. In the sense of decision theory, these subjects could be said to be approximating rational behavior. Since the subjects had no knowledge of game or decision theory, this result poses an interesting problem for the psychology of learning. Can we account, in terms of principles of individual learning, for the manner in which these pairs of interacting subjects have used the information gained solely by experience in the experimental situation to progress toward "rational" strategies?

1.3 Comparison of Experimental Results with Predictions from a Learning Model. Before we can apply contemporary theories of individual two-choice learning to the present experiment, we must be able to specify the probability that each combination of payoffs will constitute an effective reward, or *reinforcement*, for each of the two subjects. The only simple way of accomplishing this specification that has occurred to me is to assume that the probabilities of effective reinforcement are proportional to the payoff values. If we apply this assumption, the payoff matrices for the two games studied can be transformed into matrices of effective reward probabilities: for Game 1,

$$
\begin{array}{cc}
& \begin{array}{cc} B_1 & B_2 \end{array} \\
\begin{array}{c} A_1 \\ A_2 \end{array} &
\left[\begin{array}{cc} 0,\ 1 & \tfrac{1}{2},\ \tfrac{1}{2} \\ \tfrac{1}{4},\ \tfrac{3}{4} & 1,\ 0 \end{array} \right] ,
\end{array}
$$

and for Game 2,

$$
\begin{array}{cc}
& \begin{array}{cc} B_1 & B_2 \end{array} \\
\begin{array}{c} A_1 \\ A_2 \end{array} &
\left[\begin{array}{cc} \tfrac{1}{4},\ \tfrac{3}{4} & \tfrac{3}{4},\ \tfrac{1}{4} \\ \tfrac{1}{2},\ \tfrac{1}{2} & 0,\ 1 \end{array} \right] ,
\end{array}
$$

where the entries in cell ij now represent the probabilities that the obtained payoff will serve to reward the responses made by the row and column player, respectively, when the response combination is A_iB_j.

We can now readily apply either the linear model, as previously extended to the two-person, right–wrong situation by Burke [2] and Estes and Suppes [8], or the Markovian, stimulus-sampling model extensively studied by Suppes and Atkinson [12]. In order to avoid the necessity of discussing the differences between the two models, I shall here make use only of the *matching theorem* that holds for both models (proved for the linear model in [5] and [8], and for the stimulus-sampling model in [9]). According to this theorem, over a sufficiently long series of trials, the proportion of choices of a given response by a subject should tend to match the proportion of instances in which that response has been reinforced. Application of the theorem enables us to make *a priori* predictions (i.e., predictions which do not require knowledge about the values of learning parameters) of the ranges of values within which the terminal response proportions should fall for each group of subjects. These predicted values are presented in table 1, and the method of derivation is described in Appendix A. Considering that in none of the four cases does the observed terminal response proportion fall within the predicted range, and noting especially the very large disparity for the group of row players in Game 1, we must conclude that the learning models, as interpreted, do not offer a satisfactory account of the observed behavior.

The one possibility for "saving" the simple learning models in this situation would be to revise the assumption of proportionality between payoffs and reinforcement probabilities. It seems apparent from inspection of the payoff matrix for Game 1, together with the corresponding data in table 1, that under this condition the row players are tending to avoid the zero payoff more strongly than allowed for by the assumption of proportionality. The theoretical bounds for this group can be brought into line with the observed response proportion by means of a scaling function of the "diminishing returns" type, i.e., one which generates a larger difference in effective reinforcement probability for the increment from 2 to 3 payoff units than for the increment from 3 to 4 units, and a still larger difference for the increment from 0 to 1 unit. Unhappily, this scaling function simultaneously increases the disparity between theory and observation when applied to Game 2.

Prospects do not seem to be promising that we will find a single scaling function that will enable the learning theory to provide a reasonable account of asymptotic choice proportions for *both* games studied in this experiment, as well as comparable data from such related studies as that of Lieberman (see chapter 14 of this volume) in which the subjects played against a mixed strategy followed by the experimenter. Nonetheless, it is important from a theoretical standpoint to decide between two principal interpretations of our results: (1) the learning models are sound but the relationship between payoff values and reinforcement probabilities depends upon particular combinations of conditions in too complex a way to be captured by any simple scaling function; or (2) revision or augmentation of the basic assumptions of the learning models is required. To gain further information relevant to this decision, we turn now to a more detailed examination of one of the learning models.

2. Analysis of a Linear Model for Individual Learning as a Function of Reward Magnitude

For convenience of exposition, this analysis will be limited to the linear model for individual learning in two-choice situations; however, it can be assumed that strictly analogous conclusions hold for any of the stimulus-sampling models that have been applied to human binary-choice learning.

During an earlier period of concentration on learning under right–wrong reinforcing conditions, I, at least, had assumed that variation in amount of reward could be readily handled simply by lifting certain restrictions on parameter values in the linear model. The appropriate generalization of the model that was developed in connection with analyses of simple probability learning was outlined in the following manner by Estes and Suppes [8]. A distinction was made between the observable outcome of a trial and the conditioning event assumed to be produced by the conjunction of this outcome with the stimulus and response conditions obtaining on the trial. In a two-choice situation, there might be any number of experimenter-defined trial outcomes O_j, $j = 1, 2, \cdots, M$ (which might, for example, be different amounts of reward), but only three reinforcing events. These events are:

E_1:   the event that the first response alternative, A_1, is effectively reinforced by the trial outcome, in which case probability p_1 of the first response receives the increment specified by the linear transform

(1) $$p_{1,n+1} = (1 - \theta)p_{1,n} + \theta ,$$

where n is the ordinal number of the rewarded trial and θ is the learning parameter, restricted in value to the interval $0 < \theta \leq 1$;

E_2:   the event that the second response, A_2, is effectively reinforced, in which case probability of the *first* response receives the decrement described by

(2) $$p_{1,n+1} = (1 - \theta)p_{1,n} ;$$

and

E_0:   the event that the trial outcome has no effect on either response, that is,

(3) $$p_{1,n+1} = p_{1,n} .$$

It was assumed that a given combination of outcome, O_j, and response, A_i, might generate any of the three reinforcing events, although in general with different probabilities. These probabilities may be represented by a set of parameters,

$$c_{ijk} = P(E_k \mid O_j A_i) .$$

One would naturally expect that when O_j is a reward and $O_{j'}$ is a non-reward, c_{iji} will be relatively large and $c_{ij'i}$ will be relatively small.

Now, over a series of trials on each of which response A_1 occurs and is rewarded with outcome O_1, the expected change in response probability on any one trial may readily be computed by weighting the right sides of equations (1), (2), and (3) by these probabilities of the corresponding reinforcing events. Dropping the i and j subscripts on the c parameters, we obtain[2]

(4) $$p_{1,n} = c_1[(1 - \theta)p_{1,n-1} + \theta] + c_2(1 - \theta)p_{1,n-1} + c_0 p_{1,n-1}$$
$$= (1 - \theta + \theta c_0)p_{1,n-1} + \theta c_1 .$$

As n approaches infinity we can obtain the limiting value of $p_{1,n}$ in the usual manner by setting $p_{1,n} = p_{1,n-1} = p_1$ in equation (4) and solving for p_1, obtaining

(5) $$p_1 = \frac{c_1}{1 - c_0} = \frac{c_1}{c_1 + c_2} .$$

It is apparent that under the conditions described, probability of the

---

[2] It should be noted that, whereas in equations (1), (2), and (3), $p_{1,n}$ denoted the response probability for some one arbitrarily selected subject on trial n, in equation (4) and henceforth through the remainder of the paper, $p_{1,n}$ denotes the response probability for a population of subjects whose learning through the first n trials has been governed by the specified set of parameters; for a full discussion of this distinction, see [8].

continuously rewarded response will go to an asymptote of unity over a series of trials if and only if the probability is zero that administration of the reward represented by O_1 following occurrences of A_1 will ever lead to strengthening of A_2, i.e., if $c_2 = 0$. If O_1 represents anything that would normally be considered a reward, human subjects will certainly be almost always found to approximate an asymptote of unity for the rewarded response over a series of trials. In this case, setting $c_2 = 0$, we note that the learning curve obtained by solving equation (4) takes the form

$$(6) \qquad p_{1,n} = 1 - (1 - p_{1,1})(1 - \theta c_1)^{n-1} .$$

The experimental interpretation of $p_{1,n}$ in this context is that it represents the probability of A_1 when trial n is a free-choice trial, with response alternatives A_1 and A_2, following $n - 1$ trials on which A_1 has been the only available response. Under the usual conditions of human learning experiments with, say, monetary rewards, a set of experimental groups (each run for a series of trials on which response A_1 always occurs and is rewarded, but with different amounts of reward assigned to different groups), would be predicted to generate a family of learning curves all going to a common asymptote of unity, but at different rates depending on the magnitudes of reward.

To proceed in the direction of the experimental situations of primary concern in this paper, we consider next an experimental routine in which response A_1, whenever it occurs, is followed by outcome O_1 and response A_2 is followed by outcome O_2. Letting $c_{jk} = P(E_k \mid O_j A_j)$, we have for the effect of an $A_1 O_1$ trial

$$(7) \qquad p_{1,n+1} = (1 - \theta + \theta c_{10}) p_{1,n} + \theta c_{11} ,$$

and for the effect of an $A_2 O_2$ trial (upon probability of A_1)

$$(8) \qquad p_{1,n+1} = (1 - \theta + \theta c_{20}) p_{1,n} + \theta c_{21} .$$

Treatment of a series of free-choice trials run under these conditions involves mathematical difficulties which have been extensively investigated by Bush and Mosteller [3], Estes and Suppes [8], Karlin [10], and Tatsuoka and Mosteller [13], among others. We can bring out the points of immediate interest while bypassing these difficulties if we consider an experimental routine in which the experimenter has insured by means of a forcing procedure that $A_1 O_1$ and $A_2 O_2$ trials occur with equal probabilities over the first n trials and in which we wish to predict the result of a free choice on trial $n + 1$. Under these circumstances, equations (7) and (8) can be weighted by their probabilities (1/2 in each case) and combined to yield the desired probability of an A_1 response on trial $n + 1$:

$$(9) \qquad p_{1,n+1} = \left[1 - \theta + \frac{\theta}{2}(c_{10} + c_{20}) \right] p_{1,n} + \frac{\theta}{2}(c_{11} + c_{21}) ,$$

which, as $n \to \infty$, tends to the asymptote

(10) $$p_1 = \frac{c_{11} + c_{21}}{2 - c_{10} - c_{20}} = \frac{c_{11} + c_{21}}{c_{11} + c_{12} + c_{21} + c_{22}}.$$

Now, if O_1 is a reward such that $c_{11} > 0$ and O_2 is nonreward, so that $c_{22} = 0$, the asymptotic probability of A_1 will vary from near zero to unity, depending on the values of c_{11} and c_{12}. If $c_{12} > 0$, then the asymptote must be intermediate between zero and unity. If $c_{12} = 0$, we again obtain a family of curves all going to a common asymptote of unity, but at different rates, depending now on the values of c_{11} and c_{21}.

So far, our results with the linear model seem quite reasonable. A less satisfactory state of affairs arises, however, if we consider the following conditions.

Suppose two rewards, O_1 and O_2, are selected such that over a series of A_1O_1 trials p_1 would go to unity and over a series of A_2O_2 trials p_2 would go to unity (and therefore p_1 to zero), but the former at the faster rate. This means, in terms of the model under consideration, that $c_{11} > c_{22} > 0$, but $c_{12} = c_{21} = 0$. Now, over a series of trials in which A_1O_1 and A_2O_2 occur with equal probabilities, equation (10) reduces to

(11) $$p_1 = \frac{c_{11}}{c_{11} + c_{22}},$$

and we have the prediction that the asymptotic probability of an A_1 response by the subject on a free-choice trial following a series reinforced under the conditions stated must have a value intermediate between zero and unity. Although I cannot cite specific experiments bearing on the prediction,[3] I cannot believe that it would generally hold for human subjects. Suppose, for example, that O_1 and O_2 were payoffs of different amounts of money, O_1 being the larger. It seems almost certain that the conditions given at the beginning of the paragraph could be satisfied, but it is even more certain that under any ordinary circumstances, p_1 would go to unity when the larger and smaller rewards were pitted against each other in the two-choice situation. The only important case in which I would expect to obtain asymptotes intermediate between zero and unity in this type of experiment is that in which the rewards given following A_1 and A_2 responses are not entirely discriminable, so that the subject sometimes believes he has received the larger reward when in fact he has been given the smaller (for some evidence bearing on this assumption, see [6]).

In the light of this analysis, I can see little promise in the notion of accounting for human learning as a function of reward (in one-person situations, let alone in two-person interactions) by any of the models hitherto utilized in the interpretation of simple probability learning with only informative feedback. It appears that some revision of the basic assumptions will be required. One direction these revisions might take is alteration of

---

[3] A study meeting these specifications closely has, however, been conducted by Bower [1] with rats as subjects and different amounts of food as rewards; his results agree with those that I am conjecturing would hold for human subjects (see section 3).

the learning axioms, done, for example, in Atkinson's extension of the Markovian pattern model (see chapter 2 of this volume). Another direction is to leave the learning axioms unchanged but to introduce some modification of the response rule (in the terminology of the statistician or economist, the decision rule) relating the state of learning to the overt choice response. The latter possibility will be explored in the following section.

3. A Provisional Model for Human Learning as a Function of Reward Magnitude

A frequently useful strategy is to assume that relationships between variables established in simpler situations continue to hold when the same variables are imbedded in a more complex situation, even though it may not be possible to make the same observations or measurements in the more complex case. Considering experiments on learning in relation to reward magnitude with this idea in mind, one may note that the simpler experiment on probability learning is, in a sense, imbedded in the reward situation. In the typical experiment on probability learning, the task set for the subject is to predict on each trial which of two reinforcing lights will appear; if these lights have been programmed by the experimenter to appear with fixed probabilities, the usual result is that over a series of trials the subject's probability of predicting a given light comes to match its actual probability of occurrence. If the reinforcing lights were replaced by two magnitudes of monetary payoff, again programmed to occur with fixed probabilities independently of the subject's behavior, there is little doubt that the subject's probability of predicting a given reward would approach the actual probability of occurrence of that reward, with the course of learning described by the same models that have been applied to the standard experiment on prediction of lights. The key assumption now to be proposed for a theory of human learning under differential reward is that this type of probability learning does in fact occur whenever different responses are followed by different rewards with fixed probabilities, even though it is not explicitly called for by instructions to the subject. Whenever each member of a set of response alternatives, $\{A_i\}$, $i = 1, 2, \cdots, r$, is followed by different magnitudes of reward, $\{O_j\}$, $j = 1, \cdots, M$, with probabilities π_{ij}, the subject's tendency to expect reward O_j following response A_i is assumed to change from trial to trial in accord with the usual reinforcement axioms for simple probability learning, approaching π_{ij} as the number of A_i occurrences becomes large. On each free-choice trial, the subject is considered to scan the set of available response alternatives, generating for each alternative a prediction of the reward that will be received if the response is made, and then to make the response which he predicts will yield the largest reward.

A full presentation of this theory must include exact specifications of (1) the random-walk process whereby the subject considers the various response alternatives and arrives at an overt choice on any given trial; (2) learning axioms for the implicit responses of predicting the outcomes that will follow different responses; and (3) learning axioms for the responses of choosing or rejecting the response leading to a given predicted outcome (or, in other terms, for developing a scale of reward values for different outcomes). In the present paper, we shall present only the aspects of the model relevant to our immediate purpose of accounting for asymptotic choice probabilities in human learning experiments involving exactly two different reward magnitudes. Further, we shall limit the present discussion to situations in which the two possible rewards, O_1 and O_2, are clearly discriminable, with one being uniformly preferred over the other, as, for example, would certainly be the case with monetary payoffs to adult subjects.

Subject to the simplifying assumptions mentioned above, asymptotic performance in a two-choice situation can be analyzed as follows: On each trial, the subject considers both responses and predicts the reward that will follow each. On denoting predictions of the more and less preferred rewards by 1 and 0, respectively, and true probabilities that the more preferred reward will follow responses A_1 and A_2 by π_1 and π_2, respectively, application of the probability matching theorem (discussed in section 1.3) yields the following probabilities that the subject will predict each of the four possible combinations of outcomes following responses:

A_1	A_2	Probability
1	1	$\pi_1\pi_2$
1	0	$\pi_1(1 - \pi_2)$
0	1	$(1 - \pi_1)\pi_2$
0	0	$(1 - \pi_1)(1 - \pi_2)$

The subject's "decision rule" in this situation is to make response A_1 with probability 1 when he predicts the outcome combination $(1, 0)$, and with probability 0 when he predicts $(0, 1)$. When the subject predicts either of the outcome combinations $(1, 1)$ or $(0, 0)$, he makes whichever response he first considers on the given trial. The probability that A_1 will be the first response considered differs depending on whether the response alternatives are presented to the subject in a randomized or a fixed arrangement. In the first case, each response has probability 1/2 of being considered first, and therefore response A_1 is made with probability 1/2 on trials when $(1, 1)$ or $(0, 0)$ are predicted. In the second case, the probability that A_1 will be considered first on these trials is equal to the current choice probability $P(1)$ for the A_1 response on all types of trials.

With these assumptions, the asymptotic probability of an A_1 choice can readily be computed for either of the two experimental conditions: For the case of randomized presentation order,

$$(12) \quad P(1) = \frac{1}{2}[\pi_1\pi_2 + \pi_1(1 - \pi_2) + (1 - \pi_1)(1 - \pi_2)] + \frac{1}{2}[\pi_1(1 - \pi_2)]$$

$$= \frac{1}{2}(1 + \pi_1 - \pi_2) ;$$

and for the case of fixed presentation order,

$$P(1) = P(1)[\pi_1\pi_2 + \pi_1(1 - \pi_2) + (1 - \pi_1)(1 - \pi_2)] + [1 - P(1)][\pi_1(1 - \pi_2)] ,$$

which, solved for $P(1)$, yields

(13)
$$P(1) = \frac{\pi_1(1 - \pi_2)}{\pi_1 + \pi_2 - 2\pi_1\pi_2} .$$

It may readily be shown that if $\pi_1 > \pi_2$, then the expression for $P(1)$ given by equation (13) is always greater than that given by equation (12) (except for the special case of $\pi_1 = 1$, $\pi_2 = 0$, where the two are equal). This relation is just what would be expected on psychological grounds. When the presentation arrangement of the response alternatives is fixed, as in the standard key-pressing situation (see [7] and [12, ch. 3]), the subject can learn to consider the more preferred alternative first on each trial; but when the arrangement of alternatives is randomly varied from trial to trial, as in Suppes and Atkinson's "paired-comparison" learning experiment ([12, ch. 11]), it is a matter of chance which alternative first comes to the subject's attention on any trial.

As an illustrative application of the model to the case of randomized alternatives, we may conveniently take the experiment of Suppes and Atkinson, just mentioned. On each trial of this experiment, the experimenter presented orally some combination of two or all three of the letters A, B, and C (all combinations occurring equally often, and order of presentation of the letters within a presentation set being randomized) and the subject chose one of the proffered alternatives. Probabilities that choices of each alternative would be "correct" were A: .67, B: .40, and C: .20. For one group of 48 subjects each correct choice received a payoff of one cent, and for a second group of 48 subjects a payoff of five cents. The choice proportions for the two groups differed very little; consequently, we shall pool their data for our present purposes. Predicted asymptotic proportions of choices of A from A, B; A from A, C; and B from B, C may be computed simply by substituting the appropriate pairs of values of π_i in equation (12), and prove to be .64, .74, and .60, respectively. To predict the probability of a choice of A from A, B, C, we require an extension of the model to the case of three alternatives. No new assumptions are needed, and the same method of derivation used in the case of equation (12) yields

(14a)
$$P(1) = \pi_1(1 - \pi_2)(1 - \pi_3) + \frac{1}{2}[\pi_1\pi_2(1 - \pi_3) + \pi_1\pi_3(1 - \pi_2)]$$

$$+ \frac{1}{3}[\pi_1\pi_2\pi_3 + (1 - \pi_1)(1 - \pi_2)(1 - \pi_3)]$$

$$= \frac{1 + 2\pi_1 - \pi_1 - \pi_3}{3} - \frac{\pi_1\pi_2 + \pi_1\pi_3 - 2\pi_2\pi_3}{6} ,$$

and similarly,

(14b)
$$P(2) = \frac{1 + 2\pi_2 - \pi_1 - \pi_3}{3} - \frac{\pi_2\pi_3 + \pi_1\pi_2 - 2\pi_1\pi_3}{6} ,$$

(14c) $$P(3) = \frac{1 + 2\pi_3 - \pi_1 - \pi_2}{3} - \frac{\pi_2\pi_3 + \pi_1\pi_3 - 2\pi_1\pi_2}{6}.$$

When the appropriate values of π_i are inserted, equations (14) yield .54, .30, and .16 for the probabilities of choice of A, B, and C, respectively, from A, B, C. Weighting the choice probabilities by the relative frequencies of occurrence of the various combinations of alternatives, we obtain the predicted values which are compared in table 2 with the observed values reported

TABLE 2

PREDICTED AND OBSERVED ASYMPTOTIC CHOICE PROPORTIONS FOR THE THREE
ALTERNATIVES IN A PAIRED-COMPARISON LEARNING EXPERIMENT

Alternative	Observed Proportion	Predicted Proportion
A	.475	.476
B	.290	.316
C	.235	.207

by Suppes and Atkinson [12, p. 254] for choices on the last 100 trials of a 400-trial series. The predictions do not come quite as close to the data as those of two other models that have been applied to the same experiment (see chapter 2 of this volume and [12, ch. 11]), but, on the other hand, the present model is in the comfortable position of allowing for the possibility that the subjects' choice proportions might not have quite reached asymptote by the end of the experimental session.

To illustrate application of the present model to an experiment with a fixed arrangement of alternatives, it will be of interest to consider a study described by Atkinson (see chapter 2 of this volume). In Atkinson's experiment, the subject's task on each trial of a 340-trial series was simply to operate one or the other of two keys; when the choice was correct the subject was paid five cents and when it was incorrect he was fined five cents. Three groups of 20 subjects each were run on three simple contingent reinforcement schedules. In table 3 are presented the combination of π_i values for each group, the asymptotic probabilities of the A_1 response

TABLE 3

PREDICTED AND OBSERVED ASYMPTOTIC A_1 CHOICE PROPORTIONS FOR
ATKINSON'S EXPERIMENT ON SIMPLE CONTINGENT REINFORCEMENT
WITH TWO PAYOFF VALUES

Probability of Higher Payoff		Observed Proportion	Predicted Proportion
π_1	π_2		
.6	.5	.601	.600
.7	.5	.685	.700
.8	.5	.832	.800

predicted from equation (13), and the corresponding observed response proportions over the last 100 trials of the experiment. The fit of calculated to observed values is not quite as good as that reported by Atkinson for his "strong and weak conditioning" model, but it should be noted in this regard that the predictions from the present model require no evaluation of parameters from the data.

An important limitation of the present model in the simplified form presented above is that no means are provided for handling different absolute payoff values. Suppose, for example, that we attempted application to an experiment reported by Siegel and Goldstein [11] in which conditions were similar to those of the study by Atkinson represented in table 3 except that the three groups had the same reinforcement probabilities, $\pi_1 = 1 - \pi_2 = .75$, but different payoff combinations: Group I, simply information as to correctness of the subject's prediction; Group II, five cent payoff for correct responses and zero for errors; and Group III, five cent payoff for correct responses and five cent fine for errors. Both Group II and Group III represent cases for which equation (13) should hold, and there is no way within the present formulation of distinguishing between the two conditions. Applying equation (13), we obtain a prediction of .90 for asymptotic probability of the A_1 choice, which may be compared with the observed estimates of .86 and .95 for Groups II and III, respectively. The predicted value is not far off in either case; but it would be desirable to account also for the difference in outcomes for the two payoff combinations. Alternative ways of achieving this desideratum within the theory outlined in this section are currently under investigation.

Application of the present model to the prediction of asymptotic choice proportions in two-person situations such as those discussed in section 1.1 above is straightforward (see Appendix B) but wholly satisfactory results cannot be expected until a suitable way of handling different absolute payoff values has been incorporated into the theory. In the case of Game 1, the predicted outcome is an asymptotic A_1 probability of 0 for the row player and a B_1 probability of 1 for the column player, which is distinctly more promising than the prediction from the simple linear model (see table 1). But for Game 2, the theoretical asymptotic probabilities are .62 both for response A_1 of the row player and B_1 of the column player; the model comes close to the average for the two players, but fails to predict the observed difference between them. In the case of another similar experimental game studied in the Indiana laboratory,[4] again with 20 pairs of subjects and "points" as payoffs, and with the same payoff matrix as that of Game 2, the prediction of .62 for the asymptotic probability of both A_1 and B_1 agrees quite well with the observed terminal proportions of .58 and .62, respectively. This experiment differed procedurally from the one described in section 1.1 only in that the subjects were not permitted to see their opponents' payoffs. Thus the suggestion arises that a fully adequate theory will have to take explicit account of this variable.

---

[4] This study, conducted by Michael Cole and Allen Schneider, was reported at the fall 1961 meetings of the American Psychological Association.

Another two-person experiment to which the present model can readily be applied has been reported by Lieberman (see chapter 14 of this volume). With the matrix

$$
\begin{array}{cc}
 & B_1 \quad\; B_2 \\
\begin{array}{c} A_1 \\ A_2 \end{array} &
\left[\begin{array}{cc} 3 & -1 \\ -9 & 3 \end{array}\right]
\end{array}
$$

of payoffs to the row player, two groups of ten subjects played for 300 trials against the experimenter who made his choices of B_1 and B_2 in accordance with a random "mixed strategy" of .25–.75 for one group and .50–.50 for the other. Payoffs were in chips, exchangeable for money. Predicted asymptotic probabilities of the A_1 choice are .31 and .67 for the .25–.75 and .50–.50 groups, respectively, and may be compared to observed proportions over the last 50 trials of .38 and .67.

On the whole, the "scanning model," even in the highly simplified form presented in this paper, appears to represent a distinct advance over the simple linear or stimulus-sampling models for the interpretation both of individual learning as a function of reward and of two-person interactions with varying payoffs. It should be emphasized, however, that scarcely a start has been made toward solving the mathematical problems of deriving statistics of learning data for the scanning model or toward handling the differential effects of different absolute magnitudes of reward.

APPENDIX A

Derivation of Asymptotic Choice Proportions for a Two-Person Game by Application of the Matching Theorem

We consider a two-person situation described by the matrix

$$
\begin{array}{cc}
 & B_1 \quad\;\; B_2 \\
\begin{array}{c} A_1 \\ A_2 \end{array} &
\left[\begin{array}{cc} a_{11} & a_{12} \\ a_{21} & a_{22} \end{array}\right]
\end{array},
$$

where a_{ij} represents the probability that player A is effectively rewarded on a trial when the choices of players A and B are A_i and B_j, respectively; and the corresponding reward probability for player B is $1 - a_{ij}$. We shall denote by α and β the asymptotic probabilities of an A_1 choice by player A and a B_1 choice by player B, respectively. According to the matching theorem, the long-term proportion of occurrences of a given choice should equal its long-term proportion of reinforcements. To simplify the exposition, we shall here make use of the fact that in the case of both the linear model [8] and the stimulus-sampling model [9], the asymptotic probabilities α and β are known to exist. Noting also that in a two-choice situation a response is assumed to be reinforced either when it occurs and is rewarded or when the alternative response occurs and is not rewarded, we can write the "matching equations,"

(A1) $\alpha = u_{11} + u_{12} = u_{11}a_{11} + u_{12}a_{12} + u_{21}(1 - a_{21}) + u_{22}(1 - a_{22})$,

and

(A2) $\beta = u_{11} + u_{21} = u_{11}(1 - a_{11}) + u_{21}(1 - a_{21}) + u_{12}a_{12} + u_{22}a_{22}$,

where u_{ij} denotes asymptotic probability of the joint choice A_iB_j. Once the reward probabilities are specified for any particular experiment, we can solve the system consisting of equations (A1) and (A2) together with $\sum_{i,j}u_{ij} = 1$, obtaining, in general, expressions for any three of the u_{ij} in terms of the fourth and the reward parameter.

In the case of the matrix for Game 1 given in section 1.3, we have, substituting the a_{ij} values into equations (A1) and (A2), respectively,

$$u_{11} + u_{12} = \frac{1}{2}u_{12} + \frac{3}{4}u_{21} ,$$

and

$$u_{11} + u_{21} = u_{11} + \frac{3}{4}u_{21} + \frac{1}{2}u_{12} + u_{22} ,$$

which yield the solutions

$$u_{12} = \frac{3}{4} - 2u_{11} , \qquad u_{21} = \frac{1}{2} , \quad \text{and} \quad u_{22} = u_{11} - \frac{1}{4} .$$

Since u_{11} is a probability, its value must obviously fall in the range $.25 \leq u_{11} \leq .375$, and, using these bounds on u_{11}, we can in turn generate bounds on α and β:

$$.375 \leq \alpha = u_{11} + u_{12} \leq .500 \quad \text{and} \quad .750 \leq \beta = u_{11} + u_{21} \leq .875 .$$

The same procedure applied to the second game matrix of section 1.3 leads to the bounds given for that game in table 1 (p. 135).

APPENDIX B

Derivation of Asymptotic Choice Proportions for a Two-Person Game by Application of the Scanning Model

The technique of deriving asymptotic choice probabilities (assuming that they exist) for the type of situation discussed in this paper can conveniently be illustrated in terms of the two experimental games discussed in sections 1.1 and 1.2. For Game 1, the possible combination of outcomes with their associated conditional probabilities are as follows:

PLAYER A			PLAYER B		
A_1	A_2	Probability	B_1	B_2	Probability
0	1	β^2	4	2	α^2
2	1	$(1 - \beta)\beta$	4	0	$\alpha(1 - \alpha)$
0	4	$\beta(1 - \beta)$	3	2	$(1 - \alpha)\alpha$
2	4	$(1 - \beta)^2$	3	0	$(1 - \alpha)^2$

If we consider the first row for player A, and refer to the appropriate payoff matrix of section 1.1, the true asymptotic conditional probability that an A_1 choice will eventuate in the outcome of 0 payoff is β, and the probability that an A_2 choice will eventuate in a payoff of 1 is also β. Thus, according to the theory, the probability that player A (when he considers his two possible responses on any given trial) will expect this combination of outcomes should asymptotically equal β^2. The other probabilities are obtained similarly. Now the theoretical probability that player A will choose A_1 is equal to the probability that he will expect A_1 to yield the greater payoff, and the same holds for player B's probability of choosing B_1. Therefore, we have

$$\alpha = (1 - \beta)\beta ,$$

and

$$\beta = \alpha^2 + \alpha(1 - \alpha) + (1 - \alpha)\alpha + (1 - \alpha)^2 = 1 ,$$

whence $\alpha = 0$.

For Game 2, the combinations of outcomes and conditional probabilities are as follows:

PLAYER A			PLAYER B		
A_1	A_2	Probability	B_1	B_2	Probability
1	2	β^2	3	1	α^2
1	0	$\beta(1 - \beta)$	3	4	$\alpha(1 - \alpha)$
3	2	$(1 - \beta)\beta$	2	1	$(1 - \alpha)\alpha$
3	0	$(1 - \beta)^2$	2	4	$(1 - \alpha)^2$

These yield

$$\alpha = \beta(1 - \beta) + (1 - \beta)\beta + (1 - \beta)^2 = 1 - \beta^2 ,$$
$$\beta = \alpha^2 + \alpha(1 - \alpha) = \alpha ,$$

whence $\alpha = \beta = .618$.

REFERENCES

[1] BOWER, G. H., Response strengths and choice probability: a consideration of two combination rules, in *Logic, Methodology and Philosophy of Science, Proceedings of the 1960 International Congress*, E. Nagel, P. Suppes, and A. Tarski, eds., Stanford, Calif: Stanford Univ. Press, 1962.

[2] BURKE, C. J., Applications of a linear model to two-person interactions, chap. 9 in *Studies in Mathematical Learning Theory*, R. R. Bush and W. K. Estes, eds., Stanford, Calif.: Stanford Univ. Press, 1959.

[3] BUSH, R. R., and F. MOSTELLER, *Stochastic Models for Learning*, New York: Wiley, 1955.

[4] ESTES, W. K., Of models and men, *Amer. Psychologist*, 1957, **12**, 609–17.

[5] ESTES, W. K., Theory of learning with constant, variable, or contingent schedules of reinforcement, *Psychometrika*, 1957, **22**, 113–32.

[6] ESTES, W. K., and M. JOHNS, Probability learning with ambiguity in the reinforcing stimulus, *Amer. J. Psychol.*, 1958, **71**, 219–28.

[7] ESTES, W. K., and J. H. STRAUGHAN, Analysis of a verbal conditioning situation in terms of statistical learning theory, *J. Exptl. Psychol.*, 1954, **47**, 225–34.

[8] ESTES, W. K., and P. SUPPES, Foundations of linear models, chap. 8 in *Studies in Mathematical Learning Theory*, R. R. Bush and W. K. Estes, eds., Stanford, Calif.: Stanford Univ. Press, 1959.

[9] ESTES, W. K., and P. SUPPES, "Foundations of statistical learning theory, II: The stimulus sampling model for simple learning," Technical Report No. 26, Contract Nonr-225(17), Institute for Mathematical Studies in the Social Sciences, Stanford University, Stanford, Calif., 1959.

[10] KARLIN, S., Some random walks arising in learning models, *Pac. J. Math.*, 1953, **3**, 725–56.

[11] SIEGEL, S., and D. A. GOLDSTEIN, Decision-making behavior in a two-choice uncertain outcome situation, *J. Exptl. Psychol.*, 1959, **57**, 37–42.

[12] SUPPES, P., and R. C. ATKINSON, *Markov Learning Models for Multiperson Interactions*, Stanford, Calif.: Stanford Univ. Press, 1960.

[13] TATSUOKA, M., and F. MOSTELLER, A commuting-operator model, chap. 12 in *Studies in Mathematical Learning Theory*, R. R. Bush and W. K. Estes, eds., Stanford, Calif.: Stanford Univ. Press, 1959.

10

Le Théorème de Bayes et les Processus d'Influence Sociale

Claude Flament, *Laboratoire de Psychologie Expérimentale de la Sorbonne, Paris*

1. Introduction

Nous étudions les processus d'influence sociale tels qu'ils nous paraissent agir dans des situations semblables à celle de l'expérience classique de Asch [1]. Par exemple, on demande aux sujets de désigner le plus long de deux segments de droite; les sujets qui répondent d'abord sont des compères (*"stooges"*) de l'expérimentateur; le sujet expérimental, naïf, répond en dernier; on constate en général que sa réponse est influencée par celles des compères.

Ce type de situation se distingue de bien d'autres situations d'influence sociale par deux aspects fondamentaux:

(1) Le sujet expérimental doit donner une réponse *exacte*, et il sait que l'exactitude de sa réponse peut être vérifiée objectivement. Par opposition, il n'existe sans doute pas de critère objectif de réponse dans une épreuve de jugement purement esthétique.

(2) La réponse du sujet est influencée par des évènements (les réponses des compères) qui ont lieu entre la présentation du stimulus (les deux segments à comparer) et le moment où le sujet donne sa réponse. Par opposition, dans les situations du type "mouvement autocinétique" (Shérif), l'influence sociale s'exerce en partie d'un essai à l'autre, la réponse d'un sujet au $\lambda^{\text{ième}}$ stimulus influençant la réponse d'un autre sujet au $(\lambda + 1)^{\text{ième}}$ stimulus.

Certes, dans les situations qui nous intéressent, la succession des essais peut modifier les processus se développant au cours de chaque essai. Mais alors que des modèles comme ceux de Cohen [4, ch.7] étudient cette succession des essais, notre modèle se préoccupe d'abord de ce qui se passe entre la présentation d'un stimulus et la réponse à ce stimulus—sans nier, cependant, que le passé du sujet, ce qui précède la présentation du stimulus, peut avoir une grande importance dans la détermination du processus étudié, tout au moins, de ses paramètres.

Maintenant à: Département de Psychologie Sociale du Laboratoire de Sciences Sociales d'Aix en Provence.

Les processus de ce genre sont très généralement étudiés au niveau des *probabilités* (*objectives*) qu'a le sujet de donner chacune des réponses possibles. Mais nous avons vu que le sujet cherche à donner une réponse exacte, et on peut considérer le *sentiment d'exactitude* qu'il attache à chaque réponse possible. C'est à ce niveau que se place notre modèle.

Imaginons un instant le comportement qu'aurait, dans la situation décrite, un individu s'efforçant de répondre selon une *strategie* aussi *rationnelle* que possible. Il sait qu'il y a deux stimuli possibles: S_1 et S_2; deux réponses possibles: R_1 et R_2, R_i étant la réponse exacte à S_i. Avant même la présentation de l'un des deux stimuli, il estime, en fonction de son passé, les probabilités *a priori* d'apparition de chaque stimulus: $p(S_1)$ et $p(S_2)$; Un stimulus est présenté, mais le sujet ne sait pas lequel; sa perception peut être E_1^0, "je *crois* avoir vu S_1," ou E_2^0, "je *crois* avoir vu S_2."[1] Supposons que sa perception soit E_1^0; il en estime alors l'exactitude, ou, plus précisément, la probabilité $p(E_1^0 | S_1)$ de E_1^0 si S_1 a été présenté, et la probabilité $p(E_1^0 | S_2)$ de E_1^0 si S_2 a été présenté. Ces probabilités sont dites probabilités expérimentales, ou vraisemblances (*likelihood*). Le sujet utilise alors le théorème de Bayes, qui pose:

$$p(S_i | E_j^0) \propto p(E_j^0 | S_i) \cdot p(S_i),$$

$p(S_i | E_j^0)$ étant la probabilité que S_i a été présenté si le sujet a eu la perception E_j^0; Dans notre exemple, nous avons

$$p(S_1 | E_1^0) \propto p(E_1^0 | S_1) \cdot p(S_1),$$
$$p(S_2 | E_1^0) \propto p(E_1^0 | S_2) \cdot p(S_2).$$

C'est-à-dire

$$\frac{p(S_1 | E_1^0)}{p(S_2 | E_1^0)} = \frac{p(E_1^0 | S_1) \cdot p(S_1)}{p(E_1^0 | S_2) \cdot p(S_2)}.$$

Si ce rapport est supérieur à l'unité, le sujet donne R_1, la réponse exacte au stimulus S_1.

Mais si avant de donner sa réponse, le sujet entend les réponses des autres sujets, il prendra ces réponses comme des éléments d'information sur le stimulus présenté, estimera les vraisemblances, ou probabilités expérimentales correspondantes, et les intègrera à la formule du théorème de Bayes.

2. Le problème

Dans un précédent travail [7], nous avions montré, en discutant divers résultats expérimentaux, que le comportement spontané d'un sujet naïf pouvait se comparer à la stratégie bayèsienne que nous venons d'esquisser. Cependant, s'il y a *isomorphisme*, cet isomorphisme ne saurait qu'être partiel, et ceci pour deux raisons essentielles:

2.1 Les sentiments d'exactitude sur lesquels se fonde notre modèle peuvent sans doute être représentés par des nombres, mais rien ne prouve, au contraire, que l'ensemble de ces nombres ait les propriétés d'un ensemble

[1] Le choix des symboles E_i^0 pour désigner les perceptions du sujet sera justifié plus loin (section 3).

de mesures de probabilité. Par exemple, dans la stratégie bayèsienne, nous avons $\sum_i p(S_i) = \sum_j p(E_j^0 | S_i) = 1$; si nous désignons la mesure du sentiment correspondant à une probabilité en remplaçant p par π, nous pouvons très bien avoir $\sum_i \pi(S_i) \neq \sum_j \pi(E_j^0 | S_i)$.

Nous avons par exemple demandé à des sujets de donner leurs sentiments d'exactitude relatifs à trois réponses possibles (les stimuli étaient exactement ceux de l'expérience classique de Asch); à chaque réponse correspondait une ligne de 10 cm, dont les extrémités étaient libellées "Je suis absolument sûr que cette réponse est fausse" et "Je suis absolument sûr que cette réponse est exacte." Les sujets devaient cocher chaque ligne proportionnellement au sentiment correspondant. On mesurait le sentiment par la distance du point "réponse absolument fausse" au point marqué par le sujet; la somme des trois distances est extrêmement variable d'un sujet à un autre, et presque toujours très différente de 10 cm.

On peut penser qu'il s'agit là de difficultés dans le maniement par le sujet d'une échelle conventionnelle nouvelle (le phénomène est moins prononcé si on utilise des pourcentages au lieu de distances), et que ça n'empêche pas que la vérité, quelle qu'elle soit, ait un *poids constant*.

Il s'agit surtout de savoir si tous les phénomènes nous intéressant dèpendent uniquement des rapports entre sentiments—auquel cas la somme des mesures peut être arbitrairement fixée—ou si certains aspects du choix d'une réponse dépendent de la valeur réelle de cette somme. C'est ce dernier point de vue que défend Berlyne [2]. Nous verrons du reste plus loin (section 5) les dangers qu'il y aurait parfois à ne tenir compte que du rapport des mesures et non de leur somme.

2.2   Tout, dans la stratégie bayèsienne, est déterminé par les termes que nous avons considérés; et si une situation se reproduit identiquement, la réponse du sujet sera toujours la même: les probabilités estimées par le sujet bayèsien sont stables. Il ne saurait en être de même des sentiments des sujets. La répétition des caractéristiques d'une situation ne reproduira les mesures des sentiments d'exactitude que quant à leur *tendance centrale* (moyenne ou médiane, par exemple); les valeurs effectivement utilisées dans chaque cas varieront autour de ces valeurs centrales, *au hasard*, pour de multiples raisons psychologiques ou physiologiques. On peut imaginer, pour décrire ces variations, bien des distributions; celle qui sera proposée dans un instant n'a pas de justification très particulière; elle a semblé commode pour développer le modèle, et ainsi permettre une première exploration des faits; comme nous le dirons par la suite, elle s'est trouvée constituer une bonne approximation de certains résultats expérimentaux.

3. Définitions et notations

L'ensemble (fini) des stimuli possibles est
$$\mathscr{S} = \{S_1, S_2, \cdots, S_\sigma\};$$
l'ensemble (fini) des réponses possibles est
$$\mathscr{R} = \{R_1, R_2, \cdots, R_\rho\};$$

rien d'essentiel n'est changé dans le modèle si l'on pose $\sigma = \rho$; on établit alors une correspondance biunivoque (1-1) entre $\mathscr{S}$ et $\mathscr{R}$, définissant l'exactitude des réponses: R_i est la réponse exacte à S_i.

Le sujet dont nous étudions les réponses sera désigné par O.

On distingue des moments $k = 0, 1, 2, \cdots, n$; le moment 0 est celui de la présentation du stimulus; le moment $k\,(k > 0)$ est celui où le $k^{\text{ième}}$ compère donne sa réponse. Le sujet O donne sa réponse après la réponse du $n^{\text{ième}}$ compère.

$\mathscr{E}^k = \{E_1^k, E_2^k \cdots\}$ est l'ensemble (fini) des évènements pouvant advenir au moment k; ainsi, $\mathscr{E}^0$ est l'ensemble des perceptions possibles du sujet O à la présentation d'un stimulus; $\mathscr{E}^k\,(k > 0)$ est l'ensemble des réponses possibles du $k^{\text{ième}}$ compère. Eng énéral, pour tout k, l'effectif de $\mathscr{E}^k$ est $\rho = \sigma$.

Le passé du sujet O sera désigné par E^{-1}; il sera parfois considéré comme un évènement.

Les sentiments d'exactitude dont nous avons parlé seront appelés des *plausibilités*, d'après la terminologie de Pólya [15]. Nous distinguons trois types de plausibilité:

$\pi_i^{-1} =$ plausibilité que S_i soit présenté, étant donné E^{-1} (*plausibilité a priori*).

$\pi_i^k =$ plausibilité que S_i ait été présenté, étant donné la suite constatée des évènements $E^{-1}, E_h^0, E_{h'}^1, \cdots, E_{h''}^k$ (*plausibilité résultante*).

$\epsilon_{h|i}^k =$ plausibilité de l'apparition de l'évènement E_h^k, étant donné la suite des évènements $E^{-1}, E_h^0, \cdots, E_{h'}^{k-1}$, et en supposant que S_i a été présenté (*plausibilité experimentale*).

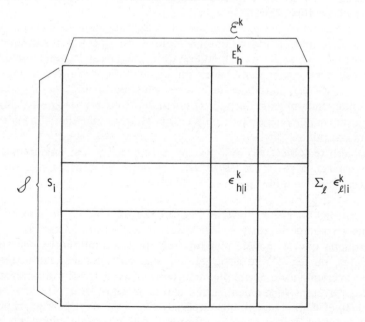

FIG. 1

Remarquons qu'à chaque moment k, le produit cartésien $\mathscr{S} \times \mathscr{E}^k$ définit un ensemble de plausibilités expérimentales (figure 1).

L'évènement E_h^k s'étant produit, on ne tient compte que des valeurs de la *colonne* correspondante. Mais si les plausibilités expérimentales somment à une valeur constante, comme les probabilités, c'est dans les *lignes* que le phénomène apparaîtra.

4. Les hypothèses du modèle

H_1. Pour tout i, k, h

$$\pi_i^{-1} \geqq 0; \qquad \pi_i^k \geqq 0; \qquad \varepsilon_{h|i}^k \, 0 \, ;$$

et au moins pour un stimulus S_i on a $\pi_i^n > 0$.

H_2. Les plausibilités a priori et expérimentales effectives dans le choix d'une réponse sont extraites au hasard de distributions logarithmo-normales indépendantes.

H_3. $\pi_i^k \propto \pi_i^{k-1} \cdot \varepsilon_{h|i}^k$.

H_4. La réponse finale du sujet O est R_i si $\pi_i^n = \max_j\{\pi_j^n\}$.

Les hypothèses H_3 et H_4 posent l'isomorphisme entre le comportement du sujet et la stratégie bayèsienne; les hypothèses H_1 et H_2 montrent en quoi cet isomorphisme n'est que partiel.

H_1 pose la possibilité de mesurer les plausibilités par des nombres réels *non-négatifs*, la notion de plausibilité négative étant sans doute à ne pas considérer. On affirme de plus qu'à la fin du processus, il est impossible que le sujet pense que toute réponse est absolument fausse; c'est là plus un problème de mise en situation, de réalisation pratique de l'expérience, qu'un problème théorique.

H_2 a, en fait, déjà été discutée (section 2.2); rappelons que si une variable x suit une distribution logarithmo-normale, c'est que $\log x$ suit une distribution normale; et si $\hat{x}$ est la médiane des x, $\log \hat{x}$ est la moyenne des $\log x$. De plus, si x et y sont distribuées indépendamment de façon logarithmo-normale, $(ax^\alpha y^\beta)$ est distribuée de même, puisque si $\log x$ et $\log y$ sont distribués indépendamment de façon normale, $(\log a + \alpha \log x + \beta \log y)$ est distribuée normalement; en particulier, (xy) et (x/y) sont distribuées de façon logarithmo-normale.

La probabilité (objective) φ_i d'obtenir la réponse R_i est calculable, comme nous le verrons, à partir de H_2 et H_4; ces deux hypothèses pourraient être remplacées, par exemple, par

H_0: $\varphi_i = \pi_i^n / \sum_j \pi_j^n$;

Nous aurions alors un modèle très proche du modèle de choix de Luce [12]; nous en avons du reste étudié certains aspects ailleurs [8].

Remarquons que le modèle pourrait très bien s'appliquer à des situations non sociales, où les $\mathscr{E}^k$ ne désigneraient pas les réponses des autres sujets, mais des évènements quelconques en relation avec le stimulus présenté.

De plus, n étant le moment après lequel le sujet doit répondre, on peut poser $n = 0$, et définir une simple expérience de jugement perceptif; ou même, $n = -1$: le sujet doit prévoir le stimulus, qui s'appelle alors, en général, un renforcement.

Nous avons expérimenté ces situations, en particulier la dernière $(n=-1)$; le modèle se réduit alors à H_1, H_2, et H_4; on a pu montrer que les hypothèses H_2, H_4 étaient nettement préférables a l'hypothèse H_0, définie il y a un instant [9].

5. Plausibilités et probabilités subjectives

Nous pouvons toujours dèfinir les quantités suivantes:

$$(1) \qquad p_i^k = \pi_i^k \Big/ \sum_j \pi_j^k, \qquad e_{h|i}^k = \varepsilon_{h|i}^k \Big/ \sum_l \varepsilon_{i|i}^k.$$

Si la somme des plausibilités est constante (*v. supra*, section 2.2), on peut, dans H_3 et H_4, remplacer π et ε par p et e sans rien changer à la description du phénomène. Qu'en est-il dans le cas de somme *non* constante? Le problème a quelque importance, car bien des techniques visant à faire exprimer par le sujet ses plausibilités partent, en fait, d'une hypothèse de somme constante. Par exemple, lorsqu'il y a deux réponses possibles, et que le sujet se contente de donner le pourcentage de chances d'exactitude d'une seule réponse, étant entendu que la mesure de l'autre réponse est le complément à 100: on oblige ainsi le sujet à effectuer lui-même les transformations définies en (1).

Si K est le coefficient de proportionnalité impliqué par H_3, on a $\pi_i^k = K\pi_i^{k-1}\varepsilon_{h|i}^k$, ou

$$\left(p_i^k \cdot \sum_j \pi_j^k \right) = K \left(p_i^{k-1} \cdot \sum_j \pi_j^{k-1} \right) \left(\varepsilon_{h|i}^k \cdot \sum_l \varepsilon_{l|i}^k \right).$$

Posons $K' = K \cdot \sum_j \pi_j^{k-1} \big/ \sum_j \pi_j^k$. Ce coefficient ne dépend pas de i; c'est un coefficient de proportionnalité, et

$$p_i^k \propto p_i^{k-1} e_{h|i}^k \sum_l \varepsilon_{l|i}^k;$$

le terme en ε peut dépendre de i, et ne pas être éliminé. Remarquons que pour éliminer ce terme, il n'est pas nécessaire de supposer que la somme de tout ensemble de plausibilités est constante, mais seulement que, dans la table des plausibilités expérimentales au moment k (*v. supra*, section 3), la somme des lignes est constante, tout en variant peut-être d'une table à l'autre.

Si cette hypothèse (assez faible) n'est pas valide, la méthode des pourcentages évoquée plus haut ne permet pas de tester le modèle.

6. Plausibilités et probabilités des réponses

D'après H_4, la probabilité (objective) que le sujet, dans un cas donné, réponde R_i est

$$\varphi_i = \mathrm{prob}\left[\pi_i^n = \max_j \{\pi_j^n\} \right].$$

L'étude des situations où $\rho > 2$ conduit à des formules générales peu maniables, et, semble-t-il, sans grand intérêt de principe.

Nous allons examiner le cas $\rho = 2$, très fréquent en laboratoire. Soit $\mathscr{R} = \{R_1, R_2\}$. Dans ce cas, on a $\varphi_i = \mathrm{prob}\,[\pi_i^n/\pi_j^n > 1]$. Nous désignons les médianes des plausibilités par le même symbole surmonté d'un accent circonflexe ($\wedge$). Par H_2, les plausibilités non résultantes (π^{-1} et ε) sont indépendamment distribuées de façon logarithmo-normale; il en est donc de même de leur produit ou de leur rapport. Soit s l'écart-type de la distribution normale des log π_i^n/π_j^n; on a

$$\varphi_i = \frac{1}{\sqrt{2\pi}}\int_{-\infty}^{N} e^{-z^2/2}dz \; ,$$

où

$$N = \frac{\log \hat{\pi}_i^n/\hat{\pi}_j^n}{s} \; ,$$

ce que nous écrirons conventionnellement

$$\varphi_i = \mathcal{N}\left(\frac{\log \hat{\pi}_i^n/\hat{\pi}_j^n}{s}\right) .$$

On a par ailleurs $\pi_i^n/\pi_j^n = p_i^n/p_j^n$, et log $\hat{\pi}_i^n/\hat{\pi}_j^n = $ logit $\hat{p}_i^n$; d'où

$$\varphi_i = \mathcal{N}\left[\frac{1}{s}\text{logit}\,\hat{p}_i^n\right] .$$

La figure 2 montre comment φ varie en fonction de $p = \hat{p}^n$, et de s. On

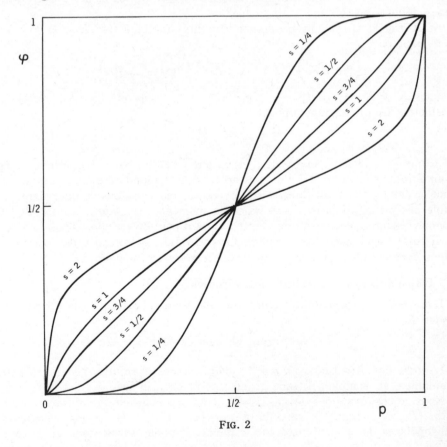

FIG. 2

voit que, comme on pouvait s'y attendre, le sujet a un comportement tendant vers la stratégie maximale lorsque s tend vers zéro; ce résultat est évidemment général (ρ quelconque).

Le modèle ne prévoit pas les facteurs déterminant la valeur de s; ils sont sans doute très divers; le problème réclamerait une étude particulière. On admettra peut-être que s varie en fonction inverse de l'attention que le sujet apporte à sa tâche. Cette attention sera sans doute augmentée par l'importance de la sanction entraînée par la réponse; on peut voir là une hypothèse permettant de comprendre certains effets constatés par Suppes, notamment, selon lesquels les sujets en situation d'apprentissage de probabilité tendent vers la stratégie maximale lorsque le gain monétaire attaché aux réponses exactes augmente.

Inversement, la fatigue peut abaisser l'attention, et augmenter la valeur de s; au moins c'est ce que nous avons constaté au cours d'une expérience assez longue [9].

7. Dépendance des évènements

H_2 pose l'indépendance des variations aléatoires des plausibilités, mais la définition des plausibilités expérimentales fait dépendre la tendance centrale à un moment k des évènements survenus aux moments antérieurs. En ce sens, il y a dépendance, et ceci peut conduire à des conséquences importantes pour l'étude des situations d'influence sociale.

Pour plus de simplicité, nous considérons seulement deux réponses possibles: R_1 et R_2. Dans les situations expérimentales habituelles, le sujet O est naïf, et les sujets k sont des compères ("stooges") de l'expérimentateur. On s'arrange pour que la réponse latente de O soit R_1 après présentation du stimulus; on a donc $\hat{\pi}_1^0/\hat{\pi}_2^0 > 1$. Les compères répondent R_2, ce qu'on notera en désignant les évènements par $E_{2|i}^k$; le sujet O parle en dernier.

En général O n'a aucune raison de penser que ses compagnons ont tendance à se tromper; en d'autres termes, $\hat{\epsilon}_{2|1}^k/\hat{\epsilon}_{2|2}^k \leq 1$ pour tout $k > 0$. Il en résulte que

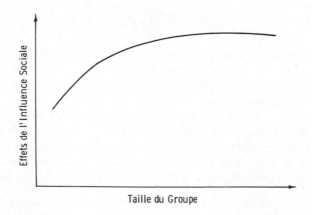

FIG. 3

$$\frac{\hat{\pi}_1^k}{\hat{\pi}_2^k} = \frac{\hat{\pi}_1^{k-1}}{\hat{\pi}_2^{k-1}} \cdot \frac{\hat{\varepsilon}_{2|1}^k}{\hat{\varepsilon}_{2|2}^k} < \frac{\hat{\pi}_1^{k-1}}{\hat{\pi}_2^{k-1}} .$$

O, qui initialement penchait pour R_1, a de plus en plus tendance à préférer R_2, sous l'influence des réponses de ses compagnons; c'est le processus de conformisme habituellement constaté.

Mais quelle peut être la courbe d'évolution de $\hat{\pi}_1^k/\hat{\pi}_2^k$ en fonction de k?

Il est vraisemblable que O a conscience du changement de son opinion, et pense qu'un phénomène analogue se produit chez ses compagnons. Il estime que la réponse du $k^{\text{ième}}$ sujet n'est pas indépendante des réponses des $k-1$ premiers sujets; donc, quand k augmente, les $\hat{\varepsilon}_{2|i}^k$ $(i = 1, 2)$ dépendent de moins en moins des stimuli, et $\hat{\varepsilon}_{2|1}^k/\hat{\varepsilon}_{2|2}^k \to 1$. Il en résulte que, plus ou moins rapidement, $\hat{\pi}_1^k/\hat{\pi}_2^k$ ne varie pratiquement plus en fonction de k.

On conclut donc à une valeur asymptotique des effets de l'influence sociale en fonction de la taille du groupe.[2] De certaines expériences de S. Asch, il semble ressortir que l'asymptote est atteinte pour 3 ou 4 sujets.

8. Conformisme et influence sociale

Les auteurs anglo-saxons parlent généralement de processus conformistes; nous préférons parler de processus d'influence sociale. La notion est évidemment plus générale. Il y a conformisme quand la réponse latente du sujet O est modifiée *dans le sens* des réponses des sujets; mais diverses expériences ont montré que, dans certaines situations, le sujet O a tendance à modifier sa réponse pour la rendre aussi dissemblable que possible de celle des autres sujets.

On peut, soit considérer qu'il y a là un phénomène fondamentalement distinct du précédent, soit tenter une explication générale des deux situations, qui ne se distingueraient que par la valeur de certains paramètres du modèle.

Notre modèle est de ce dernier type.

8.1 Soit

$$\varepsilon_i = \prod_{k=1}^n \varepsilon_{\cdot|i}^k .$$

Il n'y a que deux réponses possibles; les sujets k répondent R_1; il y a conformisme si $\varepsilon_1/\varepsilon_2 > 1$; il y a anticonformisme si $\varepsilon_1/\varepsilon_2 < 1$. Dans le premier cas, O pense que ses camarades n'ont pas une tendance marquée à se tromper; au contraire, dans le second cas. C'est ce qui se passe lorsqu'on fait précéder l'expérience d'influence sociale d'une phase préparatoire au cours de laquelle on fait croire à O que ses camarades se trompent presque toujours.

8.2 Pour préciser certains cas, supposons qu'il n'y a qu'un seul sujet, A, influençant O $(n = 1)$. Les plausibilités attachées aux réponses de A sont $\varepsilon_{1|1}^1$ et $\varepsilon_{1|2}^1$ si A répond R_1, et $\varepsilon_{2|1}^1$ et $\varepsilon_{2|2}^1$ si A répond R_2; en fait, dans des

---

[2] Coleman (chapter 8), par une voie très différente, conclut à l'existence de phénomènes très voisins.

situations de type classique, il y a une certaine symétrie entre les deux réponses, et nous avons constaté expérimentalement que le sujet O n'estimait que deux plausibilités: la plausibilité $\varepsilon^1_{1|1} = \varepsilon^1_{2|2}$ d'exactitude des réponses de A; et la plausibilité d'erreur, $\varepsilon^1_{1|2} = \varepsilon^1_{2|1}$. Dans ce cas, la condition de constance de la somme des plausibilités expérimentales est automatiquement vérifiée.

On aura de même $\varepsilon^0_{1|1} = \varepsilon^0_{2|2}$, la plausibilité d'exactitude de la perception initiale de O, et $\varepsilon^0_{1|2} = \varepsilon^0_{2|1}$, la plausibilité d'erreur correspondante. Enfin, dans les situations classiques d'influence sociale, les stimuli sont *a priori* équiplausibles: $\pi_i^{-1} = \frac{1}{2}$.

Dans ces conditions, on peut poser

$$p = \frac{\varepsilon^0_{1|1}}{\varepsilon^0_{1|1} + \varepsilon^0_{2|1}} = \frac{\varepsilon^0_{2|2}}{\varepsilon^0_{2|2} + \varepsilon^0_{1|2}},$$

$$e = \frac{\varepsilon^1_{1|1}}{\varepsilon^1_{1|1} + \varepsilon^1_{2|1}} = \frac{\varepsilon^1_{2|2}}{\varepsilon^1_{2|2} + \varepsilon^1_{1|2}}.$$

Si la réponse initiale de O est égale à la réponse de A (*accord*), la probabilité résultante d'exactitude de cette réponse commune est

$$\frac{pe}{pe + (1-p)(1-e)};$$

etc. La figure 4 définit alors quatre cas.

Le tableau 1 donne la réponse finale de O, en supposant que O pense initialement R_i.

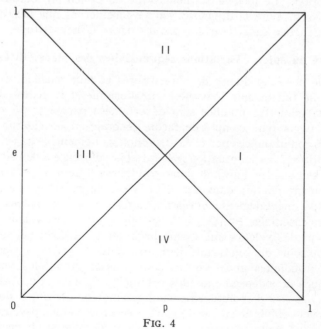

FIG. 4

TABLEAU 1

RÉPONSE FINALE DE O, EN SUPPOSANT QUE O PENSE INITIALEMENT R_i

Cas	Réponse de A	
	R_i (Accord)	R_j (Désaccord)
I	(1) R_i	(5) R_i
II	(2) R_i	(6) R_j
III	(3) R_j	(7) R_j
IV	(4) R_j	(8) R_i

Il y a conformisme évident en (6) et (7), et anticonformisme évident en (3) et (4); en (1), (2), (5), et (8), O ne modifie pas sa réponse; les phènomènes ne peuvent qu'être jugés au niveau des plausibilités, variable expériméntalement bien plus difficile à observer que la réponse finale de O.

8.3 Si nous avons plus de deux réponses, une plus grande variété de phénomènes peut apparaître. Par exemple, si les réponses sont ordonnées d'une certaine manière (c'est-à-dire si, R_i étant la réponse exacte, R_j est d'autant plus inexacte que $|i - j|$ est grand), on peut s'attendre à observer souvent des réponses finales de O *intermédiaires* entre la réponse initiale de O et la réponse de A. Ce sont les "réponses de compromis" de Asch [1], qu'il nous semble difficile d'interpréter convenablement dans la théorie de cet auteur; les subjets ne se conforment ni à l'opinion du groupe, ni à leur perception. Le modèle mathématique de Cohen [4], établi sur les résultats de Asch, évite la difficulté, en ne considérant que des réponses exactes ou inexactes, sans tenir compte du degré d'inexactitude.

9. Le passé du sujet. Variations séquentielles des plausibilités

Le modèle pose l'existence de plausibilités et leur mode d'utilisation par le sujet; il ne fait aucune hypothèse sur l'origine et la genèse de ces plausibilités. On admettra qu'elles sont déterminées par le passé du sujet, ce dont nous avons tenu compte de façon générale en considérant toutes les plausibilités conditionnées par E^{-1}. Psychologiquement, le sujet doit estimer les plausibilités dans la situation présente par référence à des situations plus ou moins semblables figurant dans son passé. Le seul moyen d'étudier scientifiquement ce fait dans ses détails est de créer un passé immédiat contrôlé expérimentalement, *en répétant ν fois de suite la même situation* définie par les ensembles $\mathscr{S}$, $\mathscr{R}$, $\mathscr{E}^k$ ($k = 0, \cdots, n$). Les valeurs au λ^{ieme} essai dépendent des valeurs aux essais précédents, et ainsi peuvent dépendre du passé "absolu" du sujet, antérieur au premier essai. Cependant, si des propriétés ergodiques apparaissent, pour ν assez grand, les valeurs seront asymptotiques et indépendantes des premières valeurs et du passé "absolu" du sujet. Les lois d'évolution peuvent néanmoins dépendre du passé "absolu" du sujet. Mais il en est de même pour toute étude psychologique. Si les mêmes lois sont constatées sur beaucoup de sujets, on peut leur attribuer légitimement un grand degré de généralité.

Nous ne voulons pas étudier ici un modèle spécial d'évolution séquentielle, mais seulement voir dans quelle mesure les modèles classiques d'apprentissage, auxquels on doit évidemment se référer ici, sont compatibles avec notre modèle.

Nous devons d'abord nous poser quelques questions:

(1) Doit-on étudier les lois d'évolution au niveau des probabilités objectives (φ_i), des probabilités subjectives $(p_i^k, e_{h|i}^k)$, ou des plausibilités $(\pi_i^k, \varepsilon_{h|i}^k)$? Puisque notre modèle fait dépendre les φ et les p des plausibilités, seules supposées réelles dans l'expérience du sujet, nous devons donc nous placer au niveau de l'évolution des plausibilités; ceci nous conduit à confronter notre modèle aux modèles d'apprentissage de Luce [12, ch. 4], qui portent sur des *forces*, formellement analogues à nos plausibilités.

(2) Doit-on étudier l'évolution des plausibilités résultantes (π_i^k) ou des plausibilités non résultantes $(\pi_i^{-1}, \varepsilon_{h|i}^k)$? Pour les mêmes raisons que précédemment, nous devons adopter ce dernier point de vue. Notre problème est donc de savoir dans quelle mesure on peut appliquer les hypothèses des modèles de Luce aux plausibilités non résultantes, et de voir ce qui s'en suit au niveau des plausibilités résultantes, en particulier au niveau de π_i^n.

(3) Enfin, doit-on se placer au niveau des plausibilités médianes $(\hat{\pi}_i^{-1}, \hat{\varepsilon}_{h|i}^k)$? Nous ne pouvons pas considérer que les plausibilités effectives à un essai déterminent les plausibilités effectives à l'essai suivant: H_2 serait sans objet. Mais on peut supposer que, d'un essai au suivant, la détermination se fait de plausibilité effective à plausibilité médiane, ou de plausibilité médiane à plausibilité médiane. Ces deux hypothèses conduiront en général à des évolutions fort différentes des φ_i observables, mais il n'est pas nécessaire de choisir pour l'étude préliminaire que seule nous voulons aborder ici.

9.1 Le modèle α de Luce. Ce modèle se définit par diverses conditions, qui peuvent très bien être valides pour nos plausibilités non résultantes. Mais alors le modèle α ne décrit pas l'évolution des plausibilités résultantes.

Supposons que le modèle α décrive l'évolution des π_i^{-1} et des $\varepsilon_{h|i}^0$; on a alors [14, p. 108]:

$$\text{(2)} \qquad \pi_i^{-1}(\lambda + 1) = \sum_j a_{ij}\pi_j^{-1}(\lambda) \, ,$$

$$\varepsilon_{h|i}^0(\lambda + 1) = \sum_j b_{ij}\varepsilon_{h|j}^0(\lambda) \, .$$

Par H_3 on a $\pi_i^0(\lambda + 1) = K \cdot \pi_i^{-1}(\lambda + 1)\varepsilon_{h|i}^0(\lambda + 1)$, et, par (2):

$$\text{(3)} \qquad \pi_i^0(\lambda + 1) = K\left[\sum_j a_{ij}b_{ij}\pi_j^0(\lambda) + \sum_{k \neq l} a_{ik}b_{il}\pi_i^{-1}(\lambda)\varepsilon_{h|i}^0(\lambda)\right] .$$

Si le modèle α était valide pour les plausibilités résultantes, nous aurions

$$\text{(4)} \qquad \pi_i^0(\lambda + 1) = \sum_j c_{ij}\pi_j^0(\lambda) \, .$$

En comparant (3) et (4), on voit qu'il faut poser $c_{ij} = Ka_{ij}b_{ij}$, et

$$\sum_{k \neq l} a_{ik}b_{il}\pi_i^{-1}(\lambda)\varepsilon_{h|i}^0(\lambda) = 0 \, ,$$

ce qui en général ne sera pas vérifié.

9.2 Le modèle β de Luce. Si toutes les plausibilités non résultantes suivent le modèle β, il en est *presque* de même des plausibilités résultantes. En effet, le modèle β implique [12, p. 109]:

$$\pi_i^{-1}(\lambda + 1) = a_i\pi_i^{-1}(\lambda) \, ,$$
$$\varepsilon_{h|i}^0(\lambda + 1) = b_i\varepsilon_{h|i}^0(\lambda) \, .$$

Par H_3

$$\pi_i^0(\lambda) = K(\lambda) \cdot \pi_i^{-1}(\lambda) \cdot \varepsilon_{h|i}^0(\lambda) \, ;$$
$$\pi_i^0(\lambda + 1) = K(\lambda + 1) \cdot \pi_i^{-1}(\lambda + 1) \cdot \varepsilon_{h|i}^0(\lambda + 1) \, ;$$

d'où

$$\pi_i^0(\lambda + 1) = K(\lambda + 1) \cdot [a_i\pi_i^{-1}(\lambda)][b_i\varepsilon_{h|i}^0(\lambda)]$$
$$= K(\lambda + 1) \cdot a_ib_i[\pi_i^{-1}(\lambda) \cdot \varepsilon_{h|i}^0(\lambda)]$$
$$= {}^{\cdot}K(\lambda + 1) \cdot K(\lambda) \cdot a_ib_i \cdot \pi_i^0(\lambda) \, .$$

D'une façon générale, on obtient $\pi_i^k(\lambda + 1) \propto \beta_i\pi_i^k(\lambda)$, où β_i est le produit des termes $a_i, b_i, \cdots$.

On remarque la présence dans le résultat de termes de proportionnalité pouvant varier en fonction de λ; cette différence avec le modèle de Luce disparaît si nous passons aux probabilités subjectives résultantes:

$$p_i^k(\lambda + 1) = \frac{\pi_i^k(\lambda + 1)}{\sum_j \pi_j^k(\lambda + 1)} = \frac{\beta_i\pi_i^k(\lambda)}{\sum_j \beta_j\pi_j^k(\lambda)}$$
$$= \frac{\beta_i \cdot \pi_i^k(\lambda)/\sum_h \pi_h^k(\lambda)}{\sum_j \beta_j \cdot \pi_j^k(\lambda)/\sum_h \pi_h^k(\lambda)} = \frac{\beta_i p_i^k(\lambda)}{\sum_j \beta_j p_j^k(\lambda)} \, ,$$

ce qui est l'expression à laquelle aboutit Luce, et sur laquelle Lamperti et Suppes [11] ont établi les formules asymptotiques du modèle β.

Voyons rapidement ce qui en résulte au niveau des probabilités objectives φ_i, lorsque $\rho = 2$, et en supposant que l'évolution se fait de plausibilités médianes à plausibilités médianes. On peut sans doute supposer que s_λ, l'écart-type des $\log \hat{\pi}_1^n(\lambda)/\hat{\pi}_2^n(\lambda)$, est pratiquement stable, au moins d'un essai à l'autre: $s_{\lambda+1} = s_\lambda = s$. Dans ces conditions, on obtient facilement

$$\varphi_1(\lambda + 1) = \varphi_1(\lambda) + \frac{1}{\sqrt{2\pi}}\int_M^N e^{-z^2/2} \, dz$$

où

$$N = \frac{1}{s}\log\frac{\beta_1\hat{\pi}_1^n(\lambda)}{\beta_2\hat{\pi}_2(\lambda)} \, , \qquad M = \frac{1}{s}\log\frac{\hat{\pi}_1^n(\lambda)}{\hat{\pi}_2^n(\lambda)} \, .$$

Un modèle linéaire ne saurait rendre compte de l'évolution des φ.

10. Etude expérimentale du modèle

Jusqu'à présent, aucune expérience achevée n'a étudié le modèle dans son entier. Divers aspects ont cependant été étudiés séparément.

Une expérience d'apprentissage de probabilité ($n = -1$), au cours de laquelle les sujets exprimaient les plausibilités π_i^{-1} ($i = 1, 2$) en pourcentage de chances que la réponse soit exacte, nous a permis de valider H_2; l'évolution séquentielle peut être décrite en faisant intervenir des opérateurs du type "stimulus sampling theory," dépendant des trois derniers renforcemments; les paramètres de ces opérateurs évoluent, en début d'expérience, avec la perception que le sujet a de la fréquence des divers stimuli [9].

Rouanet [16], dans une expérience où $n = 0$, a montré que le comportement des sujets était au moins partiellement bayèsien.

Diverses expériences nous ont permis de montrer l'importance des plausibilités π^0[6], et π^1[5] lorsque $\mathscr{E}^1$ est constitué par les réponses d'un sujet A; l'évolution séquentielle de ces dernières semble être de type oscillatoire, en fonction de l'accord ou du désaccord entre la réponse de A et la réponse finale de O (les sujets évitent une trop longue séquence de désaccords, et aussi bien, une trop longue séquence d'accords).

Une expérience actuellement en cours se place dans les conditions décrites en section 8.2. Après une période préparatoire (en individuel), on communique aux sujets des informations (fausses) sur leurs performances; on répartit ainsi les sujets dans les cadrans de la figure 4; les sujets expriment, à chaque essai, les plausibilités π^{-1}, π^0, et π^1; on peut alors tester tous les aspects du modèle. Les premiers résultats sont encourageants.

11. Conclusion. Comparaison avec quelques autres modèles d'influence sociale

Notre modèle étudie la détermination d'une réponse au sein d'une structure du type A-B-X de Newcomb [13](X étant le stimulus), et à certains points de vue, évoque les modèles se situant dans cette structure: équilibre de Cartwright et Harary [3], puissance sociale de French [10], congruence d'Osgood et Tannenbaum [14]. En fait, quatre aspects au moins nous séparent de ces modèles:

(1) Ces modèles ne supposent en général que des processus purement sociaux, alors que nous pensons que ces processus peuvent s'expliquer par des mécanismes déjà constatables dans des processus de psychologie individuelle.

(2) Ces modèles ne se préoccupent pas de la nature du critère de choix des réponses, alors que nous pensons que le caractère objectif de certains critères permet de considérer les divers évènements comme des sources d'information sur le stimulus—ce qui n'a pas grand sens lorsque le critère est subjectif.

(3) Notre analyse est de type probabiliste.

(4) Enfin, les mécanismes psychologiques supposés par ces modèles sont plutôt de type affectif, alors que nous pensons que le comportement du sujet est isomorphe, au moins partiellement, à l'une des conduites les plus rationnelles qui soient: la stratégie bayèsienne.

Les modèles de Cohen [4] et de Suppes et Atkinson [17, ch. 12] sont séquentiels: ils concentrent leurs efforts mathématiques sur l'évolution du phénomène, mais ils se basent sur certaines hypothèses relatives aux mécanismes jouant à chaque essai. Dans le modèle de Cohen, ces mécanismes semblent très proches de ceux discutés brièvement plus haut.

Suppes et Atkinson, tout comme nous, prennent leur inspiration dans la psychologie individuelle: celle de l'apprentissage par conditionnement, la nôtre étant plutôt celle de la décision. Les deux perspectives ne s'opposent pas forcément. On peut penser que les plausibilités, dont nous avons décrit l'usage, s'apprennent par un processus de conditionnement; c'est ce qui nous a amené, en collaboration avec J.-F. Le Ny (Paris), spécialiste du conditionnement, et M. Ritter (Tübingen), à réaliser une expérience de conditionnement des plausibilités (en cours d'analyse). L'axiomatique reste à préciser, les développements mathématiques à faire; il se pourrait bien qu'ils empruntent beaucoup à la "théorie de l'échantillonnage des stimuli."

SUMMARY

The situation to be studied is the Asch-type situation of social influence. The response given by the subject can be influenced by events which are the responses of "stooges." The presented model deals with the process that takes place between the first stimulus presentation and the final response to that stimulus. Such a process is generally studied at the objective probability level. Here the feeling of being correct possessed by the subject is considered and represented by numbers that do not necessarily have all properties of a probability measure. They are called *plausibilities*.

The model considers a (finite) number of stimuli and for each one of them a correct response. Then events are introduced, corresponding to the responses given by the different stooges. Four hypotheses characterize the model: H_1 postulates the existence of positive plausibilities; H_2 stipulates that the plausibilities are extracted at random from independent lognormal distributions; H_3 expresses a multiplicative law on plausibilities at the different stages of the process; and H_4 gives the final decision rule governing the subject's response. From the preceding set of hypotheses, the objective probability of observing a particular response can be derived.

The paper proceeds by discussing the concepts of conformity *vs.* social influence, as well as various implications of the model, which is compared with Luce's alpha and beta learning models. Finally, evidence of experimental validation is mentioned: various aspects of the model have been tested already and a comprehensive experiment is now being conducted.

Bibliographie

[1] ASCH, S. E., Studies of independence and conformity: I. A minority of one against a unanimous majority, *Psychol. Monog.*, 1956, **70** (9) (whole no. 416).

[2] BERLYNE, D. E., Uncertainty and conflict: a point of contact between information-theory and behavior-theory concepts, *Psychol. Rev.*, 1957, **64**, 329–39.

[3] CARTWRIGHT, D., and F. HARARY, Structural balance: a generalization of Heider's theory, *Psychol. Rev.*, 1956, **63**, 277–93.

[4] COHEN, B. P., A probability model for conformity, *Sociometry*, 1958, **21**, 69–81.

[5] FLAMENT, C. Influence sociale et perception, *Année Psychol.*, 1958, **58**, 377–400.

[6] FLAMENT, C. Ambiguité du stimulus, incertitude de la réponse et processus d'influence sociale, *Année Psychol.*, 1959, **59**, 73-92.

[7] FLAMENT, C., Modèle stratégique des processus d'influence sociale sur les jugements perceptifs, *Psychol. Française*, 1959, **4**, 91-101.

[8] FLAMENT, C., Comportement de choix et échelle de mesure, *Bull. C. E. R. P.*, 1960, **9**, 165-86.

[9] FLAMENT, C., Probabilités objectives et subjectives dans des choix séquentiels, paper presented at the XVI International Congress of Psychology, Bonn, 1960.

[10] FRENCH, J. R. P., JR., A formal theory of social power, *Psychol. Rev.*, 1956, **63**, 181-94.

[11] LAMPERTI, J., and P. SUPPES, Some asymptotic properties of Luce's Beta learning model, *Psychometrika*, 1960, **25**, 233-41.

[12] LUCE, R. D., *Individual Choice Behavior*, New York: Wiley, 1959.

[13] NEWCOMB, T. M., An approach to the study of communicative acts, *Psychol. Rev.*, 1953, **60**, 393-404.

[14] OSGOOD, C. E., and P. H. TANNENBAUM, The principle of congruity in the prediction of attitude change, *Psychol. Rev.*, 1955, **62**, 42-55.

[15] PÓLYA, G., *Mathematics and Plausible Reasoning*, Princeton, N.J.: Princeton Univ. Press, 1954.

[16] ROUANET, H., Etudes expérimentales de décisions et calcul des probabilités, paper presented at the *Colloque International du C. N. R. S. sur la Décision*, Paris, 1959.

[17] SUPPES, P., and R. C. ATKINSON, *Markov Learning Models for Multiperson Interactions*, Stanford, Calif.: Stanford Univ. Press, 1960.

11

The Structure of Interpersonal Behavior in the Dyad

Uriel G. Foa, *The Israel Institute of
Applied Research and Bar Ilan University*

Everyday language has a great variety of terms for describing the behavior of a person interacting with another. This abundance of terms makes it necessary for the scientist who wishes to observe and describe the interaction to find some parsimonious and meaningful method of classifying such behavior. Studies of small group interaction, socialization, and the like cannot begin before this problem is solved. We can achieve parsimony by showing that a small number of basic concepts, combined in various ways, provides one basis (among others) for classifying many different kinds of behavior.

Most theories of behavior, popular as well as scientific, involve attempts to achieve simple classification schemes by disregarding certain aspects of behavior and concentrating on certain others that are deemed to be more important. The disagreement that may exist on what is important and what is not leads to different proposals. A given proposal recommends itself when it leads to the systematic predictions of empirical results. For this purpose, however, the classification scheme alone is not sufficient. We also need a metatheory that provides rules for making the transition from conceptual scheme to empirical findings. If the prediction proves correct, both the scheme and the metatheory can be regarded as adequate. If the prediction fails, there is no way to tell whether the classification, or the metatheory, or both are to blame.

One metatheory that has been proposed [1] is the contiguity principle. A requirement of a classification scheme is that it tell which variables are similar to each other and which are not. The contiguity principle suggests that variables described as similar are statistically interrelated more closely than variables described as dissimilar. In this study the application of the principle is modified by introducing the new concept of semantic principal

The substantive research reported in this paper was supported by grant M-2669 from the National Institute of Mental Health of the National Institutes of Health, U. S. Public Health Service. The development of the general methods of research design and analysis, of which the application in this study is a special case, was sponsored by the Office of Aerospace Research, United States Air Force, through its European Office, under Contract No. AF 61(052)-121.

component. In substance, the problem is to devise concepts for classifying behavior in such a way that the definition of the categories and the use of a metatheoretical principle will predict their statistical interrelation. A link is thus created between conceptual and empirical structure. In recent years the structure of interpersonal behavior has received considerable attention, and several investigators, working independently, have obtained data indicating that such a structure may be circular. A re-analysis of their results has led to a new theory [2]. Only a brief outline of this theory will be given here. The main purpose of this paper is to present some recent findings in support of the structural theory.

1. Theoretical Outline

Behavior in the dyadic relation is the subject of our study. Since both partners exhibit behavior, a distinction between *actors* is implied. Furthermore, the behavior of each actor is perceived by both the actor himself and the other. This distinguishes between *observers*. Again, each observer ascribes a certain perception to himself and a certain perception (not necessarily identical) to the other. This distinguishes between *aliases*. Finally, the behavior can be actual (what is done), or ideal (what ought to be done). This distinguishes between *levels* [3].

Let us now consider the behavior of one of the actors in the dyadic relation, at a given level, perceived by a given observer, and ascribed by the observer to a given alias.

It is proposed that such behavior expresses the relationship of the actor with both partners of the dyad, himself and the other, in two modes, the emotional and the social. The emotional mode refers to the immediate relationship of the actor with himself and with the other. The social mode refers to the status positions that the actor assigns to both partners within a larger reference group. The relationship of the actor with either partner can be one of acceptance or of rejection.

It is thus suggested that behavior in the dyadic relationship is made up of three facets:

1. The *content* of the relationship: acceptance and rejection;
2. The *object* of the relationship: self and other;
3. The *mode* of the relationship: emotional and social.

These three facets give rise to eight types of relationship, such as emotional acceptance of self, social acceptance of other, emotional rejection of other, and the like. We can arrange these eight types, first by content, then by object, and, finally, by mode, in the manner given in table 1.

Note that the three facets behave as semantic principal components of the proposed order. Content behaves as the first principal component and has no bending points. Its value changes only once. Object behaves as the second principal component, forming a curve with one bending point. Its value changes twice: other, self, and then other again. Mode behaves as the fourth principal component, forming a curve with three bending points. Its value changes four times: social, emotional, social, emotional,

TABLE 1
THE CIRCULAR ORDER OF TYPES OF RELATIONSHIP

Type	Content	Object	Mode
1			Social
2		Other	Emotional
	Acceptance		
3			Emotional
4		Self	Social
5			Social
6		Self	Emotional
	Rejection		
7			Emotional
8		Other	Social

social. These two last components are symmetrical, suggesting circularity. An alternative order that maintains this behavior of the facets can be obtained by reversing the values of the mode: emotional, social, emotional, social, emotional. The order proposed in table 1 assumes that people tend to relate similarly to themselves and to the other in the emotional mode, rather than in the social mode. The reverse order would suggest the contrary. These two alternatives will be discussed in presenting the results.

Since the proposed order is circular, reversing the values of the content, or the object, or both, would not produce an alternative order. The present proposal differs from an earlier one [2] with regard to the object facet.

We could not obtain the suggested order by applying the principle of contiguity alone. Each type has three neighbors differing from it in one of three facets. For example, the type "Social acceptance of other" has three neighbors, "*Emotional* acceptance of other," "Social acceptance of *self*," and "Social *rejection* of other," differing from it, respectively, in the value of the mode, object, or content facet. In such a situation there is no way of arranging the types simply by contiguity: some other rule is needed to differentiate among the various facets. This is done by the new concept of semantic principal component. The principal components determine the role of each facet in the order pattern: If we know how each facet behaves as a component we can establish the order. It is suggested that the closer to each other any two types are in the order, the higher their coefficient of correlation. Then the matrix of the intercorrelations between the eight types will present the characteristic circumplex pattern [4]. The design of the study for testing the circumplex hypothesis is described in the next section.

2. Design of the Study

For each one of the eight types of relationship three brief stories were prepared. For example, the three stories referring to the husband's social acceptance of the wife run as follows (similar stories and questions were prepared for the behavior of the wife):

Abraham has consideration for his wife and displays toward her respect and esteem.

Isaac thinks his wife is very successful and especially esteems her personality and her actions.

Jacob is sure that everything his wife does is important and good and there is no limit to the esteem and importance that he attributes to her. After each story the following four questions were asked:

1. Do you behave toward your wife as does the husband in the story?
    Almost always
    Generally
    Sometimes
    Seldom
    Almost never
2. Do you think that a husband should behave as does the hushand in the story in relation to his wife?
    Absolutely
    Yes
    Perhaps yes
    Perhaps no
    No
    Imagine that we are reading the same story to your wife. Try to guess what she would say about the husband in the story.
3. Would your wife say that you resemble the husband in the story?
    She would say that I resemble him very much
    She would say that I resemble him quite a bit
    She would say that I resemble him slightly
    She would say that I do not resemble him so much
    She would say that I do not resemble him at all
4. Would your wife say that a husband should behave thusly?
    She would say that a husband should alway behave thusly
    She would say that a husband should generally behave thusly
    She would say that a husband should only sometimes behave thusly
    She would say that a husband should behave thusly only in exceptional cases
    She would say that a husband should never behave thusly

These questions were designed to find out how well each story fits the picture of behavior of the actor, ascribed by the respondent to the self and to the other, at both the actual and the ideal level.

The answers to the *same* question, for the three stories belonging to the *same* type, were analyzed and were found to form a Guttman scale. It was, therefore, possible to assign to each respondent a score on each scale. The scores were ranked from negative (low acceptance or high rejection) to positive (high acceptance or low rejection). For each actor, alias, and level, eight scores were assigned to each respondent, one for each one of the eight types of relationship to the dyad. The 28 coefficients of correlation between all the possible pairs of these eight scores were computed.

In each correlation matrix the observer (or respondent), actor, alias, and level are constant. Since there are two kinds of observer (wife and husband), as well as two kinds of actor, alias, and level, 16 correlation matrices were obtained, one for each given profile of observer, actor, alias, and level.

The questionnaire was administered to a sample of 633 married couples in Jerusalem, Israel. Husband and wife were interviewed separately and simultaneously in their home by two field workers. The results presented here concern the basic structural hypothesis of the study. Nevertheless, they present only part of the picture. A more detailed analysis of the data is now under way. Let us now turn to the findings.

3. Results

The results presented here consist of 16 intercorrelation matrices, each matrix being characterized by a given kind of respondent (observer), actor, alias, and level. Each matrix gives the correlation coefficients between all the possible pairs of the eight types of relationship. In the matrix the types are, of course, arranged according to their hypothesized circular order.

The first two tables refer to the responses given by the wife; i.e., the wife is the observer. In the next two tables the observer is the husband. Within each pair of tables the first table refers to the behavior of the self (the observer), the next to the behavior of the other. In each table the first two parts refer to the perception ascribed to the self and the next two parts to the perception ascribed to the other. In each table the first and third parts refer to actual behavior and the second and fourth to ideal behavior.

It should be recalled at this point that in order to provide a single meaning, scores were arranged on a scale from negative to positive. Thus low acceptance and high rejection were scored low, while high acceptance and low rejection were scored high. As a consequence, a positive correlation between acceptance and rejection indicates that the *higher* the acceptance, the *lower* the rejection tends to be.

A simple inspection of tables 2–5 suggests that the coefficients tend to follow the typical circumplex pattern: as we move away from the main diagonal, the size of the coefficients decreases and then increases again as the second diagonal is approached. Thus the highest coefficients appear along the diagonals and the lowest ones in the cells farthest from the diagonals.

For example, in the first row of table 2 the first coefficient on the left is .65. As we move to the right, the size decreases to .06 in the fifth cell and then increases again to .45. In the third row of the same table the coefficient at the right of the main diagonal is .52. As we move to the right, the size decreases and reaches the lowest point in the cell four steps from the main diagonal, .01. Then the coefficients increase again to .07

and, as we move to the left side, to .27 and .28. Since the order is circular, the last variable on the right is a neighbor of the first variable on the left.

The same pattern of coefficients that decrease in size and then increase again tends to repeat itself in each row of table 2 and in the other three tables as well, thus providing support for the hypothesis of the circumplex structure of interpersonal behavior.

The order of the coefficients reveals some deviations from the predicted pattern. For example, in table 2, fourth row, the second coefficient from the left, .16, is lower than the first one, .24, although according to the prediction it should have been higher. It is of interest to note where in the table these deviations occur and in which table they are most frequent. The deviation appearing in the fourth row of part 1 of table 2 suggests that the order between social acceptance of the other (first column) and emotional acceptance of the other (second column) should be reversed. The reversal would eliminate this particular deviation. All but three of the 85 deviations from the circumplex pattern appearing in the four tables are like this one, suggesting a reversal of the order between the emotional and social modes of relationship. If deviations were distributed randomly, only half of them would be of the kind just described. Thus the observed distribution of deviations is quite different from the one expected under chance conditions.

In proposing the circular order of the eight relationships it was noted that the only alternative order maintaining the component-like properties of the facets was provided by the reversal of the emotional and social values of the mode facet. The difference between these two alternative orders concerns the interdependence between the relationship to self and the relationship to other. One order suggests that they are more related in the emotional mode, while the other suggests a stronger interdependence in the social mode. The fact that the deviations from the circumplex are related to this particular facet may indicate that in certain respondents, or in certain types of responses, or in both, the social bond is stronger than the emotional one. In this connection it may be noted that the number of deviations is consistently larger in the ideal level than in the corresponding actual level. In some of the tables referring to ideal behavior the alternative order would fit the data nearly as well as the order that has been adopted.

The results reported so far refer to the *internal* relations among the eight types. It is of interest to find out whether the structure will also hold when the eight types are correlated with *external* variables pertaining to the dyadic relationship. In this case it will be expected that an external variable will correlate highest with one or two types on the circle and that its correlations with the other types will progressively decrease as we move away along the circle. Such a finding will provide additional evidence in favor of the structural hypothesis being tested.

An example of the relations among the variables of the circle and two external variables is given in table 6. This table reports the coefficients of correlation between general and sexual satisfactions with marriage and the

TABLE 2
Intercorrelations Among the Eight Types of Relationship
Observer: Wife; Actor: Wife

Alias Level	Type	Acceptance				Rejection			
		Other		Self		Self		Other	
		Soc.	Em.	Em.	Soc.	Soc.	Em.	Em.	Soc.
		1	2	3	4	5	6	7	8
Self/Actual	1	...	.65	.27	.24	.06	.20	.35	.45
	2	.65	...	.28	.16	.09	.20	.36	.40
	3	.27	.28	...	.52	.28	.17	.01	.07
	4	.24	.16	.52	...	.31	.17	−.11	−.01
	5	.06	.09	.28	.31	...	.39	.18	.24
	6	.20	.20	.17	.17	.39	...	.34	.35
	7	.35	.36	.01	−.11	.18	.34	...	.53
	8	.45	.40	.07	−.01	.24	.35	.53	...
Self/Ideal	1	...	.62	.34	.28	−.08	−.05	.13	.23
	2	.62	...	.25	.17	−.01	−.04	.14	.15
	3	.34	.25	...	.51	.10	.04	−.10	−.03
	4	.28	.17	.51	...	.13	.13	−.19	−.05
	5	−.08	−.01	.10	.13	...	.39	.21	.27
	6	−.05	−.04	.04	.13	.39	...	.18	.25
	7	.13	.14	−.10	−.19	.21	.18	...	.38
	8	.23	.15	−.03	−.05	.27	.25	.38	...
Other/Actual	1	...	.76	.37	.28	.10	.15	.40	.47
	2	.76	...	.37	.27	.08	.11	.36	.38
	3	.37	.37	...	.62	.22	−.12	.05	.10
	4	.28	.27	.62	...	.25	.14	.01	.00
	5	.10	.08	.22	.25	...	.35	.23	.27
	6	.15	.11	−.12	.14	.35	...	.35	.33
	7	.40	.36	.05	.01	.23	.35	...	.57
	8	.47	.38	.10	.00	.27	.33	.57	...
Other/Ideal	1	...	.57	.28	.19	−.03	.20	.06	.30
	2	.57	...	.23	.11	.07	−.01	.20	.23
	3	.28	.23	...	.52	.11	.08	.00	.02
	4	.19	.11	.52	...	.15	.13	−.10	−.01
	5	−.03	.07	.11	.15	...	.38	.23	.25
	6	.20	−.01	.08	.13	.38	...	.14	.17
	7	.06	.20	.00	−.10	.23	.14	...	.39
	8	.30	.23	.02	−.01	.25	.17	.39	...

TABLE 3

TABLE 3

INTERCORRELATIONS AMONG THE EIGHT TYPES OF RELATIONSHIP

Observer: Wife; Actor: Husband

Alias Level	Type	Types of Relationship							
		Acceptance				Rejection			
		Other		Self		Self		Other	
		Soc.	Em.	Em.	Soc.	Soc.	Em.	Em.	Soc.
		1	2	3	4	5	6	7	8
Self/Actual	1	...	.74	.23	.18	.02	.06	.45	.52
	2	.74	...	.15	.07	.08	.06	.56	.53
	3	.23	.15	...	.62	.21	.18	− .05	.09
	4	.18	.07	.62	...	.29	.25	− .13	− .10
	5	.02	.08	.21	.29	...	.41	.22	.14
	6	.06	.06	.18	.25	.41	...	.17	.14
	7	.45	.56	− .05	− .13	.22	.17	...	.68
	8	.52	.53	.09	− .10	.14	.14	.68	...
Self/Ideal	1	...	.66	.35	.31	− .03	.08	.07	.32
	2	.66	...	.29	.25	− .01	.01	.13	.25
	3	.35	.29	...	.63	.00	.15	− .09	.07
	4	.31	.25	.63	...	.04	.19	− .07	.10
	5	− .03	− .01	.00	.04	...	.38	.29	.24
	6	.08	.01	.15	.19	.38	...	.18	.25
	7	.07	.13	− .09	− .07	.29	.18	...	.44
	8	.32	.25	.07	.10	.24	.25	.44	...
Other/Actual	1	...	.73	.35	.30	.01	.09	.32	.37
	2	.73	...	.33	.23	.09	.11	.35	.34
	3	.35	.33	...	.69	.14	.10	− .05	− .05
	4	.30	.23	.69	...	.21	.13	− .07	.06
	5	.01	.09	.14	.21	...	.42	.23	.15
	6	.09	.11	.10	.13	.42	...	.29	.22
	7	.32	.35	− .05	− .07	.23	.29	...	.54
	8	.37	.34	− .05	.06	.15	.22	.54	...
Other/Ideal	1	...	.77	.29	.30	.02	.03	.26	.40
	2	.77	...	.24	.21	.01	.02	.30	.39
	3	.29	.24	...	.65	.07	.07	− .10	.04
	4	.30	.21	.65	...	.12	.12	− .12	.03
	5	.02	.01	.07	.12	...	.41	.23	.20
	6	.03	.02	.07	.12	.41	...	.11	.21
	7	.26	.30	− .10	− .12	.23	.11	...	.56
	8	.40	.39	.04	.03	.20	.21	.56	...

TABLE 4

INTERCORRELATIONS AMONG THE EIGHT TYPES OF RELATIONSHIP

Observer: Husband; Actor: Husband

Alias Level	Type	Types of Relationship							
		Acceptance				Rejection			
		Other		Self		Self		Other	
		Soc.	Em.	Em.	Soc.	Soc.	Em.	Em.	Soc.
		1	2	3	4	5	6	7	8
Self/Actual	1	$\cdots$	.64	.37	.30	.03	.09	.33	.50
	2	.64	$\cdots$	.45	.26	$-.05$	.11	.26	.34
	3	.37	.45	$\cdots$	.60	.11	.09	.04	.13
	4	.30	.26	.60	$\cdots$	.19	.06	$-.07$	.02
	5	.03	$-.05$	.11	.19	$\cdots$	.38	.25	.18
	6	.09	.11	.09	.06	.38	$\cdots$	.28	.28
	7	.33	.26	.04	$-.07$	.25	.28	$\cdots$	.60
	8	.50	.34	.13	.02	.18	.28	.60	$\cdots$
Self/Ideal	1	$\cdots$	.60	.38	.31	$-.02$	.06	.22	.31
	2	.60	$\cdots$	.31	.25	$-.06$	.13	.19	.23
	3	.38	.31	$\cdots$	.62	.02	.13	$-.06$	.08
	4	.31	.25	.62	$\cdots$	.10	.05	$-.11$	$-.01$
	5	$-.02$	$-.06$	.02	.10	$\cdots$	.42	.67	.20
	6	.06	.13	.13	.05	.42	$\cdots$	.23	.29
	7	.22	.19	$-.06$	$-.11$	.67	.23	$\cdots$	.52
	8	.31	.23	.08	$-.01$	.20	.29	.52	$\cdots$
Other/Actual	1	$\cdots$	.76	.44	.34	.11	.17	.41	.51
	2	.76	$\cdots$	.40	.27	.07	.17	.34	.38
	3	.44	.40	$\cdots$	.59	.14	.20	.11	.19
	4	.34	.27	.59	$\cdots$	.19	.13	.00	.01
	5	.11	.07	.14	.19	$\cdots$	.45	.31	.29
	6	.17	.17	.20	.13	.45	$\cdots$	.34	.34
	7	.41	.34	.11	.00	.31	.34	$\cdots$	.65
	8	.51	.38	.19	.01	.29	.34	.65	$\cdots$
Other/Ideal	1	$\cdots$	.61	.34	.25	.08	.00	.19	.25
	2	.61	$\cdots$	.25	.21	.00	$-.05$	.30	.11
	3	.34	.25	$\cdots$	.59	.00	.09	$-.07$	.05
	4	.25	.21	.59	$\cdots$	.07	$-.01$	$-.10$	$-.06$
	5	.08	.00	.00	.07	$\cdots$	.57	.30	.30
	6	.00	$-.05$	.09	$-.01$	.57	$\cdots$	.18	.27
	7	.19	.30	$-.07$	$-.10$	.30	.18	$\cdots$	.54
	8	.25	.11	.05	$-.06$	.30	.27	.54	$\cdots$

TABLE 5

INTERCORRELATIONS AMONG THE EIGHT TYPES OF RELATIONSHIP

Observer: Husband; Actor: Wife

Alias Level	Type	Types of Relationship							
		Acceptance				Rejection			
		Other		Self		Self		Other	
		Soc.	Em.	Em.	Soc.	Soc.	Em.	Em.	Soc.
		1	2	3	4	5	6	7	8
Self/Actual	1	· · ·	.72	.38	.31	.13	.15	.38	.49
	2	.72	· · ·	.27	.18	.12	.14	.41	.47
	3	.38	.27	· · ·	.56	.25	.17	.04	.09
	4	.31	.18	.56	· · ·	.26	− .09	− .07	− .04
	5	.13	.12	.25	.26	· · ·	.31	.30	.27
	6	.15	.14	.17	− .09	.31	· · ·	.26	.28
	7	.38	.41	.04	− .07	.30	.26	· · ·	.69
	8	.49	.47	.09	− .04	.27	.28	.69	· · ·
Self/Ideal	1	· · ·	.61	.42	.29	.12	.06	.21	.31
	2	.61	· · ·	.36	.26	.08	.02	.21	.21
	3	.42	.36	· · ·	.61	.22	.05	.02	.16
	4	.29	.26	.61	· · ·	.22	.07	− .07	.09
	5	.12	.08	.22	.22	· · ·	.27	.31	.31
	6	.06	.02	.05	.07	.27	· · ·	.19	.26
	7	.21	.21	.02	− .07	.31	.19	· · ·	.52
	8	.31	.21	.16	.09	.31	.26	.52	· · ·
Other/Actual	1	· · ·	.72	.46	.40	.15	.13	.14	.34
	2	.72	· · ·	.43	.32	.13	.11	.27	.26
	3	.46	.43	· · ·	.64	.32	.12	.06	.13
	4	.40	.32	.64	· · ·	.31	.13	− .05	.00
	5	.15	.13	.32	.31	· · ·	.33	.30	.27
	6	.13	.11	.12	.13	.33	· · ·	.26	.27
	7	.14	.27	.06	− .05	.30	.26	· · ·	.60
	8	.34	.26	.13	.00	.27	.27	.60	· · ·
Other/Ideal	1	· · ·	.70	.44	.37	.08	.05	.28	.37
	2	.70	· · ·	.34	.25	.08	.00	.26	.27
	3	.44	.34	· · ·	.62	.15	.04	.05	.17
	4	.37	.25	.62	· · ·	.15	.10	− .04	.01
	5	.08	.08	.15	.15	· · ·	.38	.38	.16
	6	.05	.00	.04	.10	.38	· · ·	.27	.28
	7	.28	.26	.05	− .04	.38	.27	· · ·	.56
	8	.37	.27	.17	.01	.16	.28	.56	· · ·

eight types of relationship. The types refer to the actual behavior of the respondent as ascribed to himself, i.e., they are identical with those of table 2, part 1, and table 4, part 1, respectively. General and sexual satisfactions with marriage were measured by two Guttman scales included in the questionnaires of both husband and wife.

General satisfaction with marriage correlates highest with social acceptance of the other and (lack of) social rejection of the other. Sexual satisfaction correlates highest with social and emotional acceptance of the other.

As we move away from the best neighbors of the two satisfaction variables, the correlations decrease regularly and then increase again when the best neighbors are approached from the other side of the circle. Thus the positioning of the eight variables on the circle determines their relationships with the two external variables. This finding suggests that the two satisfactions are situated in the same plane as the circle, but not necessarily on the circle itself. Indeed an attempt to fit the correlations of table 6 into the circumplex patterns of table 2, part 1 (for the responses of the wife) and table 4, part 1 (for the responses of the husband), respectively, did not produce satisfactory results; the two satisfactions do not seem to belong to the circle. The contrary would have been surprising, since the satisfactions differ conceptually from the behavioral variables of the circle. Their common feature is that both pertain to the interpersonal relation. Their common plane may perhaps be called the plane of the dyadic relationship. An interesting question is whether the two satisfactions are situated inside or outside the area delimited by the circle. The comparison of certain coefficients of correlation suggests that both satisfactions are within the circle. In this case they should correlate with the variables farthest from their best neighbors and *higher* than the best neighbors themselves, since the distance between a point inside the circle and any point on the circumference is always smaller than the diameter. This is what actually happens. For example, the two best neighbors of general satisfaction are social acceptance of the other and (lack of) social rejection of the other.

TABLE 6

INTERCORRELATIONS BETWEEN GENERAL AND SEXUAL SATISFACTIONS
AND THE EIGHT TYPES OF RELATIONSHIP

Respondent	Satisfaction	Types of Relationship							
		Acceptance				Rejection			
		Other		Self		Self		Other	
		Soc.	Em.	Em.	Soc.	Soc.	Em.	Em.	Soc.
Wife	General	.45	.39	.06	.09	.11	.28	.44	.45
	Sexual	.44	.42	.09	.12	.17	.27	.37	.41
Husband	General	.52	.47	.22	.11	.07	.24	.43	.57
	Sexual	.40	.39	.21	.12	.10	.19	.30	.37

The variables with the lowest correlation with these two are precisely those found on the opposite position on the circle: social rejection of self and social acceptance of self, respectively. The correlation of general satisfaction with these two last variables is always *higher* than the correlation between them and the best neighbors of general satisfaction. Thus general satisfaction occupies an intermediate position between opposite variables on the circle; i.e., it is inside the circle. The same is true for sexual satisfaction. The two satisfactions are fairly closely related to each other, the correlation being .64 for the wife and .58 for the husband.

These findings suggest that the circular structure can be used as a framework for determining the position of other variables that do not belong to the circle but pertain to the dyadic relationship.

4. Discussion and Conclusion

Let us now consider the possible significance of the findings and some of the problems they raise.

The eight types of relationship should be considered elementary components of behavior rather than concrete kinds of behavior. More than one type of relationship is likely to appear in the same act. The same behavioral act may well express the emotional relationship of the actor with himself and with the other, and, at the same time, may indicate the social position of each in the wider group. An act referring to the self alone or to the other alone, emotionally or socially, seems quite unusual. In fact, considerable difficulty was encountered in preparing questionnaire stories expressing only one of these components of behavior. Ordinary language tends to express these relationships in combination rather than separately. The richness of the vocabulary dealing with interpersonal relations is due to the fact that so many different combinations of relationships are possible and do actually occur. The fact that the eight relationships form a definite structure indicates, however, that certain combinations of relationships are more frequent than certain others. When, for example, we find a high correlation between emotional and social acceptance of the other, it may mean that these two components are likely to appear in the same act. Thus the frequency of a given act may, at least in part, be related to the contiguity of its components on the circular structure. This structure is based on three facets: Content (Acceptance—Rejection); Object (Self—Other), and Mode (Emotional—Social). The empirical results support the hypothesis of a circular order, thus indicating that these three facets are meaningful and provide a sound basis for the observation and analysis of interpersonal behavior. Many other classification schemes of behavior could be and have been suggested. The soundness of a scheme lies in its ability to predict empirical results.

The suggested order is provided by the successive dichotomization of the three facets: first, content; then, object; and finally, mode. This sequence may correspond to the sequence of development of these concepts in the child.

The hypothesis that discrimination between acceptance and rejection develops first seems to be supported by a number of considerations such as the following.

   a. Other facets of behavior, such as object, actor, and so on, cannot become meaningful before some elementary coding is developed for recording the content of the action, thus permitting the neonate to become an *observer*.
   b. Accepting and rejecting may be seen as a psychological equivalent of the physiological mechanisms of sucking and excreting, inhaling and exhaling.
   c. Studies of imprinting in animals [6, pp. 128–29] show that animals first develop the response of following (or accepting), later the response of flight (or rejecting), thus becoming capable of discriminating between objects to be accepted and objects to be rejected.

The dichotomy acceptance—rejection should not be confused with the dichotomy pleasure—pain. The first refers to behavior and the second to emotion. Both accepting and rejecting may give either pleasure or pain, depending on what is rejected or accepted.

The next discrimination seems to be between I and non-I (Self—Other) as *objects* of behavior. This discrimination is suggested by Piaget [5]. Piaget also suggests that at this stage the child does *not* discriminate between self and other as *actors*. For him there is no actor except himself. He is the cause of what is perceived.

The third discrimination, that between emotional and social modes, cannot appear before the child widens his social world from the dyadic relation with the mother to the larger group of the family.

A more complete theory of the sequence of development of concepts of interpersonal behavior in the child should also include facets such as actor, observer, alias, and level, which have been kept constant in the findings presented here. It is of interest at this point to note that the sequence of dichotomization of the facets in the order may correspond to the sequence of development of the facets during socialization. If so, the sequence is indicated by the order of the semantic principal components, the first component, content, developing first, followed by the second, object, and then by the fourth, mode.

It is also of interest that relationships differing only in the mode facet are precisely those having the highest coefficients of correlation. In this connection there is another problem that should be considered. The analysis presented here has been based on the coefficient of correlation between pairs of relationships. This coefficient expresses the monotonic relation between variables. Inspection of the joint occurrence tables shows, however, that some relations tend to be slightly U-shaped. This occurs when the variables differ in the content or the object facets rather than when they differ in the mode facet. The great majority of the respondents tend to be more accepting, the less rejecting they are. There exists, however, a minority with strong feelings of *both* acceptance and rejection. Likewise, most respondents tend to relate to themselves in a manner similar to their relationship to the other. A minority of respondents, however, tend to accept (or reject) themselves more strongly, the less they accept (or reject) the other. On the other hand, emotional and social relationships seem always to go together. The existence of these minorities suggests that the structure of their interpersonal behavior should be analyzed separately from that of the main group of respondents. The problem is, of course, to find a variable that will distinguish between these groups. When this is done, it may be possible to obtain intercorrelation tables with a better fit to the circumplex hypothesis. The tables obtained fit chiefly because the majority of the population belongs to a particular type.

Interestingly enough, conflicting relationships seem more likely to appear in relation to the content and object facets, which may have developed in an earlier stage, than in relation to the last developed one, the mode.

In conclusion, some of the main points suggested by the findings are as follows.

1. A new concept for ordering variables, the semantic principal component, has been introduced and its usefulness proved.
2. A close fitting of the theoretical and empirical structure of interpersonal behavior has been achieved, indicating that the proposed concepts are meaningful as well as parsimonious.
3. The circle of interpersonal behavior provides a starting point for extending the map of the interpersonal relations to include other variables such as general and sexual satisfactions.

REFERENCES

[1] FOA, U. G., The contiguity principle in the structure of interpersonal relations, *Hum. Relat.*, 1958, **11**(3), 229–38.
[2] FOA, U. G., Convergences in the analysis of the structure of interpersonal behavior, *Psychol. Rev.*, 1961, **68**(5), 341–53.
[3] FOA, U. G., "Dyadic interaction: theory and experiment," paper presented at the XVI International Congess of Psychology, Bonn, August 1960 (to be published in *Proceedings of the XVI International Congress of Psychology*).
[4] GUTTMAN, L., A new approach to factor analysis: the radex, chap. 6 in *Mathematical Thinking in the Social Sciences*, P. F. Lazarsfeld, ed., Glencoe, Ill.: Free Press, 1954.
[5] PIAGET, J., *The Construction of Reality in the Child*, New York: Basic Books, 1954.
[6] SOLLEY, C. M., and G. MURPHY, *Development of the Perceptual World*, New York: Basic Books, 1960.

12

Two-Alternative Learning in Interdependent Dyads

Robert L. Hall, *University of Minnesota*

A number of recent learning experiments have been conducted in two-person settings of greatly simplified social interaction (see [1]-[3], [8], [10]-[14]). The particular experimental task used by Atkinson and Suppes [1], [15] and by Burke [3] is an adaptation of the two-alternative predictive task commonly used in studies of individual probability learning (e.g., [4], [6], [7], [9]), and hence performance of this task lends itself readily to analysis by statistical learning theory. Pairs of subjects perform simultaneously for a considerable number of trials, predicting which of two lights will light up, with the outcome of each trial for each subject contingent upon the responses (predictions) of both. The form of this contingency is varied experimentally.

This paper reports a theoretical analysis of and an experiment on certain forms of contingency in this simplified interaction setting. The outcome of each trial in this study is fully determined by the pair of responses (one by each subject) that occurs on that trial. In other words, reinforcement of each subject is contingent upon the responses of both, and the conditional probabilities of reinforcing events, given a particular pair of responses, are either 1 or 0. The matrices of conditional probabilities of reinforcing events are varied experimentally for one subject in each dyad, leaving the matrix for the other subject constant in all conditions. The experimental conditions selected for study are all competitive, in the sense that both subjects in a dyad cannot be correct on the same trial, but they are not zero-sum, since it is possible in all conditions for both subjects to be incorrect on the same trial.

1. Experimental Design

One subject in each pair was designated A, and the other, A'. Following Burke's (1959) labeling [3], the two alternative responses for A were desig-

This investigation was supported in part by a grant from the Graduate School, University of Minnesota, and in part by research grant M-2472 from the National Institute of Mental Health, U. S. Public Health Service. Thanks are due D. LaBerge and S. Rosenberg for reading the manuscript, and Rochelle Johnson for assistance in the experiment.

nated A_1 and A_2, the outcome light corresponding to A_1 was called E_1, and the other outcome light, E_2. Hence A made response A_1 to predict outcome E_1, and A_2 to predict E_2. The responses and outcomes for A′ were similarly called A_1', A_2', E_1', and E_2'.

Each pair of subjects was assigned randomly to one of five sets of response–outcome contingencies, which remained constant over 380 trials. These conditions are summarized in table 1. Each conditional probability is either 1 or 0; in other words, each possible *pair* of responses is a sufficient condition for the occurrence of a particular reinforcing event. The five experimental conditions were created by varying the contingencies of outcome or response for A′, while leaving the response–outcome contingencies for A the same in all conditions. Specifically, the necessary and sufficient condition for A to be correct on any trial was the joint occurrence of A_1 and A_1' on that trial, and therefore the occurrence of A_1 was a necessary condition for A to be correct. In other words, when A made response A_2, outcome E_1 always occurred. When A made response A_1, he received outcome E_1 if A_1' occurred and outcome E_2 if A_2' occurred.

The necessary and sufficient conditions for A′ to be correct were different in each of the five experimental conditions, as shown in table 1. Also given in table 1 are the matrices of the conditional probabilities of occurrence of E_1 and E_1', in the form suggested by Burke.

2. Theoretical Analysis[1]

Since response A_2 is *never* followed by E_2, one line of reasoning would suggest that A_2 would extinguish, resulting in fixation on A_1, which is partially reinforced. This reasoning is based on the assumptions that success in prediction is the only important reinforcer in this situation and that an overt key press is the unit of behavior subject to learning.

On the other hand, if it is assumed that E_1 has the same effect no matter which response precedes it (one assumption underlying the linear model), the linear model of statistical learning theory [5], [6] might apply. Atkinson and Suppes [1] have extended the linear model with two-person, zero-sum game situations and have reported an experiment in such a situation. Burke has provided a general treatment of the application of the linear model to two-person situations and has reported research on several cases that meet the "diagonal-sums restriction" described by him. The experimental conditions of the present study, as described in table 1, are not zero-sum games, and they do not satisfy Burke's diagonal-sums restriction. However, it is possible to obtain limited predictions concerning asymptotic response probabilities of the two subjects and, with an additional assumption, to obtain exact predictions.

The general procedure for obtaining predictions for two-person situations has been described by Burke. The procedure will not be repeated in detail here but will be illustrated for Condition I (see equation 7), working from Burke's formulas.

[1] The author is indebted to C. J. Burke and S. Rosenberg for helpful suggestions on the theoretical analysis in this section.

TABLE 1

The Experimental Conditions

Condition	Necess. and Suff. Resp.		Cond. Prob.	
	A	A'	E_1	E_1'
I	$A_1 \wedge A_1'$	$A_1 \wedge A_2'$	$\begin{array}{c} & A_1' & A_2' \\ A_1 & [1^* & 0] \\ A_2 & [1 & 1] \end{array}$	$\begin{array}{c} & A_1' & A_2' \\ A_1 & [0 & 0^*] \\ A_2 & [0 & 1] \end{array}$
II	$A_1 \wedge A_1'$	$A_2 \wedge A_1'$	$\begin{array}{c} & A_1' & A_2' \\ A_1 & [1^* & 0] \\ A_2 & [1 & 1] \end{array}$	$\begin{array}{c} & A_1' & A_2' \\ A_1 & [0 & 1] \\ A_2 & [1^* & 1] \end{array}$
III	$A_1 \wedge A_1'$	$A_2 \wedge A_2'$	$\begin{array}{c} & A_1' & A_2' \\ A_1 & [1^* & 0] \\ A_2 & [1 & 1] \end{array}$	$\begin{array}{c} & A_1' & A_2' \\ A_1 & [0 & 1] \\ A_2 & [0 & 0^*] \end{array}$
IV	$A_1 \wedge A_1'$	$(A_1 \wedge A_2') \vee (A_2 \wedge A_1')$	$\begin{array}{c} & A_1' & A_2' \\ A_1 & [1^* & 0] \\ A_2 & [1 & 1] \end{array}$	$\begin{array}{c} & A_1' & A_2' \\ A_1 & [0 & 0^*] \\ A_2 & [1^* & 1] \end{array}$
V	$A_1 \wedge A_1'$	A_2	$\begin{array}{c} & A_1' & A_2' \\ A_1 & [1^* & 0] \\ A_2 & [1 & 1] \end{array}$	$\begin{array}{c} & A_1' & A_2' \\ A_1 & [0 & 1] \\ A_2 & [1^* & 0^*] \end{array}$

* Indicates response combinations for which subject's outcome is "correct."

The conditional probabilities in the matrices for Condition I (table 1) may be substituted in Burke's formulas [3, eq. (9)], which then simplify to:

$$(1) \qquad p_{n+1} = p_n \theta(\overline{p_n p'_n} - 2p_n + 1),$$

$$(2) \qquad p'_{n+1} = p'_n + \theta'(\overline{p_n p'_n} - 2p'_n - p_n + 1),$$

where p_{n+1} is the mean expected probability of A_1 on trial $n + 1$, p_n is the mean expected probability of A_1 on trial n, $\overline{p_n p'_n}$ is the mean expected probability of joint occurrence of A_1 and A'_1 on trial n, θ is the usual parameter for learning rate or stimulus sampling, and the corresponding values for A' are $p'_{n+1}, \overline{p_n p'_n}$, and θ', respectively.

Asymptotic probabilities are then obtained by setting $p_{n+1} = p_n = p$ and $p'_{n+1} = p'_n = p'$. Since θ and θ' are nonzero, it follows that the terms in parentheses must equal zero. That is, letting p and p' be the mean asymptotic probabilities of A_1 and A'_1, respectively, and letting $\overline{pp'}$ be the mean asymptotic probability of the joint occurrence of A_1 and A'_1, it follows that

$$(3) \qquad \overline{pp'} - 2p + 1 = 0,$$

and

$$(4) \qquad \overline{pp'} - p - 2p' + 1 = 0.$$

From these equations it can be shown that, at asymptote, the mean response probabilities of both subjects will match the probabilities of corresponding outcome events; i.e., $p = \hat{\pi}$ and $p' = \hat{\pi}'$, where $\hat{\pi}$ and $\hat{\pi}'$ are the mean asymptotic probabilities of occurrence of E_1, respectively.[2] By reference to the matrices in table 1 that define the experimental condition, the equations for $\hat{\pi}$ and $\hat{\pi}'$, in terms of response probabilities, can be written

$$(5) \qquad \hat{\pi} = \overline{pp'} + (1 - p),$$

and

$$(6) \qquad \hat{\pi}' = 1 - (p + p' - \overline{pp'}).$$

A simple rearrangement of terms in equations (3) and (4) then shows that $p = \hat{\pi}$ and $p' = \hat{\pi}$; this condition holds for *all five* experimental conditions. Equations (1), (3), and (5) also apply in all five experimental conditions.

Subtracting equation (3) from equation (4) also yields a prediction of a simple linear relation between mean asymptotic response probabilities of the two subjects, namely, Condition I:

$$(7) \qquad p = 2p'.$$

Intervals within which p and p' fall are established by using the inequalities

$$(8) \qquad 0 \leq \overline{pp'} \leq p' < p < 1,$$

and by rewriting equation (3) in the form

---

[2] The circumflex is a reminder that $\hat{\pi}$ and $\hat{\pi}'$ are determined by the responses of the two subjects, while π in most experiments is programmed by the experimenter.

(9) $p = \overline{pp'}/2 + 1/2$,

which implies $p \geq 1/2$. Substituting in (9) yields $p \leq p'/2 + 1/2$, and therefore, by reference to equation (7), $p \leq p/4 + 1/2$, or $p \leq 2/3$. Thus in Condition I the intervals and relation between p and p' are established as

(I) $1/2 \leq p \leq 2/3$, $1/4 \leq p' = \leq 1/3$, and $p = 2p'$.

Similar procedures yield predictions for Conditions II, III, IV, and V, as follows:

(II) $2/3 \leq p \leq 3/4$, $1/2 \leq p' \leq 2/3$, and $p' = 2(1 - p)$;

(III and IV) $1/2 \leq p \leq 3/4$, $1/4 \leq p' \leq 1/2$, and $p + p' = 1$;

(V) $p = 2/3$, $1/3 \leq p' \leq 2/3$, and $\overline{pp'} = 1/3$.

From equations such as (3) and (4), it is apparent that the difficulty in solving to obtain exact theoretical values for p and p' rests in the fact that the expected cross-product term $\overline{pp'}$ has not been evaluated. Exact theoretical values can be obtained by making a simplifying assumption about this term. Therefore the assumption is made that within each condition,

(10) $\overline{pp'} = pp'$.

That is, the assumption is that after many trials the mean probability of joint occurrence of A_1 and A_1' is the product of the mean probabilities of their separate occurrence.

Departures from this assumption, such that $\overline{pp'} > pp'$, would occur (a) if the probabilities p and p' are positively correlated over the pairs of subjects within a condition, which might occur as a consequence of the particular outcome matrices, or (b) if the occurrences of A_1 and A_1' are positively correlated on the average within pairs, which might occur as a consequence of systematic response sequences by one subject that are discriminable for the other subject. Negative correlation of either kind tends to make $\overline{pp'} < pp'$. However, if condition (b) were the case, assumptions of the linear model would be violated. The reasonableness of assumption (10) in the present conditions will be assessed below.

Adopting assumption (10), equations (3) and (4) then become

$$pp' - 2p + 1 = 0 , \quad \text{and} \quad pp' - 2p' - p + 1 = 0 .$$

The substitution of equation (7) in these equations yields a quadratic equation in p and a quadratic equation in p', namely

$$p^2/2 - 2p + 1 = 0 , \quad \text{and} \quad 2(p')^2 - 4p' + 1 = 0 ,$$

which solve to $p = .59$ and $p' = .29$. But for rounding to two decimal places, these predicted values satisfy the weaker prediction expressed in (7).

An analogous procedure for each of the other experimental conditions yields predictions of p and p' as given in columns (a) and (f) of table 3 below, assuming that $\overline{pp'} = pp'$. It may be noted that these predictions fall approximately at the midpoints of the respective intervals of p and p' in each condition, as derived above from the linear model alone.

3. Monte Carlo Trials

Monte Carlo trials were run in each experimental condition primarily to assess the validity of the simplifying assumption (10). The Monte Carlo trials also served to provide the only available estimate of the theoretical variability of asymptotic response probabilities and an additional estimate of the means.

A Univac 1103 scientific computer was coded to behave in accordance with the model and the conditions of this study[3]. Since the validity of assumption (10) and the variability of asymptotic probabilities both depend upon the size of θ and θ', two values of these parameters were selected. The value .05 was selected as a reasonable estimate, and .50 was selected as a very high estimate (see [1, p. 376]). All four combinations of θ and θ' values using .05 and .50 were run within each experimental condition. Since Conditions I and II are identical as systems, except for labeling of subjects and responses, Condition II was omitted from the Monte Carlo trials. Hence there were four experimental conditions and four combinations of θ and θ', for a total of 16 cells. Within each cell, 60 pairs of stat-subjects were run. Results are given in table 2.

Comparing $\overline{pp'}$ and pp' in table 2, it is evident that discrepancies are small, especially for small values of θ and θ'. Within each of the sixteen cells a t test was conducted to determine whether $\overline{pp'}$ departed significantly from pp' at the .05 level. Only in one cell (III, $\theta = \theta' = .50$) was the departure statistically significant. From equation (9), which is valid in all five conditions, it is apparent that the magnitude of error in theoretical p, introduced by using assumption (10), will equal $\frac{1}{2}(\overline{pp'} - pp')$. For a "reasonable" value (.05) of θ, this error never exceeds .005 in the Monte Carlo trials, while for very large $\theta(.50)$, the error ranges from about .002 to .025. Hence for a reasonable value of θ it appears that if assumption (10) introduces any error, the error is minor. As further confirmation of the adequacy of assumption (10) for practical purposes, only one of the 16 Monte Carlo p values in table 2 differs significantly ($p < .05$) from the corresponding estimate using the assumption, and that one (III, $\theta = .05, \theta' = .50$) differs in magnitude by only about .01.

4. Experimental Procedure

Experimental data were obtained in the conditions described above with eight pairs of subjects in each of the five conditions. The subjects were 80

---

[3] The coding of the computer was performed jointly by the author and David Campbell. We are indebted to the Numerical Analysis Center, University of Minnesota, for making computer time available.

TABLE 2

MONTE CARLO ESTIMATES OF THEORETICAL PROBABILITIES

($N = 60$ in each cell)

Condition	θ	θ'	Asymptotic Probability						Product pp'
			A_1		A_1'		$A_1 \wedge A_1'$		
			Mean (p)	σ	Mean (p')	σ	Mean (pp')	σ	
I	.05	.05	.571	.075	.292	.059	.169	.049	.167
	.05	.50	.596	.067	.288	.218	.175	.134	.172
	.50	.50	.614	.221	.336	.218	.229	.175	.206
	.50	.05	.578	.238	.290	.048	.171	.083	.168
III	.05	.05	.614	.055	.386	.055	.234	.012	.237
	.05	.50	.609	.031	.399	.198	.241	.116	.243
	.50	.50	.584	.224	.416	.224	.194	.053	.243
	.50	.05	.592	.255	.384	.044	.220	.084	.227
IV	.05	.05	.623	.076	.387	.063	.244	.060	.241
	.05	.50	.616	.068	.432	.293	.276	.195	.266
	.50	.50	.614	.239	.389	.267	.274	.233	.239
	.50	.05	.650	.252	.374	.049	.248	.109	.243
V	.05	.05	.658	.054	.511	.060	.335	.038	.336
	.05	.50	.670	.052	.582	.266	.382	.166	.390
	.50	.50	.625	.187	.591	.228	.352	.166	.369
	.50	.05	.647	.233	.499	.064	.320	.116	.323

undergraduates, predominantly sophomores, who signed up for added credit in their classes in introductory psychology.

Each subject was seated in a separate booth with walls 5 ft high so that subjects could not see one another. Subjects were used four at a time in most instances but two at a time in a few cases. On a shelf in front of each subject was a $13\frac{1}{2} \times 9$ in. panel. At the top of the panel were two white lights 1 in. in diameter (the outcome lights) with their centers 9 in. apart. At the bottom center of the panel was a spring-centering, lever-type switch, mounted so that it could be pushed to the right or left. Immediately above the switch was another white light (the signal light). Subjects were randomly assigned to conditions with a counter-balancing of right and left.

Standard instructions, read to all subjects, said (1) that the signal light would be followed on each trial by either the right or left light; (2) that subject should guess which light would go on and indicate his guess by pushing his switch; (3) that subject should keep trying and should make as many correct guesses as possible; and, finally, (4) "You will be working with another person throughout the experiment. The way the other person moves his switch may help or hinder *your* guess, and you may help or hinder his guess. You may neither talk to your partner nor see him, but what he does may make a difference in the number of correct guesses you get."

The instructions were followed by 380 automatically timed trials. Each trial consisted of the following: (1) a 2-sec interval during which the signal light was on, and subjects made their responses, (2) a $\frac{1}{2}$-sec interval during which either the right or left light was on, (3) a $\frac{1}{2}$-sec inter-trial interval.

Since only 2 secs were allowed for responses to be made on each trial, there were some trials on which subject failed to respond within the interval, and there were also a few cases in which subject made both right and left responses. Since 80 subjects were given 380 trials each, there were 30,400 possible responses. Of these, 230 were "missed," or about 3/4 per cent of all responses. Of the 230, 17 were early, 153 were late, 15 were double (both right and left), and there were 45 cases of no response. The maximum number of missed responses for a pair of subjects used in the experiment was a sum of 16 for the two subjects.

In addition to the 40 pairs reported in the experimental data, 14 pairs of subjects were run in the experiment and excluded from data analysis: 10 of these pairs because of apparatus failures, three pairs because subject violated instructions blatantly by holding his switch closed over many trials and switching it back and forth during the S^r interval (which caused erratic behavior of the apparatus), and one pair because their 18 missed responses exceeded the arbitrarily imposed limit of 16.

5. Experimental Results

Predictions concerning mean asymptotic response probabilities were tested by computing the mean proportion of A_1 and A_1' responses on trials 281 through 380 for the eight pairs in each condition. These obtained values of p and p' are shown in columns (b) and (g) of table 3. In computing all asymptotic response probabilities, only trials with one and only one response

TABLE 3
RESPONSE AND OUTCOME PROBABILITIES ON LAST 100 TRIALS
($N = 8$ in each cell)

Condition	Response A_1			Outcome E_1		Response A_1'			Outcome E_1'	
	Pred. Mean*	Obt. Mean	Obt. σ	Obt. $\hat{\pi}$	σ	Pred. Mean*	Obt. Mean	Obt. σ	Obt. $\hat{\pi}$	σ
	a	b	c	d	e	f	g	h	i	j
I	.59	.65	.142	.43	.150	.29	.14	.072	.27	.102
II	.71	.81	.095	.67	.109	.59	.58	.149	.52	.191
III	.62	.72	.179	.50	.062	.38	.27	.152	.50	.065
IV	.62	.66	.144	.52	.198	.38	.30	.178	.35	.145
V	.67	.72	.147	.60	.091	.50	.43	.180	.52	.050

* This prediction requires assumption (10), explained in text.

by each S within the response interval were included. If all responses (even early and late ones) are included, nine of the ten obtained means reported in table 3 are unchanged, and p' for Condition V increases by .01. Also given in table 3 are the obtained $\hat{\pi}$ (mean proportion of E_1 outcomes for A) and the obtained $\hat{\pi}'$, (mean proportion of E_1' outcomes for A'), both based on the last 100 trials.

The linear model without further assumption predicts $p = \hat{\pi}$ and $p' = \hat{\pi}'$ within each condition. An inspection of results for A subjects in table 3 reveals [comparing columns (b) and (d)] that $p > \hat{\pi}$ in each of the five conditions. An analysis of variance of the individual discrepancies between response probability and outcome probability reveals p significantly larger than $\hat{\pi}$ ($F = 20.5$; df $= 1$, 35; $p < .001$) and no difference among conditions in the magnitude of the discrepancy ($F < 1$; df $= 4$, 35).

The matrix of conditional outcome probabilities for A subjects is the same in all five conditions, and A_1 is the only response that is ever "correct." Hence the A subjects give the response that can be "correct" more often than would be the case if they were matching the probability of E_1.

A quasi-replication of this result is available in three conditions by examining results for the other member of each dyad. That is, for the A' subjects in Conditions I to III, as for all A subjects, only one of the alternative responses can ever be correct. In each of these conditions the discrepancy between response probability and outcome probability for each subject was computed. Signs of these discrepancies were assigned so that a positive discrepancy meant that the probability of the response that is a necessary condition for the subject to be correct exceeded the probability of the corresponding outcome. Hence the discrepancies were $p' - \hat{\pi}'$ in Condition II, and $\hat{\pi}' - p'$ in Conditions I and III. An analysis of variance of these discrepancies reveals the response probability significantly larger than would be predicted by probability matching ($F = 9.7$; df $= 1$, 21; $p < .01$), and no difference among conditions in the magnitude of the discrepancy ($F = 1.2$; df $= 2$, 21). Hence the result for those A' subjects for whom only one response can be correct is identical with the result for A subjects.

For Conditions IV and V, where both A' responses can be correct, the obtained values of p' and $\hat{\pi}'$ were compared by F tests. There was no significant difference between p' and $\hat{\pi}'$, nor between the two conditions.

The linear model, together with assumption (10), predicts exact mean asymptotic probabilities of A_1 as given in column (a) of table 3. In each of the five conditions this prediction underestimates the obtained mean reported in column (b), though for both p and p' the rank order agreement between prediction and data is good. An analysis of variance of the individual discrepancies between obtained and theoretical p reveals a significant over-all discrepancy ($F = 9.9$; df $= 1$, 35; $p < .01$) and no difference among conditions in the magnitude of the discrepancy ($F < 1$; df $= 4$, 35).

As above, for the prediction of probability matching a quasi-replication is obtained on A' subjects in Conditions I, II, and III. As before, the signs of the discrepancies were so assigned that a positive discrepancy meant an excess above prediction of the response that is a necessary condition for subject to be correct. An analysis of variance reveals a significant over-all positive discrepancy ($F = 10.1$; df $= 1$, 21; $p < .01$) and no significant difference among the three conditions in the magnitude of the discrepancy ($F = 3.3$; df $= 2$, 21; $.05 < p < .10$), which is the same as the result for A subjects.

In Conditions IV and V, where both A' responses can be correct, the obtained mean probability was below prediction. An analysis of variance of the discrepancies shows no significant over-all departure from prediction ($F = 3.2$; df $= 1$, 14; $.05 < p < .10$) and no significant difference between the two conditions in the magnitude of the discrepancy ($F = 3.3$; df $= 1$, 14; $.05 < p < .10$).

It might be noted, comparing tables 2 and 3, that the Monte Carlo values of p are equal to or less than the values predicted by using assumption (10). Hence departures of obtained p from the Monte Carlo values are also significant.

As suggested above, one line of reasoning would predict that A subjects would fix on A_1, the only response ever "correct." Out of the 40 A subjects, only one (in Condition III) was fixated for the last 100 trials. Three A subjects (one each in I, II, and III) were fixated for the last 20 trials, but one of these fixated on A_2—the response *never* correct.

The Monte Carlo trials provided estimates of the theoretical standard deviations of asymptotic response probabilities, as reported in table 2. The corresponding observed values are reported in table 3. In both tables, σ refers to the estimate of population variability. The observed σ is invariably larger than the theoretical σ for "reasonable" θ and invariably smaller than the σ for "large" θ. All 8 comparisons for σ_p with $\theta = .05$ are significant by the F-test ($p < .01$, two-tailed). None of the 8 for σ_p with $\theta = .50$ is significant at the .05 level. Of the 8 comparisons for σ_p, with $\theta' = .05$, the two in Condition I are non-significant, and the remaining 6 are significant. Of the 8 comparisons for $\sigma_{p'}$ with $\theta' = .50$, only the two in Condition I are significant.

6. Discussion

The response–outcome contingencies studied in this paper have some peculiar features. First, for all A and most A' subjects, only one of the two alternative responses is *ever* "correct"—in the sense of being followed by the corresponding outcome light. Second, $\hat{\pi}$ is inversely geared to p, so to speak. That is, the outcomes are contingent upon the responses of both subjects in such a way that, in general, a very high probability (p) of the potentially correct response by one subject is likely to result in a lower probability ($\hat{\pi}$) of the corresponding outcome because of the second response.

Under these conditions, the mean asymptotic response probabilities depart significantly from probability matching, and from predicted levels, in the direction of performing the response that can be correct. However, the alternative that is never "correct" does not, in general, extinguish. The mean probability p always falls between the level predicted by the linear model and 1.0. This is in contrast to results reported by Burke for other two-person conditions, in which mean probabilities generally fell between predicted levels and 0.5.

The linear model does not predict mean asymptotic probabilities in this experiment very well. The results would be accounted for if E_1 following A_1 has greater reinforcing effect than E_1 following A_2—which would be a change in a basic assumption of the linear model. However, such a change to patch up the model has little meaning without a more general model that can predict the circumstances under which the effects are different and the magnitude of the difference.

Variability of terminal response probabilities was greater than for those the linear model predicts for θ and θ' of .05. This is similar to the findings of Atkinson and Suppes [1] for quite different response–outcome contingencies. However, unlike the Atkinson and Suppes study, the present study found variability did *not* exceed predictions for θ and θ' of .50. It may be that values of θ in two-person contingent situations will generally be higher than the .02 to .10 often found in one-person, non-contingent situations. Possibly θ may increase as a consequence of discriminable changes in $\hat{\pi}$ over time.

It is interesting to note the theoretical predictions for this study that would be generated by the Markov learning model recently developed by Suppes and Atkinson [15]. Their one-element model makes the same prediction of asymptotic probability matching, $p = \hat{\pi}$ and $p' = \hat{\pi}'$, as is predicted by the linear model. This prediction was shown to be empirically false in the present study. That model also predicts the same linear relations between asymptotic p and p' for Conditions I, II, III, and IV, as given above, and the same asymptotic values in Condition V, namely $p = 2/3$, $1/3 \leq p \leq 2/3$, and $\overline{pp'} = 1/3$.

With the additional assumption that $\theta_A = \theta_B$, that is, that the learning rates of the two subjects within each pair are equal, bounds can be established on asymptotic p and p' that correspond closely to those established above by the linear model but that are narrower for Conditions I, II, III, and IV. The intervals are as follows:

$$
\begin{array}{lll}
\text{I} & 4/7 \leq p \leq 2/3 & 2/7 \leq p' \leq 1/3 \\
\text{II} & 2/3 \leq p \leq 5/7 & 4/7 \leq p' \leq 2/3 \\
\text{III} & 1/2 \leq p \leq 2/3 & 1/3 \leq p' \leq 1/2 \\
\text{IV} & 3/5 \leq p \leq 2/3 & 1/3 \leq p' \leq 2/5
\end{array}
$$

From table 3, columns (b) and (g), it may be noted that obtained p in two of the four cases is outside the interval, and obtained p' is outside in three out of four cases.

The phenomenon of asymptotic probability matching has been observed in numerous experiments and is built into many theoretical models of simple learning. Under the particular conditions of the present study, probability matching did not occur.

7. Summary

Eighty subjects performed for 380 trials at the usual two-alternative predictive task of probability-learning experiments. The outcome events for each subject were determined by his own responses *and* the responses of another simultaneously performing subject in such a way that both could not be correct on the same trial. Eight pairs of subjects performed in each of five different conditions defined by the conditional probabilities of outcome events, given a particular pair of responses. For both subjects in three conditions, and one subject in the other two conditions, the performance of one of the alternatives is a necessary condition for the subject to be "correct"; i.e., only one response is ever followed on the same trial by the corresponding outcome.

The linear model of statistical learning theory predicts that, at asymptote, the mean response probabilities will match the probabilities of corresponding outcomes in each condition. The one-element Markov learning model makes the same prediction. The response probabilities departed significantly from the outcome probabilities in such a way that the response that can be correct occurred more often than its corresponding outcomes. This departure was not significantly different in different conditions.

With an added assumption that was found reasonable in Monte Carlo trials, the linear model makes exact quantitative predictions of mean asymptotic response probabilities in each condition. Obtained mean response probabilities follow roughly the predicted rank order but depart systematically and significantly in the direction of the response that is necessary for a "correct" outcome of the trial.

Variances of terminal response probabilities were predicted by Monte Carlo trials on the linear model for two different assumed values of the parameter θ. Observed variances in all conditions fell between the value predicted for $\theta = .05$ and the value predicted for $\theta = .50$.

REFERENCES

[1] ATKINSON, R. C., and P. SUPPES, An analysis of two-person game situations in terms of statistical learning theory, *J. Exptl. Psychol.*, 1958, **55**, 369-78.

[2] AZRIN, N. H., and O. R. LINDSLEY, The reinforcement of cooperation between children, *J. Abnorm. Soc. Psychol.*, 1956, **52**, 100-2.

[3] BURKE, C. J., Applications of a linear model to two-person interactions, chap. 9 in *Studies in Mathematical Learning Theory*, R. R. Bush and W. K. Estes, eds., Stanford, Calif.: Stanford Univ. Press, 1959.

[4] ESTES, W. K., Of models and men, *Amer. Psychologist*, 1957, **12**, 609-17.

[5] ESTES, W. K., and C. J. BURKE, A theory of stimulus variability in learning, *Psychol. Rev.*, 1953, **60**, 276-86.

[6] ESTES, W. K., and J. H. STRAUGHAN, Analysis of a verbal conditioning situation in terms of statistical learning theory, *J. Exptl. Psychol.*, 1954, **47**, 225-34.

[7] GRANT, D. A., H. W. HAKE, and J. P. HORNSETH, Acquisition and extinction of a verbal conditioned response with differing percentages of reinforcement, *J. Exptl. Psychol.*, 1951, **42**, 1-5.

[8] HALL, R. L., Group performance under feedback that confounds responses of group members, *Sociometry*, 1957, **20**, 297–305.

[9] NEIMARK, E. D., Effects of type of nonreinforcement and number of alternative responses in two verbal conditioning situations, *J. Exptl. Psychol.*, 1956, **52**, 209–20.

[10] ROSENBERG, S., The maintenance of a learned response in controlled interpersonal conditions, *Sociometry*, 1959, **22**, 124–38.

[11] ROSENBERG, S., Cooperative behavior in dyads as a function of reinforcement parameters, *J. Abnorm. Soc. Psychol.*, 1960, **60**, 318–33.

[12] ROSENBERG, S., and R. L. HALL, The effects of different social feedback conditions upon performance in dyadic teams, *J. Abnorm. Soc. Psychol.*, 1958, **57**, 271–77.

[13] SIDOWSKI, J. B., Reward and punishment in a minimal social situation, *J. Exptl. Psychol.*, 1957, **54**, 318–26.

[14] SIDOWSKI, J. B., L. B. WYCKOFF, and L. TABORY, The influence of reinforcement and punishment in a minimal social situation, *J. Abnorm. Soc. Psychol.*, 1956, **52**, 115–19.

[15] SUPPES, P., and R. C. ATKINSON, *Markov Learning Models for Multiperson Interactions*, Stanford, Calif.: Stanford Univ. Press, 1960.

13

Some Aspects of Power in Small Groups

Georg Karlsson, *Uppsala University*

Power is one of the most important social phenomena. For many years social philosophers have pondered on the problems of social power. More recently, many social scientists have tried to define the concept of power in such a way that it can be used in empirical research. In spite of all these attempts, I think it is fair to say that no really satisfactory definition of power has so far been suggested, and that the potential uses of the concept in social research have been only partially realized.

I shall not try to solve all problems relating to power in this paper. I shall instead discuss the intuitive meaning of power and suggest a definition of social power. I shall also apply this definition to some models and theories of power that are already in existence, and show some further uses of the concept.

1. Definition of Power

The term "power" as used in everyday language has an intuitive meaning. For our purpose, we must capture as much as possible of this intuitive meaning in a precise definition, at least if we have no theoretical reasons to depart from the established meaning, and I see no such reasons at present.

There are two aspects of the intuitive meaning of power that I should like to stress in particular. First, power is a dispositional concept in the sense of Carnap [3]; i.e., it is an attribute that characterizes a person throughout a given period of time, but it can be observed only under special circumstances. A person may have power over another person even if he does not exercise his power. Second, power is different from influence. The powerful person must be able to inflict some damage or punishment to or withdraw some reward from the person he has power over in case the latter does not yield to the powerful person [11]. Thus power is the ability to influence because undesirable consequences would follow for the influenced person if he does not yield. This requirement rules out many otherwise valuable definitions, e.g., the one given by Dahl [4], which in my terminology is a definition of influence.

Let us define *elementary power* as an attribute that characterizes an individual (or a position in a group) in relation to another individual (or position). Given this basic concept, we can define a concept of *extended power* in relation to a set of individuals (positions). This latter concept is restricted to members of the same group. In this paper no attempt is made to go beyond this restriction.

Suppose that we have a group of n members. Time is discrete, divided into equal periods $t_0, t_1, t_2, \cdots$. During each period the group members do something. Their behaviors are denoted by $a_1, a_2, \cdots, a_n$; if necessary, by $a_1(t_j), \cdots, a_n(t_j)$. The result of the behavior of the group members during a period, $x(t_j)$, is some function of these activities:

$$(1) \qquad x(t_j) = g(a_1(t_j), \cdots, a_n(t_j)) \ .$$

It is assumed that there exists for each group member a utility function

$$(2) \qquad u_i(t_j) = u_i(x(t_j)) \ ,$$

which determines completely his evaluation of the group result and his consequent activities and which does not change during the time the group is studied. Given such utility functions, we can skip the result x and define the vector of u's as a function of the vector of a's:

$$(3) \qquad u(t_j) = f(a(t_j)) \ .$$

For brevity we will refer to the utilities as u_i, etc., henceforth.

Consider two group members i and j. There is a set of group acts $\{a\}$ such that members other than i or j will not change their behavior (i.e., it is constant or shows variations that do not influence u_i and u_j), and j chooses his acts so as to maximize u_j. Under these circumstances i can choose from the set available to him acts which make u_j vary. He will choose only those acts that keep u_i above a certain level u_i^*. Otherwise he will do himself a disservice. Among the other acts there is one (or more) that results in the highest u_j, and one or more that results in the lowest u_j. These u_j's are denoted $u_{ij\max}$ and $u_{ij\min}$, respectively. The *elementary power* of person i over person j is now defined as the difference between these extreme utilities:

$$(4) \qquad p_{ij} = u_{ij\max} - u_{ij\min} \ .$$

This definition of elementary power is limited in several ways. It is relative to the group for which the group products are computed. It presupposes constant behavior levels of all group members except i and j. It does not include indirect power, i.e., power wielded over a group member k via power over l, m, and others. Power through coalitions of two or more members is not included. Finally, person j may have elementary power over person i. The important thing then is the relative elementary power [11] of i over j. Several of these complications will be discussed later in the paper.

Given the elementary power p_{ij} we can define a person's *group power* as the sum of his elementary powers in the group, $\Sigma_{j=1}^{n} p_{ij} = p_i$. The power structure of the group is given by the matrix $[p_{ij}]$. Sometimes more compact expressions of the power structure are desirable. One such is the vector (p_i) of group powers of the group members. The power structure can also be characterized by the mean group power of the individuals $\sum_{i=1}^{n} p_i/n = \bar{p}$. We may also want to compute the variance of the power distribution

$$\frac{\sum (p_i - \bar{p})^2}{n} \, ,$$

which gives a measure of the degree of inequality of the power distribution.

The elementary power expresses how much punishment one person can inflict upon another, but it does not tell us how strongly motivated he is to exercise his power. The exercising of power consists in making the other person behave as the person with power wishes, i.e., in influencing his behavior. The motivation of the powerful person must be related to the utility he himself derives from the group activities. Let us say that his motivation is proportional to the difference between the u_i that he receives when j performs the a_j that is the best i can make him do and the u_i that would result otherwise:

(5) $$m_{ij} = b_i(u_{ji\max} - u_{ji\text{neut}}) \, .$$

The situation is complicated at this point by the fact already mentioned, that if i has power over j, so may j have power over i. The relative power of the two persons obviously influences what i can make j do, i.e., $u_{i\max}$. The relative power may operate in two ways, both of which are intuitively reasonable and may be assumed to occur in different situations. One is that the person with the greatest relative power completely dominates the relationship and exercises the influence that his elementary power entitles him to. The person with the smaller relative power has no motivation to exercise his power at all.

The other situation occurs when the two persons bargain some way and reach some sort of agreement on how much they will be allowed to influence each other's behavior. The actual exercising of power so far as two persons are concerned is thus determined by m_{ij}, which in turn is partially determined by the relative power between the two. The set of a_j's that i can make j perform to determine $u_{i\max}$ and the extent to which i can force his wishes upon j are partially determined by the power of i and j. Thus a person's motivation to exercise his elementary power depends on the amount of his power, which is as it should be.

We have so far treated pairs of group members in isolation. Actually this is a great simplification. The power relations in a group are in general determined by an intricate web of subgroups. We shall call these subgroups *coalitions* and consider their effects in some detail. First, however, I want to discuss the simpler case of no coalitions and some models based on this assumption.

For a theory of power in small groups as here conceived, the problem is to describe and explain the position of different individuals in given power structures, and to describe and explain the exercise of power in groups with given power structures. The theory can be developed for the simple case of no coalitions, and it becomes further complicated when coalitions are introduced.

The basic definitions that have been introduced are on a purely theoretical level. No attempts have been made to furnish operational counterparts to the theoretical definitions. For example, it is assumed that a utility function exists for each individual, but no way of measuring these utilities is indicated. I feel that it is justifiable to do some theorizing on this level to make clear what it is one would need to measure in order to test the theory to see if it includes the important variables. But some consideration should also be given to the empirical side of the theory. Therefore we will consider next a simple special case which can be tested empirically.

2. Peck Orders and Related Models

Rapoport and Landau [5]–[10] have discussed at length the properties of peck orders and dominance relations in animal groups. Their theories can be formulated as a special case of social-power relations.

Consider a group of n members. During each time period each member meets all the other members, one at a time, and fights them. In the encounter between group members i and j, the behavior a_{ij} of i can take two values:

w_j if i fights j and wins,

l_j if i fights j and loses.

The behavior a_i during a period is the vector (a_{ij}), $j = 1, \cdots, n$, $i \neq j$. The a_{ji}'s are the inverse of the a_{ij}'s; that is, $w_j = l_i$ and $l_j = w_i$.

Suppose that $u_i = \Sigma_j u_{ij}$, where $u_{ij} = 1$ if $a_{ij} = w_j$ and $u_{ij} = 0$ if $a_{ij} = l_j$. Suppose further that w_j implies that i might choose l_j instead, but l_j implies that i might not choose w_j. We then have

$$\text{(6)} \qquad p_{ij} = \begin{cases} 1 & \text{if } a_{ij} = w_j, \\ 0 & \text{if } a_{ij} = l_j. \end{cases}$$

Since the behaviors are reciprocal, the relative power equals p_{ij}. In this case i's exercise of his power over j is the same as w_j. The only behaviors in the group that matter are the exercise of power. The motivation of i to exercise his power over j thus is directly proportional to p_{ij}:

$$\text{(7)} \qquad m_{ij} = k_i p_{ij} \qquad k_i > 0,$$

which is 0 when he loses the encounter and k_i when he wins. Thus he will always choose to win if he can.

The power matrix of such a group will then contain 1's or 0's in the cells. Rapoport and Landau's matrices of dominance relations are such matrices. Their theories are applicable to groups in which the power relations have been defined in this simplified manner. It is easy to define their descriptive measures in our more general terms. Their score structure is given by the p_i's. The mean power in this special case is $(n-1)/2$. Thus the variance becomes

$$\frac{\sum\{p_i - [(n-1)/2]\}^2}{n} .$$

If we multiply the power variance by $12/(n^2 - 1)$, we get the hierarchy index h developed by Landau.

A more general case is the following. Let us denote the relative power of person i over person j by

(8) $$r_{ij} = p_{ij} - p_{ji} .$$

Suppose that when r_{ij} is greater than a certain value r_{ij}^* (a characteristic of j) j will always do as i wishes. Suppose also that the r_{ij}'s are independent of what the other group members do or that neither i nor j can influence the behavior of the other group members. Otherwise there are no restrictions on the behavior in the group.

In such a case the dominance structure of the group can be described by a matrix $[d_{ij}]$ with entries 1 if $r_{ij} > r_{ij}^*$, 0 if both $r_{ij} \leq r_{ij}^*$ and $r_{ji} \leq r_{ji}^*$, and -1 if $r_{ji} > r_{ji}^*$. This dominance matrix looks only slightly more complicated than the power matrix of a peck order. If we assume that a dominant person will always exercise his power, it will even result in the same kind of behavior as that occurring in a peck order but without the fights which are assumed to occur regularly in a peck-order group. Since we have no restrictions on the utility functions f_i, the motivations will be more complex in the present case. In particular, the changes in the power structure may be heavily influenced by these motivations.

The assumptions that the person with less relative power always follows the wishes of the more powerful person in a pair and that the more powerful always uses his power are quite restrictive. Many other ways of resolving the problem are possible. We shall next consider one further possibility.

3. Linear Utility Functions

Suppose we have a group with linear utility functions for the group members; i.e., their utilities as functions of their behavior can be expressed as

(9)
$$u_1 = c_{11}a_1 + c_{12}a_2 + \cdots + c_{1n}a_n ,$$
$$\cdots\cdots\cdots\cdots$$
$$u_n = c_{n1}a_1 + c_{n2}a_2 + \cdots + c_{nn}a_n .$$

This means, of course, that all the activities a_i can be given numerical values along some dimension, not necessarily the same for all members, and that it is only these values that determine the utilities of the group members. The c_{ij}'s can take any values, positive or negative.

In such a group the elementary power of the members is independent of the behavior of the other group members in the sense that no cross products of behavior occur. In discussing the power relationships between two members, i and j, we can limit the discussion to the activities a_i and a_j and their contribution to the utilities u_i and u_j:

(10)
$$u_i = \cdots + c_{ii}a_i + c_{ij}a_j + \cdots ,$$
$$u_j = \cdots + c_{ji}a_i + c_{jj}a_j + \cdots .$$

The elementary power of i over j is then defined as $c_{ji}(a_{i\max} - a_{i\min})$, $c_{ji} > 0$, where $a_{i\max}$ is the maximum amount of activity that i reasonably can be supposed to put in, and $a_{i\min}$ is 0 if $c_{ii} \leqq 0$ or if $c_{ii} > 0$ and u_i^* allows i to cease his own activity in the group; otherwise $a_{i\min}$ will be a positive quantity. For $c_{ji} < 0$, the elementary power becomes $c_{ji}(a_{i\min} - a_{i\max})$.

In what follows let us assume that $c_{ji} > 0$. The same reasoning applies to the case where $c_{ji} < 0$ with obvious modifications. In a group with linear utilities, the motivation of person i to exercise his power over j is positive only if two other conditions are fulfilled.

(i) Let $c_{ii} < c_{ji}$. If it is not, i will reduce his own utility as much as or more than j's when sanctioning j; he would be punished more than j if he should exercise his power, and thus will not do so.

(ii) Suppose that $c_{ji} < c_{ij}$, $a_{i\max} = a_{j\max}$, and $a_{i\min} = a_{j\min}$; then $c_{ji} > c_{ij}$.[1] If this is not the case, i will have less relative power than j. Thus the smaller the difference $c_{ji} - c_{ii}$ and the greater c_{ij}, the more strongly will group member i be motivated, assuming that $a_{i\min}$ is not affected and that $c_{ji} - c_{ii}$ remains positive. On the other hand, the greater c_{ji}, the greater will be his power over j. Given the above limitations, a person i who wants to influence the coefficients in a linear system of this kind will try to keep c_{ji} both high and low: as small as possible, but greater than c_{ii}, and as large as possible so that c_{ij} will be as high as possible. This means that c_{ii} would tend to be almost equal to c_{ij} and both would be pushed as high as possible.

If the linear system is given, several outcomes of the power relations are conceivable. Three different cases should be considered separately.

(i) $c_{ii} > c_{ji}$ and $c_{jj} > c_{ij}$. Neither one is motivated to use the power he might have. No attempts to influence the other will be made.

(ii) $c_{ii} < c_{ji}$ and $c_{jj} > c_{ij}$. Member i is motivated to use his power over j, and j has no defense against this power. The outcome is that i will force j to do as he wishes, so long as i does not perceive any danger that j may try to force a change in the given linear system.

(iii) $c_{ii} < c_{ji}$ and $c_{jj} < c_{ij}$. Both have some power that can be used; let

---

[1] If the persons have different maxima or minima for their activities, the one with the greater maximum or the smaller minimum has advantage in power. In the former case he can reward his opponent more and can thus require more from him; in the latter case he can punish the opponent more and thus threaten him with more harm if the opponent does not yield to him.

us call it *bargaining power*. Suppose for definiteness that the bargaining power of i, in this case the relative power, is greater than that of j. A power equilibrium can then be reached according to at least two different principles: (1) that i forces j to obey him completely as in (ii) above, and (2) that i and j bargain in some way about the adjustment of activities that seems to correspond to the power relations. One bargaining principle is that both should benefit equally from a change in the amount of activity. If we denote a change in activity by Δa_j, we can express this principle by requiring that

$$(11) \qquad c_{ii}\Delta a_i + c_{ij}\Delta a_j = c_{ji}\Delta a_i + c_{jj}\Delta a_j .$$

This results in a certain proportionality between the changes in the two activities:

$$(12) \qquad \Delta a_j = \Delta a_i \frac{c_{ji} - c_{ii}}{c_{ij} - c_{jj}} .$$

In the simple case of linear utility functions we have been able to discuss various possibilities fairly extensively. This case hardly ever occurs in real life, of course, but it still may be useful to examine the relations that occur in a simple system. In more complex systems some of these relations may still hold approximately. Since we have no idea of the form these utility functions may take, it does not seem worth while to study such systems with respect to relations between single individuals until we do know more about the forms they are likely to take.

4. Coalitions

A *coalition* in a group is a subgroup of two or more members who act as a unit; i.e., the behavior of the members of the coalition is decided for them by the coalition in some way and the individual members then comply with this decision. The forming of a coalition can give greater power to the coalition than to the coalition members in two ways. First, the production function of the group may be unchanged, but by coordinating their behavior the members may change the $u_{ij\max}$ and $u_{ij\min}$ so that the difference between them increases in comparison with the best that any coalition member can accomplish on his own (i here stands for the coalition). Second, the formation of a coalition may change the production function itself, so that the coalition receives more power. Both of these situations probably occur in practice.

The formation of a coalition in a group thus means that the number of units decreases; the power relations between these units have been covered in the previous discussion. But a new problem appears—the question of the power of the members of the coalition. Power within a coalition may be distributed as in a group. One possible way to measure the power of each individual in a coalition is to consider his power over the other coalition members and their power over each other, and to multiply the power of the coalition by the quantity

$$(13) \qquad\qquad c_i = \frac{p_i^c}{\sum\limits_{j} p_j^c} \,,$$

where p_i^c is the power of member i within the coalition.

The power structure of a group with coalitions would thus be given by the power of each member not in a coalition, the power of each coalition over the other members and other coalitions, and the power structure within each coalition.

The motivation of the coalition members to exercise their power through the coalition depends upon (1) m_{cij}, i.e., what the coalition can get out of the group product by influencing the rest of the group as measured by the utility of member i, (2) how the gain for the coalition is distributed through the members, and this depends on the power structure within the coalition; and (3) how the group decision for the coalition is made, which also depends on the power structure within the coalition. These relations are too complicated to go into here except in the purely formal manner:

$$(14) \qquad\qquad m_{ij}^c = f_c(m_{cij}, d_c, b_c) \,,$$

where d_c is the distribution rule within the coalition and b_c the decision rule for the coalition. The function increases with an increase in m_{cij}, with a change in d_c that gives more to i, and a change in b_c that means more influence for i on the group decisions.

The motivation to form a coalition is equal to the sum of the motivations to exercise power through the coalition over all the group members not in the coalition:

$$(15) \qquad\qquad m_{ic} = \sum\limits_{j \notin c} m_{ij}^c \,.$$

Caplow has formulated a theory of coalition formation in the triad [1], [2]. In our terminology, Caplow assumes that he knows the power of the individual members of the triad. The only aspect of the group product that he takes into account is the power of the members over each other. A member with greater relative power will control completely a member with less relative power. An individual's power is the same in relation to all members of the group and can thus be denoted by a number (whether natural, integer, rational, or real is not clear from his papers—and immaterial for his reasoning since he uses a graphical representation). The power of a coalition is the sum of the powers of the coalition members. An individual wants to control as many group members as possible. Control via coalition is valued as highly as direct personal control. The number of persons controlled by a coalition member is thus equal to the number controlled by the coalition plus the number of other members of the coalition controlled by him.

It is evident that this is a very simplified special case of the general coalition-formation situation. Caplow has developed a theory for what coalitions will be formed in three-person groups. The power of the group members is fixed, and it is assumed that the power of one person over another in no case is great enough to force him to enter a coalition. Experiments have been carried out to test the theory (e.g., [12]). Attempts have also been made to generalize the theory to four-person groups and to test this generalization experimentally (by R. Willis in an experiment not yet published).

Caplow's treatment of even the three-person theory is complicated, and the four-person theory becomes more so with his graphical method. A simpler and more general formulation of the general result of the theory can be obtained by considering the partitions of the group that occur with different coalition patterns. Suppose we have a group G with n members. Each one of the n members has a power x_i. When these powers are given we can associate to each partition of G, n natural numbers m_i, $i = 1, \cdots,$ n, the number of persons dominated by member i, indirectly by his coalition and directly within the coalition. If we denote by γ_i the functions on g, where g is an element of the set of all partitions of G into the natural numbers determined by this rule of calculation, we get

$$(16) \qquad\qquad m_i = \gamma_i(g) \ .$$

Then a possible rule for coalition formation is that the person i will try to establish one partition g which is an element of the set of partitions for which m_i is greatest. If he cannot establish a partition which gives him a higher m_i than does the partition that already exists, he will not attempt to change the partition (i.e., form any new coalition). One additional restriction on this rule for coalition formation is that an individual will try to establish only those partitions that he can think of and calculate the m_i for. As n increases, this restriction becomes more important.

5. Institutionalized Power

So far we have treated power as a quality either personal or belonging to a coalition of persons. We also have the case, however, where the whole group forms a coalition and exercises power over its members. This occurs when it is advantageous to the group to act as a unit, i.e., with all the members' behavior coordinated—or rather, when it is to the advantage of enough of the influential members so that they can force the decision on the other members.

In such a coordinated system, different members have positions which entail different degrees of control over group members. This ability to control is a sort of power which is often impersonal and is always connected with the position. The power is inherent in the whole group, and disobedience brings punishment from the whole group according to the rules in force for that group.

This institutionalized power may occur in small groups, but it is more common in larger groups. It brings problems of its own kind, and we are not going to enter into its complexities here. But we must mention this additional complication which a complete theory of social power must cover.

6. Summary

In this paper I have tried to define social power in a way that captures the intuitive idea that power is a kind of potential influence due to the powerful person's ability to punish the person who does not do as he wishes. I have also tried to distinguish between power as such and the motivation to exercise the power. In doing this I have had to introduce a very general notion of utility. I am aware that measurements of such a utility do not exist at the present time, but I have found it necessary to use the notion in order to make clear the theoretical context of the problem. It is important to use the latent variables to develop a theoretical problem and thus to indicate the need for measures of these crucial variables.

Using these basic definitions, I have tried to develop descriptive expressions for the power structure of groups in the simple case with no coalitions and in the more complicated case with coalitions. I also have showed that some theories about power, in particular the Rapoport–Landau theory of peck orders and Caplow's theory of coalitions, are simple special cases of the general situation to which a more general theory of power should be applicable. A discussion of the ways in which a power equilibrium is reached in a group is carried out in some detail for the group members where the group result (product) is represented by linear weighted sums of the activities of the group members.

REFERENCES

[1] CAPLOW, T., Theory of coalitions in the triad, *Amer. Sociol. Rev.*, 1956, **21**, 489–93.

[2] CAPLOW, T., Further development of a theory of coalitions in the triad, *Amer. J. Sociol.*, 1959, **64**, 488–93.

[3] CARNAP, R., Testability and meaning, *Phil. Sci.*, 1936, **3**, 419–71, and 1937, **4**, 1–40.

[4] DAHL, R. A., The concept of power, *Behav. Sci.*, 1957, **2**, 201–15.

[5] LANDAU, H. G., On dominance relations and the structure of animal societies: I. Effect of inherent characteristics, *Bull. Math. Biophys.*, 1951, **13**, 1–19.

[6] LANDAU, H. G., On dominance relations and the structure of animal societies: II. Some effects of possible social factors, *Bull. Math. Biophys.*, 1951, **13**, 245–62.

[7] LANDAU, H. G., On dominance relations and the structure of animal societies: III. The conditions for a score structure, *Bull. Math. Biophys.*, 1953, **15**, 143–48.

[8] RAPOPORT, A., Outline of a probabilistic approach to animal sociology: I, *Bull. Math. Biophys.*, 1949, **11**, 183–96.

[9] RAPOPORT, A., Outline of a probabilistic approach to animal sociology: II, *Bull. Math. Biophys.*, 1949, **11**, 273–82.

[10] RAPOPORT, A., Outline of a probabilistic approach to animal sociology: III, *Bull. Math. Biophys.*, 1950, **12**, 7–17.

[11] THIBAUT, J. W., and H. H. KELLEY, *The Social Psychology of Groups*, New York: Wiley, 1959.

[12] VINACKE, W. E., and A. ARKOFF, An experimental study of coalitions in the triad, *Am. Sociol. Rev.*, 1957, **22**, 408–14.

14

Experimental Studies of Conflict in Some Two-Person and Three-Person Games

Bernhardt Lieberman, *Harvard University*

1. Introduction

The theory of games of strategy has fascinated workers in a number of disciplines including mathematics, economics, psychology, sociology, and political science. If we ask why it has had such a pervasive appeal, one answer would seem to be that it has applied the abstraction, the intellectual depth, the power, and the techniques of genuine mathematics to questions of social import.

It has become obvious to many that conflicts of interest, even among reasonable individuals, are inevitable. Since social conflicts are often characterized by their complexity and are too often resolved by destructive and mutually harmful acts, efforts have been made to develop techniques and understanding that will increase the likelihood of nondestructive solutions.

Numerous attempts have been made to comprehend the essential elements of social conflicts. Game theory is one such attempt; it is a mathematical construction designed to analyze social conflicts and then prescribe a resolution of the situation that should be reasonable to the participants. It is an intellectual construction of depth and significance that makes use of the rigor of the mathematical discipline. By a process of simplification, abstraction, and analysis, the theory provides insights into situations of pure conflict and situations in which there are elements of both conflict and cooperation.

Game theory deals with situations in which persons[1] are contesting for a

Much of this work was done during my tenure as a Public Health Service Postdoctoral Research Fellow of the National Institute of Mental Health, in the Department of Social Relations, Harvard University, before my affiliation with the State University of New York, Stoney Brook.

I wish to thank Professor R. Duncan Luce for his substantive contributions to these studies. Discussions with Professors Frederick Mosteller and Howard Raiffa were most helpful.

[1] In the game theory literature and in this chapter the term person refers to a *set of interests* rather than a single individual. Thus, bridge and a war between two nations are both two-person games.

quantifiable commodity or object of value—situations in which the persons in conflict wish to obtain a maximum amount of this commodity or object. Given these conditions, the theory attempts to present a normative resolution of the conflict; it attempts to prescribe proper or appropriate behavior to one or more persons in such situations.

If a theory is normative and we discover that persons have, without knowledge of the theory, been behaving as it prescribes, the logical construction has descriptive value. Thus, the prescriptive and descriptive aspects of a primarily normative theory are not unrelated. In an age that has recognized and emphasized the irrational (or nonrational) factors that drive and govern man's behavior, it would be refreshing to discover that in certain situations a sensible resolution of conflicts is the course people normally adopt. We shall see that to some small extent this anachronistic notion about behavior is true.

One of the contributions of von Neumann and Morgenstern was to provide an interesting and useful way of classifying and looking at various types of conflict in small groups. Two distinctions of value were made: one between zero-sum and non-zero-sum games and the second between two-person and n-person games.[2] These two classifications yield four classes of games. They are: the two-person, zero-sum game; the two-person, non-zero-sum game; the n-person, zero-sum game; and, finally, the n-person, non-zero-sum game. In only one of these classes, the two-person, zero-sum game, do we have a situation of pure conflict. In each of the three other classes there is usually some element of joint effort or cooperation among the players.

Only in the simplest situation, the two-person, zero-sum game where we have a condition of pure conflict, do we have what is generally accepted to be an adequate normative solution of the conflict. Where cooperation is mixed with conflict, where people are opponents and simultaneously have to coordinate their interests, we do not have anything that approaches the convincing solution we have for the two-person, zero-sum game.

Conventional game theory requires that payoffs be presented (or be capable of being presented) in explicit matrices. Many interesting social conflicts do not satisfy the rather stringent requirements of game theory. These considerations and others have led many to criticize the limitations of game theory. Some have leveled the criticism that the theory is too abstract and does not include many features that are essential to the understanding of social conflicts.

Thomas Schelling [5] has suggested an alternative classification of the range of socially interesting games. He suggests that rather than discuss

---

[2] A zero-sum game is one in which, on each play of a game, the sum of the payments is zero. Card games such as poker are zero-sum games since whatever one or more players have won the remaining players have lost. Non-zero-sum games do not have this requirement. It is common to refer to two-person and n-person games. The latter refers to the general game where n is equal to or greater than three. For a more complete discussion of these basic terms see Luce and Raiffa [3].

zero-sum and non-zero-sum games, we should consider social conflicts on a scale from those that involve pure conflict to those of pure cooperation. The pure conflict game, the two-person, zero-sum game, is one extreme; the coordination game, where two people receive payoffs only if they coordinate their activity and cooperate, is the other. In the coordination game, maximum payment comes to the players simultaneously; and so neither player has any incentive to reduce the rewards to the other players. Between these two types of interactions there is what Schelling calls the *mixed-motive* game. This is a game that, by conventional classification, would be an n-person, zero-sum game or a two- or n-person, non-zero-sum game.

The studies to be reported in the rest of this chapter deal with the simplest types of conflicts described by game situations. Three experimental studies will be discussed: the first deals with a two-person, zero-sum game which has a saddle point;[3] the second deals with a two-person, zero-sum game which requires the use of mixed strategies for its solution; and the third deals with two variants of the three-person, zero-sum majority game.

The three studies reported here are concerned with the rationality and nonrationality of intelligent human subjects. If one is interested in specifying the situations in which intelligent individuals are rational (in a game theory sense) and those in which they are not rational, it is necessary to study the very simplest situations—where rational solutions exist. These studies were designed to compare the actual behavior of intelligent individuals with the behavior prescribed by zero-sum game models. They are descriptive; they provide some picture of how groups of intelligent individuals behave in situations of conflict described by zero-sum game models.

2. Study One: Behavior in a Strictly Determined 3×3 Matrix Game[4]

The first study describes how intelligent individuals behave when playing a strictly determined 3×3 zero-sum, matrix game. The two-person, zero-sum game with a saddle point is a model of only a limited number of two-person conflicts. However, we cannot say that such a game is not a model of any important conflicts. Haywood [3, p. 64] gives an example of quite a significant conflict that was resolved by choices of optimal strategies. His analysis of the battle of the Bismarck Sea in World War II indicates that both the Japanese and American commanders adopted minimax strategies.

The experimental game of Study One is described by the following matrix.

---

[3] A two-person, zero-sum game with a saddle point (a strictly determined game) is one in which each player should choose a single strategy. A game that requires mixed or randomized strategies is one in which the players should choose from two or more available strategies, choosing each strategy with a given probability.

[4] This study has been described in detail elsewhere; see Lieberman [2]. In this study and the two described below, the payoff matrix was known to the subjects. A matrix game board or payoff table was in front of the subjects throughout the experimental session.

Player Red

$$\text{Player Blue} \begin{bmatrix} +15 & 0 & -2 \\ 0 & -15 & -1 \\ +1 & +2 & 0 \end{bmatrix}$$

Note that the minima are -2, -15, and 0 for rows 1, 2, and 3, and that the maxima are $+15$, $+2$, and 0 for columns 1, 2, and 3, respectively.

In the above game the minimax model dictates that both players choose strategy 3, 100 per cent of the time.

Fifteen pairs of subjects played 200 repetitions of the game. Payments were in cents: $+15$ indicates a 15-cent payment from red to blue and -15 indicates a payment from blue to red. The subjects were given $\$2.50$ at the start of the game and were allowed to keep the amount they had in their possession at the conclusion of the 200 plays.

Approximately half of the subjects, after some experience with the game, adopted the minimax strategy.[5] Even those subjects who did not choose strategy 3 100 per cent of the time were, on the final trials, making the optimal choice 85 per cent of the time. On the final 20 trials, 94 per cent of the subjects' choices were of the optimal choice, strategy 3.

These data do have something to tell us. In situations where subjects can see the essential elements of a game (such as this two-person, zero-sum game with a saddle point) and where the subjects have the intellectual abilities to solve the game, we may expect rational behavior to be the modal behavior.

3. Study Two: A Failure of Game Theory to Predict Human Behavior

The mixed success of the model as a descriptive theory in Study One led to an investigation of its adequacy when randomized strategies are necessary for the solution of a game. This second study describes how people behave both against a rational opponent and against a nonrational opponent in a two-person, zero-sum game requiring the use of mixed strategies.

Certain probability learning phenomena may be considered analogous to such games. In some two-alternative experiments subjects' choices of one alternative are rewarded with a probability p, and their choices of the second alternative are rewarded with the probability $(1 - p)$. In these studies it is possible to think that the subject is engaged in a matrix game against nature, where nature behaves as if she were playing in accordance with some mixed strategy. It is well known that in the above experiment subjects' choices often match the probability of reward. Where subjects receive a unit reward for each correct prediction and suffer a unit loss (or no loss) for each false prediction, and $p = .50$, matching behavior is optimal in the

---

[5] When a player adopts a minimax strategy he is behaving in a manner that will assure him that he will minimize the maximum amount he can lose, no matter what the second player does. This is essentially the same as maximizing the minimum amount he can win. See Luce and Raiffa [3] for a more complete definition.

minimax sense. Where rewards and losses are unit values, and $p \neq .50$, subjects should choose the more frequently rewarded side on every trial to maximize the number of rewarded choices. Edwards [1] studied a number of probability learning situations which can be thought of as 2×2, zero-sum, matrix games. The elements of some of his matrices were varied from unit values, and from the results it appears that his subjects did not behave in conformity with the minimax solution. Siegel and Goldstein [6] studied probability learning situations in which amounts of money could be lost. Again, their subjects did not behave as the minimax model might indicate they should. In both of the studies, subjects were not playing against a human opponent who was, apparently, attempting to win money from them; thus a critical assumption of game theory was not satisfied. It should be said that neither the Edwards nor the Siegel and Goldstein study was designed to test the adequacy of a game theory model.

In the present study the subjects were faced with an opponent who stated he was attempting to win money from them. One of the two game situations involved was designed to satisfy the assumptions of the theory of games; the second situation yielded information about play against a nonrational opponent.

3.1 Method. A single game was used, with variations in the experimenter's responses to two groups of subjects.

The Game. A single subject played the following matrix game 300 times against the experimenter.

$$
\begin{array}{cc}
 & \begin{array}{cc} \text{E1} & \quad \text{E2} \end{array} \\
\begin{array}{c} \text{S1} \\ \text{S2} \end{array} & \begin{bmatrix} +3 & -1 \\ -9 & +3 \end{bmatrix}
\end{array}
$$

On each play of the game both the experimenter and the subject have a choice of playing a 1 or a 2. If S1–E1 occurred, the subject received three cents from the experimenter. If S1–E2 occurred, the experimenter received one cent from the subject. The other two payoffs were similarly determined. The minimax solution of this game requires that the subject play S1 with a probability .75 and S2 with a probability .25. The experimenter should play E1 with a probability .25 and E2 with a probability .75.

The above game was designed so that the prescription of the minimax model was in contradiction to a matching prediction. If in this situation subjects' choices were to match (or tend to match) the probability of reward, they would choose S1 with a probability .25 and S2 with a probability .75 when the experimenter played rationally. Given the Edwards and the Siegel and Goldstein data cited above, there was little reason to believe that the subjects' choices would match the probability of reward, but such an outcome was considered possible.

Another feature of the game is of some interest. The value of the game is zero; when the experimenter played rationally, the expected outcome of the game was zero no matter what choices the subjects made. This fact affects the interpretation of the results and will be discussed below.

Subjects. The subjects were twenty men, undergraduate students of Harvard College in residence during the academic year 1958–59.

Materials. The materials used consisted of a matrix game board that identified the payoffs; $5.00 in cash for each game; 600 red and 600 blue choice cards; red, white, and blue chips; written instruction sheets; pencils and scrap paper; screens that hid each player's choice cards from his opponent's view.

Procedure. The subjects were divided randomly into two groups of 10 each. Against the first, Group O, the experimenter played in an optimal manner over the entire 300 plays of the game. Against the second, Group N, he played optimally for the first 100 repetitions of the game and then changed to a nonoptimal, randomized strategy—choosing E1 and E2 with equal probability for the final 200 trials.

Both the experimenter and subject had $2.50 at the start of the game. Each exchanged $2.00 in cash for chips and used these to make payments during the course of play. Both held a number of their colored choice cards in their hands. A play of the game, a trial in the experiment, consisted in each player's selecting a choice card from his hand with a 1 or a 2 on it. Each placed his card face down in front of him on a table, and, after both choices were made, the cards were turned over, revealing the choices and determining the outcome of the play. Chips were exchanged after each play of the game, and, when the 300 choices were completed, the subject received an amount of money equal to the value of the chips remaining in his possession.

The experimenter's choices were all fixed in advance and were the same for each of the 10 games against the subjects of Group O. The first 100 choices against the players of Group N were identical to those against Group O. The last 200 against the subjects of Group N were identical for all members of that group but, of course, differed from the choices against Group O.

An essential assumption of game theory is that a player is in conflict with a responsive opponent who is attempting to win some quantified object from him. If the subjects perceived that the experimenter's choices were fixed in advance, an argument could be made that the game theory model could not be disconfirmed as a descriptive theory by the present study. To avoid this problem, screens were used to prevent the subject from seeing how the experimenter selected his choice card for each play of the game.

Questionnaire. At the completion of the experimental session, each subject completed a questionnaire containing questions about how he played the game and how he believed the experimenter played the game.

3.2 Results. Results for the two groups were as follows.

Group O. The results presented in figure 1 indicate quite clearly that the subjects of Group O did not play as the minimax model commands. The mean percentages of choices of S1 for the 10 subjects, considered in

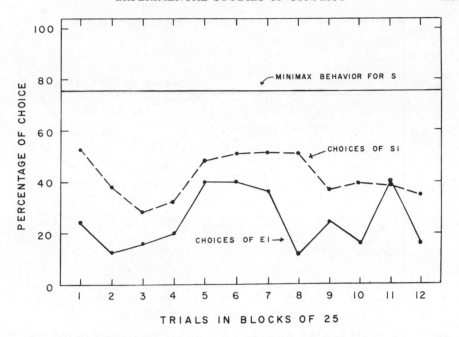

FIG. 1. Choices of S1 where the experimenter played rationally on all 300 trials—Group O. The experimenter's choices of E1 are included in the figure.

trial blocks of 25, differed grossly and significantly from the prescription of the minimax model (random fluctuation around 75 per cent).[6] The percentages of choices of S1 varied from a high of 52.8 per cent to a low of 28.0 per cent; S1 was chosen 40.9 per cent of the time over the entire 300 plays of the game. From inspection of figure 1, it appears that the mean curve may have reached a stable level of response at about 40 per cent.

In addition, it was not the case that some of the ten players adopted the minimax strategy while others did not. Inspection of the data of the individual subjects (not presented here) indicated that not one of the 10 subjects chose S1 approximately 75 per cent of the time.

Group N. The mean percentages of choice of S1 for the subjects of Group N, presented in figure 2, were similar to those of Group O over the first 100 trials: S1 was chosen 37.8 per cent of the time by the subjects of Group O and 42.8 per cent of the time by those of Group N. After the 100th trial, when the experimenter played nonrationally against the players of Group N, their choices of S1 increased rapidly, approaching the 75 per cent line, remaining, however, consistently below it. Over the last 200 trials, the mean percentage of choice of S1 was 65.1 per cent; the high

---

[6] A t test led to a rejection of the null hypothesis ($\alpha = .05$) that the choices of S1 were drawn from a population of responses in which the probability of choice of S1 was .75.

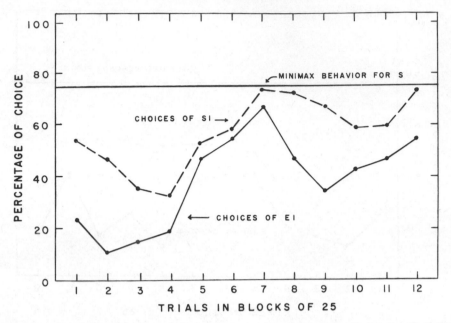

FIG. 2. Choices of S1 where the experimenter played nonrationally on the final 200 trials—Group N. Choices of E1 are included.

point, 74.4 per cent. Comparisons of the obtained behavior with the minimax behavior indicate obvious and statistically significant differences.[7]

Analyses of the behavior of the individual subjects of Group N over the final 200 plays of the game indicate that some did, on some blocks of trials, choose S1 with a frequency greater than 75 per cent. The subjects could have exploited the weakness in the experimenter's play by choosing S1 100 per cent (or perhaps only 80.0 to 90.0 per cent) of the time. However, when the entire 200 trials are considered, only two subjects chose S1 with a frequency greater than 75 per cent; one subject chose S1 80.5 per cent of the time and another 76.5 per cent of the time. From the data presented in table 1 (the percentages of the choice of S1 by the individual subjects of Group N) it is obvious that, with one possible exception, the subjects did not exploit the weakness in the experimenter's play. Since the experimenter was playing nonrationally over the final 200 plays of the game against Group N, the relationship of the subjects' choices to the minimax solution is a bit complicated and will be considered in some detail in the subsequent discussion.

The Game as a Probability Learning Situation. It is possible to subject the present data to analyses carried out in probability learning experiments. To do this, it is necessary to make some identifications. For Group N on

---

[7] A *t* test led to a rejection of the null hypothesis ($\alpha = .05$) that choices of S1 (for the subjects of Group N over the final 200 trials) were drawn from a population of responses in which the probability of choice of S1 was .75.

the first 100 trials and for Group O throughout, the probability of reward of the choice of S1 was .25; for Group N on the final 200 trials the probability of reward of the choice of S1 was .50.

Edwards [1] has offered a theoretical notion to explain behavior in probability learning situations in which reward and loss values are varied from zero and unit amounts. He offers a relative expected loss minimization rule (RELM) based on Savage's concept of *regret* or *loss*, which is applicable to the present study. Edwards found considerable correspondence between his results and the predictions of the RELM rule.

When the rule is applied to the present data, it yields a prediction for Group N over the final 200 trials. The rule predicts that subjects should choose alternative 2 more often than 1. The subjects of this study did just the opposite. The reasons for this are fairly clear and will be discussed below.

Although there does not appear to be any precise quantitative theoretical explanation of the subjects' behavior, there is one analysis of the data that yields an interesting observation. The experimenter's choices have been described variously as optimal and nonoptimal, with given numerical probabilities. Actually, he adopted two randomized strategies, one against Group O and another against Group N. This resulted in variations from trial block to trial block in the experimenter's choices of E1 and E2. The variations in behavior, together with the subjects' behavior, are presented in figures 1 and 2. There appears to be a marked responsiveness of the subjects' choices to the random fluctuation in the experimenter's choices of E1. This responsiveness is even more marked in the case of Group N where the subjects' choices follow the shift in the experimenter's change from the optimal to the nonoptimal strategy. The reader can make more detailed observations to see the extent to which subjects were responsive to the trial block variation.

TABLE 1

PERCENTAGES OF CHOICE OF S1 OVER THE FINAL
200 TRIALS BY SUBJECTS OF GROUP N

Subject	Choice of S1, %
1	80.5
2	71.0
3	67.5
4	50.5
5	61.0
6	46.5
7	76.5
8	73.0
9	64.5
10	59.0

Responses to Questionnaire. The subjects' answers to questions about their manner of play indicated that most did believe they were opposed by a player who was responsive and attempting to win money from them. Sixteen of the 20 stated that they did use some plan of play in an attempt to increase their winnings; the same number stated that the experimenter was responsive to their choices, that what he did depended on their choices. Eleven of the 20 stated they varied their choices in an attempt to influence the decisions of the experimenter.

3.3 Discussion. The behavior of the subjects of Group O indicates quite clearly that in a game requiring the use of a randomized strategy, the minimax model (which is primarily a normative model) is not adequate as a descriptive theory of behavior. Previous results indicated that in a simpler matrix game with a saddle point some people did behave as the minimax model prescribes. The current results indicate that this may be the limit of rationality of intelligent individuals in two-person, zero-sum matrix game situations.

The interpretation of the behavior of the subjects of Group N requires some consideration of the definition of rationality employed. As has already been indicated, game theory, including the minimax model, was created to prescribe what an individual should do on a single play of a game when in conflict with an opponent who is believed to be intelligent and rational. The game played by the subjects of Group N cannot be said to be such a situation. The subjects played the final 200 repetitions of a game in which, if they had adopted the minimax strategy, their expectation was zero. However, in the course of play, they might have learned that they could increase their winnings by deviating from the minimax .strategy. We cannot say that a rational player should not have attempted to exploit the weakness in the experimenter's play by deviating from the prediction of the minimax model. It might be appropriate to say that after some experience with the experimenter's choices over the last 200 plays of the game, the subjects of Group N should have chosen S1 100 per cent (or 80 per cent to 90 per cent) of the time. But since the subjects were led to believe that they were being opposed by a responsive opponent who would exploit any obvious weakness in their play, such as the adoption of a pure strategy, such a prescription may not be appropriate. Since minimax theory does not prescribe how a player should exploit an opponent's weakness, it seems clear that the situation for Group N was not a test of the minimax model as a descriptive theory.

In the two-person game played, if one player adopted the optimal strategy, as the experimenter did against Group O, the expectation of the game was zero, no matter what the subject did. It might be argued that the subjects of Group O had no incentive to be rational, since no matter what their choices were, they obtained the same expected payoff. This fact, that subjects' choices do not affect their expectation, must be seen as characteristic of utilizing the minimax model as a descriptive theory. A strict interpretation of minimax theory requires that the subjects of Group O adopt the optimal solution if only to prevent the experimenter from exploiting any weakness in their play that might exist were they not rational. Thus, the game played by the subjects of Group O was a reasonable and demanding, but not uncomplicated test of the minimax model.

From observations of the subjects during the experimental session and their responses to the questionnaires, it was obvious that they did not perceive the task facing them as one in which they should find a systematic manner of playing the game, a plan which would assure them of receiving the minimax value. Subjects tended to look for patterns in the experimenter's play and anticipate his response on each trial in an attempt to win the small amounts of money involved. Many appeared to behave in a manner similar to humans making decisions in a probability learning situation. The analyses reported above indicate that Edwards' RELM rule does not explain the behavior for Group N over the final 200 trials. Edwards states that two tendencies make the RELM rule work. The first is a preference for high probabilities of reward and the second is a preference for large amounts of reward over small amounts. Neither of these tendencies could operate in the situation facing the subjects of Group N. The experimenter adopted a .50–.50 mixed strategy, and the amounts of reward were identical no matter which alternative the subject chose. In addition, S1 had a 1-cent loss associated with it and S2 presented the possibility of a 9-cent loss. Given these factors, it is understandable that the RELM rule did not predict accurately. The present study should not be considered a good test of the rule. However, it should be recognized that, given these factors that would tend to make the rule fail, it did fail.

4. Study Three: Behavior in Two Three-Person, Zero-Sum Games

The third study to be described gives us information about how certain groups of intelligent individuals behave in two three-person conflicts which are described by zero-sum game models. The two previous studies indicated that in social interactions described by two-person, zero-sum models, people were rational in some situations but not in others. The present study, which follows in the line of the previous work, raises some new and interesting problems. The moment a third person enters a situation of social interaction, the possibility of the alignment of two against one is raised. In fact, von Neumann and others believe that this is one of the central problems in understanding the significant features of three-person interaction.[8]

Unlike the two-person, zero-sum game, the three-person, zero-sum game has no generally accepted, unambiguous solution. A small number of three-person, zero-sum games do have what we might consider precise solutions, but the larger number do not. A number of solutions of varying types have

---

[8] In the three-person game being played by the United States, the Soviet Union, and the Mainland Chinese, a very significant feature to date has been the coalition of the two communist countries against the United States. A most interesting question, and one about which there has been much speculation, is whether the coalition of the Soviets and the Chinese will remain stable.

been offered for three-person games. Von Neumann and Morgenstern offer one. However, on examination, this solution can be seen as not giving a precise prescription of how a player should conduct himself; rather, it yields a class of solutions. Shapley has offered a value for three-person, zero-sum games whose meaning is somewhat ambiguous.

In the present study two games were used. One was a three-person game which has what we may consider an obvious, specific solution. The second was a three-person game which did not have a solution in the sense that there was a precise prescription of play for each subject on every play of the game. The type of game selected virtually required the subjects to form coalitions and, in the second game, to divide the winnings obtained. The experimental situations enable us to study rigorously aspects of the phenomena of conflict, cooperation, coalition formation and communication in three-person groups.

4.1 Method. Two three-person, zero-sum majority games were employed. Eight sets of subjects played each game.

The Games. In the first game each player (designated 1, 2, 3), by a personal move, chose the number of one of the two other players. If two chose each other's numbers a couple or coalition was formed. Three distinct couples were possible; on any one play of the game only one couple or none at all could occur. The coalition that formed won an amount of money from the third player. In the first game, described by table 2, a winning coalition received 6 cents from the third player. The rules of the game provided for different distributions of the 6 cents among the winners. When the coalition (1, 2) or (1, 3) formed, player 1 received 4 cents and player 2 or 3 received 2 cents. When coalition (2, 3) formed, each player received 3 cents.

The second game is described by table 3. This game involved coalitions of different strength. The coalition (1, 2) received 10 cents from 3; (1, 3) received 8 cents from 2; and coalition (2, 3) received 6 cents from 1. The winning pairs had to decide by the use of written communications how to divide the winnings.

Procedure. In both games written communications among the players were permitted between moves. At the moment of decision each player was uninformed of the choices of the others. Choices were made by placing

TABLE 2

GAME 1

Choice of Player			Couple	Loser	Payoff		
1	2	3			1	2	3
2	1	1	(1,2)	3	+4	+2	−6
2	3	1	—	—	—	—	—
2	3	2	(2,3)	1	−6	+3	+3
3	1	1	(1,3)	2	+4	−6	+2
3	1	2	—	—	—	—	—

TABLE 3
GAME 2

Choice of Player			Couple	Loser	Payoff	
1	2	3			Couple	Loser
2	1	1	(1,2)	3	+10	−10
2	3	1	—	—	—	—
2	3	2	(2,3)	1	+6	−6
3	1	1	(1,3)	2	+8	−8
3	1	2	—	—	—	—

the card with the player's number face down on a table. The cards were then turned over simultaneously to determine the outcome of each of the 40 plays of the game.

Subjects. Forty-eight Harvard College undergraduates served as subjects. Eight groups of three played game 1, and eight different groups of three played game 2.

Materials. The materials used consisted of the following items: instruction sheets for each player; red, white, and blue chips; red, white, and blue choice cards, which contained the players' numbers; blank colored cards for communications; scrap paper and pencils for each subject; $2.50 for each player in game 1 and $3.00 for each player in game 2.

Questionnaire. After the experimental session, each player gave a description of how he played the game.

Solutions. Solution notions in three-person, zero-sum situations are quite complex. For game 1, von Neumann and Morgenstern offer an informal but convincing solution. Players 2 and 3 should unite to take 3 cents each from player 1. The basic values of the von Neumann and Morgenstern solution, a', b', and c', are all zero. The premium $\Delta/6$ to each player who is part of the coalition equals $+3$ and $-\Delta/3$ equals -6. The Shapley value for each player in game 1 is zero.

For game 2 the von Neumann and Morgenstern basic values are: $a' = +2$, $b' = 0$, $c' = -2$; $\Delta/6 = +4$, and $-\Delta/3 = -8$. For game 2, von Neumann and Morgenstern offer a solution that suggests that when coalition (1, 2) forms, player 1 should receive 6 of the 10 cents, when (1, 3) forms, player 1 should receive 6 of the 8 cents, and when coalition (2, 3) forms, player 2 should receive 4 of the 6 cents. Other sets of imputations may be considered solutions for this game. As a result, solution theory as presented by von Neumann and Morgenstern offers no simple, unambiguous prescription as minimax theory does in the two-person, zero-sum game. In game 2, the Shapley value for player 1 is $+2$; for player 2 it is 0; for player 3 it is -2.[9]

4.2 Results. Results for games 1 and 2 are as follows.

Game 1. Table 4 summarizes the outcomes of the plays of the game by the eight triples of subjects. If the subjects were to conform to the von

---

[9] For a more complete discussion of three-person solution theory see Luce and Raiffa [3, pp. 189-204] and von Neumann and Morgenstern [7, pp. 220-33].

216 BERNHARDT LIEBERMAN

TABLE 4

Data Obtained from Plays of Game 1

Trials	Percentage of Occurrence of Outcome			
	0 No Coalition	1 (1,2)*	2 (1,3)	3 (2,3)
1-5	15.0	17.5	17.5	50.0
6-10	15.0	7.5	12.5	65.0
11-15	12.5	10.0	0	77.5
16-20	12.5	15.0	5.0	67.5
21-25	15.0	5.0	12.5	67.5
26-30	20.0	5.0	0	75.0
31-35	7.5	5.0	10.0	77.5
36-40	7.5	5.0	10.0	77.5
Mean	13.2	8.8	8.4	69.7

* (1,2) indicates players 1 and 2 chose each other's numbers and formed the winning couple.

Neumann and Morgenstern solution, they should form coalition (2, 3) 100 per cent of the time. The data show that in the first block of trials, this outcome occurred 50 per cent of the time. On the last trials, outcome 3 occurred 77.5 per cent of the time. This outcome occurred more frequently than any other, approximately 70 per cent of the time over all 40 trials. It is interesting to note that the no-coalition outcome occurred at least as often as either outcome 1 or 2.

Table 5 presents the amounts each player won or lost at the conclusion of the 40 plays of the game. If the players were perfectly rational [formed the (2, 3) coalition on each of the 40 plays] player 1 would have lost $2.40 of his $2.50, and players 2 and 3 would each have won $1.20. In games (e) and (h) players 2 and 3 actually did win the maximum amount they could. In game (c) they came quite close to this maximum amount. Only in game (g) did player 1 win more than he lost.

Game 2. The relationships among the three players in game 2 are quite intricate. One might think that a simple way of resolving the conflict would be for players 1 and 2 to form a permanent coalition and divide their winnings equally. However, when this does occur, it immediately becomes obvious to player 3 that it is advantageous for him to form a coalition with one of the two others. He can make an offer to player 1 to form a coalition with him, from which player 1 can receive more than the 5 cents he can receive together with player 2. It is even advantageous for player 3 to offer 7 or even 8 cents to player 1. Thus, player 1 is tempted to break his coalition with player 2 and take the full 8 cents from player 3. Seeing this, player 2 can then make a more attractive offer to 3 or to 1. The process can be repeated.

TABLE 5

PAYOFFS TO PLAYERS OF GAME 1

Game	Amounts Won or Lost by Players (In Dollars and Cents)		
	1	2	3
(a)	−1.68	+0.80	+0.88
(b)	−1.40	+0.50	+0.90
(c)	−2.24	+1.16	+1.08
(d)	−0.84	+0.42	+0.42
(e)	−2.40	+1.20	+1.20
(f)	−0.24	+0.24	0.0
(g)	+0.02	+0.11	−0.13
(h)	−2.40	+1.20	+1.20
Mean	−1.40	+0.70	+0.70

The three players quickly learned to see the complexities of the situation. What occurred was instability, offer and counteroffer, acceptance, rejection, deception, and the "double cross." Coalitions formed and were changed; in not one of the eight games did a coalition form on the first trial and remain constant through all the 40 plays of the game.

Table 6 presents the percentages of occurrence of the possible outcomes in blocks of five trials. The no-coalition outcome occurred on 7.2 per cent of the plays; outcome 1 occurred on 35.3 per cent of the plays; outcome 2 on 18.1 per cent of the plays; and outcome 3 on 39.4 per cent of the plays. The outcome that occurred most frequently was 3, the one that yielded the smallest payoff to the winning coalition.

TABLE 6

DATA OBTAINED FROM PLAYS OF GAME 2

Trials	Percentage of Occurrence of Outcome			
	0 No Coalition	1 (1,2)	2 (1,3)	3 (2,3)
1–5	10.0	47.5	22.5	20.0
6–10	0	32.5	17.5	50.0
11–15	10.0	37.5	10.0	42.5
16–20	12.5	22.5	22.5	42.5
21–25	7.5	27.5	30.0	35.0
26–30	7.5	40.0	17.5	35.0
31–35	2.5	40.0	17.5	40.0
36–40	7.5	35.0	7.5	50.0
Mean	7.2	35.3	18.1	39.4

We may speculate a bit about such a result. It is possible that the same forces that led to the exclusion of player 1 from the coalition formation in game 1 were also effective here. If player 1 was seen as the strongest or most exploitative individual, this may have led players 2 and 3 to unite against him to form their coalition quite frequently.

Table 7 presents the frequency of the divisions of the payoffs the subjects decided upon. Since the solutions previously discussed give no precise prescription of how the subjects should play the game and divide the winnings, it is difficult to determine which of the divisions of earnings should occur most frequently. Examination of table 7 indicates that an equal division of the winnings was the most frequent outcome. On 297 of the plays of the game some payoff occurred, on 23 no coalition formed. Of the 297 payoffs a total of 182 or 61.3 per cent of the divisions were equal divisions.

4.3 Discussion. The results of game 1 describe the behavior of three individuals in a situation where two have a clear incentive to unite forces to the detriment of the third. In a majority of choices the two did just that. However, in a sizeable minority of choices this prescribed behavior did not occur. Observations of the subjects and their descriptions of the play offer a variety of reasons for this. Two can be mentioned. Some subjects felt it was not fair to do this. In other cases, the fact that player 1 received the larger share of the winnings seemed to indicate that his position was one of special privilege or power, and some players 2 and 3 sought to align themselves with him. In fact, in a number of the games player 1's position was seen initially as being advantageous, but as the relationships among the three players became clear, the weakness of his position became apparent.

The nature of game 2 made complex negotiation inevitable. The agreements, breaking of agreements, and bargaining that occurred led to an interesting result. From observation of the subjects' behavior, their written descriptions of how they played the game, and their messages, it became obvious that in a number of games the players came to realize that a maximum return on one or two plays was not important. It was far more profitable to enter into a stable, continuing agreement with one other player. Since defection was not an infrequent occurrence, the *intuitive notion of trust* was significant in determining which coalitions formed and held together. The subjects stated that they would enter into coalitions with the player they trusted, the one they believed would not be tempted to defect from their coalition for a more attractive offer on the next play of the game.

When considering the results in relation to the solutions offered, it should be kept in mind that solution theory was designed to prescribe behavior on a single play of a game. However, the following statements can be made. The Shapley value offers little help in the understanding of either the descriptive or prescriptive aspects of the two games played. If we require of a theory that it give a precise prescription of behavior and that it be completely, or virtually completely, correct, then we must reject as a *descriptive notion* the von Neumann and Morgenstern solution for the three-person situations studied here. However, if we wish to be a bit more

TABLE 7
Division of Payoffs
Game 2

Coalitions Formed	Division of Payoffs	Frequency
	10-0*	0
	9-1	0
	8-2	4
	7-3	17
	6-4†	20
(1,2)	5-5	65
	4-6	3
	3-7	0
	2-8	2
	1-9	0
	0-10	2
	8-0	0
	7-1	0
	6-2†	10
	5-3	16
(1,3)	4-4	24
	3-5	1
	2-6	1
	1-7	5
	0-8	1
	6-0	5
	5-1	0
	4-2*	2
(2,3)	3-3	93
	2-4	23
	1-5	3
	0-6	0
0		23
Σ		320

* When coalition (1,2) formed this division indicates player 1 received 10 cents and player 2 received 0 cents. Similarly, 0-10 indicates player 2 received 10 cents.

† Indicates a division of payoffs suggested by the von Neumann and Morgenstern solution.

charitable to our theories, we may concede that the von Neumann solution had a modest success in predicting the behavior obtained from the plays of game 1. In game 2, the common notion that winnings should be divided evenly is more descriptive of behavior than the von Neumann solution.

5. Conclusions

The three studies described give us a picture of behavior of some intelligent individuals in a variety of zero-sum games. The picture is a mixed one. Nowhere can we say that all individuals behave precisely as a rational theory prescribes. However, where the situation of social interaction and conflict is simple enough so that mathematical theories can prescribe precisely a form of rational behavior, we sometimes do find people actually behaving in such a way. This is true of the behavior obtained in the two-person, zero-sum game with a saddle point, and is also true in the first of the three-person, zero-sum games.

However, in the two-person mixed-strategy game (for Group O) the mathematical theory does offer a specific randomized solution. It was quite obvious in this situation that subjects did not behave in the prescribed way. The notion of a randomized strategy is nonintuitive; subjects not familiar with game theory did not learn to adopt this solution. In the second game of the three-person study, we reached a situation of social interaction and conflict in which the mathematical theory does not offer a precise prescription. It is not surprising then that the subjects exhibited varying types of behavior. In this situation an even division of winnings was the most frequent outcome.

The studies reported above are perhaps the simplest ones that could be done involving game theory notions. It is quite obvious that the mathematical theory was the primary stimulus for this work; the intent was to compare prescribed behavior with actual behavior. Now that these studies are completed, it appears that it is quite feasible to study situations of social interaction and conflict by utilizing other game models. There are any number of more interesting small group situations that may be simulated by game models. Game theory abstracts many essential elements from situations of social conflict, and ingenious experimentation may provide insight into more important social conflicts.

REFERENCES

[1] EDWARDS, W., Reward probability, amount, and information as determiners of sequential two-alternative decisions, *J. Exptl. Psychol.*, 1956, **52**, 177–88.

[2] LIEBERMAN, B., Human behavior in a strictly determined 3 × 3 matrix game, *Behav. Sci.*, 1960, **4**, 317–22.

[3] LUCE, R. D., and H. RAIFFA, *Games and Decisions*, New York: Wiley, 1957.

[4] SAVAGE, L. J., *The Foundations of Statistics*, New York: Wiley, 1954.

[5] SCHELLING, T., *The Strategy of Conflict*, Cambridge, Mass.: Harvard Univ. Press, 1961.

[6] SIEGEL, S., and P. A. GOLDSTEIN, Decision making in a two-choice uncertain outcome situation, *J. Exptl. Psychol.*, 1959, **57**, 37–42.

[7] VON NEUMANN, J., and O. MORGENSTERN, *Theory of Games and Economic Behavior*, 3rd ed., Princeton, N. J.: Princeton Univ. Press, 1953.

15

Group and Individual Behavior in Free-Recall Verbal Learning

Irving Lorge, *Columbia University,* **and Herbert Solomon,**
Stanford University

1. Introduction

An experiment in free-recall verbal learning by individuals and by groups of three is described and analyzed in the following sections. This experiment was conducted to examine the general tenability of a model of group behavior originally proposed by Lorge and Solomon [4] in some problem-solving situations. The Lorge–Solomon model gives a parsimonious account of group performance in the solution of Eureka-type problems such as mathematical tricks and parlor puzzle games. Since group performance in problem solving is obviously a function of both the type of problem and the kind and number of individuals in the group, it is of interest to see how far the applicability of the model extends.

Free-recall verbal learning in groups was suggested as a second type of problem by Professor Robert Bush. We decided to explore it for two reasons. First, it is still group behavior in an intellective framework. Second, a model for individual behavior in this context has already been advanced by Miller and McGill [8] on the basis of some experimental data obtained by Bruner, Miller, and Zimmerman [1]. Interestingly, this model is a simple Markov process which lends itself (in this situation) to the manipulations necessary to get a picture of group behavior from individual behavior. The experiment performed to test the group model also provides data that can be used to check on the Miller–McGill model previously proposed for individual behavior.

Let us now discuss prior developments leading up to the experiment and consequently to this chapter. In 1953, my colleague Irving Lorge brought to my attention some investigations into the efficiency of groups in problem solving. The issue at hand was an evaluation of optimum group size, taking into account the chance of successful group performance vs. the manpower

---

Irving Lorge died suddenly on January 23, 1961. The planning of the paper, the experiment, and the analysis were done jointly; the co-author is responsible for the exposition.

cost. For example, the Air University was interested in the efficiency bonus, if any, as group size is increased. Naturally, to make any recommendations a model of group behavior in terms of individual behavior is required.

At this point, Lorge and I went to one of the experiments in group problem solving which was most quoted in the literature, namely that reported by Marjorie Shaw [9]. After studying her data, we proposed two models of group behavior. The first simply stated that a group solved a problem if any individual in the group could solve the problem (i.e., personal interaction was not a factor). The second model allowed for ability interaction and stated that if a problem could be solved in stages, then the group would solve the problem if any individual in the group (not necessarily the same one) could successfully pass the group through each stage. Since the second model is substantively the same as the first, let us discuss the former. Briefly, we are saying that if P_g is the probability of group solution and P_I is the probability of individual solution, then

$$P_g = 1 - (1 - P_I)^k ,$$

where k is the number of individuals in the group. This is the model of group behavior that we are going to explore in free-recall verbal learning.

These two models represented reasonably well the Shaw data in which the group size was four. Subsequently, Marquart [7] reported an experiment in which she used the same problems as Shaw and where the groups were size three. Marquart's data produced significantly higher values than Shaw's for P_I, but not for P_g. This was also true in some experiments Lorge and I ran in 1957 (reported in [5]) for the same problems for groups of size five and size two, and thus the tenability of the group behavior model was weakened. One suggested explanation is that familiarization with the problems caused the higher P_I values, and we hypothesized that this may be due to greater public acceptance of puzzle solving than existed in Shaw's day, some 25 years before. Familiarization or exposure to the problem should also increase the chance of group success, but apparently the value predicted by the model was too high when compared with experimental results. Because this clouded the usefulness of the model, Lorge and I conducted in 1957 additional experimentation which took into account the possibility of previous exposure to the problem and included groups of sizes three, four, six, and seven (reported in [6]). From the results described, it appears that the original group model again becomes more tenable when some disposition is made of the variable of previous exposure to the problem. If this variable had not been taken into account some of the situations where the model does not work nicely would have been badly obscured. Although there may be more basic reasons underlying the failure of the model in these situations, some encouragement is provided by the experiment in [6] to explore the use of the model in other settings, either in different contexts or for different classes of individuals. Since we are usually limited to college students for subjects, the easiest thing to manipulate is the type of problem and this we now do.

2. Individual Free-Recall Verbal Learning Model

In Miller and McGill [8] a model is developed that reproduces some free-recall verbal learning data in a rather simple, terse, and elegant way. The data is discussed in Bruner, Miller, and Zimmerman [1], although some of the data were obviously available to Miller and McGill several years before publication. Lists of 8, 16, 32, and 64 monosyllabic words were drawn from lists reported by Egan [3] and phonetically counterbalanced to reflect the same average frequencies of occurrence. These were presented so that effectively the individuals faced a random ordering of the lists of words either 8, 16, 32, or 64 times, depending on whether the length of the list to be recalled at each trial contained 8, 16, 32, or 64 words, respectively. The subjects were given adequate time between word-list presentations for writing their responses. It appeared from the experiment that 8-word lists and 16-word lists would receive 100 per cent recall after a number of trials but that the asymptotes of the learning curves for the 32-word and 64-word lists would fall below 100 per cent recall.

Miller and McGill provide an explanation for all the experimental data for individual responses as follows. Assume each word has the same initial probability of recall and that all words are of the same difficulty for any specified individual. Also assume that learning leads to 100 per cent recall. This removes the estimation of one parameter from the model, namely the asymptote of the learning curve for the individual. Define a random variable

$$x_{i,j,n} = \begin{cases} 1 & \text{if subject } i \text{ does not recall word } j \text{ on trial } n, \\ 0 & \text{otherwise}, \end{cases}$$

and write

$$p_{i,j,n} = \Pr\{x_{i,j,n} = 1\}.$$

Then let learning take place as follows:

$$p_{i,j,n+1} = \begin{cases} p_{i,j,n} & \text{if } x_{i,j,n} = 1, \\ \alpha_i p_{i,j,n} & \text{if } x_{i,j,n} = 0, \end{cases}$$

where α_i $(0 < \alpha_i < 1)$ is the parameter describing the learning rate for subject i. Thus the probability of non-recall decreases if recall occurs but is unchanged if non-recall occurs. Also assume that $p_{i,j,0} = p_{i,0}$; that is, the probability of initial non-recall (or equivalently initial recall) is the same for every word for the ith individual. Thus two parameters, $p_{i,0}$ and α_i, determine the learning data for the ith individual. As a function of these two parameters, such descriptive values as (1) the total number of non-recalls for a word, (2) the total number of runs of non-recalls for a word, and (3) the number of trials before a word is recalled for the first time, can be developed from the model.

A good description of this model can be found in Bush and Mosteller [2, ch. 10]. This account includes methods of estimation of the two parameters from the data. Since we will also be using this model in our conjecture for group behavior in verbal recall, a brief recapitulation of the method of estimation we use for our experimental data is in order here. First let us investigate the estimation of $p_{i,0}$ which we will label p_0 with the understanding that it varies with the individual (also label by α the recall parameter α_i). An obvious estimate of p_0 is the proportion of words not recalled in the initial experimental trial. This is equivalent to N binomial trials (assuming a list of N words) each with a probability p_0 of non-recall. However, if recall of a word does not occur in the first trial or subsequent trials, the model proposed allows these additional data to be used also to estimate p_0. For each word, use the data on trials up through the trial on which recall first occurs and record the number of trials obtained by this process. Sum these for all words and denote this sum by N_0. On every such trial the probability of non-recall is p_0. Since each word can be recalled for the first time just once in a sequence, the number of recalls during the N_0 word-trials is simply N. Thus our estimate of p_0 is

$$\hat{p}_0 = \frac{N_0 - N}{N_0}.$$

(If all words are recalled on the first trial, $N_0 = N$ and $\hat{p}_0 = 0$.) This also is the maximum-likelihood estimate for this situation. In the ordinary binomial situation the variance of the usual estimate of p_0, namely

$$p_0' = \sum_{i=1}^{N} \frac{x_{i,0}}{N},$$

is $p_0(1 - p_0)/N$. The asymptotic variance of $\hat{p}_0$ is $p_0^2(1 - p_0)/N$, and thus a reduction by a factor of p_0 is obtained when we use relevant data obtained after the initial trial. This is a bit more tedious to do, but provides a payoff in the smaller variance of the estimate.

The recall parameter α can be estimated under the assumption that p_0 is known or under the assumption that p_0 is unknown. In the latter case, joint estimation of p_0 and α is required. In our analyses we will do the former by using the estimated value $\hat{p}_0$ for p_0 because this provides an estimate of α very cheaply. Bush and Mosteller have demonstrated that the difference between this estimate and the more sophisticated and better one is very slight. Since this is so, the difference between estimates will not affect our more global reasons for getting values of α, namely, examining the tenability of the model for group behavior. The estimate is

$$\hat{\alpha} = -\frac{\log_e (1 - p_0)}{T_2},$$

where T_2 is the mean number of non-recalls per word over all trials. (This nomenclature is taken from Bush and Mosteller [2, ch. 10], except that their discussion is in terms of the probability of recall.)

3. The Experimental Design

Now for the design of the experiment. We would like to have groups of individuals repeat the Bruner–Miller–Zimmerman experiment and see if the

Lorge–Solomon model for group behavior applies. Assume that for group-learning non-recall by a group of k subjects occurs if and only if all the individuals in the group fail to recall the word. Thus we are dealing with a group random variable X, similar to the one just described for individuals, x_i. Let $X_{j,n}$ represent group response for the jth word on the nth trial; then

$$X_{j,n} = \begin{cases} 1 & \text{if } \textit{all} \text{ individuals do not recall the } j\text{th word in the } n\text{th trial}, \\ 0 & \text{otherwise}, \end{cases}$$

or

$$X_{j,n} = \prod_{i=1}^{k} x_{i,j,n} .$$

Let

$$P_{j,n} = \Pr \{X_{j,n} = 1\} .$$

Thus

$$P_{j,n} = \prod_{i=1}^{k} p_{i,j,n} ,$$

where $P_{j,n}$ is the probability that a group of k individuals does not recall the jth word on the nth trial. Then the learning axiom proposed by Miller and McGill for individual subjects implies that

$$P_{j,n+1} = \begin{cases} P_{j,n} & \text{if } X_{j,n} = 1 , \\ \gamma P_{j,n} & \text{if } X_{j,n} = 0 , \end{cases}$$

where γ is the learning-rate parameter for the group and we now *assume*

$$\gamma = \prod_{i=1}^{k} \alpha_i .$$

Thus the model for a group of k individuals is identical to the model for a single individual, except that the assumption of the Lorge–Solomon model has replaced $p_{i,0}$ by P_0 and α_i by γ. The three derivable parameters of interest for the group are (1) the total number of non-recalls of a word, (2) the total number of runs of non-recalls of a word, and (3) the number of trials before a word is recalled for the first time. These are the same functions as before except that γ replaces α_i and P_0 replaces $p_{i,0}$. Also we assume as before that, for a group, the probability of initial non-recall is the same for every word, that is, $P_{j,0} = P_0$.

Before looking for subjects for the experiment, the group size and the word-list size have to be determined. Fortunately, there are some known side conditions which are helpful. First we want to assume, for simplicity, that the learning-curve asymptote is 1 for both individuals and groups. The Bruner–Miller–Zimmerman data indicated that lists of 32 words were too long for total recall by individuals. On the other hand, if lists are too short, it will be difficult to distinguish between individual and group learning; for example, a list of 8 words might not show any differences because both individuals and groups would learn too rapidly. This thinking led to a compromise of 25 words per list as one which would permit both individuals and groups to reach total recall and yet display group-learning effects.

In considering group size, we would like to get as many groups as possible from the total number of subjects and this would indicate a group of size two. On the other hand, we would like to see group behavior predicted by the model show up sharply in the experiment and this might indicate two groups each equal in size to one-half the subjects available. Another very important factor is how fast a specific group size reaches a learning asymptote equal to 1; in other words, the group size cannot be too large lest this asymptote be reached almost in the first trial. This kind of thinking led to a group size equal to three ($k = 3$), although it is obvious that decisions for $k = 2, 4$, and 5 at this point would be quite reasonable.

4. The Experiment

The subjects most easily available to the experimenter for experiments of this type are usually college students. In our situation they were graduate students in education and psychology. From a large class in educational psychology at Teachers College, Columbia University, 111 subjects were produced. These subjects performed both as individuals and in 37 groups of three on each of two days. Two lists of 25 words were taken from the Egan list. On the first day about half of the subjects performed as individuals on List 1 while the remainder were randomly put in groups of three and given List 2. Two days later, those who performed as individuals on List 1 were randomly put in groups of three and given List 2; those who performed in groups on List 2 now performed as individuals on List 1. Thus there is some necessary confounding between days and lists. The experiment was then conducted in the following way.

Each subject was told he was participating in an experiment in learning and remembering. He was told that a list of 25 words would be read 25 times and that at each trial the words would be presented in different order. He was instructed to recall and write as many words as possible after each trial. Spelling and order would not count in recall; if a subject was unsure of a word, he was told to write it down anyhow. Notebooks were provided to record the recalls.

When the subjects were operating as three-man groups, they were each to write all the words they remembered on each trial and then draw a line under the last entry on each trial. They were then to cooperate with other group members to see how many additional words could be recalled. These words were added to the list under the underlined last entry.

After this experimentation, the data was taken from the notebooks and summarized as follows. Each word not recalled was given a score of one, each word recalled received a zero score. For each individual, a listing was printed showing how the subject performed on each word on each of the 25 trials. For groups, recall of a word occurred if any of the three subjects wrote down the word either before or after group discussion. A printed listing for each group then showed group recall or non-recall by zeros or ones, respectively. From this data, p_0 and α_i were estimated for each individual, and P_0 and γ for each group. For each group, a "concocted" group score was also obtained. This is to be contrasted with the interacting group and was done in the following way. Recall scores obtained by each of the individuals in the group when they performed as individuals were lumped to secure a group response. For example, if one or more individuals in the concocted group recalled the jth word in the ith trial, then the score of 0 was recorded, otherwise a score of 1. This concocted group action therefore gave no chance for group interaction to aid in recall of a word not achieved by any subject in the group, but obviously it did permit the group to do as well as the best recaller of each word on each trial. In the tables that follow, an interacting group (group performance during the experiment) is identified by a 300 designation, a concocted group by a 900 designation; e.g., the scores for 306 are for the group of three individuals acting together, the scores for 906 are the scores for the concocted group composed of the same three individuals who performed as individuals and were then lumped together.

5. Experimental Results

The amount of collation and computation necessary to summarize the experimental data so that the group model can be tested is quite formidable. Electronic equipment was employed to make the analysis more manageable. Table 1 lists the estimates of the initial recall and learning-rate parameters for individuals and for groups under the assumption that the model is operating, and gives a global description of how well the postulated values and the experimental values for group recall are matched. It is fair to say that the hypothesized values are close enough so that more detailed study is warranted. If the differences were very large we would simply discard the group behavior model. However, a test to see how sampling fluctuations alone affect the observed differences should be investigated.

A study of the sampling problem is left to a subsequent report. Briefly, we are faced with the fact that for each individual there is some sampling variation in the estimates of α_i and p_0 and this is also true for γ and P_0 in the group they form. Whether the observed difference between P_0 and $\prod_{i=1}^{3} p_{i,0}$, and γ and $\prod_{i=1}^{3} \alpha_i$, is due solely to the sampling variations in α_i and $p_{i,0}$, and γ and P_0, requires solutions to sampling-distribution problems. If they are not mathematically tractable, perhaps some approximations may be developed.

It is interesting to note that the model predicts a better performance for the group than we observe from the data. All 37 groups have poorer learning rates than hypothesized, and for the concocted group 27 out of 37 have poorer learning rates. In initial recall, 26 out of 37 groups have poorer recall than hypothesized and for concocted groups 28 out of 37 groups do worse.

Also in initial recall, 4 times out of 37 a group contained an individual whose recall was better than that of the group. For learning rate, 14 times

TABLE 1

Estimates of Parameters for Group and Individual Learning from Experimental Data

(300 Series—Interacting Group; 900 Series—Concocted Group)

Group	α_1	α_2	α_3	$\alpha_1\alpha_2\alpha_3$	γ	p_{01}	p_{02}	p_{03}	$p_{01}p_{02}p_{03}$	P_0
301 901	.777	.893	.475	.330	.586 .494	.769	.782	.510	.307	.556 .333
302 902	.871	.729	.884	.561	.841 .650	.868	.593	.760	.391	.429 .467
303 903	.882	.824	.859	.624	.917 .745	.688	.625	.844	.363	.457 .400
304 904	.866	.908	.870	.684	.839 .811	.680	.742	.822	.415	.429 .415
305 905	.652	.804	.700	.367	.651 .494	.733	.727	.680	.362	.529 .333
306 906	.853	.877	.863	.646	.767 .817	.853	.739	.765	.482	.667 .579
307 907	.806	.836	.838	.565	.800 .862	.864	.745	.733	.472	.529 .415
308 908	.869	.875	.852	.648	.772 .742	.767	.762	.786	.459	.662 .478
309 909	.898	.778	.786	.549	.724 .651	.778	.613	.718	.342	.455 .314
311 911	.809	.790	.859	.549	.692 .669	.908	.814	.810	.599	.467 .671
312 912	.836	.870	.865	.629	.861 .826	.784	.821	.901	.580	.510 .636
313 913	.864	.824	.777	.553	.687 .728	.872	.871	.762	.579	.510 .671
314 914	.701	.857	.827	.497	.759 .558	.642	.855	.852	.468	.500 .489
316 916	.844	.859	.653	.473	.803 .551	.886	.847	.736	.552	.538 .607
317 917	.884	.790	.839	.586	.869 .645	.795	.711	.844	.477	.538 .579
318 918	.841	.856	.871	.627	.749 .740	.782	.714	.721	.403	.442 .442
319 919	.846	.725	.747	.459	.704 .505	.820	.776	.625	.398	.385 .529
320 920	.838	.859	.653	.470	.816 .589	.829	.745	.786	.485	.333 .538
321 921	.891	.846	.821	.619	.694 .746	.855	.817	.800	.559	.538 .613
322 922	.837	.774	.838	.543	.655 .689	.758	.833	.750	.474	.400 .400
324 924	.862	.873	.747	.562	.754 .683	.767	.836	.765	.491	.400 .593
325 925	.839	.868	.868	.632	.849 .782	.808	.826	.680	.454	.467 .489
326 926	.840	.762	.860	.550	.757 .647	.791	.839	.688	.457	.368 .520

TABLE 1 (Cont'd)

ESTIMATES OF PARAMETERS FOR GROUP AND INDIVIDUAL LEARNING
FROM EXPERIMENTAL DATA

Group	α_1	α_2	α_3	$\alpha_1\alpha_2\alpha_3$	γ	p_{01}	p_{02}	p_{03}	$p_{01}p_{02}p_{03}$	P_0
327	.805	.860	.870	.602	.639	.625	.883	.692	.382	.455
927					.642					.467
328	.882	.872	.514	.395	.775	.820	.636	.657	.343	.385
928					.421					.385
329	.868	.831	.795	.573	.744	.830	.810	.730	.491	.564
929					.717					..613
330	.835	.834	.760	.529	.581	.870	.718	.696	.435	.385
930					.676					.442
331	.886	.902	.704	.563	.849	.739	.714	.520	.274	.607
931					.681					.273
332	.764	.855	.882	.567	.753	.671	.836	.832	.467	.564
932					.621					.510
333	.539	.879	.797	.378	.572	.556	.636	.556	.197	.688
933					.410					.172
335	.882	.911	.840	.675	.734	.704	.753	.652	.346	.680
935					.755					.455
336	.833	.876	.852	.622	.826	.714	.784	.791	.443	.607
936					.771					.368
337	.771	.866	.859	.574	.639	.676	.750	.776	.393	.586
937					.775					.351
338	.851	.852	.818	.593	.786	.832	.711	.827	.489	.657
938					.631					.556
339	.900	.653	.861	.506	.725	.688	.684	.700	.329	.547
939					.537					.467
340	.836	.876	.697	.510	.783	.750	.838	.647	.407	.619
940					.526					.455
342	.821	.844	.885	.613	.712	.782	.762	.700	.417	.579
942					.723					.529

out of 37 a group contained at least one individual whose learning was faster than that of the group.

Some of this may be due to the confounding of the two lists with the two experimental days. In our comparison of groups and individuals we are, in each case, using two different lists of words and two different dates. In table 2, the mean values and standard deviations of α and p_0 are given for each list and for each day. Since it was possible to retrieve information on individuals when they worked in groups (individuals first recalled and recorded words, then drew a line, and then discussed recall with other members of the group and added words) we have two sets of information on each list and on each day. Thus table 2 gives some descriptive information on initial recall and learning rates for the population of individuals. There is some variation in the means of α and p_0 which suggests variation due to list or day but for a final answer we should look into the interaction between list and day for α and for p_0.

TABLE 2

MEANS, STANDARD DEVIATIONS, STANDARD DEVIATION OF MEANS OF ESTIMATES FOR
INITIAL NON-RECALL AND LEARNING RATE BY WORD LISTS AND DAYS
FOR INDIVIDUALS

No.		$\bar{\alpha}$	σ_α	$\sigma_{\bar{\alpha}}$	$\bar{p}_0$	σ_{p_0}	$\sigma_{\bar{p}_0}$
				Individuals			
60	List 1	.849	.0505	.0065	.717	.0525	.0068
59	List 2	.838	.0569	.0074	.616	.0876	.0114
64	Day 1	.855	.0428	.0054	.680	.0800	.0100
55	Day 2	.831	.0623	.0084	.651	.0946	.0128
				Individual in Groups			
59	List 1	.839	.0599	.0078	.775	.0697	.0091
60	List 2	.818	.0834	.0108	.730	.0797	.0103
55	Day 1	.838	.0613	.0083	.747	.0814	.0010
64	Day 2	.821	.0815	.0102	.757	.0752	.0094

Table 3 gives summaries for individuals, groups, and concocted groups.
The mean values of α and p_0, .821 and .755, are in the same neighborhood
of those found for individuals by Miller and McGill. It is interesting to
see that initial recall and learning rate seem much better for concocted
groups than for interacting groups. While groups do better than individuals, interacting groups seem to have a damping effect on group performance
since they do not do as well as when three individuals are left to their own
efforts and then combined into the concocted group. On the other hand, the
variability in learning rate and non-recall is higher for concocted groups.
This indicates that the simple assumption $\gamma = \Pi \alpha_i$ may not be realistic
and requires modification.

The major purpose of this chapter has been to report the experimental
results. Work is under way on the sampling distributions mentioned above

TABLE 3

MEANS AND STANDARD DEVIATIONS FOR LEARNING RATE AND NON-RECALL
FOR INDIVIDUALS, GROUPS, AND CONCOCTED GROUPS

Category	N	Learning Rate		Non-Recall	
		$\bar{\alpha}$	σ_α	$\bar{p}_0$	σ_{p_0}
Individuals	119	.821	.0804	.755	.0846
		$\bar{\gamma}$	σ_γ	$\bar{P}_0$	σ_{P_0}
Groups	37	.748	.0780	.514	.0996
Concocted Groups	37	.662	.118	.474	.114

which are necessary to test the group model. Also to be contained in a future report is the effect of group size. We are in the fortunate position here of being able to get concocted groups of varying sizes and then checking the tenability of the model. Analyses are being made of 2-, 4-, and 5-subject concocted groups, to get some ideas on the relationship between r and the α_i's for the development of new models.

REFERENCES

[1] BRUNER, J. S., G. A. MILLER, and C. ZIMMERMAN, Discriminative skill and discriminative matching in perceptual recognition, *J. Exptl. Psychol.*, 1955, **49** (3), 187-92.

[2] BUSH, R., and F. MOSTELLER, *Stochastic Models for Learning*, New York: Wiley, 1955.

[3] EGAN, J. P., Articulation testing methods, *Laryngoscope*, 1948, **58**, 955-91.

[4] LORGE, I., and H. SOLOMON, Two models of group behavior in the solution of Eureka-type problems, *Psychometrika*, 1955, **20**, 139-48.

[5] LORGE, I., and H. SOLOMON, Individual performance and group performance in problem solving related to group size and previous exposure to the problem, *J. Soc. Psychol.*, 1959, **48**, 107-14.

[6] LORGE, I., and H. SOLOMON, Group and individual performance in problem solving related to previous exposure to problem, level of aspiration, and group size, *Behav. Sci.*, 1960, **5** (1), 28-38.

[7] MARQUART, D. I., Group problem solving, *J. Soc. Psychol.*, 1955, **41**, 103-13.

[8] MILLER, G. A., and W. J. McGILL, A statistical description of verbal learning, *Psychometrika*, 1952, **17**, 369-96.

[9] SHAW, M. E., Comparison of individuals and small groups in the rational solution of complex problems, *Amer. J. Psychol.*, 1932, **44**, 491-504.

16

Some Puzzling Aspects of Social Interaction

Omar K. Moore and Alan R. Anderson,
Yale University

1. Folk-Models

In a recent paper [7] we introduced the notion of an *autotelic folk-model*, and made some suggestions concerning application of the idea. Our purpose here is to spell out these suggestions in more detail. But to forestall possibly irrelevant criticism we will begin by mentioning some similarities between our heuristic position and certain systems of what we shall call "synthetic philosophy" (for example, Whitehead's metaphysics).

One striking point of similarity is this: there is a sense in which we feel we do not know what we are talking about. By this we mean that our remarks to follow do not constitute a *theory*. And as evidence for this contention we cite the fact that we have no logically valid arguments to support what we say. To be sure, we believe ourselves to be in very good company in this respect, at least so far as the behavioral sciences and systems of synthetic philosophy are concerned—we do not believe others know what they are talking about, either (in the technical sense defined above). Whitehead, for example, gives us very few arguments in favor of his metaphysics—he just tells us how the world looks to him. In this paper we will be presumptuous enough to try to tell you how the world looks to us. At worst the picture we draw will be misleading; at best it may suggest some experimental or formal problems of interest.

With this *caveat*, we begin by summarizing briefly the principal thesis of our earlier paper, which is in part founded on the following two observations. First we note that there are very few theories, with any mathematical depth at all, which have been found to have applications in the behavioral sciences. These are principally theories of games of chance ("probability theory") and theories of games of strategy (after von Neumann). Second, we observe that each of these theories grew directly out of the study of *autotelic* activities—that is, activities undertaken by human beings solely because of their intrinsic interest. Engaging in social games, playing with puzzles or aesthetic objects, simply being sociable, are autotelic activities, which are, or should be, undertaken solely because they are enjoyable.

As regards the second point: the close connection between game theory and probability theory on the one hand and social games on the other is not open to question. It is simply a fact of history that for both theories, the first models to be considered were ordinary social games. But one may wish to raise doubts about the claim that social games and the like are *autotelic*, especially if one belongs to one of the more austere schools of social psychology which holds that it is not possible for *anyone* ever to do *anything* just for fun. To such critics we make a minor concession, perhaps putting the matter in a way which will satisfy even the most puritanical: even if no one ever does enjoy anything, the rules of our society make it clear that people are under an *obligation* to enjoy *some* things, at least. There are severely sanctioned rules, for example, to the effect that one should take part in sports only because one wants to play. We are all supposed to give short shrift to grand-standers, cheaters, and people who "let the side down" or otherwise exhibit "bad form." And the rules governing autotelic activity, which have the effect of *keeping* the activity autotelic, are remarkably pervasive. We may not do business at a party; we may not go to the opera in order to be seen there by the right people; we may not join the country club simply to meet the right people; quite the opposite. People break these rules, of course; but it seems clear that there *are* such rules to be broken, and also that *some* behavior is autotelic in the required sense, i.e., that *sometimes* these rules are consciously complied with.[1] Arnold Lunn [17, p. 22], for example, writes: "The essence of sport is the invention of an artificial problem for the fun of solving it. Nobody plays golf because some obscure need is satisfied or complex resolved by putting little white balls into round holes . . . Golf is an artificial problem invented for the amusement of man, the problem of propelling a ball in the minimum number of strokes round an eighteen hole golf course."

Now the striking fact that both probability theory and game theory have models not only in the autotelic activities which led to their development, but also in the successful conduct of the more serious matters of survival and welfare, suggests the possibility that in acting autotelically we are "modeling" our own more serious behavior. This idea seems to be at the bottom of "formal sociology" in the sense of Simmel [25], who talks, for example, about sociability as the "play form" of sociation: at a party we

---

[1] As we have mentioned, a folk-model *must* be inexpensive, and most of them obviously are, in the sense that little of importance hangs on victory (unless we are soreheads, or gloaters, i.e., poor sports). And where substantial personal risks may be involved, as for example in mountaineering, delicate problems arise in an effort to keep the matter autotelic. (We would classify mountaineering (as a sport) as a "team puzzle model," and as a sport it is just as artificial as crossword puzzles.) However, risky sports must also be surrounded by rules that minimize the risk if the sport is to be kept truly autotelic. R. L. G. Irving [16] quotes with understandable annoyance the definition, "sport is any activity which manifests itself by measuring force against resistance, and the motives for which are the attainment of personal distinction." Lunn also deplores the introduction of extraneous elements such as international rivalry into a sport.

engage playfully in competition, cooperation, deceit, love, hostility, and the thousand and one other forms that social behavior may take—but we *play* at it, for no stakes.

The essence of our previous paper is then: It might prove fruitful to look at autotelic cultural products (puzzles, games of chance, games of strategy, plays, novels, and the like) as *models* in the folk-culture, or *folk-models*, of the serious concerns of survival and human welfare— models with the help of which we come to understand and "be at home with" our natural and social environments. So put, the thesis risks banality; what gives the thesis such teeth as it has, is the fact that social games and certain serious (say) economic problems are models of the same theory (regardless of the actual behavior of players, buyers, and sellers) and so may be said to have a formal similarity sufficient to lend some credibility to our contention.

2. Games and Puzzles

For the purpose of this essay, we will ask you to assume that puzzles, games, and the like are inexpensive models, with the help of which we come to learn about the world in which we live. In order to clarify this assumption, we will first enlarge a little on *interactional* models, especially games of strategy.

It is characteristic of social interaction that I cannot maximize my own utility without "taking into account" (in some vague sense which we understand only darkly) what *you* are up to. I must have some theories or intuitions about how you are likely to behave, how you will respond to my actions, and the like. Worse than that, I must be aware that you are very likely doing the same thing in regard to me, and I have to take *that* possibility into account as well. But of course you may know that I am aware of this possibility, and you adjust your behavior accordingly. And so it goes—we are both involved in a tortuous labyrinth of relations, and though we act in this way quite easily and freely, it is better than even money that neither of us could even begin to give an explicit account of how we do it. It is the complexity of this kind of behavior, together with our inability to explain it, which lends plausibility to the suggestion that we *learn* to behave in this way by playing games of strategy. This is exactly the kind of behavior that hide-and-seek (say) requires—but in hide-and-seek failure to win is relatively inexpensive.

The interactional models provided by games of strategy may be contrasted with the noninteractional models found in puzzles. It is of course true that we can regard puzzles as one-player games—but it still seems clear that puzzles do not share the interactional features of games of strategy. Once the conditions of a puzzle are set, they do not change on us suddenly with a view to thwarting our efforts at a solution; indeed this is exactly how we distinguish between "puzzles" and "games."

Now if we are correct in our estimate of the importance of such folk-models as puzzles and games of strategy for the process which sociologists call "socialization," we should expect that their influence would be pervasive and that their presence in the backs of our minds might, in subtle ways, not only intervene in much of our thinking, but even constitute the warp and woof of many of our thought patterns. Acting on this assumption, we shall now try to develop some plausible relations between these folk-models and scientific inquiry.

We observe first that both natural and behavioral sciences are, among other things, social enterprises, undertaken in a societal context, and that they both presuppose social selves in the sense of Mead [18], capable of social *interaction*. Now our own informal observations lead us to believe that the principal problems faced by, and produced by, infants, at least as they begin to learn speech, are interactional in character: the problems faced have to do with certain social rules, as laid down, enforced or exemplified by other human beings. There are many examples: talking in accord with linguistic conventions, eating, toilet-training, playing together peaceably, respecting seniors. All of these activities are rule-ridden,[2] and it seems plausible to suggest therefore that in the socialization process social games should be prior, both temporally and in order of importance, to puzzles. Even non-interactional folk-models, say puzzles, presuppose social interaction, in the sense that they require a social context and an ability to understand the restraints put on those artificial problems we call "puzzles."

Indeed, we find some support for the notion that interactional models have a deep hold on us from the prevalence of animistic thinking in so-called "primitive" societies. In fact, it is hard to eradicate even in "civilized" societies; many research scientists half-believe Finagle's Laws (which presuppose that inanimate objects are out to get us).

In social interaction we recognize that our opposite number is potentially friendly, hostile, or indifferent to us and our concerns. It would moreover seem quite natural, especially in a state of ignorance, to endow nature with these same attributes. This is in fact a sound conservative strategy and one we have all followed from time to time. A person finding an inert bat on his doorstep does well to treat it as if it were alive until he is pretty certain that it is not. If we know little of nature generally, it might do trivial harm, and considerable good, if we were to treat nature as if it *might*, suddenly, turn on us.[3]

Now it seems to us to require a vertiginous act of abstraction to *remove* the interactional elements from our view of nature. "De-humanizing" an anthropomorphic nature ought to require a sizable wrench, as experience with civilizing primitive peoples indicates. It is therefore not altogether surprising that it took millenia of human history before the natural sciences

---

[2] The importance of the concept *following a rule*, especially a linguistic rule, has probably been recognized more clearly by Wittgenstein [31] than by anyone else in the history of philosophy, sociology, or psychology.

[3] We note that this fiction of a hostile, animistic nature, lies behind Wald's treatment [29] of confidence levels in the behavioral sciences. For a similar idea see Moore [19].

developed, especially if it is conceded that physics demands an abandonment of animism. It is central to the classical Newtonian view of natural phenomena that they be regarded as isolated systems, which run entirely by themselves and are not influenced at all by us. Nature is, in short, assimilated to a puzzle.[4] *People* (as opposed to *bodies*) have been eradicated from the picture as ruthlessly and as completely as may be, and we are left with a mindless mechanism which dominated, and still dominates, the attitude of many working natural scientists. No one of course can maintain that as a heuristic principle, mechanism has been unsuccessful in the natural sciences—our astonishing theoretical and technological progress would seem to indicate that in physics this is precisely the right view to take.

In view of the success of the puzzle model in the natural sciences, it is not at all surprising that those interested in the behavioral sciences should have tried equally to remove *people* from their considerations. The principal thesis of behaviorism, at least in its early and crude forms, was that a human organism is a black box, subject to certain inputs and outputs, which should be studied like any other physical system. Social and psychological processes were to be regarded as isolated phenomena of a mechanistic sort, to be studied in complete abstraction from the social, interactional context in which they occur. Such an attitude is at least strongly suggested by the preoccupation in the first half of this century with rote-learning experiments and psycho-physical measurements, and more recently by attempts to simulate various kinds of problem-solving on computers.

In this section we have thus far been concerned primarily to push the folk-model thesis to the following point: there are important differences between interactional models (games) and noninteractional models (puzzles). Theoretical and technological successes in the physical sciences have "depended," in some sense, on looking at nature from the point of view of a puzzle model rather than a social-interactional model; we may say alternatively that the puzzle model is *appropriate* to physics in a way in which the interactional model is not. At any rate, we would like again to take this vague contention as a heuristic assumption.

We want to make one further observation: It seems quite clear that the most important and impressive applications of descriptive mathematics have been in those areas where puzzle models are most appropriate. Of course it is true that we have enjoyed almost three hundred years of applications of high-powered mathematical methods to solve problems in physics, and we have devoted barely thirty years to the elaboration of the same kinds

---

[4] It might be objected that a conception of natural processes devoid of social interaction was known to several early Greek cosmologists, for example Democritus, and that consequently we are on shaky ground historically. In reply we explain that we do not mean to hold the position in such a sharp form. It must at least be conceded that Homer and Hesiod had a view of nature which was pervaded by social interaction—and all we wish to claim is that the latter kind of view is likely to come first. Even so, the classical views which pervaded western attempts at science up until the scientific Renaissance were those of Aristotle, which, if not involving social interaction explicitly, at least embodied many anthropomorphic norms.

of methods in the behavioral sciences. In the latter case one may even genuinely doubt that the significance of such empirical results as have been obtained justifies the sophistication of the mathematical methods employed. Surely no one would argue that anything remotely like celestial mechanics has resulted from the mathematical study of human behavior; and *we* would still advise a person interested in the human condition to read Durrell's *Alexandria Quartet* [12] rather than an equal number of volumes of some professional journal in the behavioral sciences.

There is of course no *a priori* reason why this should be so; it may well be that the paucity of impressive results arises directly from the youth of the enterprise. After all, social scientists have been trying to apply mathematical methods in the behavioral sciences for only a fraction of the time the physicists have had; maybe we have not yet located our Archimedes. We have used this line of defense often enough to have feelings of great attachment for it. Still, it may be that now the time is ripe for those of us on the side of the angels to scrutinize the devil's claims a little more carefully (to draw on one highly-touted dramaturgical folk-model).

3. Puzzle Models and Social Interaction

We now propose that the attempt to apply the descriptive mathematical methods appropriate to the puzzle model in the social sciences is a mistake (in a certain sense we should like to get clear about). There are principally three considerations which move us to this feeling, of which the first is rather minor, though not without interest on its own account.

1. The mechanistic ideal of nineteenth-century physics has, even in the natural sciences, been crumbling in this century. Nothing could be more foreign to that ideal than the notion that the position or velocity of the observer could make a difference to the observations (as relativity theory indicates). The same anti-mechanistic idea is implicit also in Heisenberg's Uncertainty Principle, namely, that even making a physical observation jiggles things a little bit—the "totally isolated" system is affected even by being observed. Even Church's theorem may be looked upon as a limitation on what *we* can do. In short, even in physics and mathematics *people* (or at any rate scientific people) are creeping back into the picture in ways unimaginable to natural scientists of the last century.

2. Second, and more important, there is a difference between the relation of a natural scientist to his subject matter, and that of a behavioral scientist to his subject matter, which seems to us to have received insufficient attention in the literature. One sometimes gets the idea that behavioral scientists would like to *predict* human behavior in much the way that a weather man predicts the weather, and to contrive mathematical theories which will enable these predictions to be even more accurate. What seems frequently to be overlooked is that though the weather is unlikely to change its character *because* we have made a prediction about it, people, on the other hand, are quite likely to change their behavior *because* we have predicted that they will behave in such and such a way.

There is a delightful tale, no doubt apocryphal, to the effect that a group of freshman interviewees at Yale (for a psychological study) decided that each member of the group would manage somehow in the course of the interview to mention white horses. The group of subjects was substantial, and so was the consternation of the interviewers when they compared notes. The tangle was finally unravelled, owing to what we regard as weakness of character on the part of one of the freshmen. He confessed. But the episode illustrates a point: subjects *need* have no serious purpose in confounding a study in the behavioral sciences—they may do it just as a practical joke. (A "practical" joke is, by our reckoning, a non-autotelic joke, at least for the victim.)

More to the point, it seems plausible to suppose that if people are given a reasonably good theory, which enables them to cope conceptually with a broad class of problems, they will *use* it, and in that respect, at least, alter their (perhaps social) behavior. There can be no doubt, for example, that the theory of games of strategy *has* been used occasionally in formulating policy, and it would seem that the resulting behavior could be sensibly accounted for most economically by the assumption that the persons involved knew the theory and were using it.

In short, a decent theory is likely to influence the behavior of those who know it. This means that our predictions of human behavior may go wrong if we tell our subjects all we know, i.e., if we give them the techniques required to solve the problems we set. (And notice that if we deliberately conceal our theories, we violate one of the ideals of the scientific enterprise, namely, that scientific results should be public; in principle, in the behavioral sciences the roles of investigator and investigatee are interchangeable. This is not true in physics, chemistry, or mathematics.)

3. Third, the distinction between those who have predominately puzzle models and those who have predominately interactional models in the backs of their heads seems to us to shed some light on a factional dispute among intellectuals, which has been causing uneasiness in certain quarters recently. We have in mind the kind of situation considered by C. P. Snow [26]. It seems reasonable to suppose that people who are concerned with, and perceptive of, the nuances of social interaction, and who think of the world as a place inhabited by others who are also experiencing major or minor successes or frustrations in living their lives—people with such interactional preoccupations are more likely to become literary intellectuals: novelists, or playwrights, or psychoanalysts, or historians. From this standpoint it is not difficult to see that what the black-box enthusiasts are doing must seem monumentally irrelevant to the important aspects of social human behavior. "Who *cares* about 'tests of significance' which are not tests of significance? What could be a more blandly inane way to approach or evaluate any important aspect of our lives with other people?"

To the scientific intellectuals, on the other hand, at least those who see nature and society through the same polarized lenses, the work of the *literati* must seem so much idle vapouring. "The concepts are not clear, there is a lot of wild talk about Minds, and Intentions, and Emotions, and the like—

not a shred of anything that looks even remotely as if it could be treated as a puzzle, or mathematized in any way at all. No insights of any interest can possibly be gained in this way about anything, much less about anything as complicated as human behavior—so let's leave all that to the dilettantes, and get back to the old drawing board."

Of course we have drawn the split more sharply than it deserves; still, it seems clear that some such divisiveness is in evidence; and differences among the kinds of models we have been considering look to us relevant to the dispute.

4. A Mathematical Treatment of Social Interaction

Such, then, is a rough general picture of the role we believe folk-models to play and the influences we think they have. We will now show that they are relevant to our topic. In particular, we will consider, from the point of view we have been outlining, a recent application of mathematics to social interaction.

In a recent interesting book, Suppes and Atkinson report some elegantly designed experiments concerning two-player games, the results of which are then analyzed from two points of view: their own variation of learning theory (black-box heuristics), and game theory (social-interaction heuristics). We find their interpretations of their experimental results of particular interest, since they are so sharply at divergence with our own. They write as follows [28, p. 3]:

... we have been concerned with the application of learning theory to situations involving social interaction. From this standpoint, we have ignored concepts like friendliness, cohesiveness, group pressure, and opinion discrepancy, which have been important in the recent investigations of many social psychologists, and have attempted instead to explain the detailed features of social interaction situations in terms of conditioning concepts. The exchange of information between players in a game, for instance, can be successfully analyzed in terms of an organism's ability to discriminate between stimuli, the important point being that this information may be treated in terms of the notion of stimulus in exactly the same way that perceptual stimuli in a one-person situation are handled. The social situation, *qua* social, does not require the introduction of new concepts. We do not claim that our experiments on highly structured game situations justify the inference that no new fundamental concepts are required to explain any social behavior. But we think it is important to demonstrate in empirical detail and with quantitative accuracy that no new concepts are needed for a substantial class of social situations.

We can agree with them at the outset that the results show clearly that game theory is less effective in predicting behavior (in the experiments they consider) than is the learning theory they apply. But their experiments have one feature which leads us to question their more general conclusions.

In order to eliminate stimuli which are difficult to measure (facial expressions, nuances of voice, body movement, etc.) and to get some control over the situation, players are separated by a screen and communicate only by lights and buttons (which are in addition under the experimenter's control). The plays of the game then consist of various ways of pushing buttons, observing lights, and receiving rewards. Indeed, in some cases there is no communication at all between players after the play begins.

Now it seems to us that the fact that game theory is less effective *in these situations* than the authors' learning theory might lead to one of two conclusions: Either (1) "social behavior may be analyzed without remainder in terms of the concepts of stimulus, response, and reinforcement and the processes of stimulus sampling and conditioning" [28, p. 256]; or (2) the abstractions required to make learning theory apply (i.e., the control of stimuli, leading to elimination of any effect even of players observing each other) have in effect eliminated *social* interaction between the players.

Of course we are not arguing that game theory is somehow superior as a descriptive theory for the experiments considered; it seems to us that the evidence presented by Suppes and Atkinson is conclusive on this point. We do question the broader claim that "the social situation, *qua* social, does not require the introduction of new concepts." Nor are we arguing that black-box heuristics have no place in psychology; people engaged in basic research have a legitimate right to be interested in whatever interests them; and learning experiments certainly have the stability and informativeness required of scientific theories, however irrelevant they may be to (say) problems of formulating public policy, or the problem of designing an experiment.

Our conclusion is essentially that the experiments did not involve social interaction in the sense meant by most sociologists and social psychologists; in evidence we offer two considerations.

In the first place, the experimental arrangement was such that the only way in which the subjects could tell whether social interaction was involved, was from the words of the experimenter. In fact, each of the experiments could have been carried out in such a way that the experimenter was in complete control—issuing rewards and punishments entirely at his own discretion and without regard for plays by opposing players.

We do not mean to deny, of course that *some* social interaction was involved. There was certainly social interaction between the experimenters and the subjects, and between the subjects and laboratory personnel before they entered the experimental situation. (On this point see Criswell [11].) Nor do we deny that in certain formal respects, social interaction was present in the experimental situation, at least in the sense that game-theoretical notions could be applied. Nor do we mean to deny that it is of interest to see whether subjects can treat a situation as interactional even when the usual clues are missing, and the subjects have to be *told* that the situation is interactional. (Notice, incidentally, that the subjects must already have an idea of what is involved in social interaction in order to interpret meaningfully the information the experimenters provide about the game-like character of the task.) Nor, finally, do we wish to deny that experimental schematizations of full-bodied interactional patterns are of interest; one of us has himself done experiments that were highly schematized.

But we do submit that when "social interaction" (in the important sense that everyone finds so difficult to explain) is really present, the situation involved in the experiments does not obtain. People do not in general need to be told that they are in an interactional situation—such a situation bears its interactional character on its face.

This is the first of our reasons for doubting that social interaction was involved in the experiment. The second is as follows:

In the experiments under consideration, the subjects had to *learn* what strategies were realistically, in terms of pay-off, available at all—as opposed to *using* interactional strategies already available. We acknowledge of course that interactional strategies must be learned—a matter which is perplexing enough in its own right. But learning good chess strategies inductively is a different enterprise from employing such strategies in a play of the game.

It is clear that one important aspect of the task set for subjects in the experiment was that of *learning* strategies for playing the game. This fact alone might (possibly) account for the fact that learning theory applied. But as "social interaction" is usually conceived, we do not say that A is interacting (as opposed to *learning* to interact) with B, unless A has some conception of the structure of the social situation of which he is a part, i.e., unless he has some idea as to how his actions affect his "utilities." This amounts in effect to having some strategies already in mind, which are relevant to the interactional encounter, and among which the participant may choose.

The contention that social interaction may be "reduced" to individual psychology becomes even more dubious if we consider the probable result of letting the subjects in on the secret. Surely if, in those experiments where the pay-off matrix was displayed, the subjects were loyal to the experiment and were on top of game theory, their behavior would have approximated the latter much more closely.

With this last point we close our case. Suppose we grant that the success of learning theory over game theory, in making predictions, supports the view that no peculiarly social concepts are required to explain social interaction. Then parity of reasoning would seem to require that if game theory had been more successful, then characteristically "social" concepts *would* be required to explain social interaction. But it is not at all difficult to imagine a situation in which game theory would be more successful than learning theory: namely a situation in which (1) the subjects knew game theory, (2) game theory was applicable, and (3) the subjects used it.

We hope to have shown, at a minimum, that the claim that social interaction requires (as we shall put it) no extra-psychological concepts is a philosophical, or methodological, or heuristic thesis, rather than a scientific theory. We hasten to add that nothing that Suppes and Atkinson say would require them to deny this minimal claim. They have, characteristically, been careful to qualify what they say. For example, they write [28, p. 265]: "The experimental problem involves exact and clear identification of the stimuli. At present, we may not always be able to identify the relevant stimuli experimentally, for many of the nuances of social communication and activity depend on a long history of verbal usage and interaction. Nevertheless, we are convinced that ultimately such an analysis can be provided."

We hope we have also made it clear that we have no objections to black-box heuristics; as we remarked (in effect) before, any heuristic orientation which produces interesting and elegant results is welcome.

But we do feel that no one has *shown* that extra-psychological concepts are unnecessary in explaining social interaction. Nor, of course, have we shown that such concepts are necessary. It is like proofs of the existence of dryads. No one has proved their existence to our satisfaction, and in our heart of hearts we know that it cannot be done. But we have no *proof* that it cannot be. Similarly we have no proof that specifically social, as opposed to psychological, concepts are required to understand social interaction. But we would like to turn now to some considerations which might lead one to believe that such is the case.

5. Rules

Consider the following problem. Suppose you were to find yourself on a lifeless moon, with no possibility of returning to, or communicating with, the earth. Suppose also that you were in a frame of mind to do something bad. What would you do?

In informal conversation, this question has elicited a wide variety of initial responses, but after a little thought the answer generally settles on the following point: the only way to do something bad in those circumstances is somehow to break some *rule*. It may be moot whether there are any rules to break in the quasi-solipsistic universe we are considering; the examples we have heard (spitting, say, or offending God or oneself by committing suicide) have a farfetched ring to them. But note that even this kind of outrageous rule-breaking is doing something *against* someone or some thing: the idea of rule-breaking in which no one (or nothing) gets hurt in any way, seems, or seems almost, self-contradictory. (See, e.g., Anderson [1], [2], Prior [23], or Nowell-Smith and Lemmon [22].)

In this paper we have been trying (from time to time) to appear to be sane arguers and also (from time to time) to say what we believe, even without the kind of evidence we would like to have. Here we come on one of the latter points. The "conclusion" seems to us inescapable that *self-consciously acting in accordance with a rule* (or formulating such rules) is one of the fundamental aspects of social interaction, and any experimental studies which neglect this point simply have nothing to do with that topic. Indeed this is implicit in our earlier claims that social games of strategy are *models* of social interaction; obedience to game rules must be self-conscious. The whole point is, as Hume [15, p. 210] says in comparing games with other social interaction:

> In societies for play, there are laws required for the conduct of the game; and these laws are different in each game. The foundation, I own, of such societies is frivolous; and the laws are, in a great measure, though not altogether, capricious and arbitrary...The comparison, therefore, in these respects, is very imperfect. We may only learn from it the necessity of rules, wherever men have any intercourse with each other...It is impossible for men so much as to murder each other without statutes, and maxims...

6. Prediction and Control in Sociology

We have been trying to "establish" two points: (1) The descriptive mathematics appropriate to puzzle models simply does not fit social interaction; and (2) one principal characteristic which distinguishes group sociology from individual psychology is the concept of *self-consciously following and formulating social rules*.

Now if we are right on the first point, one might very reasonably demand that we suggest some alternatives. If social interaction does not have the puzzle-like features appropriate to descriptive mathematical treatment, then what are those of us who are interested in the scientific study of social interaction to do?

One might incorrectly draw from our remarks the conclusion that we take a dim view of applications of mathematical or logical techniques in the behavioral sciences; this is far from the truth. In our earlier paper [7] we tried to suggest some ways in which formal analyses could be brought to bear on problems concerning human behavior.[5] It seems to us, however, that the most fruitful approach is likely to be indirect. It is a mathematical commonplace that a satisfactory theory requires simplifying assumptions, and in a sense we have been arguing that folk-models are based on the same principle. We can look at chess as a quasi-mathematical abstraction from serious social interaction; so viewed it is not quite so surprising that a mathematical treatment of games as cultural objects is possible. Of course the theory of games is not a mathematical theory of human behavior; it is rather a theory of cultural objects which people have invented and (or so we claim) used to help shape their behavior. But without intending to minimize in any way von Neumann's monumental achievement in formulating the theory of games, it still seems to us that only the barest beginning has been made in the formal analysis of autotelic cultural objects. For example, the whole domain of aesthetic objects is virtually untouched.

Even a complete analysis of existing folk-models would, however, still leave us with major problems. If we are correct in holding that folk-models

---

[5] In the present volume, Anderson's paper (chapter 1) also offers a formal treatment of the typically social behavior which we have discussed, the application of a rule.

constitute the theoretical arm of a society's culture, it would seem that in relatively stable, static societies, the theoretical problems have in this sense been solved (i.e., stability is ensured, granted no major changes in population, size, technology, etc.). And in a slowly evolving society, one might expect gifted individuals to come up with new models reflecting the changes. By and large, few societies have failed to develop socializing techniques sufficient to produce members of the society in good standing: on the whole the record for stable societies in the past has not been one of consistent failure.

But presently existing folk-models are not enough. They have evidently been produced on a hit-or-miss basis, and in societies which have been stable enough to tolerate many mistakes. But we, in common with many others,[6] feel that modern industrial societies, especially in relation to populous underdeveloped areas, are in a state of unstable, dynamic disequilibrium, and it seems to us doubtful whether we can risk continuing to be so haphazard in our construction and dissemination of autotelic socializing models.

Traditionally of course, no one has thought of a social scientist's job as that of creating folk-models. The task for social scientists has been thought of as similar to the task of any other scientist—namely, to learn to predict, and in some measure control, certain aspects of our environment (however one may wish to interpret these vague words). But when the objects we wish to make predictions about, and to control, are other *people*, the goals of prediction and control take on a faintly ominous ring.

To take the notion of control first, there are obvious senses in which we wish to control the behavior of others; criminal codes are designed to do just that. So are civil methods for obtaining remedies and redress. But one of the principal tenets of what we like to think of as a democratic society is that the liberty of action for individuals shall be restricted, or controlled, as little as possible, consonant with the continued existence of the society. There *have* been behavioral scientists who take the attitude that what is required is a strong effort to produce a society like that of *Brave New World*. (For a frightening example see Halmos [13].) But the idea of exerting this kind of fierce control over our fellow-men may well worry others as much as it does us. The control we wish to exercise, at least from the ideological standpoint we espouse, should be as minimal as possible.

Again there are obvious senses in which we wish to be able to predict

---

[6] We cite for example, Whitehead [30, p. 756]: "Our sociological theories, our political philosophy, our practical maxims of business, our political economy, and our doctrines of education, are derived from an unbroken tradition of great thinkers and of practical examples, from the age of Plato in the fifth century before Christ to the end of the last century. The whole of this tradition is warped by the vicious assumption that each generation will substantially live amid the conditions governing the lives of its fathers and will transmit those conditions to mould with equal force the lives of its children. We are living in the first period of human history for which this assumption is false."

correctly the behavior of others. We like to feel confident that a taxi driver will take us where we tell him; we are pretty certain that if a person is dropped from an airplane, he will go down (rather than up); and it may be of interest to know how fast people can (on the average) memorize nonsense. We might even be interested in trying to predict with accuracy and in detail how people will solve serious and difficult intellectual problems, such as that posed by the Michelson-Morley experiment.

Under this head we have two remarks to make. In the first place, if we could have predicted that Einstein would come up with the Special Theory of Relativity, we would have been in a position to solve the problem ourselves. "What were the inputs?" we would ask. "Well, with those inputs, and with that history, we get the following outputs," we would answer. Our theory of behavior would then simultaneously have an enormous impact on both physics and international politics.

Surely no one seriously envisages anything of the kind. Even those of us who have conducted experiments designed to enable us to predict some rather trivial aspect of human behavior have taken some pride in the novelty and ingenuity of our experimental design. We couldn't have predicted, two years before, that we were going to do just *that*, and we know ourselves as intimately as anyone does.

Secondly, there is, from an intellectual point of view, something disappointing about the possibility of predicting *how* people will solve problems. We may sometimes be able to do it, of course. If a person really wants to know the solutions to the equation $5x^2 + 3x + 2 = 0$ and if he knows enough algebra, it is not hard to guess what he will do. But we also have the feeling that such problems are trivial. If we give someone an algorithm for a class of problems, it is reasonable to expect that he will use it to solve problems in that class. The interesting problems, whether of an interactional or puzzle character, are the difficult ones—the ones that neither we nor others know the answer to.

This observation brings us back to the "major problems" mentioned at the top of the previous page. We have pointed out that in stable, relatively static societies we might expect folk-wisdom (and available folk-models) to suffice for the job of socializing the members of the society. Familiar problems get codified, and abstract, schematized folk-models may be explored autotelically, so that members of the society can learn about various aspects of their environment in an inexpensive way.

We would like to suggest that in a dynamic society of the kind mentioned earlier, something new in the way of folk-models will be needed. If we can't tell what kinds of problems are likely to face us, we can even less predict the kinds of solutions they will require. In such a situation, it becomes urgent to supply not only new folk-models but also models which will enable people to cope with situations in which the rules are continually changing. We are all familiar with the anxiety produced in children when they don't know what is expected of them (not that they necessarily *do* what they are required to do—but even when they don't behave, they *know* they are being bad). The stresses involved in (say) "civilizing" a group of "primitives" point to the same moral. Autotelic activities in which the rules are constantly changing may provide one way of acclimating people to a world of constantly and rapidly shifting norms.

We began this section with a promise to offer some alternatives to the standard view of behavioral science as a program for predicting and controlling human behavior; obviously our remarks thus far have been abstract and programmatic. As inadequate examples of the kind of thing we have in mind, we will mention some formal and experimental work that has been suggested by the heuristic considerations we have been trying to expound in this paper.

1. One of us has been constructing a family of dynamic autotelic responsive environments,[7] designed to elicit creative behavior on the part of children. These responsive environments are experimental, in the sense that they require experimental equipment (e.g., a special-purpose computer to serve as a companion to the "subjects"), and of course children for the environment. It is also experimental in the sense that detailed records of the children's behavior are kept (and also, finally, in the sense that "experiments" in the narrower sense can, and will, be run). But the studies and the heuristic considerations which motivated them are not offered as a "theory of human behavior." The experimental techniques stem rather from an abstract analysis of the cultural objects to which the children are to be exposed, and a rough formal analysis of possible kinds of environments.

The principal aim of this work is to produce novel, creative behavior, and new cultural objects, both inside and outside the artificial environment. Harking back to our previous remarks about predictability, one can easily see that we would be deeply disappointed if the children's behavior were predictable in any detail. As matters now stand there is at least one thing we feel that can be safely predicted—the children will return to interesting responsive environments with apparent pleasure, though the option of not coming is always available. That is, these are "experiments" in which it is not necessary to coerce, cajole, trick, or hire, subjects. In fact they learn more from the situation than the experimenters do.[8]

---

[7] By a "responsive environment" we mean an environment which satisfies the following conditions: (1) it permits subjects to explore freely; (2) it is self-pacing, i.e., events happen in the environment at rates determined by the subjects; (3) the environment retains its lawful aspects, in spite of (2), so that subjects cannot distort the environment (e.g., by going so fast that things blur); (4) it permits subjects to make full use of their capacities for making inductive and deductive inferences about the events in the environment: it is non-didactic, in the sense that it does not teach, though subjects learn; (5) it is probable that subjects will make a series of interrelated discoveries about aspects of the physical, social, or cultural world, selected by the experimenter; and (6) it is dynamic, in the sense that each discovery can be used in the course of making new discoveries. Space does not allow a fuller discussion. Accounts of the matter may be found in Moore [20] and Moore and Anderson [21].

[8] Mention should also be made in this connection of some elegant work of Suppes [27]; our own brief experience with these materials convinces us that children enjoy returning to these books, and that experience with them is in that sense autotelic.

What is sought is an environment in which "subjects" emerge (if anything) superior in some abilities to the experimenter, and are prepared to undertake and solve problems which are beyond the abilities of the experimenter. Ideally they would become experimenters of the same sort, and be superseded by their own "subjects." Of course this is a coöperative undertaking, with (initially) junior and senior partners—but the relation between subject and experimenter in the behavioral sciences has always been necessarily cooperative, if success is to be achieved at all (cf. the white horses mentioned in section 3).

2. Cooperating, or operating together on some task, requires two things: some idea of a goal to be attained, and some structure of rules within which the operation of attaining the goal is to be carried on. A second "application" of the general heuristic scheme we have been describing is in the formal or mathematical analysis of the notion of a *rule*. Before 1920, there were scarcely any attempts to apply formal techniques to anything of a normative character. (One might want to count probability theory as a counter-example, especially if it is associated with "degree of rational belief"—but other counter-examples would be hard to find.) The advent of the theory of games, and more recently of deontic logic,[9] seems to indicate that a broader range of cultural objects is amenable to mathematical analysis. Again these are *not* "theories of human behavior"; they are rather an analysis of what constitutes "strategically correct" play for one who wants to win, or "correct" inferences as to what is enjoined, permitted, or forbidden, by a set of rules. After some ten years of investigation by a number of people, the topic is still in a rudimentary state, but some aspects of the matter are becoming clearer. Five years ago it was not at all obvious how the *relevance* of one proposition to another could be handled formally. We now have at any rate one explication of the notion that seems to suffice for certain purposes.[10]

As we see matters, one of the principal activities of social scientists will be, or should be, to continue the work begun (for our civilization) by Homer and Hesiod, i.e., to continue the job of constructing folk-models for the instruction and diversion of our fellow-creatures. We have no reason to believe that a more scientific, and less haphazard, approach to the problem will ensure success or even survival. But here again we are in good company; Bishop Butler [9] had misgivings too:

And though it is our business and our duty to endeavour, within the bounds of veracity and justice, to contribute to the ease, convenience, and even cheerfulness, and diversion of our fellow-creatures: yet, from our short views, it is greatly uncertain, whether this endeavour will, in particular instances, produce an overbalance of happiness upon the whole; since so many and distant things must come into the account. And that which makes it our

---

[9] See, e.g., Anderson [3] and [4], Anderson and Moore [8], Castañeda [10], Hintikka [14], Rescher [24], and von Wright [32].

[10] See Anderson and Belnap [5] and [6], and the paper in this volume by Anderson (p. 11).

duty is that there is some appearance that it will, and no positive appearance sufficient to balance this on the contrary side; and also, that such benevolent endeavour is a cultivation of that most excellent of all virtuous principles, the active principle of benevolence.

REFERENCES

[1] ANDERSON, A. R., "The Formal Analysis of Normative Systems," Technical Report No. 2, Office of Naval Research, Contract SAR/Nonr-609(16), NR 170-044, with Yale University, 1956.

[2] ANDERSON, A. R., The logic of norms, *Logique et Analyse*, 1958, **2**, 84-91.

[3] ANDERSON, A. R., On the logic of "Commitment," *Philosoph. Studies*, 1959, **10**, 23-7.

[4] ANDERSON, A. R., A reduction of deontic logic to alethic modal logic, *Mind*, 1958, **67**, 100-103.

[5] ANDERSON, A. R., and N. D. BELNAP, JR., The pure calculus of entailment (to be published in *The Journal of Symbolic Logic*).

[6] ANDERSON, A. R., and N. D. BELNAP, JR., Tautological entailments, *Philosoph. Studies*, 1962, **13**, 9-24.

[7] ANDERSON, A. R., and O. K. MOORE, Autotelic folk-models, *Sociol. Quar.*, 1960, **1**, 203-16.

[8] ANDERSON, A. R., and O. K. MOORE, The formal analysis of normative concepts, *Amer. Sociol. Rev.*, 1957, **22**(1), 11-17.

[9] BUTLER, J. (Bishop), *The Analogy of Religion*, 2d ed., London: Knapton, 1736.

[10] CASTAÑEDA, H. N., The logic of obligation, *Philosoph. Studies*, 1959, **10**, 17-22.

[11] CRISWELL, J. H., The psychologist as perceiver, chap. 8 in *Person Perception and Interpersonal Behavior*, R. Taguiri and L. Petrullo, eds., Stanford, Calif.: Stanford Univ. Press, 1958.

[12] DURRELL, L., *The Alexandria Quartet*, London: Faber and Faber, 1957-60.

[13] HALMOS, P. R., *Towards a Measure of Man*, New York: Humanities Press, 1957.

[14] HINTIKKA, K. J. J., Quantifiers in deontic logic, *Soc. Scient. Fennica: Commentat. human. litt.*, 1957, **23**, 2-23.

[15] HUME, D., *Enquiries Concerning the Human Understanding and Concerning the Principles of Morals* (L. A. Selby-Bigge, ed., 2d ed.), Oxford: Clarendon Press, 1951.

[16] IRVING, R. L. G., *The Romance of Mountaineering*, New York: Dutton, 1935.

[17] LUNN, A., *A Century of Mountaineering, 1857-1957*, London: Allen & Unwin, 1957.

[18] MEAD, G. H., *Mind, Self, and Society*, Chicago: Univ. of Chicago Press, 1934.

[19] MOORE, O. K., Divination—a new perspective, *Amer. Anthro.*, 1957, **59**, 69-74.

[20] MOORE, O. K., Orthographic symbols and the preschool child—a new approach, *Creativity: 1960 Proceedings of the Third Minnesota Conference on Gifted Children*, E. Paul Torrence, ed., Univ. of Minn., Center for Continuation Study, 1961, 91-101.

[21] MOORE, O. K., and A. R. ANDERSON, *Early Reading and Writing* (motion picture), Part I: "Skills," Part II: "Teaching Methods," Part III: "Development," Guilford, Conn.: Basic Education, Inc., 1960.

[22] NOWELL-SMITH, P. H., and E. J. LEMMON, Escapism: the logical basis of ethics, *Mind*, 1960, **69**(275), 289-300.

[23] PRIOR, A. N., Escapism, the logical basis of ethics, chap. 5 in *Essays in Moral Philosophy*, A. I. Melden, ed., Seattle, Wash: Univ. Washington Press, 1958.

[24] RESCHER, N., An axiom system for deontic logic, *Philosoph. Studies*, 1958, **9**, 24–30.

[25] SIMMEL, G., *The Sociology of Georg Simmel*, Glencoe, Ill.: Free Press, 1950.

[26] SNOW, C. P., *The Two Cultures and the Scientific Revolution*, Cambridge: Cambridge Univ. Press, 1960.

[27] SUPPES, P., *Set and Numbers, Book I*, Stanford, Calif.: the author, 1960.

[28] SUPPES, P., and R. C. ATKINSON, *Markov Learning Models for Multiperson Interactions*, Stanford, Calif.: Stanford Univ. Press, 1960.

[29] WALD, A., *Statistical Decision Functions*, New York: Wiley, 1950.

[30] WHITEHEAD, A. N., *Adventures of Ideas*, New York: Macmillan, 1933.

[31] WITTGENSTEIN, L., *Philosophical Investigations*, New York: Macmillan, 1950.

[32] VON WRIGHT, G. H., *An Essay in Modal Logic*, Amsterdam: North-Holland, 1951.

17

Speed and Accuracy of Cognitive Achievement in Small Groups

Frank Restle, *Michigan State University*

College students spend much of their time solving problems, often as members of small, accidental groups. In reaching solutions, a cooperative group has an advantage over an individual in that the group can solve a problem as soon as any member suceeds in doing so, as long as the solution is generally accepted. In addition, the group can "remember" all of the items that individual members remember and report. Furthermore, groups are less likely to accept wrong answers than are individuals, for it is usually difficult to get a whole group to agree on a single wrong answer. Although there are exceptions to these rules, it is relatively easy to find experimental conditions that show clearly the advantages of the cooperative group.

The small, accidental group is an attractive subject of study for the experimental psychologist. A sample of subjects can be drawn from a population such as the students in an introductory psychology course. Some subjects can be tested individually, and others formed at random into groups which are tested together. The independent variable is the size of the group, and the dependent variable is the level of achievement. The question is, how does achievement vary with the size of the group, other things equal (or randomized).

This paper describes the elementary theory for predicting the effects of group size. The theory, to be viable, must take account of how the subjects interact in the group, and this in turn depends on the nature of the problem. Since the theory of group performance on a problem depends on the theory of individual performance, some remarks about group and individual performance in the tasks of problem-solving and memorizing, are introduced.

1. Theory

The models used below are based on two assumptions. The first is the *pooling assumption*, i.e., the assumption that people are just as effective

The work reported in this paper was done while the author was a Faculty Research Fellow of the Social Science Research Council. He is now at Indiana University.

in groups as they are as individuals, which leads to the conclusion that the success of a group can be predicted by estimating parameters of the distribution of individual accomplishment and then combining these parameters. The second is the *waiting-time assumption*, i.e., that for a fairly homogeneous population of college students, success or failure and time to solution can be treated as simple stochastic variables and that in particular, the probability of any unitary cognitive achievement in a given trial or short interval of time is independent of time.

These are simple assumptions that do not take account of the complexity of group life. Their purpose is to define the simplest kind of experimental outcome, one which would be thought relatively uninteresting, and at the same time to provide reasonable predictions on the basis of simple and limited information.

1.1 Pooling. Lorge and Solomon [3] developed two models of group behavior in the solution of multiple-stage problems. Theirs is a "non-interactional ability model," which assumes that people working in groups are precisely as good as they are working alone, and that differences in performance depend upon differences in ability. In the Lorge–Solomon Model A, the population is divided into solvers and non-solvers. Data gathered from tests of individuals are used to estimate P_I, the proportion of individuals who can solve. Then, if the groups are randomly formed and consist of k people each, the probability that a group contains a solver is

(1) $$P_G = 1 - (1 - P_I)^k .$$

According to this model, a group will solve the problem if and only if the group contains at least one solver.

In the data used by Lorge and Solomon, which had been collected by Shaw [7], this model failed to give an accurate prediction of performance on one of three problems, the group's performance being better than predicted. The erroneous prediction was corrected by assuming that the problems might involve several stages, so that two individuals, each of whom can do only one stage (and neither of whom can solve the problem) might in a group, complement one another and attain group success. Lorge and Solomon referred to this "multiple-stage" model as Model B. Because of the difficulty of isolating stages and abilities of subjects on several stages, this model has never been put to a real experimental test.

The Lorge–Solomon models pool ability. The facts that some individuals succeed and others fail, and that people who succeed take different lengths of time to do so, are attributed to fixed differences between people. The success of a group depends upon whether it has a solver in it, and also, it is assumed, on the speed of the fastest solver in the group.

Another method for predicting performance is to pool accomplishment. Suppose, for example, that the probability is φ that any person in the population may solve the problem within a given minute, given that the problem is not already solved. The probability that someone in a group of size r will solve is $1 - (1 - \varphi)^r$, just as in equation (1). The difference between pooling ability and pooling accomplishment is that the latter depends on a rational theory of the distribution of accomplishments, and leads to a distribution of group accomplishments. Predictions can be more detailed than they would be if abilities were pooled. Furthermore, pooling accomplishments leads one to examine the experimental situation carefully for factors that will affect accomplishments, in the hope of finding the same factors in data on groups as in data on individuals.

The method of pooling is merely one of several possible methods of analyzing achievement. If the group solves whenever an individual in the group solves, accomplishments are pooled. In other situations, the group may solve when all members of the group have solved their problems. For example, the problem may be to agree on one of several interpretations of a sentence. One might suppose that each member must arrive at the solution before a unanimous agreement is reached. A third kind of problem might require that a majority of the group arrive at the same opinion, so that the probability of group agreement (and solution) becomes the same as the probability of majority agreement.

Each of these ways of completing the group task leads to a statement of the form, "the group solves if and only if..." followed by a specification of the conditions imposed on individuals in the group. The statement, an hypothesis about the relation of individual performance to group performance, will often determine the form of a mathematical model relating group and individual attainment. "Pooling" is a special case—"the group solves if and only if some individual in the group arrives at the correct solution."

1.2 Elementary Theory of Waiting Times. Consider a unitary event that may occur on any one of a sequence of occasions or trials, $1, 2, \cdots$. Suppose that p is the probability that the event occurs at trial 1. Assume that the term "unitary event" refers to an event that either occurs completely or does not occur at all; in other words, exclude the possibility that the event "partly occurs" in any sense. If the event does not occur at trial 1, then nothing has happened and the probability of its occurring on the next trial should be unchanged, p.

This concept of a unitary event leads to the idea that the probability that the event will occur on the next trial, given that it has not already occurred, is a constant p. Then the probability that the event first occurs on trial n is

$$(2) \qquad\qquad p(n; p) = (1 - p)^{n-1} p ,$$

which is the geometric or negative binomial distribution.

If the event can occur in continuous time, the usual limiting arguments are applied. Let $p(h)$ be the probability that the event will occur during the interval $(t, t + h)$, given that it has not occurred by time t. Then, since $p(h)$ does not vary with time t, the limit of $[p(h)/h]$ approaches a constant λ, and the density function, corresponding to the probability of solution at trial n, becomes the exponential

$$(3) \qquad\qquad f(t; \lambda) = \lambda e^{\lambda t} .$$

The geometric and exponential distributions for trials and continuous time, respectively, are the basic elements of the theories of learning and problem solving used in this discussion.

Suppose that the final solution of a problem, or some final response, requires that k stages be completed, a possibility envisaged by Lorge and Solomon. Suppose further that the time to solution of stage 2 is independent of the time taken to complete stage 1, and so on. Then the mean time to completion of the problem is the sum of the means required by the k stages, and the variance of the total time is the sum of the variances of the stages. The distributions of these compound trials or times are the convolutions of the component stage distributions. By using the theory given by Feller [1], the moment-generating functions of all possible compounds can be calculated in a routine way from the known component generating functions; hence a great variety of statistical predictions can be made. The general theory permits easy proof of the assertions in this paper as well as of many important generalizations and extensions which are not included here.

If all stages have the same probability of solution (p or λ), then the compound distributions take simple forms. In discrete trials the geometric distribution becomes the negative binomial

$$(4) \qquad P(n; k, p) = \binom{n-1}{k-1} p^k (1-p)^{n-k} ,$$

and in continuous time the exponential distribution becomes the gamma distribution

$$(5) \qquad g(t; k, \lambda) = \frac{\lambda}{(k-1)!} e^{-\lambda t} (\lambda t)^k .$$

These simple waiting-time models, with the notion of simple non-interactional pooling of accomplishment, make up the theory to be applied.

Note that the present models attribute the distribution of accomplishments (that is, the differences between subjects in success or time taken to finish) to the intrinsic variability of discrete events. For simplicity, the models disregard individual differences in parameters such as p and λ. Indeed, the experimental results given below, derived from data on subjects from elementary psychology courses, suggest that individual differences comprise only a small portion of the observed variance in the performance of the tasks used. This is perhaps more plausible if these simple memorizing and problem-solving tasks are considered to be intelligence tests.

2. Experimental Tests of the Models

2.1 Memorizing. A very simple test of the validity of the present approach is based on data collected by Perlmutter and deMontmollin [4]. Individuals and groups of three subjects memorized lists of two-syllable nonsense words. On each trial the list was presented to the subjects, who

TABLE 1

OBTAINED AND PREDICTED MEANS, INDIVIDUALS
AND GROUPS OF THREE

(Perlmutter and deMontmollin)

Trial	Individual Means	Group Means	
		Obtained	Predicted
1	2.3	5.5	6.1
2	5.4	10.2	12.0
3	7.7	14.8	15.0
4	9.7	17.3	16.8
5	11.4	18.2	17.8

then attempted to recall the words. The resulting individual and group learning curves are available.

Suppose that the height of the individual learning curve represents the proportion of syllables learned, and interpret this as the probability that any given syllable would have been learned by any subject on the trial. Then the expectation of group performance is given by using equation (1). In this case, p is the proportion of items learned by individuals, taken from the individual learning curve, and $k = 3$ is the size of the group. Predicted and observed performances for groups are given in table 1, and observed results are seen to be quite close to those predicted.

Ronald Hoppe has repeated the experiment with more subjects and a shorter list of syllables [2]. This replication confirms the *a posteriori* conclusions from the Perlmutter–deMontmollin data and also provides the detailed data on which statistical tests can be performed. Hoppe used the same technique of immediate recall, changing the order of presentation of items randomly on each trial.

Shown in table 2 are the proportions of items recalled for individuals and groups of three subjects, as well as the proportions predicted from equation (1). Note that the predictions are quite accurate except for trial 1, the first recall. On trial 1, groups do not reach the predicted level of achievement.

Closer inspection of the data reveals the reason for this discrepancy. Direct applicability of equation (1) to the learning curves depends upon the assumption that all individuals and all items are equal. We do not know about the individual differences, but the items differed widely in difficulty because of a surprisingly powerful serial position effect. The first and last syllables in the list were usually remembered after the first presentation, and the middle items were almost never remembered. The performance of individuals on trial 1, with the proportion of correct responses as a function of serial position, is as follows:

Serial Position   1   2   3   4   5   6   7   8
Proportion Correct   .70 .48 .09 .02 .09 .02 .28 .32

TABLE 2

OBTAINED AND PREDICTED MEANS, INDIVIDUALS
AND GROUPS OF THREE

Trial	Individual Means	Group Means	
		Obtained	Predicted
1	2.0	3.4	4.6*
2	3.3	6.1	6.3
3	4.5	7.6	7.3
4	5.6	7.7	7.8
5	5.8	7.8	7.8
6	6.4	7.9	7.9
7	6.4	7.9	7.9
8	6.7	7.9	8.0
9	7.2	7.9	8.0

* Prediction significantly wrong. When corrected for serial position effect, prediction is 3.8, not significantly different from the obtained value.

The serial position effect from a single presentation of a list of nonsense words was found again when one trial was given to a large class of undergraduates.

Equation (1) can be used for each item in the list, and the results summed over items to yield a prediction of group performance on trial 1. This more appropriate calculation gives a good prediction of the group score, as shown in table 2 (corrected for serial position). The correction applies mainly to trial 1 because the items were presented in different orders on successive trials and the serial-position effects should cancel out rapidly.

2.2 Solving Verbal Puzzles. In a study by Davis, individuals and groups of four subjects were compared in their ability to solve puzzles.[1] The puzzles were quite simple, and 12-minute time limits were sufficient to draw answers, right or wrong, from almost all subjects and groups. A total of 187 individuals and 22 groups, drawn with reasonable care from our pool of Introductory Psychology students, were tested on each of three problems.

Davis designed his study to provide a close analysis of the Lorge–Solomon theory that problems might involve several stages. He used three problems, one involving a trick of interpretation (which seemed to be nearly a one-stage problem), one requiring the subject to untangle a sequence of cancelling clauses in a complex sentence (which seemed to involve three to five stages), and a third, a slight complication of the "water-jug" problem, which seemed to involve several stages, perhaps five or six. Of course it was

[1] Davis, J. H., Models for the classification of problems and the prediction of group problem-solving from individual results. Unpublished Ph.D. dissertation, Michigan State University, 1961.

impossible to be certain of how many stages these problems involved, but they were designed to differ in apparent number of stages.

Davis applied the waiting-time theory to the distribution of solution times of those subjects who solved the problems correctly. In order to get a reasonable estimate he assumed that all stages were equally difficult (i.e., had the same parameter λ), so that the appropriate continuous-time model generated a gamma distribution. Tests of goodness of fit indicated that the distributions on the three problems were adequately described by the gamma distributions. Further investigations made it possible to subtract the time required to read the problems, which should not be included in problem-solving time.

A useful fact about the gamma distribution is that the number of stages, k, is equal to the squared mean divided by the variance. This rather rough estimate seemed most appropriate for Davis's data, and gave very interesting results. The estimated numbers of stages in the three problems were 1.3, 3.0, and 5.0, quite close to the original, intuitive expectations, and also quite close to the number of detectable stages or parts in the answers required. In a subsequent study at Miami University (Ohio), college students who had solved the problems estimated the number of stages in each. Mean estimates were 2.8, 4.0, and 6.3, fairly close to the values of squared mean divided by variance. Since the estimated number of stages was shown to be quite reasonable, and varied in agreement with the experimenter's intention and ratings by students, the waiting-time model gained some plausibility.

When predicting group performance from individual performance, however, Davis was faced with a difficulty. On the two multiple-stage problems, approximately half the individuals failed to solve the problem correctly. Almost all subjects arrived at some answer, but there seemed to be many mistakes possible and subjects erred in a variety of ways.

The Lorge–Solomon model can be applied to the proportion of subjects who solve at the end of 12 minutes, and the calculation comes out very close to Davis's results. Unfortunately, the prediction is that almost all groups will solve, and in fact almost all groups do solve, so that the test is very weak. As in Hoppe's experiment, one can apply the Lorge–Solomon model [equation (1)] at any time t. If this is done, the predictions are very inaccurate. Some points of the cumulative distributions for individuals and groups are shown in table 3 with the simple Lorge–Solomon prediction. Notice that group performances are greatly inferior to these predictions.

Also shown in table 3 are the predictions, based on the Lorge–Solomon model in which each problem is assumed to consist of two independent stages. Since increasing the number of stages increases the theoretical advantage of groups, it makes the predictions even less accurate. All of these predictions, except for that concerning the one-stage problem which most of the individuals solved, are significantly at variance with the data.

In discussions, Davis and I arrived at the following hypothesis [5]:[2] Any subject who makes an error continues to take part in group discussions, but

---

[2] Also Davis, J. H., *op. cit.*

TABLE 3

PROPORTION OF SOLUTIONS BY TIME t, GROUPS OF
FOUR SUBJECTS, PREDICTED AND OBSERVED
(Davis)

Problem	Solutions	Time in Minutes (t)					
		2	4	6	8	10	12
Rope	Obtained	.48	.77	.87	.87	.97	.97
	Predicted (1 stage)	.53	.98	1.00	1.00	1.00	1.00
	Predicted (2 stages)	.76	1.00	1.00	1.00	1.00	1.00
Word Tangle	Obtained	.14	.31	.58	.60	.65	.77
	Predicted (1 stage)	.19	.53	.77	.90	.92	.97
	Predicted (2 stages)	.37	.77	.87	.97	.98	.99
"Water Jug"	Obtained	.05	.26	.36	.48	.55	.77
	Predicted (1 stage)	.04	.28	.45	.77	.85	.92
	Predicted (2 stages)	.12	.46	.76	.90	.95	.98

does not contribute toward solution—in fact, his contributions amount to "dead time" as far as the group's progress is concerned. Hence a group with two people who will solve and two who make errors would actually be slower than a group with two solvers and no others.

Suppose, now, that subjects who have made an error consume only their share of the group's time. We know approximately what proportion of subjects will make errors, from data on the proportion of false answers given by individuals. In a group of four, the number of subjects who go wrong may be from zero to four, and should follow a binomial distribution.

Consider a particular group of r subjects of whom A are solvers and $r-A$ make errors. Let the rate of an individual be λ. Then the A solvers have a rate of $A\lambda$ during the time they are working, but because of the dead time consumed by non-solvers, they work only A/r of the time. Hence the effective "rate" of such a group is $(A\lambda)A/r = A^2\lambda/r$, and the distribution of solution times for a number of such groups would be a gamma distribution with k stages and this new rate. Recall that A, the number of solvers in a group, has a binomial distribution. The actual distribution of group performance is calculated by averaging the distributions that arise when $A = 0, 1, 2, \cdots, r$, weighting each according to the binomial distribution. While the algebra is fairly complex, the calculation is not particularly difficult. The predicted distributions are shown, with data from groups, in table 4. To date, statistical investigations have failed to reveal any significant discrepancy between these predictions and the observed distributions.

2.3 Solving the Doodlebug Problem with Errors Corrected. In more recent work, Hoppe has been collecting group and individual data on the "Doodlebug" problem used by Rokeach [6]. This is a multiple-stage problem, somewhat like a chess problem, but involving initial conditions which many

TABLE 4

PROPORTION OF SOLUTIONS BY TIME t, GROUPS OF FOUR,
PREDICTED USING INTERFERENCE MODEL, AND OBTAINED

(Davis)

Problem	Solutions	Time in Minutes (t)					
		2	4	6	8	10	12
Rope	Obtained	.48	.77	.87	.87	.97	.97
	Predicted	.54	.87	.90	.91	.98	.99
Word Tangle	Obtained	.14	.31	.58	.60	.65	.77
	Predicted	.16	.36	.60	.65	.71	.75
"Water Jug"	Obtained	.05	.26	.36	.48	.55	.77
	Predicted	.04	.24	.36	.53	.60	.70

subjects find difficult to accept. Because this problem is quite difficult and very few of our subjects can solve it without aid, the experimenter answered questions during the solution period and prevented subjects from making very deep excursions into wrong solutions.

This experiment is very like Davis's except for a crucial point; by keeping the individuals and groups from arriving at wrong solutions, Hoppe removed an important element used in explaining Davis's results. Davis's groups fell below the Lorge–Solomon pooling level, and our explanation was that they were retarded by group members who had made an error. Hoppe's groups were aided by the fact that no members could long stay in error, hence their performances should equal the Lorge–Solomon pooling level. I shall not present Hoppe's data here, for he intends to repeat and extend his study, but the performances of his groups of two and three are very close to the Lorge–Solomon pooling level, one distribution being above and the other below prediction. This result agrees very well with our present understanding of the situation, though it is hardly conclusive.

3. Discussion and Implications

The results above arise from combining two mathematical models, a description of the process of solving the problem, and a simple model for pooling accomplishments. I should like to describe the ground rules under which we have played this theoretical game, so that the results can be evaluated appropriately.

Our basic rule is that any data on individual performance can be used in predicting group performance. For example, in Hoppe's memorizing study we found a serial position effect. Since that effect appeared in individual data, it was used in the prediction of group performance. We think it was wise, however, to repeat the individual experiment, at least roughly, to assure ourselves that the serial position effect was really there. Similarly, we used the fact that some people gave wrong answers as individuals to explain the relatively slow performance of groups in Davis's experiment.

Since subsidiary assumptions were involved in that calculation, further studies are needed. Davis did find that the social structure of his groups, in so far as it could be decided by sociograms based on "preference as a partner in further group problem solving," was equalitarian. Communication frequency was also relatively equal from subject to subject. Solvers and contributors in groups could not be distinguished from non-solvers by the experimenter-observer. These facts support the idea that subjects who have made a mistake would probably take their full share of the group time. Hoppe's experiment, while it involved many changes from Davis's, differed especially in that Hoppe did not let his subjects arrive at wrong answers. Hoppe did not find the retardation of groups that Davis had found. Thus there are a few elements of support for the analysis of Davis's results.

Some aspects of evaluation of the results should be made clear. First we are testing genuine extrapolative predictions. This is not like asking whether a utility function can be found to agree with a set of choices, where parameters are estimated from the very data being fit. While our predictions are certainly imperfect and it is sensible to improve them if we can, the data could be much farther from prediction than they are; the predictions are close enough to suggest that we are on the right track. Second, one could complain that we have not obtained enough data, especially enough groups, to make a good test of a particular distribution. This is true, but at present we are not willing to make the enormous investment in laboratory labor to make tests of as many as 100 four-man groups. Anyone who has tried to form groups at random and then to get all members to the laboratory on time, has some idea of the difficulties. If as many as 15 per cent of all subjects called fail to appear (and in the Michigan climate that is only to be expected), only about half of the intended four-man groups are there to be tested. This sort of problem makes each experiment a considerable undertaking.

Problems of experimental feasibility have led us to attempt to predict distributions of times to solution rather than mere proportions of solvers, so as to extract every possible bit of information from the groups we did form and test. Hoppe is now collecting protocols to increase the yield of detailed information. The memorizing experiments and similar procedures which give detailed information about each subject show promise as ways of increasing the efficiency of research.

3.1 Introduction of Social Variables. In the studies discussed above, the variables hardly seem to be those of social psychology. Conformity, communication nets, roles, interaction, and many other accouterments of social theory are missing. The strategy of our investigations tends to delay the entry of such variables. In fact, in Davis's study, the concept of a kind of interference between people was introduced to explain the results. This is genuine social psychology, if admittedly somewhat elementary. Our strategy identifies social factors in group cognition as deviations from models which predict group from individual performance. In a sense, social variables will be introduced only as they are shown to cause group attainment to differ from what would otherwise be predicted.

This strategy does not in any way reflect on the validity or importance of the usual methods of social psychology. If we have any resistance to such theory, it is only from the suspicion that roles, patterns of interaction, conformities, and so on often do not have any great effect on cognitive attainment in open, face-to-face groups. Groups may differ widely in structure and interaction without differing systematically in speed or sureness of accomplishment. Since the methods used in this chapter lead to a close analysis of group performance, however, they may help in isolating those social variables which do affect achievement.

3.2 Efficiency of Groups Compared with Individuals. In all of the experiments discussed here as well as in most others reported in the literature, groups do better than individuals. However, in a practical vein, groups cost more than individuals. The question of efficiency arises: Are groups worth the extra cost? For purposes of discussion, it is probably sensible to suppose that the cost of a group is directly proportional to its size and to the time it takes to arrive at solution. For simplicity, discussion is limited to continuous-time processes like those arising in Davis's experiment, where workers can make wrong answers. (In practical cases, no one knows the right answer to the problem in advance.)

The mean of a gamma distribution $g(t; \lambda, k)$ with rate λ for a k-stage problem, is k/λ. Consider a problem in which all individuals will eventually arrive at a correct solution. Then the waiting-time model shows that a group of size r will yield a gamma distribution with rate $r\lambda$, that is, $g(t; r\lambda, k)$. If the cost of an individual is C per hour, the cost of a group of size r is rC. But since the individual will take a mean time of k/λ, the mean cost of an individual is Ck/λ. The group takes a mean time of $k/r\lambda$; hence its expected cost is $rCk/r\lambda = Ck/\lambda$, which is the same as the cost of an individual.

The economic decision now rests on peripheral matters. It usually takes some time to get an individual or group working: travel time to the place of work, reading time, and so on. All of these subsidiary costs are greater for groups than for individuals; hence there may be an advantage in using individuals. Of course, if the value of a solution decreases with time, e.g., in a "crash" program, the group, which will get the solution sooner at the same mean cost, is more advantageous.

Now consider a problem in which some proportion of individuals will arrive at a wrong answer, as in Davis's experiment. Suppose that only a proportion P of all individuals will solve. For any group of size r, if i of the individuals solve successfully, the distribution of that group is a gamma distribution, $g(t; i^2\lambda/r, k)$, which has mean $kr/i^2\lambda$. Given a binomial distribution of i, the number of solvers, the mean cost of the solution by groups that have a solver in them is

$$(6) \qquad \mu_t = \frac{r^2 Ck}{\lambda} \sum_{i=1}^{r} \binom{r}{i} P^i (1-P)^{r-i} \frac{1}{i^2} .$$

The writer has not been able to evaluate the sum in equation (6), but some information is available. The problem is, of course, the behavior of μ_t as a function of r. Professor Herman Rubin of Michigan State was able to show that the change of μ_t is monotone in r. When $r = 1$, then $\mu_t = Ck/\lambda$, and when r becomes very large, as i/r clusters more and more closely around P, the value of μ_t approaches $Ck/P^2\lambda$. From Rubin's statement, which is not proved here, it follows that the mean cost of solution increases with increasing group size.

Whether this, in turn, means that groups are less efficient the larger they are, depends upon the importance or value of the correct solution. If an individual gets the right answer, his solution is relatively cheap. However, with a large proportion of non-solvers ($P \ll 1$) it is quite possible that an individual will give a wrong answer. A group has a smaller probability of arriving at a wrong answer. If the correct answer is sufficiently valuable, it may be more efficient to use the group. For example, groups can be more efficient on important problems where an individual solver can easily be led astray.

In the kind of *ad hoc* group studied by Davis, we found that non-solvers in the group would retard the other members. Another way of saying this is that if subject X were to solve alone, he would solve faster alone than in a group with non-solvers in it. However, our pooling-of-accomplishments model says that we cannot predict in advance which subjects will turn out to be solvers and which will not.

One suggested method of increasing efficiency would be to have the "group" subjects work in separate cubicles. According to the theory, the same proportion of subjects would solve as in a face-to-face group, but now the solvers would not be retarded. This method of "monads" leads to the correct solution earlier than real face-to-face groups. Whether it is also more efficient is, however, questionable. A real group arrives at a single answer which, with probability $1 - (1 - P)^r$, is correct. A group of monads arrives at r answers, approximately rP of which are correct, the remainder wrong. The monads do not give a single answer, hence after they are finished some device must be arranged to decide among their answers. This is inefficient in itself. Furthermore, the deciding device does not even go into operation until all (or at least several) of the monads have finished. If it waits until all monads are finished, then monads are far inferior to groups. Monads are superior only in the sense that the *first* monad to get the right answer does so relatively quickly.

The above discussion, while it does give some preliminary results, is intended mainly to indicate how complicated and delicate the question of efficiency may be in relation to the optimal size of the group.

4. Summary

Learning and problem solving were described by a simple waiting-time model, and group work was described by a pooling-of-accomplishments model. The resulting theory was applied to two memorizing experiments and two experiments on the solution of verbal problems. With various minor modifications, the theory was reconciled with detailed data. The question of efficiency of groups was discussed in the light of the experimental results.

REFERENCES

[1] FELLER, W., *Introduction to Probability Theory and Its Applications*, 2d ed., New York: Wiley, 1957.

[2] HOPPE, R. A., Memorizing by individuals and groups: A test of the pooling-of-ability model (submitted to *J. Abnorm. Soc. Psychol.*, 1961).

[3] LORGE, I., and H. SOLOMON, Two models of group behavior in the solution of eureka-type problems, *Psychometrika*, 1955, **20**, 139-48.

[4] PERLMUTTER, H. V., and G. DEMONTMOLLIN, Group learning of nonsense syllables, *J. Abnorm. Soc. Psychol.*, 1952, **47**, 762-69.

[5] RESTLE, F., *Psychology of Judgment and Choice*, New York: Wiley, 1961.

[6] ROKEACH, M., *The Open and Closed Mind*, New York: Basic Books, 1960.

[7] SHAW, MARJORIE E., Comparison of individuals and small groups in the rational solution of complex problems, *Amer. J. Psychol.*, 1932, **44**, 491-504.

18

Subtask Phasing in Small Groups

Thornton B. Roby, *Tufts University*

The tendency to break tasks down into segments, or subtasks, in order maximally to employ the time, energies, and talents of group members seems to be an ubiquitous feature of group performance. Any distribution of labor may, however, be self-defeating unless provision is made for the subtasks to be performed in proper sequence in relation to each other and to outside events. The purpose of the present paper is to suggest a formulation of the temporal coordination problem, to describe certain classificatory distinctions, and to sketch out mathematical models for studying various special aspects. The problems with which we shall be concerned include the initial definition of task segments, the ordering relations among these segments, and the behavioral problem of adhering to a certain phasing structure after it has been established.

Phasing is only one aspect of the over-all problem of group behavior, itself a very special type of organismic adjustment [3]. A first step in describing the phasing problem is therefore to give it a setting within a more general context.

The immediate circumstances of a group at a particular time will be referred to as an E-state—a specific constellation of values for relevant environmental conditions. In the present discussion we shall assume that these E-state conditions affect all group members in the same way, that the group can in fact be considered a unitary organism except for the dispersal of actions over group members.

The E-states are subject to at least partial control by group members' behavior, and we define the classes of behaviors having certain effects as action units. That is, an action unit (AU) is defined by a particular set of E-state transitions or instrumental effects. A given AU may take a variety of forms in terms of observable motor behaviors.

In principle, at least, it will be possible to represent the behavior and progress of a group by a sequence, say,

$$A E_1 = E_2 ,$$

$$B E_2 = E_3 ,$$
$$C E_3 = E_4 ,$$

in which the successive E-states, $E_1 \cdots E_4$, operated on by AU's, A, B, C, give place to new E-states.

It is conventional, in discussing operator effect, to combine several steps — for example,

$$C B A E_1 = C B E_2 = C E_3 = E_4 ,$$

to indicate successive application of the operators in right to left order. The central problem of this paper, then, is the analysis of these AU's which, considered as environmental operators, do not commute; e.g., $A B E_1 \neq B A E_1$ for at least some E's.

The physical conditions under which environmental operators will or will not commute are of great interest, but go well beyond the scope of this report. It will not be possible, either, to discuss the mathematical properties of these operators in any detail. Even so, the succinct terminology suggested by the operator formulation is helpful in outlining the main conditions and parameters of the general phasing problem.

To fix ideas, we shall employ the above notation to formalize a very well-known—and very often mishandled—problem in military tactics.

Suppose that an Invader is hoping to establish a beachhead at a certain point in Enemy country. The state of this geographical spot (the putative beachhead) may be any of the following:

E_1: Occupied by the Enemy; defensible ;

E_2: Occupied by the Enemy; indefensible ;

E_3: Occupied by the Invader; indefensible ;

E_4: Occupied by the Invader; defensible .

The Invader has at his disposal three distinct action units: Bombardment (A), Troop landing (B), and Supply drop (C). These are associated with the following operator mappings:

A		B		C	
E_1	E_2	E_1	E_1	E_1	E_1
E_2	E_2	E_2	E_3	E_2	E_1
E_3	E_3	E_3	E_3	E_3	E_4
E_4	E_3	E_4	E_4	E_4	E_4

Each operator is associated with a particular set of transitions between E-states, brackets indicating E-states that behave the same under a particular operator.

An Invader will ordinarily be faced with the problem of changing the beachhead condition from E_1 to E_4 and he will attempt to employ the sequence of action units, $A B C$ in that order. In the terms given above;

$$CBAE_1 = CBE_2 = CE_3 = E_4 .$$

In the present case it is obvious that no sequence of action units will be successful that does not contain ABC, or some trivial variant, as a terminal sub-sequence. All sequences other than $A, B,$ and C entail greater cost or are unsuccessful. Note that, in this example, there are two E-state "dimensions"—that is, the occupancy of the beachhead, on the one hand, and its defensibility on the other. A and C operate only on the "defensibility" dimension and are, in fact, mutually inverse. B influences only the "occupancy" dimension, and then only if the "defensibility" dimension is at a particular value. This dimensionalizability is typical of tasks which incorporate non-commutative operators, and hence phasing effects. Although, in the present case, the problem of determining an optimal sequence is trivial, the problem of adhering to it exactly is exceedingly difficult.

1. Principal Definitions

In order to allow sufficient space for a discussion of the phasing problem proper it will be necessary to begin with some rather sweeping assumptions. Specifically, we must suppose that any ordered sequence of AU's can be assigned a value which, in some sense, reflects its instrumental effectiveness. This effectiveness will be greater to the extent that the general welfare of the group is promoted as a consequence of the instrumental sequence. Clearly, it will be necessary to evaluate the sequence within a particular set of environmental conditions, preexisting and coexisting. It may be possible, however, to assign statistical values to sequences within a broad environmental context. In general, then, the *instrumental value* of a sequence is the extent of improvement of the E-state at the end of the sequence as contrasted with the initial state.

In this paper we shall be concerned exclusively with the comparison of sequences which, considered as unordered sets, are identical. That is, we are interested in the effects of reordering a set of AU's to different agents; the replacing AU will be homologous (i.e., functionally equivalent) to the replaced one. This rather considerable restriction of the problem also permits us to overlook "cost" factors in evaluating sequences—at least to the extent that the intrinsic cost of a set of responses is typically independent of the order in which they are applied.

In addition to evaluating total instrumental sequences it will be convenient to have a terminology for evaluating individual AU's at a certain position in a sequence. By a "building function" we shall mean an evaluative function defined on a truncated sub-sequence of AU's and any particular AU. Thus the function $B(S_1, A)$ evaluates the effectiveness of a sequence S_1 of AU's followed by A. For illustrative purposes, we might propose that the measure B on this set could be the maximum of all instrumental values obtained by completion of the truncated sequence. Then the "partial instrumental value" of A in this context can be defined as the difference (necessarily nonpositive) between the value of the set S_1 before appendage of A and after A is added on. This convention permits the analysis of a total sequence as an additive function of the partial instrumental values of its components.

Fortunately, our further discussion of the phasing problem does not seem to require a complete resolution of all of the questions of evaluation and analysis suggested above. If we have here indicated the general nature of these issues and given some hint to their possible treatment, this will provide a sufficient background for the use of the phrases introduced above in the following section.

Four sets of classificatory distinctions will now be introduced. It is believed that all of these can be refined to meet prescribed standards of rigor. The present exposition, however, aims at heuristic value rather than logical precision. Furthermore, the distinctions are presented in black and white terms even though only mixed cases or continuous gradations may occur in real life.

1.1 Plastic and Dynamic Environments. A task environment will be referred to as plastic [2] if the only operators affecting E-states are group-produced AU's. If, on the other hand, there are other forces shaping the environment, it will be called a dynamic environment. A stochastic or "chancy" environment is a special type of dynamic environment in which the AU's remain the only explicit operators affecting the E-states but in which other changes are interposed in unpredictable fashion.

Truly plastic environments probably occur only in the laboratory situation. However, the plastic paradigm may describe almost any task environment to a degree of approximation and over the short run (as in the beachhead example given above). If the environment is strictly plastic, all that is required for perfect adherence of group members to a phasing program is for each group member to be aware of the behavior (or intentions) of other group members. This is obviously not enough, however, if the group is contending with a dynamic environment. In the latter case their AU's must be placed in with each other and also in with the additional operators interposed by nature.

1.2 Temporal Conditions. We can distinguish crudely between phased sequences that need only be ordered and those for which precise chronological relationships hold. This is probably adequate for most purposes, but it fails to bring out some of the more interesting facets of the problem. For example, it is broadly true that tasks occurring in plastic environments require only ordering of the AU's, whereas more delicate temporal relations obtain under dynamic conditions. There are exceptions, however. A string quartet operates on an essentially plastic environment, yet the temporal relations among AU's are exquisitely critical.

For the purpose of setting up models of the phasing problem in any particular situation, it is necessary to determine whether the AU's themselves are to be treated as points in time, as temporal units of modular length, or as units of variable length. Clearly this distinction affects the meaningfulness of various problems that might be considered. For example, exact coincidence is a meaningful criterion with modular AU's but not with punctate or variable-interval AU's.

Speaking broadly, and depending on the types of AU's involved, there are two classes of phasing criteria. Coincidence criteria depend on the closeness in time of two AU's. The criterion function may be positive or negative according to whether the AU's are mutually facilitative or interfering. However, the criterion function will be symmetric with respect to the AU's. That is, if A and B are the two AU's concerned, it is just as important for A to be close to (or removed from) B as the reverse.

Precursion criteria, on the other hand, depend on whether one AU comes before or after the other AU, and perhaps on how long before or after. Criterion functions in this class will not ordinarily be symmetric.

1.3 Coupling. We shall here distinguish between *process* coupling and *product* coupling of two AU's. Process coupling implies that the performance of a given AU affects the operator mapping of a second AU, favorably or unfavorably; product coupling means that the output of the AU becomes the input of a second AU.

The coupling interactions suggested in the beachhead problem are of the product type. Each AU "sets up" new conditions for the succeeding AU's. We can suppose, though, that there are other "support" functions that interact process-wise with the illustrative AU. For example, unless adequate combat training (say, D) precedes troop landing B, the latter will not result in the transformation of E_2 to E_3, even though a "troop landing" is nominally executed.

Although the distinction between process coupling and product coupling seems logically unambiguous, it is not always clear how it applies in particular cases. One of the most interesting forms of coupling, for example, occurs when the information resulting from the performance of one AU is used to guide the performance of a second AU. In this case, it is not immediately clear whether the coupling should be considered as the process or product type. The decision in this case hinges on whether or not we choose to include environmental information in our description of E-states. Generally speaking, the process vs. product distinction is clear once AU's and E-states are defined, but the latter definitions are largely a matter of convenience.

1.4 Necessary and Preferential Orderings. Finally, it will be useful to distinguish between necessary ordinal relationships and preferential ordinal relationships.

Necessarily, A precedes B if all AU sequences with positive instrumental value containing B also contain a prior occurrence of A. Thus A must either make B possible (process interaction) or be required so that B will lead to some improved E-state (product interaction).

For preferential order relationships, on the other hand, there may be AU sequences with positive instrumental value containing A and B in either order, but one of the orders (say, A first and then B) leads to more favorable outcomes or to lower "cost" of the AU's.

Here again a certain measure of arbitrariness appears to be justified on heuristic grounds.

2. Specific Models

The models presented here are intended to highlight problems and to pinpoint parameters for more intensive theoretical and empirical study; they are in every case too specialized and limited to stand as definitive treatments. The following topics are considered:

(a) Given a method of describing interactions among the AU's, how does one determine what the optimal sequencing or phasing of AU's should be? For the preferential situation, we discuss both the indicated measures and the prospect of an algorithm to arrive at the optimal phasing. A variant of this problem occurs whenever the order relationships are necessary, and where the second model considered is one in which it is shown that exact inter-segment spacings can be derived as a function of necessary precursions.

(b) Given normative solutions of the problem of how AU's should be ordered, it is possible to derive indices that describe the task from the standpoint of its phasing requirements. A model is proposed which incorporates an information-theory approach to the computation of such an index. It is demonstrated that information in the "negentropy" sense is in this case related to information in terms of group communications. It is shown that increasing specialization and division of labor incurs a calculable cost in terms of coordination requirements.

(c) A close look at real-life tasks reveals that they often entail a tradeoff problem between uncertainty on the one hand, and delay or communication costs on the other. For certain specified conditions a model is developed for estimating the relative importance of these cost sources.

2.1 Normative Ordering. If there are a number of task segments or AU's that can be used in various orders, the considerations of the foregoing sections lead us to expect different final-outcome values for each such ordering, even if all orderings lead to completion of the task. Ordinarily, however, it will not be feasible to determine directly the over-all outcome values for all the possible permutations of a large set of AU's. However, it may be possible to determine the influence that any one AU has on the effectiveness of other AU's performed later. Our present model attempts to show how an optimal over-all ordering may be obtained from a set of values defined for the ordered pairs of AU's.

The specific assumptions are as follows:

1. For every ordered pair of AU's (say, a, b), a value V_{ab} is defined that indicates the increment in the value of b if it is preceded by a.

2. The values V_{ab} are independent of the time or number of AU's intervening between a and b.

3. The total value of an instrumental sequence is the aggregate of values for all component AU's as modified by their predecessor AU's.

Our assumptions permit us to express all of the relevant information for all AU's in a matrix (table 1) in which AU's are listed along rows and columns and a given cell entry opposite c and beneath f indicates that, if c precedes f, the value of f is increased by six units; conversely, if f precedes c, the value of c is increased by two units.

Suppose the AU's were to be performed in the order indicated in this matrix. Then the relevant V_{ij} would be those entries above the main diagonal of the matrix; i.e., each unit would be assisted only by those units to the left of it. The boldface entries indicate the independent partial instrumental values of the AU's, that is, the values that the AU's have apart from their precursors. Thus c performed in the order indicated would have a value of $5 + 4 + 1$, or 10. The total value of the sequence would be the sum of the values on or above the main diagonal, which in the present case is 88. It is instructive to consider how the action units with such a building function can be reordered so as to maximize the total value of the sequence.

It is clear that the over-all objective is to make the matrix as asymmetric as possible—that is, to get high values in the upper right-hand corner of the matrix and low values in the lower left-hand corner. A simple interchange of the position of two AU's will accomplish this in specific cases, but it would also disrupt the effects of each of these AU's on intervening AU's. Hence, it is desirable to get an initial ordering such that the number of required interchanges is minimized.

The column totals as given in table 1 indicate the general dependency of each AU on preceding AU's. Similarly, the row totals indicate the contribution of each AU to potential successor AU's. Evidently, the AU's for which the row totals are high and the column totals are low should go early, and those AU's for which the row totals are low and column totals high should go later. These criteria may be combined by taking the difference between the row and column totals for each AU (shown in the last column

TABLE 1

HYPOTHETICAL DATA ILLUSTRATING VALUE INCREMENTS IN AU'S
AS A FUNCTION OF PRECURSOR AU'S

	a	b	c	d	e	f	$\Sigma_j V_{ij}$	Diff.
a	**2**	3	5	9	2	7	26	5
b	1	**4**	4	1	6	2	14	−8
c	3	7	**1**	4	9	6	29	9
d	6	2	4	**5**	1	1	14	−4
e	8	3	5	1	**9**	7	24	0
f	3	7	2	3	6	**0**	21	−2
$\Sigma_i V_{ij}$	21	22	20	18	24	23		

TABLE 2

THE DATA OF TABLE 1 REORDERED ON THE BASIS OF MARGINAL DIFFERENCES

	c	a	e	f	d	b	$\sum_j V_{ij}$
c	**1**	3	9	6	4	7	29
a	5	**2**	2	7	9	3	26
e	5	8	**9**	7	1	3	24
f	2	3	6	**0**	3	7	21
d	4	6	1	1	**5**	2	14
b	4	1	6	2	1	**4**	14
$\sum_i V_{ij}$	20	21	24	23	15	22	

of table 1). Ranking the AU's according to this criterion gives the ordering of table 2. The total value of the sequence based on this ordering would be 94.

In order to make further refinements in the permutation sequence, it is convenient to work with difference scores, as shown in the following matrix.

	c	a	e	f	d	b
c		-2	4	4	0	3
a			-6	4	3	2
e				1	0	-3
f					2	5
d						1
b						

The entry -2 opposite c and under a indicates that a contributes two more units to the value of c than c does to the value of a. The obvious objective is to obtain as many positive units in the upper right-hand corner of the matrix as possible. As it happens, there are three negative units in the present matrix. One of these can be eliminated by interchange of a and e; since a and e are already adjacent, no intervening relationship can be disturbed. This leads to the following ordering:

	c	e	a	f	d	b
c		—	4	-2	4	0	3
e			—	6	1	0	-3
a				—	4	3	2
f					—	2	5
d						—	1
b							—

To answer the question whether this is the optimal ordering, the following considerations apply. First, if all difference values in the upper right-hand triangle are positive, then the ordering is surely optimal; if any two adjacent AU's yield a negative value, they should certainly be interchanged. The chief problem concerns negative values for separated AU's.

If d_{ik} is negative and units i and k are separated by only one element (say, j) then it is clear that reversal of i and k will also require changing the sign of either d_{ij} or d_{jk}. If either of these is smaller (in absolute or algebraic value) than d_{ij}, then "castling" is indicated, reversing whichever of d_{ij} or d_{jk} is least in algebraic value. Finally, if more than one unit separates i and k, then all possible castling movements must be considered. For example, if the sequence $i\,j\,h\,k$ obtains with d_{ik} negative, one must examine the alternative orderings $k\,i\,j\,h$; $j\,k\,i\,h$; $j\,h\,k\,i$, and so on. If the number of possible interchanges to be considered is too great, one can repeat, for the submatrix covered by these AU's, the transformation by row and column totals.

In the present example there remain only two negative values: d_{ca} and d_{eb}. Reversal of d_{ca} requires changing the signs of either d_{ce} or d_{ea}, both of which exceed d_{ca} in absolute value. Reversal of d_{eb} entails the reversal of at least d_{ea} or d_{fb}, both of which exceed d_{eb} in absolute value. On replacing the difference values with the original values, as shown in the matrix below, a total score of 100 is obtained:

	c	e	a	f	d	b
c	1	9	3	6	4	7
e	5	9	8	7	1	3
a	5	2	2	7	9	3
f	2	6	3	0	3	7
d	4	1	6	1	5	2
b	4	6	1	2	1	4

It seems certain that more elegant and powerful algorithms could be found for treating this problem.[1] On the other hand, our present concern is rather to indicate the considerations that confront a group in developing a task ordering. We should expect their solution of the problem to be empirical and intuitive, particularly since they would not ordinarily have value estimates as firm as the ones used here.

The foregoing discussion is concerned with preferential order relationships. If the binary relationships entail necessary precursion, there is of course no equivocality in the final ordering in so far as it concerns ordered pairs of AU's. However, there is a somewhat similar normative problem that involves the more exact relationships that are not explicitly given. Whenever the AU's require time for completion, the simple dyadic order

---

[1] Since this was originally written, a procedure has been published for handling comparable problems in industrial situations [1].

relationships between various elements may build up into a very tight time schedule. This occurs because of the transitive nature of necessary precursion. If a must precede b and b must precede c, a must precede c; if they all require modular time units for completion, then a must precede c by 2 units. This problem arises in industrial processes under the heading "lead times."

To illustrate the phenomenon and to demonstrate one mathematical approach, we shall return to the data of table 1. It is now stipulated that if any AU contributes 7 or more to the instrumental value of a second AU, the former must precede. In practice one might pick the smallest value that did not lead to inconsistencies (that is, "cycles" of the form $a > b > c \cdots > a$). The above procedure yields the matrix N of table 3 in which unit entries represent value increments of 7 or more: other entries are all zeros.

Squaring the matrix N according to standard procedures leads to a matrix N^2 in which positive entries indicate the necessity for two-step precursion. In the example, the 1 in the $a\,b$ position derives from the fact that a must precede f by one step and f must precede b by one steps. This process is continued until the final matrix power with a positive entry, in this case N^4, is obtained. If the matrix powers do not vanish after m steps, where m is the order of the matrix, then the intial criterion of precedence has permitted an inconsistency. This is guaranteed by the fact that higher powers of a triangular matrix must converge.

TABLE 3

MATRIX OPERATION FOR DERIVING LEAD TIMES FROM NECESSARY PRECURSION DATA

N							N^3					
	a	b	c	d	e	f		a	b	c	d	e	f
a	—	0	0	1	0	1	a	—	0	0	0	0	0
b	0	—	0	0	0	0	b	—	—	0	0	0	0
c	0	1*	—	0	1	0	c	0	1*	—	1	0	1
d	0	0	0	—	0	0	d	0	0	0	—	0	0
e	1	0	0	0	—	1*	e	0	1	0	0	—	0
f	0	1	0	0	0	—	f	0	0	0	0	0	1

N^2							N^4					
	a	b	c	d	e	f		a	b	c	d	e	f
a	—	0	0	0	0	0	a	—	1	0	0	0	0
b	0	—	0	0	0	0	b	0	—	0	0	0	0
c	0	1	—	0	0	0	c	1	0	—	0	0	1*
d	0	0	0	—	0	0	d	0	0	0	—	0	0
e	0	0	0	0	—	0	e	0	1*	0	1	—	1
f	0	0	0	0	0	—	f	0	0	0	0	0	—

After reaching the final power, N^4, in table 3, we have worked backward to N, placing an asterisk next to each entry that occurs in a higher matrix power. Thus the starred entry eb in N^2 indicates that e must precede b by *at least* two steps: the same entry, unstarred, in N^3 indicates that e precedes b by exactly three steps.

From the results of these manipulations, we obtain an explicit temporal interval for 13 of the 15 possible order relationships between pairs of AU's. These order relationships can be directly translated into an over-all ordering $c\,e\,a\,(d\,f)\,b$, in which d and f should evidently occur in the same space. As it happens, this technique leads to the same ordering as that derived from the earlier procedure which utilized the preferential data.

2.2 Structural Considerations. It is clear that orderings of AU's such as those obtained in the above paragraphs can be graded in terms of strictness. At one extreme each AU may fit in at only one time: at the other extreme, all permutations of the task segments may be equally effective. The purpose of this section will be to suggest a measure for the phasing requirements of a task based on the general notion of the entropy of an ensemble. This measure will then be related directly to the coordination problem posed by assignment of AU's to isolated group members.

The measure here proposed requires that we settle in advance for a certain set of acceptable sequences. This of course discards the information represented in the differential instrumental values among these sequences, but this is the "going price" for the use of information measures. An alternative, not here pursued, is to employ the variance of instrumental values over all permutations of the AU's.

The informational measure of phasing depends on the fact that if there are n AU's in a simple order (i.e., each one a necessary precursor of all following subtasks) then the correct permutation of AU's is one of $n!$ such permutations and the information is $\log n!$. If the task is less rigidly ordered, it contains less information until reaching the limit of an unordered task which contains no phasing information.

To obtain the information for intermediate cases, it is only necessary to divide $n!$ by the number of equivalent ways in which the subtasks can be arranged. For example, if there are five subtasks, of which three (say, a, b, c) must precede the other two (say, d, e) then the information is $\log$ (5!/3! 2!) or $\log 10 = 3.32$.

Table 4 shows graphs (Hasse diagrams) for a sample of partial orderings and the information contained in each. For some of these orderings, the equivalent arrangements are explicitly shown, and the following rules hold in general if there are two independent ordered sub-chains, e.g., $(b\,c)$ and $(d\,e)$ in task graph IV; then the total number of elements in these chains can be thought of as "places," and these places can be selected ad lib for the elements in either sub-chain. For example, there are two elements in both the sub-chains of task graph IV, and $\binom{4}{2} = 6$ ways of assigning places to b and c that preserve their internal ordering. This can be directly extended to more sub-chains. For example, three ordered sub-chains of re-

TABLE 4

Task Graphs and Phasing Information

I	II	III
a │ b │ c │ d │ e	a │ (b, c) │ d │ e	(a, b, c) │ (d, e)
$\log 5! = 6.907$	$\log 5!/2! = 5.907$	$\log 5!/2!3! = 3.322$

IV	V	VI
a branching to b and d; b—c, d—e	a branching to b and d; b—c—e, d—e	a branching to b and d; b—c, d—e
$\log 5!/6 = 4.322$	$\log 5!/3 = 5.322$	$\log 5!/10 = 3.585$

IV	V	VI
$a\ b\ c\ d\ e$	$a\ b\ c\ d\ e$	$a\ b\ c\ d\ e$
$a\ b\ d\ c\ e$	$a\ b\ d\ c\ e$	$a\ b\ d\ c\ e$
$a\ b\ d\ e\ c$	$a\ d\ b\ c\ e$	$a\ b\ d\ e\ c$
$a\ d\ b\ c\ e$		$a\ d\ b\ c\ e$
$a\ d\ b\ e\ c$		$a\ d\ b\ e\ c$
$a\ d\ e\ b\ c$		$a\ d\ e\ b\ c$
		$d\ a\ b\ c\ e$
		$d\ a\ b\ e\ c$
		$d\ a\ e\ b\ c$
		$d\ e\ a\ b\ c$

spective lengths k, l, m generate $\binom{k+1}{1}$ equivalent orderings $\binom{k+1+m}{m}$. An unordered sub-chain of k elements can be treated like an ordered sub-chain of equal length, but it generates $k!$ equivalent arrangements.

The chief problem of this section is to describe the communication requirements that are imposed as the AU's in table 4 are distributed over group members to satisfy various criteria. Our analysis will provide a quantitative expression of the intuitively obvious fact that the coordination requirements increased as a function of the degree of AU distribution.

First suppose that a totally ordered task (such as task I in table 4) is divided amongst two group members—e.g., a, b, and c given to one agent and d and e to the other. Then the ordering of subtasks assigned to the individual group members is not disturbed, and it accounts for part of the total ordering information. In this case the set $(a\,b\,c)$ contains $\log 3! = 2.585$ bits of information and the set $(d\,e)$ contains $\log 2! = 1.000$ bits, out of the original $\log 5! = 6.907$ bits of ordering information. The remaining 3.322 bits of information represent the coordination requirements between agents.

In order to interpret this interagent information, we assume as before an over-all task performance time broken up into five unit periods. Then the coordinating information is required to indicate to each of the presumably isolated agents which of these five periods will be occupied by his AU's. In the present case, this is $\log \binom{5}{2} = \log \binom{5}{3} = \log 10 = 3.322$ bits. In terms of explicit communication, this might mean that the agent with the set $(a\,b\,c)$ performs these three units, then relays the news of their completion to the agent with $(d\,e)$.

In principle, this provides a scheme for computing the coordination requirement in any task: it is measured by the discrepancy between the total structuring information in the task and the sum of the information for separate subtask orderings. This makes it clear that we can reduce the coordination requirement by imposing strict individual requirements. In task IV, for example, the division of AU's into the two simply ordered sets $(a\,b\,c)$ and $(d\,e)$ leaves only .737 bits of information for coordination. Explicitly, there are 10 ways in which the two subsets $(a\,b\,c)$ and $(d\,e)$ might be intermingled. Since 6 of these 10 arrangements are permissible, the coordinating information is $\log (10/6) = .737$ bits. If task VI is divided into the subsets $(a\,b\,c)$ and $(d\,e)$, no coordination at all is required between agents; they can operate in complete independence of each other.

The simplicity of this schema is impaired somewhat if either of the intra-agent orderings depends upon the ordering used by the other agent. To illustrate, consider a division of task IV into the subsets $(a\,c\,e)$ and $(b\,d)$ containing, respectively, 1.585 and .000 bits of internal ordering information. In this case, coordination is required not only with respect to when each agent may act but also with respect to which AU he will choose. Although a must be performed first, there is a choice between b and d: this choice will in turn affect the choice between c and e, etc. Hence, the $4.322 - 1.585 = 2.737$ bits for coordination in this task structure reflects qualitative information about the identity of AU's as well as purely temporal information. However, it is rather awkward to express this information in terms of explicit communications.

Before leaving this topic, it should be noted that there will often arise the question of how much of a coordination requirement is justified by the advantage in division of labor. The latter will vary widely depending on the task structure and the specific nature of the AU's. For a simply ordered task, such as task I, division of labor is indicated only if there is process interaction (e.g., fatigue) or if there is specialization of skills among group members. For most tasks, on the other hand, there will be savings in time if separate agents work on reciprocally unordered AU's. This will ordinarily entail some expense in standby time as well as in coordination costs.

2.3 Behavioral-Functional Phasing Problems. We have seen that the logic of the interaction between group and environment may dictate a certain ordering of task elements or action units; the desirability of optimal utilization of personnel calls for the distribution of AU's over group members; this distribution, in turn, imposes a need for coordinating procedures which permit the group to retain the basic subtask ordering. Using simple models, we can examine various specific mechanics by which this may be accomplished.

As noted, there will ordinarily be two kinds of uncertainty on the part of any group member concerning the performance of AU's by other agents; the identity of the AU and the time of completion (or other "phase-in" time). This uncertainty may arise from the human unpredictability of the operator or from the contingency of these data on environmental circumstances. We should expect the former facet of the uncertainty to diminish as the group members become accustomed to working with each other. However, a certain amount of environmentally based uncertainty would persist in almost any real task.

To illustrate, consider the task graph IV in table 4, with a distribution $(a\,c\,e)$ assigned to agent X and $(b\,d)$ assigned to agent Y. The agent with $(b\,d)$ is uncertain only about *when a* will be completed. His partner with c and e must, however, know whether b or d has been used. If the choice of which is used first is at the discretion of person X, then X can agree to use one or the other consistently, or Y can learn X's general proclivities. On the other hand, if the choice between b and d is determined by some environmental signal, Y must either use that signal or obtain more direct information on the actual AU. Y can use the signal as a cue only if X uses the signal predictably (according to explicit agreement or not).

In many real-life tasks, Y will generally have some inkling of whether X has or has not performed a given linked AU. His problem is whether or not his information is firm enough to justify taking action. If he does not take action, he may simply wait for more definite information or initiate some action to obtain it. There may be direct costs of information-seeking or indirect costs due to loss in value of the resulting sequence, because of time lag. In either case, the problem for Y seems to be whether to act on sketchy information or to wait for fuller information.

The actual information that Y may receive can fall into one of three types: antecedent information, process information, or outcome information. The first sort of information gives Y the context within which X's decision was made; process information tells Y what X actually did, though not necessarily how it turns out; outcome information tells Y the final results of X's actions.

To illustrate, consider the task with parameters summarized in table 5. The row and column headings E_i, E_j, E_k, E_l are four E-states relevant to the group. In this example, E_k is taken to be an E-state of positive "income" value to the group and E_l is an E-state of negative value. By this we mean that the group gains a certain amount for time spent in E_k and loses for time spent in E_l. Their objective is to maximize time in E_k, which they control by operations in E_i and E_j.

TABLE 5

Schematic Representation of a Task with Two Phased Action Units

	E_i	E_j	E_k	E_l	$\hat{E}_i$	$\hat{E}_j$	$\hat{E}_k$	$\hat{E}_l$
E_i	—	a	—	b	1	0	0	0
E_j	—	—	b	a	$\frac{1}{2}$	$\frac{1}{2}$	0	0
E_k	$f_1(t)$	—	—	—	0	0	1	0
E_l	$f_2(t)$	—	—	—	0	0	0	1

Specifically, if E_i occurs, the AU indicated by a changes the group's condition to E_j; application of b to E_j changes the group's situation to E_k—the favorable state. In the terminology suggested earlier, $b\,a\,E_i = b\,E_j = E_k$. The reverse application, however, as well as a repeated application of a, places the group in E_l. Transition from E_k or E_l to E_i is taken as a pure function of time, perhaps stochastic. Any operator effects not explicitly shown are assumed to be identities.

Suppose now that an operator agent A has control of the action a; and a second, isolated, agent B has control of b. We suppose that A gets a direct indication whenever the state E_i occurs, while B gets either delayed or uncertain information on E_i.

We shall focus our discussion on the nature and conditions of B's decision problem. First, it is clear that B has only a "when" decision to make—he has no option as to which AU he will employ. The criterial measure of B's performance depends upon how soon b is applied *after* a has been completed. It is thus a mixed coincidence criterion.

Second, the nature of B's information—and of his possible uncertainty—is clear. If he has any evidence as to the occurrence of E_i, he may assume that A has also received this evidence and has initiated a. Alternatively, B may have more direct evidence on the occurrence of a, either verbal or through other sources of inference. Finally, B may receive evidence that the situation has been changed to E_j.

Whenever all of these avenues of information are available, they will tend to fall into a hierarchy of increasing certainty but also of increasing latency. Depending on the criterial and other task parameters, it may be advisable for B to take a chance on applying b incorrectly in order to avoid the otherwise inevitable lag in obtaining better information.

In order to define a numerical problem we make the following assumptions:

1. B's information can be summarized by the second matrix of table 5, in which rows represent the true states of the world and columns represent B's resulting signal. The signal $\hat{E}_j$ is then unambiguous, but $\hat{E}_i$ may indicate either E_i or E_j.

2. A's information is perfect and he immediately initiates a. The time for completion of a is uniformly distributed over the interval $t = 0$ to $t = L$.

3. $f_1(t)$ and $f_2(t)$ are defined by stipulating that the group will remain in

either E_k or E_l until some fixed time $t = M$. They receive no income in E_l but receive an income $w\,dt$ for time spent in E_k.

Suppose then that, at time t $(0 < t < L)$, B is still receiving the signal $\hat{E}_i$. Should he wait for $\hat{E}_j$ or take a chance?

Note first that the probability that the true state is E_j if $\hat{E}_i$ appears can be calculated by the customary Bayes procedures:

$$P_t\{E_j \mid \hat{E}_i\} = \frac{P_t\{E_j \cdot \hat{E}_i\}}{P_t\{\hat{E}_i\}}$$

$$= \frac{P_t\{E_j \cdot \hat{E}_i\}}{\sum\limits_{x=i,j} P_t\{\hat{E}_i \mid E_x\} P_t\{E_x\}}$$

$$= \frac{t/2L}{t/2L + (L-t)/L}$$

$$= \frac{t}{2L - t} \, .$$

If B applies b at this time, the expected income is the product of the probability of attaining E_k and the income w for the remaining time, $M-t$. This entire expression is then

$$\left(\frac{t}{2L - t}\right) w(M - t) \, .$$

Differentiating this expression with respect to t, one obtains

$$\frac{d}{dt} = t^2 - 4Lt + \frac{2ML}{(2L - t)^2}$$

which has roots at

$$t = 2L - \sqrt{2L(2L - M)} \, .$$

Thus if $M = 0$, then $t_{\max} = 0$; if $M = L$, then $t_{\max} = (2 - \sqrt{2})L = .59L$; and if $M = 3/2L$, then $t_{\max} = L$. It is clear that B can never profit by waiting longer than L, as he can then be certain that E_j is the true state.

If B decides always to wait for the unambiguous signal $\hat{E}_j$, his expectation will be the product of the income w and the time remaining from the appearance of $\hat{E}_j$, at time t, till the time M. In this case, however, B must also have an auxiliary rule to apply b at time L, even if there is no $\hat{E}_j$ signal by then (recall that this occurs with probability .5). His expectation is therefore

$$\frac{W}{2}\left[\int_0^L \frac{M - t}{L}\, dt + M - L\right] \, .$$

This expression has a value, after integration and simplification, of

$$\tfrac{1}{4} W(4M - 3L) \, .$$

This decision rule then has a value of $WL/4$ if $M = L$. By way of contrast, the optimal application of the former rule [that is, "jumping the gun" at $(2 - \sqrt{2})L$] has a value of

$$\frac{a - \sqrt{2}}{2} \, WL \cong 1.18 \, \frac{WL}{4} \, ,$$

and is slightly advantageous.

Of course, the specific numerical results for this very artificial task are of little direct value. What these models emphasize is that the phasing aspects of compound tasks confront people with conflicting decision alternatives. Their resolution of these situations may of course reflect personality characteristics, cognitive attributes, or factors that derive from the social climate of the groups.

3. The Function of Empirical Research

We turn finally to the question of how the theoretical framework here sketched out might interact with a research program. I shall first indicate briefly the direction our own research has taken and then venture a few remarks on the long range outlook for theoretical–empirical symbiosis.

The research at Tufts has touched on each of the three areas related to the models discussed above. A study conducted by Dr. Lorraine Eyde investigated the ability of groups to discern and respond appropriately to specified normative subtask orderings. We set up preferential orderings by presenting groups with a problem which, in essence, required them to solve a crossword puzzle. Presumably, some of the words could be filled in before others and the letters would then aid the discovery of more difficult words. Necessary orderings were established in group arithmetic problems which required the use of the numerical solution to one problem segment in following segments.

A second set of investigations, conducted by Dr. Bernard Harleston and Mr. Harvey Roazen, has attempted to manipulate the tightness or strictness of task phasing and the distribution of AU assignment over group members. The tasks used in these studies have involved the requirement that group members accumulate certain specified subsets from a finite pool of objects that could be exchanged. As an example, one task requires each of the group members to compile a set of short words using a common fund of letters—a sort of consecutive anagram problem.

Finally, in studies now in progress we are examining individual decision-making behavior in situations that pose a conflict between fast but poorly informed responses and delayed decisions based on better information. The particular task we are using is a stock-market situation in which subjects have a choice between buying stocks on the spot, using "stale" information, or waiting for upgraded information but buying the stocks at penalized rates.

I shall not describe the results of these studies in any detail since they are to be made available elsewhere. Instead, I should like to call attention to a problem that has become increasingly acute for us, and may be of general significance: the problem of working out mutually complementary roles for theory and research. Of course, this is an all-pervading scientific problem, but it seems to be uniquely severe in this area, which treats the group as an economic system, and I suspect that it may take on major proportions as our theory begins to mature. I am not suggesting that we shall witness the melancholy spectacle of the research psychologist's becoming a technological sacrifice to his own theoretical cunning. It does appear, however, that the function of laboratory research may change markedly from its present one.

At present, it would appear that where research is the hand-maiden of theory in this area, it performs one of two major functions. First, it may deal with components, testing individual behavior to see if it satisfies the assumptions of theory or measuring the parameters of individual behavior that are relevant to the theory. A second form of research is concerned with total system behavior, but in a rather non-analytic way. It either demonstrates conclusions that are obvious from the most superficial theoretical analyses, or acts as a sort of organic Monte Carlo process, deriving consequences that are implicit in, but not obvious from, the theory.

What is less clear at present is how laboratory research can be used as a genuine tool of discovery in conjunction with theory of the operations analyses type. One difficulty appears to be that we have not yet developed behavior-recording or content analysis to the point where it can be used to illuminate complex processes—in fact to a point where it is anything more than a tedious nuisance. One suggestion that follows from this is that we must learn to make our laboratory operations more operational; that is, we must learn how to obtain records in free-response situations that have a clear relevance for theory.

4. Summary

This paper has presented a general formulation of the problem of subtask phasing in groups and has proposed four dimensions for classification: subject or environmental actuation, temporal relations among subtasks, necessity or degree of strictness of ordering, and the coupling or medium of interaction between subtasks.

Three broad problem areas were suggested. The normative problem is a function of the task environment only, and concerns the optimal ordering of subtasks. The distributive–structural problem is how one should assign subtasks or action units to various agents. The behavioral–functional problem is concerned with how the optimal phasing is maintained under conditions of agent isolation. A rudimentary mathematical model has been sketched out for each of these areas in order to indicate relevant parameters. Finally, we have described research growing out of this framework and have ventured some remarks on the current relation between theory and research.

REFERENCES

[1] KELLEY, J. E., Jr., Critical path planning and scheduling, *Operations Res.*, 1961, **9**, 296-320.
[2] ROBY, T. B., The mechanics of environmental adjustment, *Behav. Sci.*, 1959, **4**, 107-19.
[3] ROBY, T. B., "Contributions to a Theory of Group Performance," Institute for Psychological Research, Report No. NR 170-408, NONR Contract No. 494(15), Medford, Mass.: Tufts Univ., 1960.

19

Two-Person Interactions in a Continuous-Response Task

Seymour Rosenberg, *Bell Telephone Laboratories*

It is frequently assumed by psychologists that interaction sequences between two persons can be understood in terms of individual laws of behavior. Reactions of one individual are explained in terms of environmental conditions created in part by a second individual; reactions of the first, in turn, affect the stimulus complex and hence the subsequent behavior of the second individual. As the number of elements in such a sequence is extended, however, this type of shuttlecock analysis can become very cumbersome, even for simple interactions. In laboratory interactions, a more parsimonious method of analysis can sometimes be rendered with a quantitative model of individual behavior. The view that interactional systems may be explained with individual behavior laws is retained in this approach.

In the psychological literature, quantitative analyses of interactional systems in terms of individual behavioral laws have evolved primarily from mathematical learning theory [3], [11]. The finite-response task has received the greatest share of attention in both individual and interactional learning situations. The continuous-response task, by contrast, has had a more limited history of systematic analysis. I refer to the continuous-response task in which particular response and outcome values occur in ordered pairs over a series of discrete trials. The model proposed by Suppes [10], which is an extension of stimulus-sampling theory, appears to be the first formal treatment of the continuous-response task with discrete trials. Empirical studies of individual learning in this type of continuous-response task are exemplified by the line-drawing experiments and by a number of discrete-positioning studies imbedded in recent motor-learning literature [2]. A small number of empirical studies of two-person (dyadic) interactions using variants of a continuous-response task have also appeared recently [5]–[8].

Thanks are due E. N. Gilbert and R. Gnanadesikan for their invaluable help in a number of the mathematical aspects of the paper.

The present paper describes an individual behavior model for the continuous-response task based on somewhat different notions from those used
in the model developed by Suppes. The model will be described and applied
first to an experiment in noncontingent reinforcement in a continuous-
response task. The modifications of the experimental task to produce dyadic
reward systems will be described and will be followed by an application of
the model to these dyadic systems. Essentially, predictions about dyadic systems are derived from the solution of simultaneous linear difference equations describing changes in individual behavior over all trials. Finally, a
study of the effects of communication in various dyadic reward systems
will be reported.

1. The Continuous-Response Task

1.1 General Properties. The model is relevant to tasks with the following general properties.

(a) The responses available to a subject are ordered along a continuum.
Bounds for the continuum may or may not be explicitly specified for the
subject. Examples of tasks with explicit bounds include positioning a lever
within a fixed spatial interval, selecting a number anywhere between 0 and
100, and so on. Bounds are less explicit when they are determined by
physiological limits (e.g., number of crank turns per unit time), or by
"reasonable" restraints (e.g., the autokinetic response).

(b) All possible outcomes are either "correct" or "incorrect" on a given
trial. (The model may not be applicable to a continuum of payoffs.)

(c) Each outcome event specifies or indicates to a subject a *unique distance
and direction* of the actual response on a given trial relative to the correct
or goal response for that trial. This component of the outcome event will
be termed the "cybernetic cue." In practice, the correct response is usually
not a unique point on the response continuum but a small region on and
around a point.

(d) Responses and outcomes occur in ordered pairs over a series of
discrete trials.

The methods for displaying the distance between the correct response
and the actual response can vary considerably for different experimental
tasks. The display may show both the actual and correct responses or
simply the directional difference between them. These two types of display
correspond to the distinction between pursuit and compensatory tracking
[1]. In addition, the units of response distance may be subjected to any
of a variety of transformations and presented as a number, a physical distance, a stimulus intensity, and so on. Note, however, that if the display of
the *direction* of the correct response relative to the actual response is affected
or lost in a transformation, the task and associated behavioral processes
are seriously altered. That is, it should be obvious to the subject whether
his response on a trial was "too high" or "too low." Models or theories
for continuous-response tasks must eventually reckon with various transformations in the cybernetic cue.

1.2 The Specific Task. The particular task that will now be described satisfies the general properties described above, is convenient as a referent in the description of the model, and was used in the collection of all the data presented in this paper. It lends itself readily to studies of both individual behavior systems and dyadic systems. The task will first be described for the individual experiment.

The subject is seated in a booth that contains all the necessary display and response equipment. When two subjects are run at the same time, they are seated in separate booths and cannot see each other. Essential components of the equipment in a booth are sketched in figure 1.

A response knob in the lower left corner of the tilted panel permits the

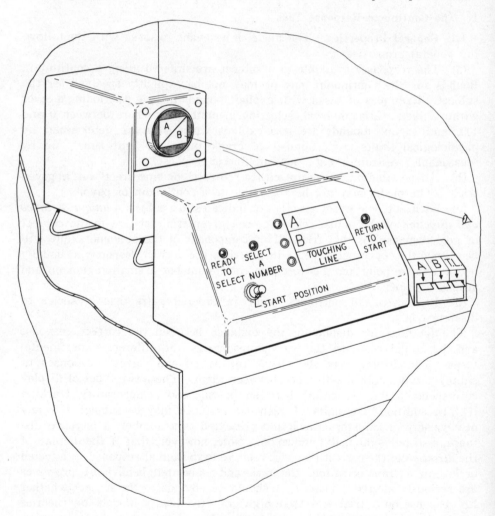

FIG. 1. A sketch of the equipment in a subject's booth.

subject to pick a number between 0 and 100 on each trial. Differently colored lights on the same panel serve as signals for the subject to respond.

At the far end of the booth, an oscilloscope (DuMont 401A) displays the outcome as a small illuminated dot on the face of the cathode-ray tube. The only part of the tube face visible to the subject is a square ($3\frac{3}{16}$ in. on each side) and the dot always appears within this square. The subject controls the horizontal displacement of the dot on the square by the size of the number that he selects and the experimenter controls the vertical displacement of the dot. The bounds on the subject's response continuum (0 and 100) correspond to the extreme left and extreme right sides of the square, respectively. Intermediate responses on the continuum correspond linearly to the horizontal displacements of the dot. A single black line $\frac{1}{64}$ in. thick is painted diagonally across the square as shown in figure 1. A correct outcome is defined for a subject as the dot's touching anywhere on the line.

In addition, a small box containing three switches is located on the right side of the table. The subject is asked to report the position of the dot on each trial by depressing one of the three switches. A corresponding light on the subject's panel goes on, automatically confirming to the subject that his report of the outcome had been received by the experimenter.

A complete trial lasts 12 to 15 sec. The subject has 5 sec to select a number. The outcome (dot on screen) then follows and lasts 3 sec. The trial terminates when the subject returns the response knob to the start position (off scale). Trials are run consecutively.

2. Basic Properties of the Model

The psychological basis for the model is as follows. In a continuous-response task the subject responds primarily to the magnitude of the distance between his actual response and the correct response and to the direction of the correct response; in short, he responds to the cybernetic cue. The cybernetic cue is symbolized $D_{x.n}$, where x in the subscript identifies the subject (superfluous for the one-person case) and n identifies the trial number. The cue $D_{x.n}$ is expressed in terms of the units of the response continuum and is either positive or negative depending on the direction of the correct response relative to actual response. In general,

$$(1) \qquad\qquad D_{x.n} = f(y_n) - x_n .$$

The term x_n is the value of the subject's response on trial n, and y_n (in the one-person noncontingent case) is a value chosen by the experimenter on the nth trial. $f(y_n)$ is the value of that x on trial n which would have been correct for that trial.

(In individual learning studies employing a continuous-response task it is sometimes possible to simplify, $f(y_n) = y_n$. In the oscilloscope task the notation $f(y_n)$ is retained, since any single-valued function of y may serve as a goal line and satisfy the general properties of the continuous-response task. In the oscilloscope task, $D_{x,n}$ is the horizontal distance of the subject's dot on trial n from his goal line in terms of response units.)

The cybernetic cue on a given trial determines the size of the response change for the next trial. That is, the subject tends to change his response in *proportion* to the distance of his response from the correct response on a given trial. If the correct response changes from trial to trial, the subject is, in effect, "tracking" the successive positions of the correct response with a lag of one trial. A subject's rate of goal approach (i.e., the size of the proportion, *per se*) is assumed to vary from trial to trial although the average rate of goal approach is positive. A reasonable argument for positive rates of goal approach can probably be made in terms of a long learning history in which approach responses related to the distance of the organism from the goal have been reinforced. Whether a goal be stationary or in motion, it is hard to cite examples of situations in which "going away" from the goal actually increases the chances of relatively immediate goal attainment. One source of variability in behavior is thus described by the notion of a variable rate of positive goal-approach behavior.

A second source of behavior variability occurs as a psychophysical error either in the subject's reproducing a response or in his judging the exact location of the correct response or in both. This variability can be quite large where an experimenter employs a response continuum in which kinesthetic cues are important to the subject's reproducing a response. Where responses and outcomes both occur on the same spatial continuum and where the continuum is visually accessible, this source of behavior variability is probably low. A similar type of variation (for purposes of the model) is introduced by the existence of a small goal area rather than a unique goal point. The subject "aims" at different parts of the goal area from trial to trial. Even when he is in the goal area on a given trial, he may change his response choice slightly on the next trial because the width of the goal area is consistent with this latitude in behavior.

These descriptive notions of goal approach behavior and response error in a continuous-response task may be summarized in the following difference equation:

$$(2) \qquad \varDelta x_n = x_{n+1} - x_n = \alpha_n(D_{x,n} + \delta_n) ,$$

where α_n is the rate of goal approach on trial n, $\varDelta x_n$ is proportional to $D_{x,n}$, and δ_n includes psychophysical and "aiming" errors in the $(n + 1)$th response as well as psychophysical errors associated with the subject's observing the nth outcome.

If we now add certain explicit assumptions about the stochastic properties of the sources of variability described above, a fairly tractable model results. The following formal properties are assumed for the random variables, α_n and δ_n.

(*a*) *For a given subject, the statistical parameters of the distribution of α_n and δ_n are independent of responses and outcomes on any previous trial.*

(*b*) *For a given subject, the values of α_n and δ_n are independent of n.*

(c) *For a given subject, the pairs of values α_n and δ_n are statistically independent of each other.*

In addition to these mathematically convenient assumptions, it will be helpful to make the psychologically reasonable assumption that δ_n has a symmetrical (probably normal) distribution with the population mean $\bar{\delta} = 0$ for each subject. Note also the psychological assumption that $\bar{\alpha}$, the population mean of α_n, is greater than 0 for each subject.

Other restrictions on the moments of α_n are required for the moments of x_n to converge in a noncontingent reinforcement situation. For example, if $0 < \bar{\alpha} < 2$, the average of x_n will converge as $n \to \infty$. Interestingly enough, the lower-bound restriction on $\bar{\alpha}$ is the same as the psychological assumption that $\bar{\alpha} > 0$ for each subject. No special assumptions about the shape of the distribution of α_n are required.

Restrictions on the moments of α_n required for stable asymptotic response moments in a noncontingent situation do not necessarily correspond to those required for convergence of response moments in a dyadic reward system. Nevertheless, estimates of moments of α_n (particularly of $\bar{\alpha}$ and σ_α^2) from data in a noncontingent situation can be used to predict behavioral stability or instability in a variety of dyadic systems. The first experiment to be described is a study in noncontingent reinforcement, the primary purpose of which will be to obtain estimates of $\bar{\alpha}$ and σ_α^2 for later prediction in dyadic systems. The model is also committed to certain predictions in the one-person noncontingent situation; some of these predictions will be examined very briefly in the following section.

3. A Study in Noncontingent Reinforcement

3.1 Experimental Conditions. The subjects were female clerks and typists. Their modal age was 18 years. They were scheduled according to the hour of the day that they could be spared from their normal work. Taped instructions explaining the signals, the response mode, and the outcome display were given through earphones.

The goal line in all conditions was a diagonal across the square as shown in figure 1. That is, $f(y_n) = y_n$. A subject was correct on any trial in which she matched the vertical displacement of the dot (plus or minus the width of the line and dot). All subjects received 150 trials.

The experimental conditions are easier to describe if one first thinks of the display square as an area in the first quadrant of the x–y plane. The subject's responses (x-axis) and the experimenter's programmed values (y-axis) both range from 0 to 100. A 2×2 factorial design was used with 16 subjects in each of the four conditions. The two orthogonal factors are the size of σ_y and the preliminary instructions to the subject.

Size of σ_y. For 32 subjects, y_n had a normal distribution with a mean of 50 and $\sigma_y = 5$. For the other 32 subjects, y_n had a normal distribution with the same mean but with $\sigma_y = 15$. Each subject was assigned to one of these two conditions for all 150 trials. On each trial, a y-value was randomly selected from the appropriate distribution. Four lists of 150 Gaussian deviates each were obtained from the RAND tables of random digits to program y-values. A list (appropriately transformed in mean and variance) was randomly assigned to a subject with the restriction that all lists occur equally often in each cell of the 2×2 design. The manipulation of σ_y is relevant to the model since $\bar{\alpha}$ and σ_α^2 are expected to be invariant across the two conditions. Other comparisons between the two conditions are also relevant to the model. A rationale for manipulating variance of y_n also obtains from the fact that y_n in a dyadic system is determined by another subject's responses (rather than by the experimenter) and that different dyadic systems "create" differences in the subject's response variability. It is important to ascertain that model parameters remain invariant in different dyadic systems. Of course, simple differences in a noncontingent schedule do not capture subtle differences between dyadic systems that may exist in the response sequences and contingencies.

Instructions. Two different sets of instructions were used, termed "social" and "asocial." The essential difference between the sets of instructions is that in the social instructions subjects were told that y-values were chosen by another subject and in the asocial instructions subjects were simply told that their job was to guess y-displacements with sufficient accuracy to obtain correct outcomes. To lend credence to the instructions, subjects were run one at a time in the asocial condition and two at a time in the social condition. The rationale for studying instructions stems directly from the application of the model to dyadic systems. Although it is easy to set up a dyadic experiment in which neither subject is aware that another subject plays a role in determining outcomes, it is also important to determine the effects, if any, of such knowledge. Data on the nature of these effects are important in determining the applicability to dyadic systems of any individual behavior model in which no special assumptions have been made about social-setting factors.

3.2 Parameter Estimates from Transition Responses. An estimate of $\bar{\alpha}$ for *each* subject is derived as follows. If we multiply equation (2) by $D_{x,n}$ (since $D_{x,n}$ may be zero) and take expected values, we obtain

$$(3) \qquad E[\Delta x_n D_{x,n}] = E[\alpha_n D_{x,n}^2] + E[\alpha_n \delta_n D_{x,n}] .$$

Using the properties assumed for α_n and δ_n, and rewriting in terms of empirical quantities, we obtain

$$(4) \qquad \hat{\bar{\alpha}} = \frac{\sum_n (\Delta x_n D_{x,n})}{\sum_n (D_{x,n}^2)} .$$

Estimates of $\bar{\alpha}$ were calculated for each subject in each of the two trial blocks, 1–75 and 76–150. The results are summarized in figure 2. The average $\hat{\bar{\alpha}}$ in each condition in each trial block is plotted. In all 128 estimates of $\bar{\alpha}$, only one estimate was less than zero and two were greater than one, specifically, $-.01 < \hat{\bar{\alpha}} < 1.09$.

An analysis of variance was performed on $\hat{\bar{\alpha}}$. The results are summarized in table 1.

The larger $\hat{\bar{\alpha}}$ values which occurred with social instructions are significantly different from $\hat{\bar{\alpha}}$ values with asocial instructions (source 1B). One interpretation or "explanation" of the effect of instructions is that a subject in the social condition assumes that the other person has the same goal line as she does and hence uses a higher rate of goal approach. In the asocial

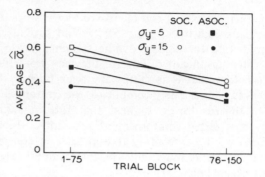

FIG. 2. Average $\hat{\bar{\alpha}}$ in each condition in each of two trial blocks.

condition, the subject does not ascribe any such cooperative motive to the experimenter when he generates y-displacements from trial to trial. The use of goal lines with slopes other than plus one and minus one in a noncontingent-reinforcement study may throw additional light on these interpretations since, in these cases, the horizontal and vertical distances of a dot outcome from the line are not the same. Any subject who assumes that the "other" has the same goal line may fractionate his or her own contribution (Δx_n) according to the relative difference between horizontal and vertical distances of dot to line, while asocially instructed subjects may not.

However, if the effect of instructions is simply to increase the size of $\bar{\alpha}$ equally for all goal lines, the utility of the model for dyadic systems is not profoundly altered with either "aware" or "unaware" subjects. In fact,

TABLE 1

ANALYSIS OF $\hat{\bar{\alpha}}$ FOR EACH SUBJECT IN EACH CONDITION FOR
TRIAL BLOCKS 1-75 AND 76-150

(See also fig. 2.)

Source	df	MS	F	Error Term
Individuals	63	0.0786		
A. $\sigma_y = 5$ vs. $\sigma_y = 15$	1	0.0187	<1	1D
B. Social vs. asocial	1	0.3623	$4.77*$	1D
C. A × B	1	0.0126	<1	1D
D. Within condition	60	0.0760	2.62†	3D
Trial Blocks	1	0.6258	21.36†	3
1 × 2	63	0.0293		
A. 1A × 2	1	0.0590	2.03	3D
B. 1B × 2	1	0.0367	1.27	3D
C. 1C × 2	1	0.0079	<1	3D
D. 1D × 2	60	0.0290		

$* \; p < .05$ $† \; p < .001$

if this simple effect of instructions were unequivocally demonstrated for various goal lines, the model would provide an interesting and nonintuitive prediction for certain dyadic systems (see *Spiral systems* in section 4.1).

The significant difference between trial blocks (source 2) refutes the assumption that $\bar{a}$ is stationary over trials. This type of nonstationarity in $\bar{a}$ does not seriously complicate the contemplated analysis of dyadic systems, but the results do suggest that rate of approach can probably be modified by specialized reinforcement schedules. In a noncontingent schedule, after $E(x_n) = \bar{y}$ no rate of goal approach is consistently reinforced, and the decrement in $\hat{\bar{a}}$ may indicate the gradual extinction of high rates of goal-approach behavior.

The absence of a significant difference between σ_y conditions (source 1A) is in accord with the model. Finally, the significant differences between individuals within conditions (source 1D) indicates that $\bar{a}$ is a consistent property of a subject.

Estimates of the second central moment σ_α^2 were obtained as follows:

$$(5) \qquad \sigma_\alpha^2 = E[(\alpha_n - \bar{\alpha})^2] = E[\alpha_n^2] - \bar{\alpha}^2 \ .$$

From equation (2), and the properties assumed for α_n and δ_n,

$$(6) \qquad E[\alpha_n^2] = \frac{E[\Delta x_n^2]}{E[D_{x,n}^2] + E[\delta_n^2]} \ .$$

The main source of difficulty in obtaining estimates of σ_α^2 is $E[\delta_n^2]$. Since there appears to be no simple way of evaluating $E[\delta_n^2]$ from data in this type of experiment, a rough estimate of the "usable" *range* of $E[\delta_n^2]$ was obtained by letting $E[\delta_n^2] = k = 0, 25, 100$ in the following equation:

$$(7) \qquad \hat{\sigma}_\alpha^2 = \frac{\sum_n (\Delta x_n^2)/N}{[\sum_n (D_{x,n}^2)/N] + k} - \hat{\bar{\alpha}}^2 \ .$$

Estimates of σ_α^2 were obtained for each of the two trial blocks by using equation (7) and the three k values. When $k = 100$, negative $\hat{\sigma}_\alpha^2$ occurred in the data of 10 per cent of the subjects. Hence the usable range of $E[\delta_n^2]$ was taken to be 0–25. This range is also in accord with the interpretations associated with δ_n; i.e., psychophysical and aiming errors are small in this task. (Experiments can probably be designed with the single purpose of obtaining precise estimates of δ_n^2 in a continuous-response task. These estimates may also provide a test of the independence assumption of $D_{x,n}$ and δ_n.) The $\hat{\sigma}_\alpha^2$ values for $E[\delta_n^2] = 0, 25$ are summarized in figure 3. The $\hat{\sigma}_\alpha^2$ were subjected to a log transformation ($t = 200 + 100 \log_{10} \hat{\sigma}_\alpha^2$) and the transformed variable t was analyzed statistically. A summary of the analysis of t is presented in table 2. In general, the results for trial blocks, and lack of difference due to σ_y differences, are similar to those found for $\hat{\bar{a}}$. The instructional difference does not appear as a significant effect, however, although figure 3 suggests the existence of such a difference.

3.3 Empirical Histograms. Detailed quantitative analyses of response moments, autocovariance, and so forth, which are relevant to the model will not be pursued here, since the main focus of the paper is the extension

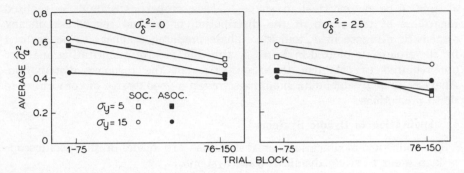

FIG. 3. Average $\hat{\sigma}_{\alpha}^2$ in each condition in each of two trial blocks. σ_{δ}^2 values are assumed.

of the model to dyadic systems. Response histograms for each condition over the last 75 trials are presented in figure 4, however, to indicate some gross properties of the behavior of each condition. The pertinent density functions of y_n are also plotted with each histogram. The effects of instructions, if any, on these data appear to be small. However, the effects of σ_y are easily discernible. With the assumption that $\bar{\delta} = 0$ and that δ_n is symmetrical, the asymptotic distribution of responses in all conditions is expected to have the same mean as $\bar{y}$, to have a variance proportional to

TABLE 2

ANALYSIS OF TRANSFORMED $\hat{\sigma}_{\alpha}^2$ FOR EACH SUBJECT IN EACH CONDITION FOR TRIAL BLOCKS 1-75 AND 76-150 AND FOR THE TWO ASSUMED VALUES OF σ_{δ}^2

(See also fig. 3.)

Source	df	MS	F	Error Term
Individuals	63	6389		
A. $\sigma_y = 5$ vs. $\sigma_y = 15$	1	407	<1	1D
B. Social vs. asocial	1	10647	1.64	1D
C. A × B	1	2608	<1	1D
D. Within condition	60	6481	4.53†	4D
Trial Blocks	1	28921	19.59†	4
$\sigma_{\delta}^2 = 0$ vs. $\sigma_{\delta}^2 = 25$	1	11542	48.90†	5
1 × 2	63	1476		
A. 1A × 2	1	6811	4.76*	4D
B. 1B × 2	1	115	<1	4D
C. 1C × 2	1	94	<1	4D
D. 1D × 2	60	1432		
1 × 3	63	236		
2 × 3	1	383	4.16*	7
1 × 2 × 3	63	92		

* $p < .05$ † $p < .001$

σ_y^2, and to be symmetrical in shape. These properties should be realized regardless of the shape of the distribution of α_n and regardless of any systematic decrease in $\bar{\alpha}$, and σ_α^2. These predictions appear to be realized for the group data plotted in figure 4, although precise quantitative analyses are required to establish these properties of the response distribution. Analyses of individual data should also reveal a good degree of conformity to these predictions.

4. Application to Dyadic Systems

The following modifications or restrictions are made in the oscilloscope task in order to study dyadic reward systems.

(a) Each subject manipulates both the *horizontal* displacement of the dot on *his own display square* and the *vertical* displacement of the dot on the *other subject's display square*.

(b) The two goal lines, one in each display square, are not necessarily the same; i.e., both subjects do not necessarily receive correct outcomes on the same trial.

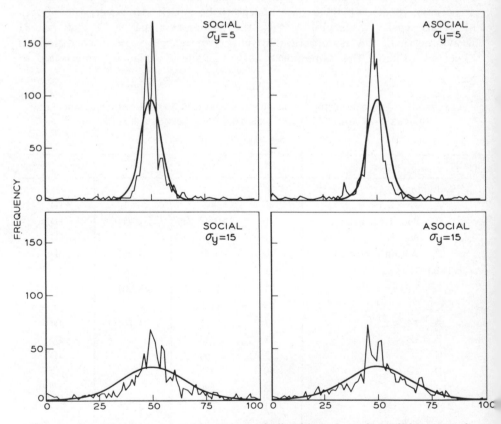

FIG. 4. Empirical histograms of response of all subjects in each condition over the last 75 trials. Density functions of y_n are also plotted.

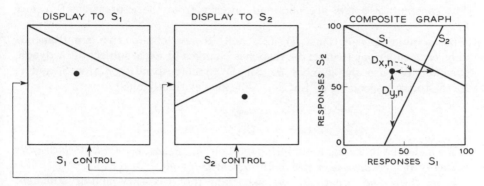

FIG. 5.   An example of a dyadic system showing a typical outcome (the dot) as it is displayed on the oscilloscope of each subject.   The terms $D_{x,n}$ and $D_{y,n}$ in the composite are explained in the text.

(c)   No communication or visual contact is permitted between the subjects. The last restriction precludes interaction behavior not explicitly identified in the model.   In all other essential respects, the task is unchanged.

An example of a dyadic reward system is shown in figure 5.   The first two squares are sketches of two typical display squares, one available to one subject, S_1, and the other available to the other subject, S_2.   The dot (exaggerated in size) in each square is an example of a simultaneous outcome on a trial in which S_1 chooses 40 and S_2 chooses 60.   Note that the horizontal displacement of the dot in the S_1 display corresponds to the vertical displacement of the dot in the S_2 display, and vice versa.   The composite graph (available to neither subject) in figure 5 summarizes all (x, y) values required for one or for both subjects to obtain correct outcomes.   All (x, y) points on the S_1 line represent response pairs required for S_1 to receive a correct outcome.   All points on the S_2 line represent response pairs required for S_2 to receive a correct outcome.   The intersection is an (x, y) value in which both subjects simultaneously receive a correct outcome.   Any (x, y) values on neither line represent incorrect outcomes for both subjects.   A dyadic reward system can be given a geometric representation similar to that of the composite graph for a variety of other continuous-response tasks and even for simple numerical outcomes.   That is, the S_1 line on the composite is the transformation used on each of the S_2 responses to determine the response required of S_1 to receive a correct outcome on each trial. Similarly the S_2 line is the transformation on the S_1 responses that determines the response required of S_2 on each trial for a correct outcome.

The S_1 and S_2 lines (transformation) are written in the forms $x = f_1(y)$ and $y = f_2(x)$, respectively, while the corresponding values of x and y that would have resulted in a correct outcome for S_1 and S_2 on trial n are denoted $f_1(y_n)$ and $f_2(x_n)$.   We restrict the ensuing discussion to linear functions.   That is,

(8)
$$f_1(y_n) = ay_n + l ,$$
$$f_2(x_n) = bx_n + m .$$

The constants a, b, l, m are obtained directly from the expressions $f_1(y)$ and $f_2(x)$.

By combining equations (1), (2), and (8) we obtain two simultaneous difference equations to describe response changes of each subject in a dyadic system. We use the symbol β_n for S_2 to correspond to α_n for S_1 and ε_n for S_2 to correspond to δ_n for S_1. The model thus yields

$$\text{(9)} \qquad \begin{aligned} x_{n+1} &= (1 - \alpha_n)x_n + \alpha_n a y_n + \alpha_n l + \alpha_n \delta_n \,, \\ y_{n+1} &= \beta_n b x_n + (1 - \beta_n)y_n + \beta_n m + \beta_n \varepsilon_n \,. \end{aligned}$$

We make the following assumption explicit: α_n, β_n, δ_n, ε_n *are all stochastically mutually independent in a randomly assembled dyad.*

From these two equations, we ascertain the necessary and/or sufficient conditions for behavioral and reward stability in a variety of dyadic reward systems. Derivations will be limited to the first two asymptotic response moments.

4.1 First-Moment Stability. We first rewrite equations (9) in terms of expected values. Let $E[x_n] = X_n$ and $E[y_n] = Y_n$. Equations (9) may be rewritten

$$\text{(10)} \qquad \begin{aligned} X_{n+1} &= (1 - \bar{\alpha})X_n + \bar{\alpha}a Y_n + \bar{\alpha}l \,, \\ Y_{n+1} &= \bar{\beta}b X_n + (1 - \bar{\beta})Y_n + \bar{\beta}m \,. \end{aligned}$$

The terms, $\bar{\alpha}\bar{\delta}$ and $\bar{\beta}\bar{\varepsilon}$, were dropped, since we assume $\bar{\delta} = \bar{\varepsilon} = 0$. Whether or not we make this assumption, these terms are not critical in determining the asymptotic stability of (X_n, Y_n).

The expected values X_n and Y_n as functions of n, initial conditions, and goal line parameters are now readily obtained by the methods of ordinary difference equations. From (10), we obtain

$$\text{(11)} \qquad \begin{aligned} X_n &= X^* + C_1\lambda_1^n + C_2\lambda_2^n \,, \\ Y_n &= Y^* + \left(\frac{\lambda_1 - 1 + \bar{\alpha}}{\bar{\alpha}a}\right)C_1\lambda_1^n + \left(\frac{\lambda_2 - 1 + \bar{\alpha}}{\bar{\alpha}a}\right)C_2\lambda_2^n \,; \end{aligned}$$

then C_1 and C_2 can be evaluated in terms of a, b, l, m and X_0, Y_0.

The roots λ_1 and λ_2 of the characteristic equation associated with (10) are

$$\text{(12)} \qquad \lambda = \frac{2 - \bar{\alpha} - \bar{\beta} \pm \sqrt{\bar{\alpha}^2 - 2\bar{\alpha}\bar{\beta} + \bar{\beta}^2 + 4\bar{\alpha}\bar{\beta}ab}}{2} \,.$$

For systems in which there is a unique intersection of the two goal lines and where $\bar{\delta} = \bar{\varepsilon} = 0$, X^* and Y^* are coordinates of the intersection. Where no unique intersection exists,

$$\text{(13)} \qquad \begin{aligned} X^* &= \frac{n\bar{\alpha}\bar{\beta}(am + l)}{\bar{\alpha} + \bar{\beta}} \,, \\ Y^* &= \frac{n\bar{\alpha}\bar{\beta}(bl + m) + \bar{\beta}m - \bar{\alpha}bl}{\bar{\alpha} + \bar{\beta}} \,. \end{aligned}$$

Values of X_n and Y_n in the limit as $n \to \infty$ are designated X and Y (subscripts dropped). Asymptotic stability of the first moments of a system depend upon the existence of a unique intersection and the values of the roots, λ_1 and λ_2. The following classification scheme obtains from derivations of X and Y.

Intersection Exists. Any system in which $ab \neq 1$ contains an intersection somewhere on the x-y plane. In these systems stability of (X, Y) at (X^*, Y^*) depends upon λ_1 and λ_2. Both X and Y are stable if and only if both $|\lambda_1|$ and $|\lambda_2|$ are less than one. Necessary and sufficient restrictions on λ_1 and λ_2 for stability of (X, Y) may be more conveniently rewritten as follows [4, p. 172]:

(14)
$$(1 - ab)\bar{a}\bar{\beta} > 0 ,$$
$$(1 - ab)\bar{a}\bar{\beta} - 2(\bar{a} + \bar{\beta}) + 4 > 0 ,$$
$$(ab - 1)\bar{a}\bar{\beta} + \bar{a} + \bar{\beta} > 0 .$$

a. Divergent systems. These are systems in which $ab > 1$. No combinations of positive $\bar{a}$ and $\bar{\beta}$ values satisfy (14) when $ab > 1$. Thus, from the results obtained in the noncontingent study, it is predicted that divergent systems are all unstable at (X^*, Y^*) for virtually *every* dyad which is assembled. An accidental choice of the response-pair (X^*, Y^*) could stabilize the first moments at the intersection if $\sigma_\delta^2 = \sigma_e^2 = 0$.

b. Convergent systems. These are systems in which $0 \leq ab < 1$. In convergent systems, (14) can be satisfied with specifiable combinations of positive $\bar{a}$ and $\bar{\beta}$ values. Figure 6, obtained from (14), shows $(\bar{a}, \bar{\beta})$ values required for (X_n, Y_n) to approach a stable value in the convergent system $ab = .25$. This system will be examined empirically in the next section. It is clear from the noncontingent study that we expect the first moments of responses to be stable at (X^*, Y^*) for virtually all dyads in the convergent system $ab = .25$.

c. Spiral systems. These are systems in which $ab < 0$. For most parameter combinations, the two values of equation (12) are complex and complete solutions are typically written in polar form. When the roots are complex, expected values (X_n, Y_n) spiral into the intersection, that is, approach a stable value, for specifiable combinations of positive $\bar{a}$ and $\bar{\beta}$. Figure 6 illustrates stable $(\bar{a}, \bar{\beta})$ values that yield stable asymptotic moments for the spiral system $ab = -4$. The dyadic system illustrated in figure 5 also has $ab = -4$.

A rather interesting prediction is pointed up by the analysis of this spiral system. If a large number of dyads were run in this system, it would take longer for subjects who were given "social" instructions to stabilize at the intersection than subjects who were given "asocial" instructions. This prediction follows from the results of the noncontingent study; viz., a larger proportion of $(\bar{a}, \bar{\beta})$ values would initially exceed the required range in figure 6. This prediction is contrary to the intuitive notion that subjects who are "socially aware" necessarily perform more adaptively.

No Intersection Exists on the x-y Plane. In these systems $ab = 1$; hence, $\lambda = 1$ and $1 - \bar{a} - \bar{\beta}$. Two distinct types of systems arise when $ab = 1$.

a. Common goal area. Both subjects have exactly the same goal line over the entire x-y plane. The asymptotic value (X, Y) will be somewhere

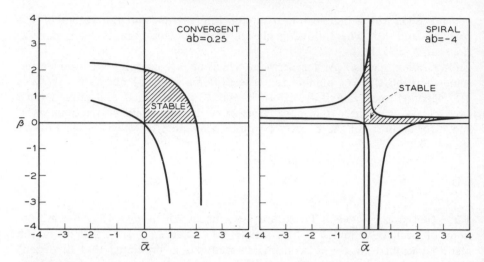

FIG. 6. Combinations of $\bar{\alpha}$ and $\bar{\beta}$ required for stability of the first moments of response in two dyadic systems.

on the goal line providing $|\lambda_2| < 1$. It is common to find this general type of reward system in social psychological experiments; that is, all participants always receive the same reward on all trials. A study by Hall [5] demonstrated the stability of this type of system in a continuous-response task.

   b. Competitive systems. Subjects do not have the same goal area anywhere on the *x–y* plane, that is, the lines are parallel and not the same. In such a case asymptotic first moments are not finite in the model. However, since most response continua are necessarily bounded, there are finite (not necessarily stable) limits on the response means of the two subjects.

   Systems Outside of the Domain of the Model. When $ab = \infty$, one or both subjects have a goal line in which no correct response can be specified for any trial. In the oscilloscope task, the goal line would be a horizontal straight line. The outcome is either "correct" or "incorrect" but no cybernetic cue exists, that is, $D_{x,n}$ or $D_{y,n}$ or both are not finite. Behavior of the subject who is given no cybernetic cue is outside the domain of the model. A dyadic system containing no cybernetic cues on any trial will be examined empirically in a later section. Although the model does not explicate behavior in these systems, they are, in a sense, limiting cases of divergent systems. Interpreted in this way, we would not expect the intersection to be a stable point for (X, Y).

   4.2 Second-Moment Stability. In systems for which the asymptotic first moments, (X, Y), are predicted to be stable, e.g., a convergent system, we are also interested in the stability and magnitudes of the second moments. Establishing the stability of (X, Y) is not sufficient to assure stability of the second moments of x_n and y_n unless α_n and β_n are assumed to be constants.

   The derivation of second moments of response in a dyadic system is straightforward. First, a translation of axes is convenient. Let (x', y') be new axes with the origin at the intersection of the two goal lines. Difference equations (9) are rewritten:

(15)
$$x'_{n+1} = (1 - \alpha_n)x'_n + \alpha_n a y'_n + \alpha_n \delta_n ,$$
$$y'_{n+1} = \beta_n b x'_n + (1 - \beta_n)y'_n + \beta_n \varepsilon_n .$$

Let

$$\xi_n = E[x'_n]^2 , \qquad \eta_n = E[y'_n]^2 , \qquad \zeta_n = E[x'_n y'_n] .$$

Expressions for ξ_{n+1}, η_{n+1}, and ζ_{n+1} are

$$\xi_{n+1} = [(1 - \bar{\alpha})^2 + \sigma_\alpha^2]\xi_n + 2a[\bar{\alpha} - \bar{\alpha}^2 - \sigma_\alpha^2]\zeta_n$$
$$+ a^2[\bar{\alpha}^2 + \sigma_\alpha^2]\eta_n + \sigma_\delta^2[\sigma_\alpha^2 + \bar{\alpha}^2] ,$$

(16) $$\zeta_{n+1} = b[\beta(1 - \bar{\alpha})]\xi_n + [(1 - \bar{\alpha})(1 - \bar{\beta}) + ab\bar{\alpha}\bar{\beta}]\zeta_n + a[\bar{\alpha}(1 - \bar{\beta})]\eta_n ,$$

$$\eta_{n+1} = b^2[\bar{\beta}^2 + \sigma_\beta^2]\xi_n + 2b[\bar{\beta} - \bar{\beta}^2 - \sigma_\beta^2]\zeta_n$$
$$+ [(1 - \bar{\beta})^2 + \sigma_\beta^2]\eta_n + \sigma_\varepsilon^2[\sigma_\beta^2 + \bar{\beta}^2] .$$

The *stability* of the second moments depends on the sizes of the three roots of the associated characteristic equation. It is necessary and sufficient that all three roots of the polynomial be less than one in absolute value. Roots of the characteristic polynomial contain the parameters, $a, b, \bar{\alpha}, \bar{\beta}, \sigma_\alpha^2$, and σ_β^2. *Stability* of the second moments does not depend on σ_δ^2 and σ_ε^2.

Convenient expressions are known [9] for testing whether or not a particular set of parametric values yields stable second moments (i.e., the characteristic polynomial has roots whose moduli are all less than unity). It is also possible to obtain an analytic estimate of the proportion of dyads in a given system for which second moments of response are stable. Such an estimate requires, in turn, an estimate of the joint probability distribution of the first two moments of α_n and β_n. While these estimates are available from data obtained in the noncontingent study, the analytic procedure is very complicated.

A simpler approach was used. First, the convergent system $ab = .25$ was selected, since this system will be examined empirically in the next section. Sixteen stat-dyads were obtained from the noncontingent study by randomly pairing subjects within the (social, $\sigma_y = 5$) condition and within the (social, $\sigma_y = 15$) condition. These experimental conditions were chosen since all subjects in the dyadic systems were also told that another subject affected vertical displacements of the dot. Using parameter estimates from the last 75 trials in these two conditions of the noncontingent study, second-moment stability of each stat-dyad was tested [9]. When $\sigma_\delta^2 = \sigma_\varepsilon^2 = 0$ was assumed, 6 out of the 16 stat-dyads were found to be unstable; when $\sigma_\delta^2 = \sigma_\varepsilon^2 = 25$ was assumed, 3 out of the 16 stat-dyads were found to be unstable. Larger assumed values of σ_δ^2 and σ_ε^2 would reduce further the estimated proportion of unstable dyads.

If we know that the second moments are stable, (ξ, η, ζ) can be obtained from equations (16) by the solution of three simultaneous equations. The second central moments of response at asymptote are denoted by ξ and η.

5. Experimental Analysis of Dyadic Systems

5.1 **Experimental Conditions.** Subjects were undergraduate female volunteers from all undergraduate classes of a girl's college. They were paid $1.50 for participating. Taped instructions, explaining the signals, the response alternatives, and the outcome display were played through earphones. Each subject was told that the vertical displacement of her dot was determined by the response of the subject in the other booth and that her response, in turn, determined the vertical displacement of the dot in the other subject's display. Pairs were randomly assembled insofar as class schedules would permit. All pairs were given 100 consecutive trials.

Four pairs were run in each of three dyadic reward systems. The three systems are: (a) convergent system with goal line parameters, $a = b = -.5$, $l = 92$, $m = 58$; (b) divergent system with $a = b = -2$, $l = 116$, $m = 184$; (c) competitive system with $a = b = -1$, $l = 116$, $m = 84$. The intersection of goal lines, (X^*, Y^*), in the convergent and divergent systems is the same, (84, 16). If (x_n, y_n) corresponds to the intersection value, both subjects simultaneously receive a correct outcome.

The predictions for each of these systems have already been discussed in the previous section. In summary, these predictions are as follows. In the convergent system, the first response moments are expected to stabilize at asymptote for virtually every dyad. The intersection (X^*, Y^*) is the stable point for (X, Y) in the convergent system. The most conservative estimate of the stability of ξ_n and η_n indicates that the majority of dyads in the convergent system will exhibit stable second moments of response. The exact proportion of dyads with stable second moments depends to some extent upon the estimation procedures for σ_α^2. In the divergent system, virtually every dyad is expected to fail to stabilize at the intersection, since the first moments are unstable. Furthermore, with certain reasonable restrictions on $\bar{a}$ and $\bar{\beta}$, the following is also derived for the divergent system:

$$\lim_{n \to \infty}(X_n, Y_n) = (X, Y), \quad \begin{cases} \text{(upper bound, lower bound)} \\ \qquad\qquad\text{or} \\ \text{(lower bound, upper bound)} . \end{cases}$$

That is, both subjects in the divergent system approach either of the two pairs of bounds of the response continuum. Finally, since no intersection exists in the competitive system, the first moments cannot stabilize at a unique and optimal point. The limiting value (X, Y) in this competitive system is the combination (upper bound, lower bound).

5.2 **Results.** Figure 7 is a graphic summary of the results. Each row of four graphs summarizes data from the reward system labeled in the first graph of a row. Each goal line is also identified in the first graph as that of S_1 or S_2. Data from 4 trial blocks of 10 trials each are presented for each reward system. Trial blocks are equally spaced over the 100 trials. Each circle in a graph represents the coordinates of average response values of a single dyad in the indicated trial block. Horizontal and vertical spokes associated with each circle represent the sizes of the standard deviations (SD) of the responses by S_1 and S_2, respectively, in that trial block. By reading a row from left to right, it is possible to obtain an impression of the dynamics of a system over time.

Visual examination of figure 7 is sufficient to verify the most important predictions. First moments of response of the four dyads in the convergent system stabilize very close to the intersection. The SD's of all four dyads are within the expected range of variation of stable dyads. If we use trials 61–100 (which includes the last two trial blocks in figure 7) to estimate the second central moments of response, (ξ, η), the four dyads yield (5.7, 181.7), (0.4, 0.3), (3.8, 0.5), and (40.2, 28.7). Estimates of the proportion of unstable dyads in the system $ab = .25$, using stat-dyads in the noncontingent study, appear to be too high. Had we assumed a larger σ_δ^2 and σ_ε^2 the proportion might have been reduced. On the other hand, evidence from actual dyads in the convergent system also indicate that most σ_δ^2 and σ_ε^2 fall within the assumed range, 0–25. For example, (ξ, η) was obtained for four randomly selected stable stat-dyads in the (social, $\sigma_y = 5$) condition assuming $\sigma_\delta^2 = \sigma_\varepsilon^2 = 25$. This condition was chosen since it most closely approximates both instructions given to the dyads in the convergent system and the range of response variation found in this system during the latter part of

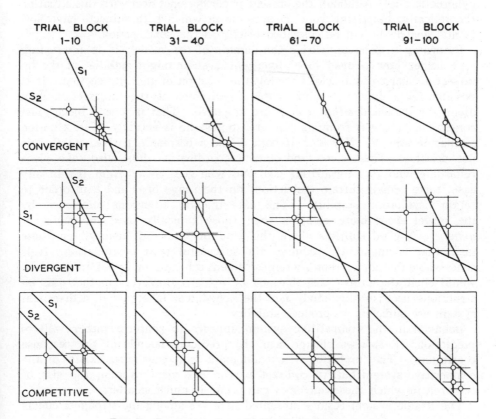

FIG. 7. Summary of results in three dyadic systems.

the experimental session. Using equation (16), the four stat-dyads yielded the following (ξ, η) values: (258.8, 18.2), (130.5, 139.5), (123.2, 233.6), (64.3, 38.0). These particular solutions of equations (16) are generally higher than empirical values cited above for the four actual dyads. Assumed values of σ_δ^2 and for σ_ε^2 less than 25 would reduce the (ξ, η) values of the stat-dyads so that they corresponded with (ξ, η) values of the actual dyads.

In the divergent system no dyad appears to have stabilized at the intersection of the two goal lines. There is a noticeable tendency for the responses to cluster at the (lower bound, upper bound), one of the two pairs of bounds predicted from the model. On the other hand, these bounds are not "absorbing barriers." It is important to note that as the pair of response values does approach the bounds of the continuum, outcomes occur on the display square for which there is no realistic horizontal distance, $D_{i,n}$, for one or both subjects. For example, if $y_n > 58$, then $x_n = f_1(y_n) < 0$, a set of values not available to S_1. A divergent system in almost any continuous-response task with response bounds will generate either extra-domain outcomes or unrealistic cues and hence is of some general interest. In the oscilloscope task, these extra-domain outcomes appear to be psychologically similar to *all* outcomes where the goal line is horizontal; i.e., there is no cybernetic cue. Although the present paper does not deal with this situation theoretically, empirical work on systems in which both subjects have horizontal goal lines will be described briefly in the next section.

Returning to behavior within the domain of the model, it is interesting to consider how a dyad in a divergent system might stabilize at the intersection short of subjects' knowing the location of the intersection. It is possible for a dyad to realize stable asymptotes at the intersection in a divergent system if *either $\bar{\alpha}$ or $\bar{\beta}$ are* negative. That is, one subject must consistently go away from his goal area unless he is actually in it, a notion similar to *umweg*. However, if both $\bar{\alpha}$ and $\bar{\beta}$ become negative, stability is not possible. Thus, some kind of tacit coordination must also take place regarding who goes toward his goal and who goes away from it. In any case, there remain certain restrictions on the range of $\bar{\alpha}$ and $\bar{\beta}$ in order to retain asymptotic stability. The experimental situations subsumed by the model seem more complex than those typically used in studies of *umweg*. Nor do subjects share the kind of "cultural history" on these tasks that is apparently required for successful tacit coordination. It is conceivable that an appropriate reinforcement schedule or set of instructions would elicit the proper distributions of $\alpha_n(\beta_n)$. However, neither the instructions used in this study nor the schedules "inherent" in a divergent system are sufficient to produce stability.

Behavior in the competitive system appears to conform rather well to prediction. Responses cluster near the predicted bounds of the response continuum. The problem of extra-domain outcomes also exists in the competitive system but, in contrast to the divergent system, the size of the area in which these outcomes can occur is much smaller.

The dyadic system results presented here are among the strongest effects suggested by the model. Statistical analyses are hardly required to establish the fact that certain predicted effects were realized. The presence of complex time-dependent, system-dependent parameters and other nonlinear effects which may arise in dyadic systems can and should now be investigated using larger samples and more incisive analyses of data obtained in dyadic systems. Quantitative explication of behavior where outcomes contain no cybernetic cue, i.e., outcomes outside the domain of the present model, are also necessary for a complete account of all dyadic systems. In general, it is profitable to explore with an explicit and complete model the view that interactive systems can be explained by individual behavior laws, although definitive tests of this question are elusive. Failures of an individual behavior model in analyses of dyadic systems may reflect an inadequate model or the presence of genuine interactive effects, or both.

6. Communication

An interesting variety of additional individual and interactive experiments are now required to test and to improve details of the model. Nevertheless, the analyses of dyadic systems that stem from the model have already yielded sufficient understanding of the basic experimental situation so that new dyadic variables can also be investigated within the same experimental situation. One of the more interesting and cogent sets of experimental variables consists of the communicative links made available to participants in a dyadic system. By communication I refer to the availability of linguistic responses between the two subjects. Linguistic responses need not be vocal. Coded switches, automated message dispensers, etc. are generally more convenient for precise control and measurement of these responses by the experimenter. It is obvious that a broader theoretical framework can be stimulated by and will benefit from a body of systematic data on communication variables.

A study illustrating an empirical exploration of a simple communicative link is summarized in this section. This study was actually run at the same time as the previously reported dyadic study and all experimental conditions in both studies were randomly ordered over time.

6.1 Experimental Conditions. Twenty dyads from the same population of female college students were assembled. Four reward systems were used. In addition to the convergent, divergent, and competitive systems already described, a system in which $a = b = \infty$ was constructed. In the latter system, both subjects have a horizontal goal line so that no $D_{i,n}$ exists on any trial. Four dyads were run in each of the four systems with the two-way communication link which will be described below. Four additional dyads were run in the system $a = b = \infty$, with no communication between the two subjects.

In addition to the paraphernalia in each booth required for a dyadic reward system, each subject in the communication condition had three coded switches and three coded lights in the booth. The three switches were labeled:

1. RAISE DOT, PLEASE.
2. KEEP DOT SAME, PLEASE.
3. LOWER DOT, PLEASE.

As soon as the dot was displayed on a trial, each subject was permitted to push one of the three switches in her booth if she wished to make a request of the other subject for the next trial. She could also abstain from making any request on any trial. Six seconds were available on each trial to push one of the request switches. Immediately following this time period, one of three lights in each booth went on, corresponding to the switch the *other subject* had pushed. The three lights were labeled:

1. HIGHER NUMBER, PLEASE.
2. SAME NUMBER, PLEASE.
3. LOWER NUMBER, PLEASE.

Communication on a trial was not possible after the display of the signals. Thus each subject always made requests without knowledge of the other's current request. The signal light remained on half way through the response period of the following trial. The subjects were told that they did not have to honor requests made by the other subjects.

6.2 Results. The results are summarized in figure 8. Consider first the three systems already studied. The addition of communicative links in the convergent system does not seriously affect the stability of responses. All dyads in the convergent system stabilize at or near the intersection very early in the experiment. The addition of communicative links in the divergent system appears to result in more stability at the intersection, although the addition of communication is not significant over the 100 trials. Two dyads in the divergent system finally achieved the degree of asymptotic stability at the intersection which rapidly characterizes virtually all dyads in the convergent system. In the competitive system, there is a significant tendency for response to cluster at the opposite set of boundaries [i.e., (lower bound, upper bound)] with communication, and this tendency persists throughout the session.

The effects of communication are most dramatic in the system $a = b = \infty$. With no communication, responses show no sign of stabilizing at the intersection. The average responses value across all eight subjects on the last trial block is 51.1, and the average of eight SD's, each taken about a subject's own mean, 23.5. With communication, responses clearly stabilize at the intersection in three dyads and are close to the intersection in the fourth dyad. The SD's are generally low in the last trial block—almost comparable to those found in a convergent system.

It is particularly interesting to compare the results in the divergent system with those in the system $a = b = \infty$. In a mathematical sense, the latter system is a limiting case of a divergent system (recall that divergent systems are those in which $ab > 1$). However, the stabilizing effects of communication apparently are very different—at first blush a rather surprising result. It is conceivable that the dramatic effects of a simple communicative link occur only in the limit of a divergent system, i.e., where

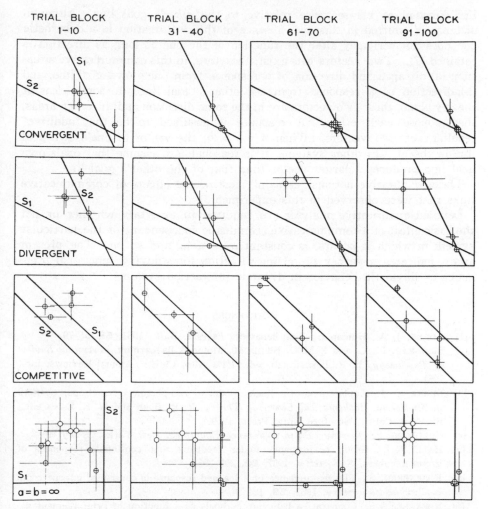

TRIAL BLOCK 1-10   TRIAL BLOCK 31-40   TRIAL BLOCK 61-70   TRIAL BLOCK 91-100

FIG. 8. Summary of results in four dyadic systems with communication between subjects. The system in the last row also shows data from four dyads with no communication. Open circles, no communication; circles with cross lines, communication.

each subject is "completely dependent" upon the other's responses for reward. In any case, an interesting and provocative difference exists between the two systems when communication is available.

Quantitative explication of effects of communicative links in dyadic systems requires more evidence on processes associated not only with these communicative response categories but with other categories of linguistic behavior as well. Results of the present study suggest a simple hypothesis for the way in which requests are likely to function. We may view the functional properties of these communicative stimuli as similar to those of a cybernetic cue. In effect, influence stimuli from another give a subject the *direction* of his response relative to the *other's* goal line. Although distance is omitted in this cue, absence of this information in a cybernetic cue does not seriously alter the function of the cue as long as direction is retained [7]. Two vectors can exist, therefore, in this communicative situation: (a) distance and direction of a response from one's own goal line, and (b) direction of a response from the other's goal line. In some areas of the x–y plane, these two vectors are in the same direction and, in other areas, they oppose each other. A response is assumed to be the "additive" resultant of two vectors. When $a = b = \infty$, the vector of one's own goal line is absent. In other systems, it is reasonable to assume that one's own goal line produces a larger vector than that of the other's goal line.

These qualitative notions "explain" most of the effects of communicative links that were observed in this experiment.

Detailed quantitative analyses are required to ascertain whether or not the basic effect of a communicative stimulus is independent of the particular system in which it occurs, is constant over time, and so on. The present study indicates a rather promising direction for studying functional properties of linguistic behavior in dynamic interaction systems.

References

[1] ADAMS, J. A., Human tracking behavior, *Psychol. Bull.*, 1961, **58**, 55–79.

[2] BILODEAU, E. A., and I. McD. BILODEAU, Motor-skills learning, in *Annual Review of Psychology*, P. R. Farnsworth, ed., Palo Alto, Calif.: Annual Reviews, Inc., 1961.

[3] BURKE, C. J., Applications of a linear model to two-person interactions, chap. 9 in *Studies in Mathematical Learning Theory*, R. R. Bush and W. K. Estes, eds., Stanford, Calif.: Stanford Univ. Press, 1959.

[4] GOLDBERG, S., *Introduction to Difference Equations*, New York: Wiley, 1958.

[5] HALL, R. L., Group performance under feedback that confounds responses of group members, *Sociometry*, 1957, **20**, 297–305.

[6] ROSENBERG, S., The maintenance of a learned response in controlled interpersonal conditions, *Sociometry*, 1959, **22**, 124–38.

[7] ROSENBERG, S., Cooperative behavior in dyads as a function of reinforcement parameters, *J. Abnorm. Soc. Psychol.*, 1960, **60**, 318–33.

[8] ROSENBERG, S., and R. L. HALL, The distribution of knowledge of results in dyadic teams, *J. Abnorm. Soc. Psychol.*, 1958, **57**, 271–77.

[9] SAMUELSON, P. A., Conditions that the roots of a polynomial be less than unity in absolute value, *Ann. Math. Stat.*, 1941, **12**, 360–64.

[10] SUPPES, P., Stimulus-sampling theory for a continuum of responses, chap. 23 in *Mathematical Methods in the Social Sciences, 1959*, K. J. Arrow, S. Karlin, and P. Suppes, eds., Stanford, Calif.: Stanford Univ. Press, 1960.

[11] SUPPES, P., and R. C. ATKINSON, *Markov Learning Models for Multi-Person Interactions*, Stanford, Calif.: Stanford Univ. Press, 1960.

20

A Topological Approach to the Measurement of Social Phenomena

Maynard W. Shelly, *Office of Naval Research*

1. Introduction

When scales of an interval variety or stronger [9] are available to either the experimenter or subjects of a group experiment, judgments of the relative closeness of two states (which could be experimental conditions, attitudes of other persons, behavior of other persons, and so on) can be made on the basis of the relative closeness of the numbers resulting from the applications of the scales. These scales, then, in a way place some structure on the set of states of interest to either the experimenter or the subjects. In the absence of such scales, there is usually a corresponding decline in the amount of structure that can be placed upon the set of states of interest. In particular, two distinct but related problems emerge.

The first is the problem the experimenter encounters in determining whether or not, for example, two experimental conditions or two responses of the subjects in his experiments are "close" to each other when he has no strong (interval or stronger) scale to measure them. The second problem is to develop a structure by which he can predict when two states (e.g., the responses or attitudes of other persons) will be close together from the point of view of the subject. A similar type of general structure might provide a basis for attacking both types of problems.

This paper represents a preliminary effort to provide a structure for a space of states (whatever they may be, e.g., the experimental conditions, the set of possible responses of a group, and so on) when there may be no strong scales available. The purpose of this structure will be to provide a framework for treating the closeness of states. The structure itself will be a topological space generated from the measurements and judgments made by either the experimenter or the subjects. This paper will then

The author wishes to thank Dorothy Gilford and Fred Rigby for listening to an initial version of this paper and making suggestions, and Carolyn Shelly for reading and helping with parts of the final manuscript.

show, in an informal way, one way in which a topology can be established on a set of states of interest either to the experimenter or the subject. It is hoped that direct extensions of these ideas will be useful to those experimenting upon and analyzing social phenomena. Whether or not the ideas will be useful for predicting the behavior of subjects will depend upon further developments not begun in this paper; it is hoped, however, that the generality of the ideas will make it at least heuristically useful in this respect.

2. Basis for Selecting a Topological Approach

A topological approach to the problem of establishing relations of closeness has been selected because of the generality of topology and because, in a loose sense, topology is concerned with problems of "closeness."

We shall combine what are usually called judgments and what are usually called measurements into a single category which we shall call measurements. In this paper, measurement will be the attachment of any symbol (geometric, linguistic, and so on) to a state in the set of states of interest. The question is then, after we have attached a number of symbols to two different states, whether or not these two states are relatively close (i.e., relative to some third state or set of additional states). This is clearly one of the reasons for using strong scales—we can determine whether or not two states are relatively close (or conversely not close) on the dimension defined by the scale.

Several, and often a very large number of, states could have the same symbol attached to them. Thus a symbol will usually be actually associated with a set of states, and the states in this set will not be distinguishable by the measurement which assigns the symbol associated with them. This is also true when we use strong scales. A large number of states may have the same number attached to them but may vary considerably in other ways. Through consideration of the sets of states which are indistinguishable by a given measure, we can establish a hypothetical structure on the space of states of interest to us. We would like to relate this structure, in some reasonable way, to some mathematical structure which lets us use sets of states to develop ideas of closeness. It is at this point that the concepts of topology seem potentially valuable.

Topology may be considered to be the abstract study of limit points, and the study of limit points must involve ideas of closeness. The study of limit points in topology is differentiated from the study of limits in, say, the calculus, by its generality; the study of limits in topology is not dependent upon any metric as in the calculus. It is therefore possible to treat ideas of closeness when there is no metric on the space of interest, even though the existence of a metric may be very useful.

A topology is defined on a set of states (or abstractly a set of points) through defining a certain class of sets having certain properties on this set of states. The sets of this class are called open sets. These open sets, together with certain definitions related to them, place a structure on the set of states. This structure, as indicated, is very general and permits very general considerations of the "closeness" between points of the set upon which the topology has been established. Furthermore, topology is the study of closeness as it is preserved under very general transformations, and although changes in the topology will not be studied in this paper, it should nonetheless be clear that if the topology is really related to the measurements we make, as we change the measures we will change, or transform, the topology on the set of states of interest to us. This is one reason that a topological approach to measurement appears to be feasible for studying social processes.

Lewin [5] has previously considered what he called a topological approach to the study of behavior. In his approach, which was not topological in any but a most general sense, he did not explicitly relate his "topology" to the judgments of, or measurements made by, the individual. This paper will show one way in which a topology can be established on a space of states where the open sets of the topology are explicitly related to the measurements an individual makes. The purpose will be to show how sets of states, indistinguishable by a given measure (a given symbol), can be used to define open sets. There is generally no unique topology which can be established on a set of states, and the topology established in this paper is one of many which could be established. Indeed, it will be indicated how a second topology could also be established on a set of states. The usefulness of a particular topology, in this case, will depend upon the applications to which it leads. It is possible, and even likely, that a topology for the experimenter, useful in designing experiments, will not be the same as that which might prove useful in interpreting a subject's behavior.

3. Two Approaches to Improvements in Experiments in Social Psychology

Most of the papers in this volume represent one approach to making improvements in experiments in social psychology. This approach is based upon finding ways to represent group processes which can be treated within extensions of existing and rigorous models such as the statistical learning model. Experiments are conducted to test the appropriateness of the extension, and some alterations are made in the statistical model (or the experimental situation is revised), and so on.

Another approach is also possible. This approach involves looking at what those experimenting with social processes are trying to understand when they investigate group processes. The goals of their experimental procedures are examined, and the concepts they use are analyzed. An attempt is made to see how improvements can be made in their methodology while retaining what we feel to be the intuitive essence of their concepts. This is the approach used, for example, by those developing specialized statistical methods for data that are not the product of strong scales.

Such an approach often has a dual application. It is useful in developing a structure to put into formal form certain of the experimental procedures and inferential methods which are currently largely informal and intuitive.

This same structure can often be applied to analyze the behavior of subjects in social psychological experimental situations as well. Indeed, it can often be used as a heuristic guide to thinking about situations far more general than those of experimental group settings. When the experimenter must act largely in an informal way (using "informal" to mean acting upon the basis of his personal experiences rather than upon formally prescribed rules) he is acting very much like the subjects with whom he is experimenting. For example, the subject does not distinguish between many aspects of behavior he considers to be irrelevant to the group's task, and the experimenter for purposes of both recording and analysis combines events into equivalence classes.

This duality between models for the methods a scientist follows and models for analyzing the behavior of persons can go in either direction. This paper is motivated more by similarities between the behavior of the person in a social situation and the scientist than by the similarity between the behavior of the scientist and the person in the social situation. The latter of these two positions has also been taken, e.g., by Kelly [4], who in essence says that the behavior of persons in everyday situations is qualitatively no different from that of scientists, especially in their desire to predict future events.

The objection could be raised that the approach presented in this paper tends to incorporate formally into scientific procedure strong personal elements. It can be argued, and indeed has been argued, that such strong personal elements are an intimate part of science. It can also be argued that the understanding we as scientists wish to achieve is qualitatively no different from that which the subjects as persons in a group experiment wish to achieve.

It does not seem to be in keeping with the behavior of scientists to say that cold, objective prediction is the only major goal of a scientist. By the sheer weight of time they consume, it is not possible to test very many predictions, and what is tested will determine in part the direction a theory takes. The modifications made in a theory will depend in part upon what aspects of it are chosen for empirical testing. Thus, in some respects, a theory takes a random walk depending upon the personal interests of the scientists interested in the theory. Additionally, few if any tests of a prediction are final because of the usually enormous complexity involved in arriving at exactly the right set of experimental circumstances. Inadequacies in the logic of induction contribute further to any lack of finality in the testing of a prediction. Perhaps even more important is that it appears that the scientist is as much, if not more, interested in the conjectures he can make as he is in confirming existing hypotheses. It is then possible that understanding, with all of its subjective aromas and hues, is an important counterpart of prediction and that we should not develop methodologies which minimize the personal satisfactions of the scientist. It thus seems as reasonable to try to add rigor to the concepts in which he is already interested as to insist that he change altogether the concepts he works with. It seems as reasonable to build on an understanding a scientist already has as to require him to acquire a completely different set of concepts.

Others have also stressed the personal elements in science. Warren Weaver [12] has questioned a possible overemphasis upon objectivity. Objectivity, he contends, cannot be called upon to select from the myriad of possible explanations of natural events. As Bridgman [2] said, "I would place as the most important mark of an adequately educated man a realization that the tools of human thinking are not fully understood, and that they impose limitations of which we are not fully aware." Poincaré contended that the least that is required to understand a mathematical proof is a grasp of the logical sequence as a purposeful procedure; whether such a proof be a part of a theory of social behavior or a purely mathematical development, objectivity has little to do with it. Polányi, in his book *Personal Knowledge* [7], rejects the ideal of scientific detachment. He does not believe that knowledge is or can be impersonal, universally established, detached, and objective. He regards knowing as an act of comprehension that involves change in the person carrying out the act of comprehension. Statistical tests, which the statistician created for the scientist wanting an objective decision procedure, have recently been objected to by Tukey [10]. He has said: "We cannot afford to cut off the heads of most of our young delicate insights in the sacred name of significance. . . . The dichotomy which some statisticians seem to uphold between (i) appearances to be disregarded entirely, and (ii) appearances to be believed implicitly, is utterly false and increasingly dangerous."

Even measurements in the physical sciences, in which it might be thought that personal elements are minimal, show consistencies not associated with the phenomena being measured. For example, Mandel [6] has studied testing methods involving a rather large number of laboratories. He asserts that the agreement between laboratories is much less than agreement within a laboratory, even for well-established methods of measurement. Thus even here there is a need for measurement models that include aspects usually omitted.

It thus would appear that an approach to measurement which would broaden it to include judgments often considered beyond the domain of science has enough support to warrant its being pursued. It is not contended that this approach represents any unique optimization of the research process in the study of social phenomena, but only that it may contribute where others do not. Indeed, it can, and has been, argued [3] that perhaps some combination of men and computers should develop theories which no component of the combination alone could understand. For example, such theories might contain many more $n$ary functions than currently accepted theories contain because men find it difficult to make conjectures upon the basis of such complex functions. Such a combination of men and computers might call for its own approach to measurement. Yet if we accept understanding as a goal of the individual scientist, a methodology based upon his capabilities and his goals would still seem to be required.

4. Elementary Measures

We shall include as a measurement the attachment of any symbol to a state. This could be the result of a measurement (in the usual narrower sense) or any judgment by the scientist (or more generally by any individual). We shall therefore begin by defining what we shall call elementary measures. These are measures which can assume only a single value and involve only observations; manipulations as a part of the measuring process will not be considered in this paper. We shall further restrict ourselves to explicit symbols. That is, we shall not consider as admissible any ideas of "betweenness" when there is no explicit symbol "between" two others.

The set of states in which we are interested will be denoted by X. Such a set of states might be all possible results of an experiment with a group under specified conditions, the states of the environment which could act as experimental conditions, the attitudes a person might have, and so on. An element of X will be denoted by x, and the inclusion indicated in the usual way, $x \in X$.

We shall accept as understood what it means to observe a state; not to do this leads to many complications which cannot be treated here. Then we assume that we observe a state and that we may attach a symbol to that state. This symbol may be a number read from a dial or otherwise obtained, a word, a personal shorthand symbol, a sentence, and so on. It will be a symbol selected from some finite set of symbols denoted by $\mathit{\Phi}$. The individual symbols, or elements, of $\mathit{\Phi}$ will be denoted by ϕ. Since there are only a finite number, we can index them by the index set $I_\phi = \{1, \cdots, n\}$.

We shall want any combination of these symbols also to be a symbol which can be applied to a state; and any combination of symbols also to be the result of a measurement. In other words we want closure under multiple application of measures. Now, rather than write out long strings of symbols when we wish to denote that a combination of symbols has been applied to a state, it is convenient to form a new set of symbols composed of sequences of symbols in $\mathit{\Phi}$. This new set, called the free semigroup formed on $\mathit{\Phi}$, will be denoted by F, and a particular sequence of ϕ's, technically known as a word, will be denoted by f. The null word, composed of no elements of $\mathit{\Phi}$, will be denoted by $\mathit{\Lambda}$.

Corresponding to the set of symbols we shall use what we will call the elementary measures which assign the symbols to the states. These may be a judgmental process or a measuring instrument or, more often, a component of either, for they will either assign or not assign a symbol to a state; hence the term "elementary." Thus for each element $\phi_i \in \mathit{\Phi}$, we shall define a corresponding elementary measure e_i. We denote the collection of the e_i by E. Consider the observed state x to be fixed, and let (x, F) be the set of all pairs (x, f) with $f \in F$. Then let the *elementary measure* e_i be a function corresponding to ϕ_i which takes $x \times F$ into $x \times F$ [or, in the notation used in this paper, (x, F) into (x, F)] and which has the property that for any fixed $f \in F$

(4.1) $$e_i: (x, f) \rightarrow \{(x, f), (x, f\phi_i)\} \; ;$$

which of the two values is assumed depends on x.[1]

The function e_i has been defined by the symbol with which it is associated. Many measuring instruments, techniques, or judgments may lead to the same symbol. Thus an elementary measure e_i may be identified with many physical processes. It is also for this reason that it is called elementary, and it will enter as a component into "more advanced" measures, e.g., scales.

When we begin to measure, for example, a condition or a response, we usually assume no information to begin with. Thus the couple we usually begin with when we apply the first elementary measure will be (x, Λ). This is not necessary. The concept of an elementary measure has been made sufficiently broad to begin with any state of information. However, through defining e_i for any f in the pair (x, f), we have implicitly said that the results of previous measurements (as used in this paper) have no effect. This would seem reasonable, because it can be assumed that it is largely the manipulations required to prepare for the measurement which alter the effects of future measurements. These latter remarks are made explicit in the following definition of a composite elementary function.

A *composite elementary measure* e_2e_1 will be a function, for a fixed x, from (x, F) to (x, F) having all the properties that the functions e_1 and e_2 have individually, and having also the property that for a fixed f

(4.2) $$e_2e_1: (x, f) \rightarrow \{(x, f), (x, f\phi_1), (x, f\phi_2), (x, f\phi_1\phi_2)\} \; ,$$

the value assumed depending upon x.

This definition makes it reasonable to also establish a free semigroup upon the set E. We shall call this free semigroup G. Obviously, F and G are in one-to-one relation to each other. This relationship then establishes a type of duality between the theorems about results of measures and theorems about the elementary measures themselves.

Although no proofs are given in this paper, some of the later theorems in this paper depend upon a relationship between individual and composite elementary functions which is not included in the definition of the elementary function. Therefore the following assumption is introduced: When symbols are attached to a state by individual elementary measures, both symbols will also be attached to that state by the composite elementary measure made up of individual elementary measures. In symbolic form we have for individual elementary measures e_1 and e_2:

(4.3) $$[e_1(x, \Lambda) = (x, \phi_1) \wedge e_2(x, \Lambda) = (x, \phi_2)] \Rightarrow e_2e_1(x, \Lambda) = (x, \phi_1\phi_2) \; .$$

---

[1] In this paper logical disjunction will be denoted by $\vee$ and logical conjunction by $\wedge$. The existential quantifier, "there exists," will be denoted by V and the universal quantifier, "for every," will be denoted by $\wedge$. Implication will be symbolized by $\Rightarrow$, and the relation of "if and only if" by the doubled-headed arrow, $\Leftrightarrow$. A single arrow $\rightarrow$ will denote "leads to."

The following is the generalization of (4.3) for an arbitrary measure $g \in G$.

$$(4.4) \qquad [g_1(x, \Lambda) = (x, f_{g_1}) \wedge g_2(x, \Lambda) = (x, f_{g_2})] \Rightarrow g_2 g_1(x, \Lambda) = (x, f_{g_1} f_{g_2}) ,$$

where f_{g_i} is the element of F corresponding to $g_i \in G$. This generalization can be shown by first showing it for g_1 and then for g_2.

It would seem that under the preceding definitions and assumptions the sequential application of elementary measures would be the same as their composite application. This is true, but before we show the relationship we shall first introduce some more notation and define an additional function.

First, let e_i be an arbitrary elementary function. Denote its domain by $D(e_i)$ and its range by $R(e_i)$. For x and f fixed, we obviously have $D(e_i) = (x, f)$. But e_i can be applied to any state in X, for it is not necessary that e_i be able to associate a symbol with that state; there is therefore no question of appropriateness. Hence for x not fixed we have $D(e_i) = (X, f)$. For any word $f \in F$, however, e_i at most adds the letter ϕ_i to form a new word, say $f' \in F$. This is true for any $f \in F$. Hence we have $D(e_i) = (X, F)$.

Note that $R(e_i)$ depends upon both x and the elementary function e_i. It should be clear that $R(e_i) = (X, F)$. It would be convenient to define a function which had as arguments x and e_i, but assumed values only in F instead of (X, F). We shall denote such a function by φ, and its value in F by $\varphi(x, e_i)$. This function enables us to write $e(x, f)$ as $[x, \varphi(e, x)]$, which makes the notation for applying the result of an elementary measure easier.

We now return to the problem of sequentially applying two elementary measures. Let the elementary measures be e_1 and e_2 and let $e_2 \triangleright e_1$ denote applying first e_1 and then e_2 to the result; i.e.,

$$(4.5) \qquad e_2 \triangleright e_1(x, f) \equiv e_2[e_1(x, f)] .$$

The results contained in (4.6) to (4.8) enable us to show that under the assumptions and definitions of this paper the sequential application is the same as the composite application of elementary measures. The needed results are

$$(4.6) \qquad R(e_2 \triangleright e_1) = R(e_2 e_1) ,$$

$$(4.7) \qquad D(e_2 \triangleright e_1) = D(e_2 e_1) ,$$

$$(4.8) \qquad \varphi(e_2 e_1, x) = \varphi(e_1, x) \varphi(e_2, x) .$$

Results (4.6) and (4.7) show that the range and domain of $e_2 e_1$ and $e_2 \triangleright e_1$ are the same. It need only be shown then that they assume the same values within that range. Equation (4.8) gives this result to us and hence the two functions are equivalent. This result can be generalized to

$$(4.9) \qquad g_2 \triangleright g_1 = g_2 g_1 .$$

In order to place a topology on the space X, we will need to define some particular measures. These will be the measures corresponding to an "inappropriate" measure and the equivalent of making no measurement [(4.11) and (4.12) below]. These measures are introduced mainly to complete the set of measures and to make certain manipulations simpler.

A measure e_i will be called a *constant measure for the state* x if

$$(4.10) \qquad\qquad e_i(x, f) = (x, f) .$$

The following measures are two types of constant measures. A measure e_i will be called a *null measure* if

$$(4.11) \qquad\qquad (\bigwedge x)[e_i(x, f) = (x, f)] ,$$

and a measure e_i will be called a *universal measure* if

$$(4.12) \qquad\qquad (\bigwedge x)[e_i(x, f) = (x, f\phi)] .$$

A universal elementary measure will be denoted by e_0 and a null measure by $e_\emptyset$.

5. Elementary Measures and Sets of States in X

Our goal is to establish a topology on the space X through the use of measures and then to use the topology to work back to relationships between the measures. In this section we take the first steps toward using our elementary measures to place a structure on X. We begin by defining sets of states based upon indistinguishability.

Consider some elementary measure $e_i(x, f)$ equal to either (x, f) or $(x, f\phi_i)$ depending upon x. We can thus partition X into sets depending upon the value of $e_i(x, f)$. Since we shall be principally interested in such partitions when $f = \varLambda$ we shall assume that we begin with no information. This does not result in any loss of generality. We define a fundamental class of sets in X:

$$(5.1) \qquad\qquad A_i \equiv (x \mid e_i(x, \varLambda) = (x, \phi_i)) .$$

This class of sets will be called *A-sets*. There are two particular A-sets which correspond to the universal and null measures. By definition $e_0(x, f) = (x, f\phi)$ for all x, and hence $A_0 = X$. On the other hand, we have $e_\emptyset(x, f) = (x, f)$ for all x, and hence $A_\emptyset = \emptyset$.

The A-sets in (5.1) are based upon $\emptyset$; we can easily extend this definition to A-sets based upon G:

$$(5.2) \qquad\qquad A_g \equiv (x \mid g(x, \varLambda) = (x, f_g)) ,$$

where f_g is again the element of F corresponding to g. Denote this class of A-sets by $\mathscr{A}_g$. We can define a single-valued transformation, say τ, from G onto $\mathscr{A}_g$, and hence another single-valued transformation, say τ', from F onto $\mathscr{A}_g$.

Consider now two states. We may be able to differentiate between them without assigning different symbols to them, but certainly if we can assign different symbols to them, we should be able to differentiate between them. Thus we may consider two states to be distinguishable if we can assign different symbols to the two states. Distinguishability is limited, however, by the limited number of measures we can apply in a bounded amount of time, and hence distinguishability is limited by the set of measures we choose to use. We can further weaken what we mean by two states being distinguishable. It seems reasonable to define two states as being distinguishable to some extent if we can assign a symbol to one state but not to the other. We may, for example, be able to say that one person is happy, but simply not be able to attach any similar adjectives to another person. We have, however, made a partial distinction between the two. It is this latter concept of distinguishability which we will use in establishing our first topology on X.

Two states x_1 and x_2 will be said to be *partially distinguishable* by the measure e_i if one and only one of the states has the symbol ϕ_i associated with it; i.e., symbolically we have

$$(5.3) \qquad x_1 \, \mathbf{D}_{e_i} \, x_2 \Longleftrightarrow [(e_i(x_1, \Lambda) = (x_1, \phi_i) \land e_i(x_2, \Lambda) = (x_2, \Lambda)]$$
$$\lor [e_i(x_1, \Lambda) = (x_1, \Lambda) \land e_i(x_2, \Lambda) = (x_2, \Lambda)] \, .$$

We shall want to extend this definition to any of the composite elementary measures in G. To do this it will first be easier to define another relation. The following relation has, for us, no important physical interpretation, but if one wished to interpret it, it could be called an asymmetric partial distinguishability. This relation, $\mathbf{P}$, is defined as

$$(5.4) \qquad x_1 \mathbf{P}_{G_1} x_2 \Longleftrightarrow (\mathbf{V} g \mid g \in G_i)[g(x_1, f) = (x_1, ff_g) \land g(x_2, f) = (x_2, f)] \, .$$

This says that one state is in relation $\mathbf{P}$ to the other state for a set of composite elementary measures $G_i \subset G$ if there is one measure $g \in G_i$ which attaches the symbol f_g to the first state but not to the second. Using this definition we can rewrite (5.3) as follows:

$$(5.5) \qquad x_1 \mathbf{D}_{e_i} x_2 \Longleftrightarrow x_1 \mathbf{P}_{e_i} x_2 \lor x_2 \mathbf{P}_{e_i} x_1 \, .$$

It should be clear then how we can define partial distinguishability on a set of composite elementary measures. Two states will be *partially distinguishable for a set of composite elementary measures* G_i if either the first state is in relation $\mathbf{P}$ to the second state for the set G_i or the second state is in relation $\mathbf{P}$ to the first state for the set G_i, or symbolically,

$$(5.6) \qquad x_1 \mathbf{D}_{G_i} x_2 \Longleftrightarrow x_1 \mathbf{P}_{G_i} x_2 \lor x_2 \mathbf{P}_{G_i} x_1 \, .$$

In particular, when $G_i = g$, for some $g \in G$, we have

$$(5.7) \qquad x_1 \mathbf{D}_g x_2 \Longleftrightarrow x_1 \mathbf{P}_g x_2 \lor x_2 \mathbf{P}_g x_1 \, .$$

The inability to partially distinguish between two states, defined by the negation of partial distinguishability, is in some ways as important a relation as partial distinguishability. For example, it is an equivalence relation and can thus be used to partition the set of states of interest to us. In an empirical sense as well, the failure to be able to partially distinguish can be important, for the size of the equivalence classes determined by the lack

of partial distinguishability limits our behavior to behave differentially toward different states. This relation of the lack of partial distinguishability
between two states, to be denoted by $x_1 \not\emptyset_g x_2$ when the two states are x_1 and
x_2 and the composite elementary measure is g, will be used directly together
with the A-sets in constructing the topology on X.

6. An Elementary Scale

We shall now use the composite elementary measures to form what will
be called an elementary scale. The concept of an elementary scale is introduced for several reasons. The first is that it is more general. The set
of all elementary scales includes the set G. For any particular state, the
set of elementary scales and the set of elementary composite measures,
both of which include that state in an A-set, are identical. Second, the
concept of an elementary scale is closer to what is usually meant by a
measure and serves to show how the elementary measures can enter into
"more advanced" types of measures as components. Third, the scale concept offers an introduction to a type of measure which is rather different
from what is usually meant by a measure. This type of scale will be introduced briefly at the end of the paper.

An *elementary scale*, α, will be a collection of measures from the free
semigroup G having certain properties. Let us denote the ith elementary
scale by α_i and its *components*, the composite elementary measures, by
$(g_{i_1}, \cdots, g_{i_n})$ where $n \geq 1$. This collection of g_{ij}'s must have the following
properties:

(6.1)
   (i) $\alpha_i(x, f) = g_{i_n} \cdots g_{i_1}(x, f)$;

   (ii) $A_{i_j} \cap A_{i_k} = \emptyset$ for all $j, k = 1, \cdots, n, j \neq k$.

There are several things which should be noted about elementary scales.
The first is that an elementary scale is really an element of G which can
be decomposed in a certain way. There is thus a lack of uniqueness to the
elementary scales α_i, for there will be other decompositions such as result
from reordering the components or from combining two or more components
into a single component. The different scales produced in this way will attach the same symbol to every state in X.

A simple type of elementary scale is one which contains two symbols,
one meaning the opposite of the other. The existence of this type of scale,
given fixed interpretations, clearly depends upon the set $\emptyset$ initially chosen.
Thus once we begin to treat more complex forms of measurement we must
begin to concern ourselves with the possibility of "enriching" $\emptyset$. In order
to define an elementary scale having more than one component even if the
proper symbols exist in $\emptyset$, there is the further problem of determining when
two measures produce disjoint A-sets. At any particular time this becomes
a trivial problem because, if it is assumed that a person can only make one
judgment at a time and an instrument give but one reading at a time, these
judgments or readings must correspond to elementary scale components.

When sequential measurements are considered, the triviality vanishes. There are, however, several considerations which will enable us to avoid the problem or provide a means for approaching a solution. First, we are not usually really sure what state the measuring instrument is in, so that we cannot be sure what reading it will give or if it will change its reading. Instruments change in their sensitivity and persons change in their frames of reference. An analysis which continued to follow this route would lead us to modify our concept of scale, and another version of a scale will be introduced in the last section of this paper. Second, whether two elements of G produce disjoint A-sets is often primarily an empirical problem. Being able to develop an elementary scale is thus made dependent upon information we can try to obtain. For an empirical science, methodology cannot be independent of the subject matter of that science. The third consideration involves a constructive alteration of $\emptyset$. Since the elements of $\emptyset$ bear no unalterable relationship to the empirical world, the components of $\emptyset$ can be redefined or others added so that measures to be used as scale components successively exclude each other. Thus, the problem of constructing an elementary scale can be reasonably met even if we choose not to adopt a substitute scale.

We shall later want to have, say, two elementary scales, each with the same number of components. To achieve this we can simply add enough null measures to the elementary scale having the least number of components so that both elementary scales will have the "same number" of components.

We shall now define what we mean by the product of two elementary scales. Let $\alpha = (g_1, \cdots, g_n)$ and $\alpha' = (g'_n, \cdots, g'_{n'})$. Then

$$(6.2) \qquad \alpha'\alpha = (g'_1 g_1, g'_2 g_2, \cdots, g'_n g_1, \cdots, g'_{n'} g_n) .$$

Considering the intersections of A-sets corresponding to the components of the product of the two elementary scales, we see that the product of two elementary scales is again an elementary scale.

It was previously remarked that we may not know what state a measuring instrument is in and that consequently there may be some uncertainty, for example, about whether the reading it gives should not be adjusted. Or there may be uncertainty about which of two successive readings is the "true" value. It was remarked that these ideas would be used to define a different type of scale. In this section we shall show only how these ideas can be incorporated into an elementary scale.

If we are uncertain about what state a measuring instrument, or more generally a person, was in, then there may be uncertainty, for example, on whether f_1 or f_2 should be attached to a state. The corresponding uncertainty among the g's is whether or not g_1 or g_2 was employed as the composite elementary measure. We shall denote this latter uncertainty by $g_1 \cup g_2$, or symbolically define the following equivalence:

$$(6.3) \qquad g_1 \cup g_2(x, f) \equiv [g_1(x, f) \vee g_2(x, f)] .$$

Using this definition, we shall define what we mean by $\alpha_1 \cup \alpha_2$. This is easiest if we do it by stages.

Let α and α' be the two elementary scales of (6.2). Suppose we know that any confusion between the two elementary scales is limited to a confusion between two components of those scales, the ith component of α and the jth component of α'. We shall indicate this situation as follows:

$$(6.4) \qquad u_{ij}(\alpha; \alpha') \equiv (g_1, \cdots, g_i \cup g'_j, \cdots, g_j, \cdots, g_n) \, .$$

The confusion on the ith component of the elementary scale α may not be this specific. For example, whenever we attach the symbol f_{g_i} to a state, we may not be certain whether we should attach this symbol or any one of the $f_{g'_1}, \cdots, f_{g'_{n'}}$ from the scale α'. Thus if we say, "There is something strange about that person," (which could be an elementary scale with a single component) we may be uncertain whether we really should have been more specific in our judgment and should have said, "He was a quiet person," or, "He was not a quiet person but looked at you strangely." We shall denote this situation by

$$(6.5) \qquad u_{i1}(\alpha; \alpha') \cdot u_{i2}(\alpha; \alpha') \cdot \, \cdots \, \cdot u_{in'}(\alpha; \alpha')$$
$$\equiv (g_1, \cdots, g_{i-1}, g_i \cup g'_1, \cdots, g'_i \cup g'_{n'}, \cdots, g_n) \, ,$$

where α and α' are the same as in (6.3).

A total confusion between α and α' would extend the situation of (6.5) to each component of α, and hence we would have

$$(6.6) \qquad \alpha \cup \alpha' = \prod_i \prod_j u_{ij}(\alpha; \alpha') \, .$$

Let x be fixed. Then there is at most one component, say g_i, of an elementary scale α, which will associate its corresponding symbol, in this case f_{g_i}, with the fixed state. This results directly from the definition of an elementary scale. Then, remembering that we are keeping x fixed, we can let A_α be the A-set for the elementary scale α. A_α will be equal to some $A_{g'}$ where g' is either a component of the elementary scale α or contained in some component of α. From this and the preceding definitions it follows that for every $A_{\alpha_1} \cap A_{\alpha_2}$ there is at least one corresponding product of elementary scales which has this intersection for its A-set. Similarly, for every $A_{\alpha_1} \cup A_{\alpha_2}$ there is at least one corresponding confusion of scales which has as its A-set this union of A-sets.

We conclude this section by extending the definition of partial distinguishability to elementary scales. Two states are *partially distinguishable by an elementary scale* α if they are distinguishable by some component of that scale:

$$(6.7) \qquad x_1 D_\alpha x_2 \Longleftrightarrow (\bigvee g \mid g \in \alpha)(x_1 D_g x_2) \, ;$$

where $g \in \alpha$ means that g is a component of α. If we use the notation $\alpha(g)$ in $x_1 D_{\alpha(g)} x_2$ to indicate that g is a component of α by which it is possible to partially distinguish between the two states x_1 and x_2, then the following conclusion becomes self-evident:

$$(6.8) \qquad x_1 D_{\alpha(g')} x_2 \Longleftrightarrow (\bigwedge g \mid g \in \alpha, g \neq g')(x_1 \not{D}_g x_2) \, .$$

7. A Topology Based on Partial Distinguishability

We shall first establish a topology for a single state and then extend it. The topology based upon a single state will be directly related to elementary measures through the use of partial distinguishability.

First, we shall define a partial ordering on the set G. We shall say that

$$(7.1) \qquad\qquad g_1 < g_2 \Longleftrightarrow A_{g_1} \subset A_{g_2}.$$

Consider now some fixed state, say x_0. There will be at most one component of α which attaches a corresponding symbol to the state. A symbol corresponding to a subword of such a component might be attached to the state instead of to the symbol corresponding to the complete component of α. Thus, as we remarked earlier, we are really concerned only with the applications of the words of g to the state x_0. Let $\mathscr{A}_{x_0}$ be the set of all A-sets including the state x_0. Then in the sense of Berge [1], this set forms a filter base; i.e., it satisfies (7.2) where I is the index set for $\mathscr{A}_{x_0}$:

$$(7.2) \qquad \text{(i)} \quad (\bigwedge i \mid i \in I)(A_i \neq \varnothing),$$

$$\text{(ii)} \quad (\bigwedge i \mid i \in I)(\bigwedge j \mid j \in I)(\bigvee k \mid k \in I)(A_k \subset A_i \cap A_j).$$

It is the fact that $\mathscr{A}_{x_0}$ satisfies (7.2) that enables us to make use of the A-sets in the way we shall.

Let C be any set contained in X. This set does not have to contain the point x_0. Let I still be the index of the set $\mathscr{A}_{x_0}$. Now choose the smallest g_i such that for any $c \in C$, $x_0 \not{D}_{g_i} c$. We know that there is at least one such smallest g_i because the A-sets containing both x_0 and C form a partially ordered subset and are themselves a filter base. Let the A-set corresponding to the smallest g_i such that $x_0 \not{D}_{g_i} c$ for any $c \in C$ be called the *least g-set covering C*, or when C is understood, simply the least g-set. It can then be shown that the taking of the least g-set for any set C acts as a closure operator, and that the complements of the least g-sets form a topology on the space X.

This topology is not a very interesting one, although it does confirm some of our intuitive ideas and thus indicates that the approach taken can lead to reasonable results. For example, in this topology based only upon x_0, the only neighborhood of the point x_0 is X, which means that regardless of how many measurements we make on a single state, we cannot determine from these alone how close this state is to any other state.

The topology based on a single state can be readily expanded into a more satisfactory topology by taking the intersections of topologies based on several states. Then we can begin to consider the relative closeness of states.

Consider the problem of the relative closeness of two states to a third. Let the principal state be x_1, and let us consider two other states, x_2 and x_3, with reference to the state x_1. The state x_2 will be at least as close to the state x_1 as the state x_3 is to x_1 if every neighborhood which includes both x_1 and x_3 also includes x_2. This means that every open set which contains x_1 and x_3 will contain an open set which contains x_1 and x_2.

Let the topology be the intersection of the topologies based upon $y_1, \cdots,$ y_n, all of which are states in X. Consider now any y_i. The states x_1 and x_2 are at least as close as the states x_1 and x_3 if for every g partially distinguishing between y_i and both x_1 and x_3 there is another g, say g', which partially distinguishes between y_i and both x_1 and x_2. This g' is such that every state not partially distinguishable from y_i by the measure g is also not partially distinguishable from y_i by the measure g'. For example, let the space of states be attitudes of persons, and let the measures be judgments about the attitudes. Then the two attitudes a_1 and a_2 are at least as close as attitudes a_1 and a_3 under the following condition. A judgment, which attaches an attribute to a fourth attitude, say a_4, and not to a_1 and a_3, may not attach different attributes to any attitude to which a judgment that distinguishes between a_4 and a_1 and a_2 does not attach different attributes. This example makes the relativity of closeness apparent.

8. A Topology Based upon Distinguishability

The topology described in the preceding section was based upon partial distinguishability. It is also possible to base a topology on the attachment of *different* symbols to two states rather than upon the ability to attach a symbol to one state and not to another.

Distinguishability of two states will depend upon a pair of composite elementary measures. We shall say that two states are distinguishable by the measures g_1 and g_2 if we can attach the word f_{g_1} to one state and not to the other, and conversely with regard to the word f_{g_2}. If the states are represented by x_1 and x_2, we can define distinguishability on a set $G_i \subset G$ by the relation $\mathbf{P}$ as follows:

$$(8.1) \qquad x_1 D_{(g_1, g_2)} x_2 \Longrightarrow [\bigwedge (g_1, g_2) \mid (g_1, g_2) \in G \times G][(x_1 P_{g_1} x_2 \wedge x_2 P_{g_2} x_1)$$
$$\vee (x_2 P_{g_1} x_1 \wedge x_1 P_{g_2} x_2)] .$$

We can extend this definition to sets of states rather than the single states themselves. Let C_1 and C_2 be two sets of states, $C_1 \subset X$, and $C_2 \subset X$. Then the condition for C_1 and C_2 being distinguishable is

$$(8.2) \qquad C_1 D_{G_i} C_2 \Longrightarrow (\bigwedge c_1 \mid c_1 \in C_1)(\bigwedge c_2 \mid c_2 \in C_2)(\bigvee g \mid g \in G_i)(c_1 D_g c_2) .$$

This concept of distinguishability between sets of states makes it possible to define a topology on X through identifying the concept of separability (see Wallace [11]) with that of distinguishability. The topology is similar to the preceding one in that roughly a closed set is one for which all states in the complement are distinguishable from those within the set.

9. The Concept of an Uncertain Scale

It was remarked before that it was possible to bring into the basic definition of a scale the concept of an uncertainty between measures. This was not done for this paper in developing the topology because of the greater difficulties in treating such a scale. In (9.1) we define such a scale.

We shall call $\alpha^* = (g_1^*, \cdots, g_n^*)$ an *uncertain scale* if the following are true:

$$(i) \quad \alpha^*(x, f) = g_n^* \cdots g_1^*(x, f) \, ;$$

$$(9.1) \quad (ii) \quad g^* = \bigcup_j^{n_i} g_{i_j} \, ;$$

$$(iii) \quad (\bigwedge g_{i_j} \mid g_{i_j} \in g_i^*)[(x \in Ag_{i_j}) \Rightarrow (\bigwedge g_j^* \mid g_j^* \neq g_i^*)(\bigvee g_{j_k} \mid g_{j_k} \in g_j^*)$$

$$(x \notin A_{g_{j_k}})] \, .$$

This definition permits us, for example, to be uncertain about what state an instrument is in, but to remain convinced that we have non-overlapping categories. It should be clear that if $g_i^* = g_i$, then we simply have the definition of an elementary scale. If condition (iii) is omitted from (9.1), the definition for $\alpha_2 \alpha_1$ (6.2) and for $\alpha_2 \cup \alpha_1$ (6.6) can be shown to lead to the same definitions for $\alpha_2^* \alpha_1^*$ and $\alpha_2^* \cup \alpha_1^*$. It can further be shown that $\alpha_2^* \alpha_1^*$ will be associated with the intersection of the A-sets, $A\alpha_2^*$ and $A\alpha_1^*$ when α_1^* and α_2^* are applied to a fixed state x_0. Similarly, it can be shown that with reference to the same x_0, the fixed state $\alpha_2^* \cup \alpha_1^*$ will be associated with the union of the A-sets $A\alpha_1^*$ and $A\alpha_2^*$. Thus it appears feasible that a topology could be established using uncertain scales in much the same way we established a topology on X, using elementary scales.

10. A Remark about Research on Social Situations

In many experimental social situations comparatively little attention is given to what information is available to the subjects. There is evidence that many reasonable definitions of information, when applied to an analysis of the social context, might make social behavior a lot less mysterious. Many of the papers in this volume indicate that when the information is experimentally controlled (i.e., the experimenters are aware of the information their subjects are receiving), some aspects of social behavior can be predicted without many additional factors now used to predict individual behavior. An experiment by Shelly [8] on types of learning conditions which might occur in multiperson interaction situations showed that initial learning rates could be approximated by a prediction based on a definition of information dependent upon the expected number of trials to eliminate uncertainty. The methods of this paper might possibly lead to further, but still psychologically meaningful, definitions of what information a subject in a social situation has available, and make his behavior in still more general social situations equally "reasonable."

REFERENCES

[1] BERGE, D., *Espaces topologiques*, Paris: Dunod, 1959.
[2] BRIDGMAN, P. W., Quo vadis?, *Daedalus*, 1958, **87**, 77–84.
[3] FEIN, LOUIS, The computer-related sciences (synnoetics) at a university in the year 1975, *Amer. Scient.*, 1961, **49**, 149–68.
[4] KELLY, G. A., *The Psychology of Personal Constructs*, New York: W. W. Norton, 1955.

[5] LEWIN, K., *Principles of Topological Psychology*, New York: McGraw-Hill, 1936.
[6] MANDEL, J., The measuring process, *Technometrics*, 1959, **1**, 251-68.
[7] POLÁNYI, M., *Personal Knowledge*, Chicago: Univ. of Chicago Press, 1958.
[8] SHELLY, M. W., Learning with reduced feedback information, *J. Exptl. Psychol.*, 1961, **59**, 209-22.
[9] STEVENS, S. S., Mathematics, measurement and psychophysics, chap. 1 in *Handbook of Experimental Psychology*, New York: Wiley, 1951.
[10] TUKEY, J. W., Where do we go from here?, *J. Amer. Stat. Assn.*, 1960, **55**, 80-93.
[11] WALLACE, A. D., Separation spaces, *Ann. Math.*, 1941, **42**, 687-97.
[12] WEAVER, W., The imperfections of science, *Amer. Scient.*, 1961, **49**, 99-113.

21

On the Reliability of Group Judgments and Decisions

William H. Smoke and Robert B. Zajonc,
University of Michigan

There is a popular misconception about unanimous group decisions. It is believed that since the likelihood of unanimity is in general so very small, when unanimity does occur it must be correct. In a recent experiment, for instance, Barnlund [1] required small groups of subjects to solve problems in logic. The subjects worked on these problems first as individuals and then discussed their own solutions as a group, finally arriving at a group decision. Barnlund reports that in cases where there was an initial unanimity among the group members, the subjects never discussed their solutions, but simply moved to the next problem. This was true not only of cases where the group was initially correct, but also where it was initially incorrect. In a similar but somewhat less recent experiment by Thorndike [3], the same result was obtained. Of 725 group judgments only three were changed when the group was initially unanimously correct. But also, of 263 group judgments only one was reversed when the group was initially unanimously incorrect.

The reasons that decisions are sometimes entrusted to groups rather than to individuals are many. Among them is the expectation that a decision arrived at by a group is more reliable than one arrived at by an individual. The reliability of group decision schemes may therefore be evaluated in terms of their superiority over individual decisions.

If p is the probability that a given individual member is correct, the group response has a probability $h(p)$ of being correct, where $h(p)$ is a function of p depending upon the type of decision scheme accepted by the group. We shall call $h(p)$ a *decision function*. Intuitively, it would seem that a group decision scheme is desirable to the extent that its $h(p)$ surpasses p, or to put it somewhat differently, to the extent that the derivative of $h(p)$ with respect to p is positive and large. The larger $h'(p)$, the more we gain by substituting a group of individuals for a single individual.

This research was sponsored by Contract Nonr-1224(34), Task NR 170-309 granted to the Research Center for Group Dynamics by the Office of Naval Research. (The first author is now at the University of California, Berkeley.)

Several group decision schemes may be distinguished, and in principle, we could evaluate them by comparing the derivatives of the corresponding functions. The different decision schemes, the corresponding decision functions, and their derivatives with respect to p are outlined in table 1.

In table 1, the decision schemes are described in terms of the responses of individual members, while the decision functions and their derivatives are written in terms of the probabilities that these responses are correct. The functions $h(p)$ have been plotted in figure 1 for groups of five individuals. It can be seen from figure 1 that quorum schemes seem to be most effective ones, that unanimity and oligarchy are inferior to dictatorship, and that a fixed decision scheme has a non-monotone function. This last conclusion is evident from the derivative, which is negative when $i < np$. It is also interesting to note that when individual probabilities are below .3, an independent decision scheme with $h(p)$ arbitrarily assumed to be equal to .5 is generally superior to all others. In general, only the minimal quorum, the independent, and the fixed decision schemes will surpass p for values of p smaller than .5. However, the fixed decision scheme reaches a maximum at $i = np$, and it can be shown that this maximum cannot be greater than .5 for $i > 0$. Of course, if there exists an independent decision scheme with C equal to one, no other scheme can surpass it. Before we attempt to evaluate the derivatives of the various $h(p)$ functions it will be useful to have a less informal way of describing decision schemes.

Let r_i denote the response of the ith individual, and R denote the group decision. For each pair of responses r_1 and r_2, let r_1r_2 be the response which is correct if and only if both r_1 and r_2 are correct, and let $r_1 \vee r_2$ be

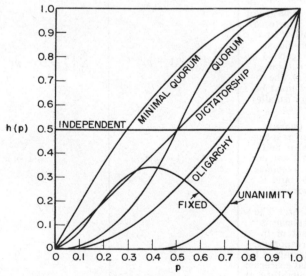

FIG. 1. Various types of decision functions for $n = 5$ and $k, i,$ and $l = 2$.

TABLE 1

Decision Scheme	$h(p)$	$h'(p)$
1. *Dictatorship*. The group response is completely determined by the response of one individual, who may be the group leader, an expert, or an advisor.	p	1
2. *Oligarchy*. The group response of a group of n individuals is completely determined by the joint response of a particular subset of k members, where $k < n$.	p^k	kp^{k-1}
3. *Unanimity*. The group response is a (or b) if and only if all members respond a (or b), and b (or a) otherwise.	p^n	np^{n-1}
4. *Fixed*. The group response is a (or b) if and only if exactly i members respond a (or b), and b (or a) otherwise. The value of i is equal to or smaller than n.	$\binom{n}{i}p^i(1-p)^{n-i}$	$\binom{n}{i}p^i(1-p)^{n-i}\left[\dfrac{i-np}{p(1-p)}\right]$
5. *Quorum*. The group response is a (or b) if and only if at least l individual members respond a (or b), and b (or a) otherwise. The value of l must be equal to or smaller than n.	$\displaystyle\sum_{i=l}^{n}\binom{n}{i}p^i(1-p)^{n-i}$	$\displaystyle\sum_{i=l}^{n}\binom{n}{i}p^i(1-p)^{n-i}\left[\dfrac{i-np}{p(1-p)}\right]$
6. *Minimal quorum*. The group response is a (or b) if and only if at least one member's response is a (or b), and b (or a) otherwise.	$1-(1-p)^n$	$n(1-p)^{n-1}$
7. *Independent*. The group response is independent of individual responses, and is determined by an external criterion whose probability of being correct is a constant C.	C	0

the response which is correct if and only if either r_1 or r_2 (or both) is correct. Thus, if R represents the *group response* of a group of two people, and r_1 and r_2 represent the individual responses, then $R_1 = r_1 r_2$ (conjunction) or $R_2 = r_1 \vee r_2$ (disjunction) are alternative possibilities for a decision about the group response.

If r_1, r_2, and r_3 represent the individual responses of a group of three people, then the possibilities for deciding the group response R are as follows:

(1) $R_1 = r_1 r_2 r_3$,
(2) $R_2 = (r_1 r_2) \vee r_3$,
(3) $R_3 = (r_1 \vee r_2) r_3$,
(4) $R_4 = r_1 \vee r_2 \vee r_3$,

plus all other combinations obtained by permuting subscripts of the individual responses r_i.

We shall assume the following basic relations to hold with respect to group decisions. We have the two *distributive* relations

(D1) $(a \vee b) c \equiv (ac) \vee (bc)$,
(D2) $(ab) \vee c \equiv (a \vee c)(b \vee c)$.

Using (D1), we can rewrite (3) as

(3′) $R_3 \equiv (r_1 r_3) \vee (r_2 r_3)$,

and using (D2), we can rewrite (2) as

(2′) $R_2 \equiv (r_1 \vee r_3)(r_2 \vee r_3)$.

We also have the two *idempotent* relations

(I1) $aa \equiv a$,
(I2) $a \vee a \equiv a$,

and the *commutative* relations

(C1) $ab \equiv ba$,
(C2) $a \vee b \equiv b \vee a$.

These allow us to write any conjunction

$$R \equiv r_{k_1} r_{k_2} \cdots r_{k_n}$$

as a conjunction

$$R \equiv r_{k_{i_1}} r_{k_{i_2}} \cdots r_{k_{i_m}}$$

in which the individual conjuncts r_{k_i} appear in increasing order, $k_{i_1} \leq k_{i_2} \leq \cdots \leq k_{i_m}$, and in which no individual conjunct appears twice,

$$k_{i_1} < k_{i_2} < \cdots < k_{i_m}.$$

We also have the following relations for conjunctions:

(S1) $a \vee (ab) \equiv a$,
(S2) $a(a \vee b) \equiv a$,

which allow us to replace a disjunction of two conjunctions in which each conjunct of the first disjunct is a conjunct of the second disjunct, by the first disjunct alone. That is

$$(r_1 r_2 \cdots r_p) \vee (r_1 r_2 \cdots r_p r_{p+1} \cdots r_q) \equiv r_1 r_2 \cdots r_p.$$

Equally we can replace a conjunction of two disjunctions in which each disjunct of the first conjunct is a disjunct of the second conjunct by the first conjunct. Thus

$$(r_1 \vee r_2 \vee \cdots \vee r_p)(r_1 \vee r_2 \vee \cdots \vee r_p \vee r_{p+1} \vee \cdots \vee r_q) \equiv r_1 \vee r_2 \vee \cdots \vee r_p .$$

We define an *elementary disjunction* as a term $R \equiv r_1 \vee r_2 \vee \cdots \vee r_n$ which contains no conjunctions, and in which every disjunct occurs at most once. Similarly, an *elementary conjunction* is a term $R \equiv r_1 r_2 \cdots r_m$ in which no disjunctions appear and every conjunct appears at most once. We can assume that the individual r_i are numbered in increasing order in both an elementary disjunction and an elementary conjunction.

Let us call a *disjunctive normal form* an expression which is a disjunction of elementary conjunctions, and in which no pair of disjuncts is such that every conjunct of one is a conjunct of the other. In the same way, a *conjunctive normal form* is an expression which is a conjunction of elementary disjunctions in which no pair of conjuncts is such that every disjunct of one is a disjunct of the other.

We can define the *length* of an elementary conjunction to be the number of individual r_i it contains, and the *width* of an elementary disjunction to be the number of individual r_i it contains. Then the *length* of disjunctive normal form is the length of an elementary conjunction of minimal length of the form, and the *width* of a conjunctive normal form is the width of an elementary disjunction of minimal width of the form.

The expressions of (1), (2), (4), and (3') are disjunctive normal forms, but (3) is not. Also, the expressions of (1), (3), (4), and (2') are conjunctive normal forms, but (2) is not. The lengths and widths of these expressions are as follows:

	Length	Width
(1)	3	1
(2)	1	
(2')		2
(3)		1
(3')	2	
(4)	1	3

Every expression may be rewritten as an equivalent expression that is a disjunctive normal form by using the relations (D1), (I1), (C1), and (S1), and this disjunctive normal form is unique. Also, every expression may be rewritten as a unique conjunctive normal form by using (D2), (I2), (C2), and (S2). The uniqueness follows from the fact that two disjunctive (conjunctive) normal forms of an expression are equivalent to the same expression, and are therefore equivalent to each other — and this, taken with the following theorem, implies that they are the same.

THEOREM. *If* $R \equiv (r_{11} r_{12} \cdots r_{1n_1}) \vee (r_{21} r_{22} \cdots r_{2n_2}) \vee \cdots \vee (r_{m1} r_{m2} \cdots r_{mn_m})$ *is a disjunctive normal form of an expression for a group response R in terms of individual responses* r_{ij}, *then R is correct if and only if there exists an index i such that each of the responses* $r_{i1}, r_{i2}, \cdots, r_{in_i}$ *is correct.* Similarly, if

$$R \equiv (r_{11} \vee r_{12} \vee \cdots \vee r_{1n_1})(r_{21} \vee r_{22} \vee \cdots \vee r_{2n_2}) \cdots (r_{m1} \vee r_{m2} \vee \cdots \vee r_{mn_m})$$

is a conjunctive normal form of an expression for a group response R in terms of individual responses r_{ij}, *then R is incorrect if and only if there exists an index i such that each of the responses* $r_{i1}, r_{i2}, \cdots, r_{in_i}$ *is incorrect.*

The proof amounts simply to observing that a conjunction is correct if each conjunct is correct, and incorrect otherwise; and that a disjunction is incorrect if each disjunct is incorrect, and correct otherwise.

Now if R and S are two equivalent disjunctive normal forms and $r_{i1}r_{i2}\cdots r_{in}$ is a disjunct of R, then R is correct if each of the r_{ij} $(j = 1, \cdots, n)$ is correct. Since S is equivalent to R, S is correct if each r_{ij} $(j = 1, \cdots, n)$ is correct, and this implies that S has a disjunct $r_{k1}r_{k2} \cdots r_{km}$ such that each r_{kl} $(l = 1, \cdots, m)$ is an r_{ij} for some $j = 1, \cdots, n$. But by the same reasoning R has a disjunct $r_{p1}r_{p2} \cdots r_{pq}$ such that each r_{ps} $(s = 1, \cdots, q)$ is an r_{kl} for some $l = 1, \cdots, m$ and therefore is an r_{ij} for some $j = 1, \cdots, n$. Then, since R is a disjunctive normal form, $p = i, q = n$, and $r_{pj} = r_{ij}$ for $j = 1, \cdots, n$. Therefore each r_{ij} is an r_{kl} for some $l = 1, \cdots, m$. Thus each disjunct of R is a disjunct of S, and conversely; and this shows that R and S are the same. Similar reasoning establishes that two equivalent conjunctive normal forms are identical. Thus we have shown

THEOREM. *The disjunctive and conjunctive normal forms of a group response are unique.*

We can now define the length and width of an arbitrary group response as follows: The *length* of a group response is the length of its disjunctive normal form, and the *width* of a group response is the width of its conjunctive normal form. The length of a group response has the intuitive significance of the minimum amount of agreement that is demanded, and the width has the significance of the maximum amount of disagreement that is tolerated. It is reasonable to require of a decision scheme that it measure high in both of these characteristics.

Suppose now that we have a group of n individuals and a decision scheme R for deciding the group response in terms of the individual responses $r_1, \cdots, r_n$. If each individual response has a probability p of being correct, then in terms of R the group response has a probability $h(p)$ of being correct. What are the properties of $h(p)$? Formulating the problem in this manner allows us to benefit from some theorems proven by Shannon and Moore [2] in their analysis of circuit reliability. The evaluation of the properties of $h(p)$ adapts their results to the present problem.

If $R = R_1R_2$, then $h(p) = h_1(p)h_2(p)$; if $R = R_1 \vee R_2$, then $1 - h(p) = [1 - h_1(p)][1 - h_2(p)]$, where R_1 and R_2 are independent. We can get another, more useful method of calculating $h(p)$ as follows: Suppose R is an expression in n individual responses r_i $(i = 1, \cdots, n)$. Then we may relate the n-tuple $(r_1, r_2, \cdots, r_n)$ to the Q^n n-tuples $(q_1, q_2, \cdots, q_n)$, where for each

i $(i = 1, \cdots, n)$ we have $q_i = p$ or $q_i = 1-p$. Each of the n-tuples $(q_1, q_2, \cdots, q_n)$ may be thought of as representing the event in which r_i is correct if $q_i=p$ and is incorrect if $q_i = 1 - p$. These events are independent and exhaust all possibilities. If Q is the set of events $(q_1, q_2, \cdots, q_n)$ for which R is correct, then, since the probability of the event $(q_1, q_2, \cdots, q_n)$ is just $q_1 q_2 \cdots q_n$, we have $h(p) = \sum_Q q_1 q_2 \cdots q_n$. Let m be the number of elements q_i of $(q_1, q_2, \cdots, q_n)$ for which $q_i = p$. Then the number of elements q_i for which $q_i = 1 - p$ is $n - m$, and the probability of $(q_1, q_2, \cdots, q_n)$ is $p^m(1-p)^{n-m}$. For each m $(m = 0, 1, \cdots, n)$ let A_m be the number of events $(q_1, q_2, \cdots, q_n)$ of probability $p^m(1 - p)^{n-m}$ for which R is correct. Then

$$(A) \qquad h(p) = \sum_{m=0}^{n} A_m p^m (1 - p)^{n-m}.$$

We can reason similarly about the probability $1 - h(p)$ that R is incorrect. If $(q_1, q_2, \cdots, q_n)$ is an event in which R is incorrect, then as before, the probability of $(q_1, q_2, \cdots, q_n)$ is $p^m(1 - p)^{n-m}$, and if B_m $(m = 0, 1, \cdots, n)$ is the number of events of probability $p^m(1 - p)^{n-m}$ for which R is incorrect, then we have

$$(B) \qquad 1 - h(p) = \sum_{m=0}^{n} B_m p^m (1 - p)^{n-m}.$$

Since there are

$$\binom{n}{m} = \frac{n(n - 1) \cdots (n - m + 1)}{m!}$$

distinct events of probability $p^m(1 - p)^{n-m}$, and Q^n events in all, we have the relations

$$A_m + B_m = \binom{n}{m} \qquad (m = 0, 1, \cdots, n)$$

and

$$\sum_{m=0}^{n} (A_m + B_m) = Q^n$$

between the A_i and B_i.

If $A_l p^l (1 - p)^{n-l}$ is the first non-vanishing term of (A), then l is the least integer for which an event $(q_1, q_2, \cdots, q_n)$ with $q_i = p$ for l elements represents an event in which R is correct. Such an event is also one in which l individual responses r_i are correct, and l is the least integer with this property. Thus l is the *length* of R. In the same way, if $B_{n-w} p^{n-w}(1 - p)^w$ is the last non-vanishing term of (B), then w is the least integer for which an event $(q_1, q_2, \cdots, q_n)$ with $q_i = (1 - p)$ for w elements represents an event in which R is incorrect. Thus w is the *width* of R. From (A) and (B) it follows that $A_l p^l$ approximates $h(p)$ in the neighborhood of $p = 0$ and that $B_{n-w}(1 - p)^w$ approximates $1 - h(p)$ in the neighborhood of $p = 1$.

Let R be a decision scheme for a group G and let r_i be the response of one of the individuals of G. Fixing attention on r_i and supposing R to be expressed in disjunctive normal form, we may reduce the decision scheme

R to two decision schemes R_1 and R_2 which do not involve r_i. Suppose first that r_i is correct. Then R is correct if and only if the decision scheme R_1 is correct, where R_1 is obtained from R by deleting r_i from each disjunct in which it occurs, and by setting R_1 equivalent to the constant value "correct" if r_i occurs alone in any disjunct. Now suppose that r_i is incorrect. Then R is correct if and only if R_2 is correct, where R_2 is obtained from R by deleting from R each disjunct in which r_i occurs, and by setting R_2 equivalent to the constant value "incorrect" if r_i occurs in every disjunct of R. Let us note first that every disjunct of R_2 is a disjunct of R_1, since R_2 contains only those disjuncts of R not containing r_i, while R_1 contains all disjuncts of R with r_i deleted—and deleting r_i does not alter those disjuncts of R not containing r_i. Thus, if $h_1(p)$ is the probability of R_1, and $h_2(p)$ the probability of R_2, we have

(C) $$h_1(p) \geqq h_2(p) ,$$

since every event in which R_2 is correct is one in which R_1 is correct. If R_1 has the constant value "correct," then $h_1(p) = 1$, and if $h_2(p)$ has the constant value "incorrect," then $h_2(p) = 0$. The event in which r_i is correct is an event of probability p, and the event in which r_i is incorrect has probability $1 - p$. Thus, if $h(p)$ is the probability that R is correct, we have

(D) $$h(p) = ph_1(p) + (1 - p) h_2(p) ,$$

since $h_1(p)$ is the probability that R is correct if r_i is correct, and $h_2(p)$ is the probability that R is correct if r_i is incorrect.

Let us call a decision scheme R for a group G of n individuals a *quorum* scheme if R is correct just in case at least l individual responses are correct. Clearly, R is of length l. The polynomial function which expresses the probability that R is correct is

$$h_l(p) = \sum_{i=l}^{n} \binom{n}{i} p^i (1 - p)^{n-i} .$$

It is called a *quorum* function. If R' is any decision scheme of length l for G, then any event in which R' is correct is one in which at least l individual responses are correct. Thus this is also an event in which R is correct. Therefore, if $h(p)$ is the probability that R' is correct, we have $h(p) = h_l(p)$.

An event in which R is incorrect must be an event in which at least $n - l + 1$ individual responses are incorrect. Conversely, every event in which at least $n - l + 1$ responses are incorrect is an event in which R is incorrect. Thus R is of width $w = n - l + 1$, and for every other decision scheme R' of width w, if $1 - h(p)$ is the probability that R' is incorrect, we have $1 - h(p) \leqq 1 - h_l(p)$, since every event in which R' is incorrect is one in which at least $w = n - l + 1$ responses are incorrect, and hence is an event in which R is incorrect. This inequality may be rewritten as follows: $h_l(p) \leqq h(p)$.

Given two quorum functions $h_l(p)$ and $h_{l'}(p)$, with $l < l'$, corresponding to quorum schemes R and R', respectively, every event in which R' is correct is one in which R is correct, but not conversely. Thus

(E) $$0 = h_{n+1}(p) \leqq h_n(p) \leqq \cdots \leqq h_1(p) \leqq h_0(p) = 1$$

with equality only for $p = 0$ and $p = 1$.

Suppose now that $h_{l,n}(p)$ is the probability function of a quorum scheme R of length l on n individuals. Then we have from (D)

$$h_{l,n}(p) = ph_{l-1,n-1}(p) + (1 - p)h_{l,n-1}(p) \, ,$$

since $h_{l-1,n-1}(p)$ is the probability that R is correct, given that a fixed one of the individual responses is correct, and this is just the probability that a quorum scheme of length $l - 1$ on the remaining $n - 1$ individuals is correct. Similarly, $h_{l,n-1}(p)$ represents the probability that R is correct, given that some fixed individual response is incorrect, and this is the probability that a decision scheme of length l on the remaining $n - 1$ individuals is correct. We can rewrite the equation as follows:

$$h_{l,n}(p) = p[h_{l-1,n-1}(p) - h_{l,n-1}(p)] + h_{l,n-1}(p) \, ,$$

and since the bracketed expression is positive except for $p = 0, 1$, we have $h_{l,n}(p) \geqq h_{l,n-1}(p)$, with equality only if $p = 0, 1$. Rewriting the equation as

$$h_{l,n}(p) = (1 - p)[h_{l,n-1}(p) - h_{l-1,n-1}(p)] + h_{l-1,n-1}(p)$$

leads to $h_{l,n}(p) \leqq h_{l-1,n-1}(p)$, with equality only for $p = 0, 1$, since now the bracketed expression is negative for $p \neq 0, 1$. Thus we have

(F) $$h_{l,n-1}(p) \leqq h_{l,n}(p) \leqq h_{l-1,n-1}(p) \, ,$$

with equality only for $p = 0, 1$.

It follows then that quorum functions form a 'Pascal's triangle:[1]

$$0 = h_{10} \leqq h_{00} = 1$$

$$0 = h_{21} \leqq h_{11} \leqq h_{01} = 1$$

$$0 = h_{32} \leqq h_{22} \leqq h_{12} \leqq h_{02} = 1$$

$$0 = h_{43} \leqq h_{33} \leqq h_{23} \leqq h_{13} \leqq h_{03} = 1$$

while their graphs against p are given in figure 2.

We have shown that if $h(p)$ is the probability function for a scheme of length l and width w on n individuals, then $h_{l,n}(p) \leqq h(p) \leqq h_{n-w+1,n}(p)$. That is, $h(p)$ is bounded below by the quorum scheme of length l on n individuals, and bounded above by the quorum scheme of width w, or of length $n - w + 1$. It is a corollary that we must have $l + w = n + 1$ for any scheme of length l and width w on n individuals, with equality if and only if the scheme is a quorum scheme.[2]

---

[1] If h is a quorum function and h_r and h_l are the two quorum functions above in the triangle to the right and left, respectively, then $h = ph_r + (1 - p)h_l$.

[2] Thus, the result in theorem 3 of Shannon and Moore does not apply to decision schemes.

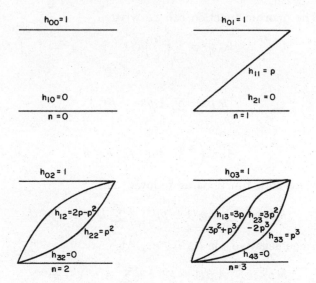

FIG. 2. Quorum functions $h_{ij}(p)$ for $n = 0, 1, 2,$ and 3.

It is clear that all decision functions $h(p)$ shown in table 1 can be written in the form

$$h(p) = \sum_{i=l}^{n} \binom{n}{i} p^{i}(1 - p)^{n-i} \, ,$$

where l is the length of the decision scheme and $n - l + 1$ its width. For instance, decision scheme 1 (dictatorship) may be written as

$$h_d(p) = \sum_{i=l}^{n} \binom{n}{i} p^{i}(1 - p)^{n-i} \, ,$$

where $n = i = 1$. Unanimity may be written as

$$h_u(p) = \sum_{i=l}^{n} \binom{n}{i} p^{i}(1 - p)^{n-i} \, ,$$

where $n = i = l$. It remains to show now that the quorum scheme has a function with a greater slope than any other scheme. Theorem 2 of Shannon and Moore is directly applicable to decision schemes.

THEOREM. *If the h curve for any quorum function involving a group of n members, say $h_Q(p)$, crosses the h curve of any other decision scheme of a group of n members, say $h(p)$, then at the point of crossing p_0, the quorum function has the greater slope, and*

$$h(p) > h_Q(p) \qquad (0 < p < p_0) \, ,$$
$$h(p) < h_Q(p) \qquad (p_0 < p < 1) \, .$$

Thus, in a reasonable sense, the quorum functions give the best increase in reliability.

PROOF. The quorum function can be written

$$h_Q(p) = \sum_{i=l}^{n} \binom{n}{i} p^i (1-p)^{n-i} ,$$

while

$$h(p) = \sum_{i=0}^{n} A_i p^i (1-p)^{n-i}$$

and

$$A_i \leq \binom{n}{i} \quad \text{for} \quad l \leq i \leq n .$$

We can rewrite both functions as follows:

$$h_Q(p) = \sum_{i=l}^{n} A_i p^i (1-p)^{n-i} + \sum_{i=l}^{n} D_i p^i (1-p)^{n-i}$$

with the D_i non-negative for $l \leq i \leq n$. Also,

$$h(p) = \sum_{i=l}^{n} A_i p^i (1-p)^{n-i} + \sum_{i=0}^{l-1} A_i p^i (1-p)^{n-i} .$$

Now each term in these sums is of the form $u(p) = B_i p^i (1-p)^{n-i}$, and

$$u' = \frac{du}{dp} = B_i [i p^{i-1}(1-p)^{n-i} - (n-i)p^i(1-p)^{n-i-1}]$$

$$= B_i \left(\frac{i}{p} - \frac{n-i}{1-p} \right) p^i (1-p)^{n-i} = \frac{i - pn}{p(1-p)} u(p) .$$

Hence $u'/u = (i - pn)/[p(1-p)]$ is a monotone increasing function of i; that is, terms for larger values of i have larger values of the ratio u'/u. If we let u_Q stand for any term in the second summand of the expression for $h_Q(p)$, and u for any term in the second summand of the expression for $h(p)$, then we have $u_Q'/u_Q > u'/u$, since each term of the first summand corresponds to a greater value of i than any term of the second. There must exist a constant K such that $(u_Q'/u_Q) > K > (u'/u)$; that is, K is a lower bound for all ratios u_Q'/u_Q and an upper bound for all ratios u'/u. Hence $u_Q' > Ku_Q$, and $Ku > u'$. Summing these inequalities over the terms u_Q and u, we have $\sum u_Q' > K \sum u_Q$ and $K \sum u > \sum u'$. Also

$$h_Q'(p) = \frac{d}{dp} \left(\sum_{i=l}^{n} A_i p^i (1-p)^{n-i} \right) + \sum u_Q' = C'(p) + \sum u_Q'$$

and

$$h'(p) = \frac{d}{dp} \left(\sum_{i=l}^{n} A_i p^i (1-p)^{n-i} \right) + \sum u' = C'(p) + \sum u' ,$$

where $C(p) = \sum_{i=l}^{n} A_i p^i (1-p)^{n-i}$. But if $h_Q(p_0) = h(p_0)$, then

$$h_Q(p_0) = C(p_0) + \sum u_Q(p_0) = C(p_0) + \sum u(p_0) .$$

Hence $\sum u_Q(p_0) = \sum u(p_0)$ and $\sum u_Q'(p_0) > K \sum u_Q(p_0) = K \sum u(p_0) > \sum u'(p_0)$. Therefore

$$h'_Q(p_0) = C'(p_0) + \sum u'_Q(p_0) > C'(p_0) + \sum u'(p_0) = h'(p_0) \, ,$$

and this proves that $h'_Q(p_0) > h'(p_0)$. Thus the quorum function has the greater slope at the point of crossing. The theorem follows from the observation that since the h and h_Q curves are continuous, they can have at most one point p_0 $(0 < p_0 < 1)$ in common without contradicting the fact that at a common point the slope of the h_Q curve is greater than the slope of the h curve.

This result supports the intuitive conviction that the "best" kind of group decision is the ordinary majority vote, at least in circumstances in which each member of the group is as likely as another to make the "correct" response. For a quorum scheme is in fact just a majority vote decision.

REFERENCES

[1] BARNLUND, D. C., A comparative study of individual, majority, and group judgment, *J. Abnorm. Soc. Psychol.*, 1959, **58**, 55-60.
[2] SHANNON, C. E., and E. F. MOORE, Reliable circuits using less reliable relays, *J. Frankl. Inst.*, 1956, **262**, 191-208.
[3] THORNDIKE, R. L., The effect of discussion upon the correctness decisions, when the factor of majority influence is allowed for, *J. Soc. Psychol.*, 1938, **9**, 343-63.

22

Analysis of Social Conformity in Terms of Generalized Conditioning Models

Patrick Suppes and Madeleine Schlag-Rey,
Stanford University

1. Introduction

The claim is often made that social interaction between several persons can be analyzed within the framework of stimulus response theory. Granted a sufficiently broad definition of stimulus and response, it would be hard to find psychologists who would disagree with this thesis. The difficulty with too broad a statement is that it becomes identical with the general methodological position, commonly labeled *behaviorism*, adhered to by social psychologists and sociologists who vary widely in their theoretical orientation. The stimulus–response psychologist who wishes to replace a general methodological thesis about social behavior with a detailed scientific theory must descend from the plateau of generalities to the lower level of detailed experimentation. This paper is the record of one such descent.

The analysis of social conformity in situations requiring the expression of a perceptual judgment has become a familiar paradigm for testing social psychological theory. The experiment we report in this paper is in this tradition. It builds directly on the earlier work of Sherif [11], Asch [1], Cohen [4], and Suppes and Krasne [13]. The theoretical ideas developed here are related to those set forth in Suppes and Atkinson [12, ch. 12]. Research that is related but less relevant to ours is to be found in Deutsch and Gerard [5], Flament [8], [9], and Di Vesta [6].

It is pertinent to review briefly the main ideas leading up to the present study. The great merit of Sherif was to consider the processes of social influence on a scale of behavior more elementary than that of attitudes or opinions. In introducing the study of simple perceptive judgments, he made the processes of social influence accessible to experimentation. Persuaded that the effects of social interaction on perceptual judgment would be

This research was supported by the Rockefeller Foundation and by the Group Psychology Branch of the Office of Naval Research under Contract NR 171-064 with Stanford University.

greatest when the object to be judged has little structure, Sherif utilized the ambiguous autokinetic effect. This effect consists of the illusion of movement of a fixed point of light surrounded by total darkness.

Asch's studies, on the other hand, have demonstrated that social pressure is equally capable of affecting perceptual judgment when it is applied to a situation whose perceptual elements are perfectly structured and non-ambiguous. It will be recalled that Asch's studies consisted of asking subjects to judge the relative length of lines after judgments of the same kind had been made by seven other subjects who were in reality accomplices of the experimenter. He found that the true subjects, that is, the last ones to make a judgment, showed a marked tendency to conform to the judgment of the majority, even when it did not agree with the true perceptual situation. However, not all subjects conformed to the judgment of the majority; he observed rather wide individual differences in this respect.

The temporal or dynamic aspects of the process of social influence have been examined by Asch [2] and Cohen [4]. Asch found little systematic tendency—probably for two reasons. In the first place his experiment consisted only of 18 trials; secondly, there was considerable variation in the perceptual situation from trial to trial. Cohen made all his trials identical and increased the number to 36. He analyzed his experiment in terms of a model consisting of a Markov chain with four states. Two of the states are transient and two are absorbing. There is a transient and absorbing state of nonconformity and a transient and absorbing state of conformity. The most obvious prediction of this model is that ultimately all subjects will be making either completely conforming responses or responses which are completely correct perceptually. Unfortunately, the number of trials selected by Cohen was not sufficient to obtain this behavior, and it is perhaps an open question whether or not this fundamental property of his model can actually be verified in an experimental situation of the Asch-type.

As far as we know, the first experiment having an adequate number of trials in the study of social conformity is that of Suppes and Krasne [13]; they ran each subject for 250 trials. However, the experimental conditions they used do not permit a direct comparison with the results of Asch and Cohen. The experiment of Suppes and Krasne, like the original Asch experiment, is concerned with perceptual judgment of parallel lines of unequal length, some vertical, some horizontal. The subject is asked to indicate the longer of two lines. As for certain subjects in the original experiment of Sherif, the social pressure is exerted *after* each individual has given his response. This pressure is exercised by the experimenter, who announces the correct judgment at the end of each trial. As in the case of the response of the majority in the Asch experiment, the result announced by the experimenter is in reality erroneous on certain trials. Operating within the framework of stimulus-sampling theory, Suppes and Krasne postulate two kinds of reinforcement on each trial. One kind is the social reinforcement provided directly by the experimenter at the end of each trial. The other is the perceptual reinforcement, not directly observable, which reinforces the response that the subject perceives as correct. The basis of this second reinforcement is secondary reinforcement from habitual perceptual discrimination made by subjects outside the experimental situation and prior to the experiment.

Suppes and Krasne use a one-element stimulus-sampling model familiar from the literature [3], [7], [12]. To handle the two kinds of reinforcement defined above, they postulate that on each trial one of three mutually exclusive and exhaustive conditions obtains: (1) The social reinforcement is effective; (2) the perceptual reinforcement is effective; and (3) neither reinforcement is effective. The probabilities of the social reinforcement or the perceptual reinforcement being effective are two parameters estimated from the response data.

The results of the experiment of Suppes and Krasne demonstrate that the presence of the majority is not necessary in order to influence individual responses, even when the perceptual judgment is easy. Because the social pressure exerted by the experimenter is exerted after the subject makes his response and because he is not a peer of the subjects, a direct comparison with the results of Asch and Cohen is not possible. In a certain sense, their experiment is related to the work of Janis, Hovland, and Kelley [10], who have studied the influence of "experts" in the transmission of information. In the experiment of Suppes and Krasne the experimenter plays the role of such an expert. The estimation of the parameters of conditioning—θ_I for the perceptual reinforcement and θ_G for the social reinforcement—confirm that the greater the perceptual ambiguity of the situation the greater the effectiveness of social influence. They observe that the ratio θ_I/θ_G is always smaller when the perceptual discrimination is more difficult. An advantage of the theoretical approach of Suppes and Krasne is that they assimilate the effects of social influence into a general theory of behavior. On the other hand, the quantitative agreement between their empirical results and theoretical predictions is not as exact as one would like. The discrepancies that exist in their study have partly inspired the present research. As will be discussed shortly, we introduce in this paper a wider class of models in order to attempt to account for detailed sequential properties of the data. In all likelihood, these models would also provide a better account of the data of Suppes and Krasne.

1.1 Aim of Our Research. Several questions do not seem to be adequately answered by the studies we have reviewed. The two principal questions we have considered are the following.

First, how and to what extent are the responses of an individual faced with making a perceptual judgment influenced by the knowledge of responses given by another individual, when

(a) the discrimination is easy;
(b) the discrimination is objectively impossible;

(c) the social information is communicated *before* the subject responds;

(d) the social information is communicated *after* the subject responds?

Secondly, is the relation between the ambiguity of the perceptual stimuli and the effect of social information the same according to whether this information is communicated before or after the response of the subject? To permit an exact study of the simple knowledge of responses given by another individual we have attempted to minimize the social factors utilized by Asch, Cohen, and Suppes and Krasne. Our experiment was conducted with pairs of subjects who were each other's peers. We have utilized neither the effect of a majority nor the prestige of an expert. Our objective has been to develop models to analyze such simple dyadic situations in terms of the general concepts of stimulus sampling and conditioning.

2. Method

In order to realize the objectives of this study, we have used an experimental situation in which the subjects are given a long sequence of trials demanding perceptual judgments. Each subject received 320 trials in approximately 43 minutes. The duration from the beginning of one trial to the next was eight seconds. The subjects were asked to judge and respond accordingly as to which of two lights illuminated at the same instant extinguished first.

In one experimental condition the interval of time separating the extinction of the two lights was sufficiently great for the probability of response to be .933 in the absence of social influence. This condition is analogous to that of Asch.

In the other experimental condition there was no actual interval of time between the extinction of the two lights, which makes an objective judgment as to which light extinguished first impossible. This condition is analogous to that of Sherif.

Two subjects participated together in a given experimental session. The experiment was presented to them as a test of perception. The instructions which they received were designed to convince them that their simultaneous participation was determined by budgetary rather than scientific considerations and that the information which they received from each other was only given in order to indicate to each when he ought to respond.

The subjects were isolated from one another but both saw the same stimuli; that is, both saw the same pair of lights.

On each trial each subject was told that his response was communicated to the other by a small light on the apparatus of his neighbor. The information actually received by the other was in reality controlled by the experimenter. The assertion that each subject was receiving information as to the response of his neighbor in order to permit proper functioning of the apparatus was challenged by no subject.

As stated, the subjects always responded in the same order. Subject A, who responded first and received after his own response information concerning the response of his neighbor, was in an experimental condition corresponding to that of Sherif and of Suppes and Krasne. The other subject, B, replied after seeing on his apparatus which response subject A made. The experimental condition for the B subjects corresponded to the experimental condition of Asch.

The combination of the two scales of difficulty of judgment ($\delta = .9$ and $\delta = .5$) and the two conditions for receiving information before or after responding determined four experimental conditions: A.9, B.9, A.5, B.5.

2.1 Choice of Subjects. The population from which voluntary subjects were recruited consisted of classes of rhetoric from five secondary schools, public and private, in Liège, Belgium. All subjects were male and between the ages of 17 and 19. All were in the last year of the secondary school. One hundred and two subjects participated in the main body of the experiment and 15 other subjects took part in the preliminary psychophysical studies. The experimental results for 76 subjects of the 102, with 19 subjects in each of the four experimental groups, are reported here. The elimination of 26 subjects was due solely to malfunction of the equipment. Each subject in the experimental group was matched with one in the three other experimental groups in order to receive exactly the same sequence of perceptual and social stimuli. This meant that when a malfunction occurred for one subject at least another pair of subjects had to be run to replace him in the grouping.

2.2 Perceptual Stimulus. We have preferred to use the judgment of the order of extinction of two lights to that of the comparison of lines projected on a screen (Asch, Cohen, and Suppes and Krasne) for several reasons. The stimuli are extremely simple and are able to differ on a trial from one another only on a single variable, the order of their extinction. This avoids the kind of interference possible from the diversity of orientation in space of horizontal and vertical lines as well as problems associated with the large visual field of lines projected on a screen. Secondly, the degree of ambiguity of the stimulation is easily controlled in a continuous manner by regulating the interval of extinction of the two lights. When the ambiguity is minimal, the situation is analogous to that of Asch. When the ambiguity is complete, that is, when the lights extinguish at the same time, the situation resembles the perceptual phenomena used by Sherif. An important aspect of the perceptual stimulus used is that subjects seem to be able to retain the impression that an objective discrimination is always possible. A typical comment of a subject in the situation when there was no objective difference in the extinction time of the two lights was the following: "C'était quasiment impossible à juger, sauf pour quelques essais où la différence était claire." The principal difference between this situation and that of Sherif is in the type of judgment demanded of subjects.

We preferred to consider the problem of discrimination at the moment of extinction of the lights rather than at the onset of the signal because the simultaneous illumination of the lights signalled the beginning of each trial. To avoid any possible side effects from one light being illuminated first, the simultaneous illumination of both lights at the same instant was carefully controlled. The order of extinction of the lights was programmed in advance. Each light had the same probability of extinguishing first: $P(S_1) = P(S_2) = .5$ where S_1 is the event occurring on a trial when the light designated "1" extinguishes first and S_2 is defined in a similar manner. The designation S_1 was applied to the light located on the left for half the subjects in each experimental group and to the light located on the right for the other half. For half of those sessions in which the stimulus S_1 was on the left the position of subject A was fixed as left, and similarly for half of the sessions when S_1 was on the right. The same 19 programs were used for all four experimental groups.

In the condition $\delta = .5$, the extinction of the lights was simultaneous and the designation of the stimuli as S_1 and S_2 was purely conventional. The other experimental condition, in which the psychophysical judgment without social influence would be correct approximately .9 of the time, was determined in the following manner. An approximation of δ between .90 and .95 was obtained with four subjects. An interval of .06 sec seemed a good approximation. A psychophysical study was then run with this time interval with 15 subjects for a total of 4,170 trials. The mean estimate for the group was .933; that is, the perceptually correct judgment was made on the average with that probability.

2.3 Social Stimulus. As already indicated, subjects were selected from a population relatively homogeneous as to sex, age, and education. We also tried to avoid effects from the existence of close personal relations between the members of a subject pair. Three kinds of pairs occurred in each experimental group: pairs with members from different schools, pairs with members from the same school but from different classes, and pairs with members from the same class. The number of pairs in each of these three categories (respectively 10, 18, 10) was exactly the same in the two conditions $\delta = .9$ and $\delta = .5$. This was the sole restriction on placing subjects randomly in one of the four experimental conditions. To minimize extensive discussion of the experiment by the subjects, all experimental sessions were completed in three weeks.

The response information that subjects were told they were communicating to each other was transmitted by small lights on the tables of their apparatus. This manner of communication reduced to a minimum possible variations in the manner in which they informed each other of their perceptual judgments. However, two sources of information could not be eliminated with our apparatus. First, the duration of illumination of the light indicating the response made by the other subject was determined solely by the duration of the time the other subject held down his response key. Second, the latency of the information received, whether before or after the subject's own response, depended upon the regularity of his response rhythms and of the other member of his pair.

As already indicated, the programming of the social stimuli was done completely in advance of the experiment and in no way depended upon the actual responses of the subject. Let σ_1 be the event of a subject's being shown that the other member of his pair predicted that the S_1 light extinguished first and let σ_2 be defined similarly. The experimentally controlled conditional probabilities of this information being correct were as follows:

$$P(\sigma_1 \mid S_1) = .2 \quad \text{and} \quad P(\sigma_2 \mid S_2) = .6 \ .$$

Of course, when $\delta = .5$, the designation of S_1 and S_2 events was made on an arbitrary random basis.

2.4 Experimental Equipment. The two subjects forming a pair were placed in a small nearly cubical room (2.5 m wide, 3 m long, and 2.5 m high). The walls of this room were of compressed wood of different density on each panel in order to avoid resonance. When the door was closed, the room was relatively insulated. An electric ventilator functioned continually in order to renew the air in the room; it also had the effect of creating a background of moderate but constant noise. A diagram of the room and the positions of the subjects are shown in figure 1.

The two subjects were seated and instructions were read while they were in position. They were not able to see each other because of a panel of 1.25 m which ran from the floor to the ceiling of the room. In front of

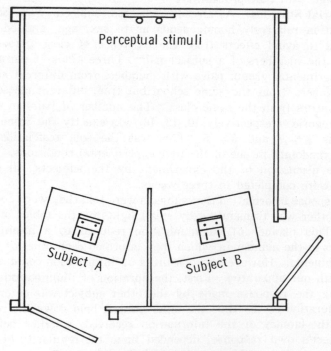

FIG. 1. Plan of the experimental room.

each subject was a table on which there was a small metallic apparatus painted gray-blue. The general shape of the apparatus resembled a portable typewriter. On the oblique plane of the apparatus were the two keys, each 7 cm in length and 1.6 cm in width, which subjects pressed to indicate their responses. The keys were painted black. They were separated from one another by a distance of 14 cm. Just beyond the keys was a small vertical panel on which there was a small neon light exactly above each key. These lights were used to inform the subject of the responses given by his neighbor. An electric light of 25 w, activated by a reduced current, was situated 1.4 m above each apparatus and served to illuminate the apparatus itself. The remainder of the room, except for the stimulus lights, was in darkness.

Two stimulus lights at the same horizontal level were on the wall of the room facing the subjects. They were two neon lights 3 cm in diameter separated from each other by 21 cm and 1.25 m from the floor, which placed them slightly below the level of the eyes of the subjects. In order to soften the image of these lights, they were covered with paper. The mean distance between the subjects and the stimulus lights was approximately 2.2 m. Because there were two subjects it was impossible to place each so that he was exactly the same distance from both lights. However, the design of the equipment as shown in figure 1 was such that there was no more than 6 cm difference in the total length of 2.2 m in the distance of each light to any subject.

The mechanical and electrical equipment containing the program of reinforcements and the record of responses was housed outside the experimental room itself.

2.5 Instructions to Subjects. The following instructions were read in French to all subjects.

Cette expérience est en réalité individuelle. Chacun de vous doit accomplir sa tâche indépendamment de l'autre et ne pas communiquer avec lui. Si l'expérience se déroule pour deux volontaires en même temps, c'est parce que le fonctionnement de l'appareil est très coûteux; en le faisant marcher pour deux personnes à la fois, nous réalisons une grande économie.

L'expérience consiste, pour chacun de vous, en une série d'épreuves successives. Au début de chaque épreuve, vous voyez les deux lampes de ce panneau central s'allumer en même temps. Ensuite, elles s'éteignent mais, chaque fois, l'une d'elles s'éteint avant l'autre. Votre tâche consiste à dire laquelle s'est éteinte la première. Pour le dire, il faut vous servir d'une des deux touches de la boîte placée devant vous: vous appuyez sur la touche gauche si c'est la lampe gauche qui s'éteint la première, sur la touche droite si c'est la lampe droite qui s'éteint la première. N'appuyez pas trop fort pour ne pas caler les touches, mais appuyez suffisamment longtemps pour que votre réponse soit bien indiquée.

(At this point the experimenter shows how to press the buttons and the subject practices pressing them.)

Pour ne pas embrouiller l'enregistrement de vos réponses, il faut que vous évitiez de répondre en même temps. Les deux petites lampes qui sont placées sur votre cadran vous permettent de savoir quand votre voisin est en train de répondre; en effet, les touches de votre voisin sont reliées à ces lampes, et l'une d'elles s'allume chaque fois que votre voisin répond. Pour ne pas embrouiller l'enregistrement, il importe aussi que vous répondiez toujours dans le même ordre. Vous qui êtes assis à gauche, vous répondrez toujours le premier. Aussi, dès que vous voyez s'éteindre une des lampes du panneau central, appuyez sur la touche correspondante, puis relâchez-la. Vous qui êtes assis à droite, dès que vous voyez sur votre écran que votre voisin a répondu, indiquez immédiatement votre propre réponse en appuyant sur la touche correspondant à la lampe que vous avez vu s'éteindre la première, ensuite relâchez-la.

Ne vous découragez pas s'il vous paraît parfois impossible de distinguer laquelle des deux lampes s'éteint la première. Certaines perceptions peuvent être correctement effectuées sans que l'on en ait conscience. C'est pourquoi vous devez donner une réponse de toute façon à chaque épreuve, même si vous n'êtes pas sûr du tout qu'elle est bonne.

Pour éviter de fatiguer votre vue, ne fixez pas tout le temps les lampes du panneau central.

Enfin, si quelque chose ne fonctionne pas bien, par exemple si les petites lampes au-dessus des touches ne s'allument pas, cessez de répondre.

3. Results

We have organized the presentation of results in the following manner. The mean learning curve and some general statistical results that do not depend on the consideration of a particular model are given first. The results of applying the one-element θ model are next indicated, and the usual difficulties of applying this model to the fine structure of the data are commented upon. We then turn to the class of models central to this paper, the generalized conditioning models of both the positional and relational sort. After defining these models, we proceed to apply them *seriatim* to each of the four experimental groups.

3.1 Mean Learning Curves. The proportions of A_1 and A_2 responses given the perceptual stimulus event S_1 or S_2 are plotted in figure 2. (The A_1 response is the prediction that stimulus event S_1 occurred.) The mean conditional proportions $P(A_2 \mid S_1)$ and $P(A_1 \mid S_2)$ are plotted in figure 2 in blocks of 40 trials. Note that these are the probabilities of incorrect responses, i.e., the probabilities of making an error in perceptual judgment. For the $\delta = .5$ groups this designation is conventional. Because $P(\sigma_2 \mid S_1) - P(\sigma_1 \mid S_2) = .4$, the spread between $P(A_2 \mid S_1)$ and $P(A_1 \mid S_2)$ is directly indicative of the mean conformity effect for each experimental group. It is quite apparent from figure 2 that this effect is most pronounced for Group B.5, the group which receives the social stimulus before making their own responses and for which an objective perceptual discrimination is impossible.

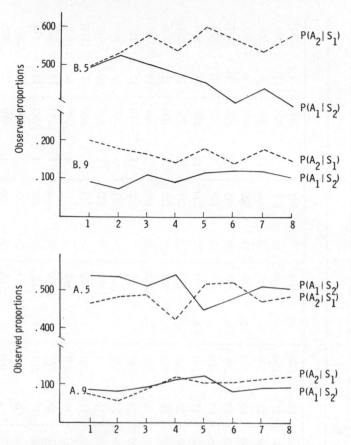

FIG. 2. Conditional proportions of A_1 and A_2 responses for all four experimental groups in blocks of 40 trials.

By comparing B.5 with A.5, and B.9 with A.9, it is also apparent from figure 2 that, independent of the difficulty of discrimination, the conformity effect is greater for the B than for the A subjects. Put another way, it is clear from figure 2 that the temporal position of the social stimulus in relation to the subjects' responses is a critical variable.

3.2 Response Dependencies. Before analyzing sequential dependencies in some detail with different models, we report at this point a rather striking difference in the $\delta = .5$ and the $\delta = .9$ groups in simple response dependency. Using the standard χ^2 test for zero-order vs. first-order Markov process in the sequence of response random variables (see [12], ch. 2), we obtained the following results. For the two $\delta = .5$ groups the zero-order vs. first-order results are highly significant. For A.5 in the test of first-order vs. second-order dependency, $\chi^2 = 9.88$, which with $2(2 - 1)^2 = 2$ df approaches significance at the .01 level. For B.5, we even approach significance at the .01 level in testing second-order vs. third-order ($\chi^2 = 13.41$, df $= 4(2 - 1)^2 = 4$).

TABLE 1

ABSOLUTE AND RELATIVE FREQUENCIES OF A_1 RESPONSES IN THE LAST 160 TRIALS FOR EACH SUBJECT AND FOR FOUR SUBSEQUENCES, GROUPS B.9 AND B.5

Subjects	$S_1\sigma_1$ .9		$S_1\sigma_1$ .5		$S_1\sigma_2$ .9		$S_1\sigma_2$ .5		$S_2\sigma_1$ .9		$S_2\sigma_1$ .5		$S_2\sigma_2$ .9		$S_2\sigma_2$ .5	
1	11	1.000	4	.364	62	1.000	15	.203	–	.000	7	.241	–	.000	7	.152
2	14	1.000	12	.667	53	.855	21	.284	4	.108	15	.577	5	.106	11	.262
3	9	.643	6	.462	52	.788	13	.200	13	.371	10	.385	18	.400	6	.107
4	14	.824	6	.333	51	.750	10	.154	13	.448	11	.306	4	.087	9	.220
5	8	.444	5	.455	26	.400	32	.500	9	.250	22	.611	5	.122	17	.347
6	14	1.000	4	.308	61	1.000	60	.800	–	.000	12	.462	–	.000	40	.870
7	13	.813	10	.714	57	.750	33	.508	4	.160	27	.730	10	.233	24	.545
8	9	.819	8	.571	45	.692	16	.246	14	.424	22	.647	18	.353	14	.298
9	12	1.000	7	.700	55	.753	32	.516	10	.345	26	.722	–	.000	21	.404
10	13	.867	9	.600	50	.862	23	.390	6	.143	22	.489	2	.044	15	.366
11	21	1.000	3	.130	60	1.000	28	.483	–	.000	5	.185	1	.019	12	.231
12	13	1.000	7	.538	48	.960	27	.587	1	.026	29	.674	–	.000	23	.397
13	11	1.000	7	.583	66	.930	31	.477	–	.000	19	.633	1	.018	29	.547
14	19	1.000	10	.476	59	.908	15	.221	1	.032	18	.621	–	.000	7	.167
15	11	.611	6	.375	48	.787	46	.767	4	.167	4	.160	4	.070	40	.678
16	24	.857	13	.591	57	.950	43	.652	–	.000	13	.464	1	.023	18	.322
17	10	1.000	2	.250	47	.758	15	.231	15	.455	9	.281	4	.073	14	.255
18	11	.786	13	.929	72	.900	33	.413	1	.034	23	.793	–	.000	13	.351
19	18	.947	20	1.000	54	.885	4	.066	–	.000	26	.929	1	.019	7	.137
$\bar{X}$		.874		.528		.838		.405		.156		.522		.082		.350
S^2		.0249		.0455		.0196		.0415		.0280		.0447		.0135		.0362

On the other hand, the results of the test of zero-order vs. first-order are not significant for either Group A.9 or B.9. For A.9, $\chi^2 = .217$, df $= 1$, $P > .50$; for B.9, $\chi^2 = .096$, df $= 1$, $P > .70$. However, if we look at the sequence of correct or incorrect responses (correct with respect to the perceptual stimulus), rather than at the sequence of A_1 or A_2 responses, dependencies are evident. The test of zero-order vs. first-order is highly significant for both groups. For A.9, $\chi^2 = 63.05$, df $= 1$, $P < .001$; for B.9, $\chi^2 = 111.50$, df $= 1$, $P < .001$. The consistency of these significance levels with the results described later for the models tested on these two groups will be evident.

3.3 Response Variance. Because, as indicated by figure 2, the effects of conformity were greater for the two B groups, we have tabulated the response variances for each subsequence $S_i\sigma_j$ in the last 160 trials. Restriction to a given subsequence $S_i\sigma_j$ entails uniformity of stimulation for the subject for that subsequence.

Another reason for selecting these subsequences is that the one-element θ model may be easily applied separately to the four subsequences. If we apply it in the form used by Suppes and Krasne [13] as described above, the two parameters of perceptual and social reinforcement, θ_I and θ_G, must be estimated from the data and thus there remain no degrees of freedom in the 2×2 response transition matrix. However, these estimates can be used to predict the variances shown in table 1. The results are given in table 2. Evidently, as shown in the third row for each group, the predicted variances are always too small. This result is of some interest because

TABLE 2

PREDICTED AND OBSERVED VARIANCES OF RESPONSES IN THE SUBSEQUENCES
$S_i\sigma_j$, LAST 160 TRIALS, GROUPS B.9 AND B.5

Quantity	Subsequence			
	$S_1\sigma_1$	$S_1\sigma_2$	$S_2\sigma_1$	$S_2\sigma_2$
B.9				
$\theta_I + \theta_G$	.793	.831	.872	.825
Predicted Variance	.0113	.0030	.0057	.0021
Observed Variance	.0249	.0196	.0280	.0135
Obs. Var./Pred. Var.	2.20	6.53	4.91	6.43
Mean No. of Trials	15.47	64.47	30.89	49.10
B.5				
$\theta_I + \theta_G$	.800	.839	.858	.866
Predicted Variance	.0241	.0051	.0104	.0062
Observed Variance	.0455	.0415	.0447	.0362
Obs. Var./Pred. Var.	1.89	8.14	4.30	5.84
Mean No. of Trials	15.05	65.11	31.68	48.16

for most of the cases reported in [12], the variance predicted by the one-element model is greater than the observed variance. We are not prepared to offer an explanation of this reversal of the usual ratio.

3.4 Definition of Generalized Conditioning Models. We now turn to the models of most direct concern in this article. These models also assume only one stimulus element but they generalize the conditioning assumptions in several directions. Their *raison d'être* is in fact the detailed study of which past events are most effective in predicting responses. The *positional* models, as we shall call them, were first introduced by Suppes and Atkinson [12], the *relational* models were introduced by us in an earlier paper [14]. Roughly speaking, in the positional models the conditioning parameters are defined in terms of positional variables like an S_1 stimulus or an S_1A_2 stimulus-response pair. (Admittedly this use of "positional" is still abstract, for the subscript 1 or 2 refers to the left lights or keys for half the subjects and right for the other half.) In the relational models, on the other hand, the conditioning parameters are defined in terms of relations between pairs or triples of perceptual or social stimuli and responses; for instance, a single parameter for the pairs $S_1\sigma_1$ and $S_2\sigma_2$, and a single parameter for the pairs $S_1\sigma_2$ and $S_2\sigma_1$.

Because of the relative complexity of the experimental situation, the notation for the various generalized conditioning models becomes somewhat cumbersome. The reader should keep in mind the central idea that in every case conditioning parameters of a certain sort are being used. We shall explicitly state the intuitive idea behind each model. We define at this point only the eight models tested on Group B.9.

The first positional model has four parameters defined as follows:

$$(1) \qquad c(i', j') = P(A_{1,n+1} \mid \sigma_{j',n+1} S_{i',n+1}) .$$

Since i' and j' each take on the value 1 or 2, we have the four parameters $c(1, 1)$, $c(1, 2)$, $c(2, 1)$, and $c(2, 2)$. If this model were to fit perfectly, it would mean that responses would be conditioned completely, even though probabilistically, to the perceptual and social stimuli on the same trial and no knowledge of earlier events such as the nature of the perceptual or social stimulus on the preceding trial (trial n) would improve prediction of response probabilities.

The other model with four parameters is a relational one. To define the parameters it is desirable to use the familiar Kronecker delta symbol:

$$\delta_{ij} = \begin{cases} 1 & \text{if } i = j , \\ 0 & \text{otherwise} . \end{cases}$$

We then define

$$(2) \qquad c(\delta_{ik}, \delta_{i'j'}) = \delta(A_{i',n+1} \mid \sigma_{j',n+1} S_{i',n+1} A_{k,n} S_{i,n}) .$$

The most interesting thing about the parameters defined by (2) is that they take into account the response on trial n and also the perceptual stimulus on that trial, as well as the perceptual and social stimuli on trial $n + 1$, and yet there are only four parameters. It is pertinent to consider the difference between these four parameters and the four of model (1). The parameters of the second model depend on the relation between the perceptual and social stimuli on trial $n + 1$, that is, the $\delta_{i'j'}$, and the relation between the perceptual stimulus and response on trial n, that is, δ_{ik}. Should this model fit perfectly it would mean that these two relationships fully determined (in a probabilistic fashion) the conditioning of responses.

It should be noticed in the tables given below that although both models (1) and (2) depend on exactly four parameters (namely, the conditional probabilities indicated), eight different predicted values of the response probability for A_1 occur for model (2) because the parameters are defined for A_i ($i = 1, 2$), whereas the parameters for model (1) are defined in terms of A_1. In the tables to follow observed data and predictions are all given for A_1.

The third model is a positional one depending on eight parameters, the perceptual stimuli on trials n and $n + 1$ and the response on trial n. If the social stimuli are important, this model should not predict responses very well.

$$(3) \qquad c(i, k, i') = P(A_{1,n+1} \mid S_{i',n+1} A_{k,n} S_{i,n}) \,.$$

For the fourth model, a relational one also with eight parameters, we need to generalize the delta notation to possible agreement or disagreement among the perceptual and social stimuli and response on a trial.

$$\gamma_{ijk} = \begin{cases} 1 & \text{if } i = j = k \,, \\ 2 & \text{if } i = j \text{ and } i \neq k \,, \\ 3 & \text{if } i = k \text{ and } i \neq j \,, \\ 4 & \text{if } j = k \text{ and } i \neq j \,. \end{cases}$$

We then define

$$(4) \qquad c(\gamma_{ijk}, \delta_{i'j'}) = P(A_{i',n+1} \mid \sigma_{j',n+1} S_{i',n+1} A_{k,n} \sigma_{j,n} S_{i,n}) \,.$$

It is clear from this definition that model (4) is defined in terms of the relation between the two stimuli on trial $n + 1$ and the relation between the two stimuli and response on trial n.

Model (5) is a mixed positional and relational model having eight parameters. It is positional with respect to trial $n + 1$ and relational with respect to trial n.

$$(5) \qquad c(\delta_{ik}, i', j') = P(A_{1,n+1} \mid \sigma_{j',n+1} S_{i',n+1} A_{k,n} S_{i,n}) \,.$$

Each of the three remaining models tested on Group B.9 involves sixteen parameters. Model (6) is purely positional, and the other two are mixed. We comment on their significance later.

$$(6) \qquad c(i, k, i', j') = P(A_{1,n+1} \mid \sigma_{j',n+1} S_{i',n+1} A_{k,n} S_{i,n}) \,,$$

TABLE 3

GROUP B.9—CONDITIONING PARAMETERS, TRANSITION PROBABILITIES, GOODNESS OF FIT OF EIGHT GENERALIZED CONDITIONING MODELS

n	$n+1$	A_1 obs.	(1) $c(i', j')$	(2) $c(\delta_{ik}, \delta_{i'j'})$	(3) $c(i, k, i')$	(4) $c(\gamma_{ijk}, \delta_{i'j'})$	(5) $c(\delta_{ik}, i', j')$	(6) $c(i, k, i', j')$	(7) $c(\delta_{ik}, j, i', j')$	(8) $c(\gamma_{ijk}, i', j')$	N
$S_1\sigma_1A_1$	$S_1\sigma_1$	.843	.874	.931	.867	.934	.897	.902	.880	.879	51
	$S_1\sigma_2$	.821	.826	.855	.867	.844	.842	.859	.824	.825	218
	$S_2\sigma_1$	.094	.140	.145	.078	.156	.118	.121	.101	.115	96
	$S_2\sigma_2$	.032	.075	.069	.078	.066	.058	.052	.065	.047	157
$S_1\sigma_1A_2$	$S_1\sigma_1$	.667	.874	.793	.717	.765	.742	.738	.742	.667	15
	$S_1\sigma_2$	.741	.826	.718	.717	.722	.727	.710	.757	.739	27
	$S_2\sigma_1$	.353	.140	.282	.227	.278	.303	.290	.368	.316	17
	$S_2\sigma_2$	.118	.075	.207	.227	.235	.188	.184	.159	.190	17
$S_1\sigma_2A_1$	$S_1\sigma_1$	.918	.874	.931	.867	.929	.897	.902	.905	.911	184
	$S_1\sigma_2$	.869	.826	.855	.867	.863	.842	.859	.849	.855	809
	$S_2\sigma_1$	.128	.140	.145	.078	.137	.118	.121	.125	.120	391
	$S_2\sigma_2$	.057	.075	.069	.078	.071	.058	.052	.055	.065	648
$S_1\sigma_2A_2$	$S_1\sigma_1$	.761	.874	.793	.717	.803	.742	.738	.741	.774	46
	$S_1\sigma_2$	.705	.826	.718	.717	.717	.727	.710	.714	.723	166
	$S_2\sigma_1$	.277	.140	.282	.227	.283	.303	.290	.279	.298	83
	$S_2\sigma_2$	.192	.075	.207	.227	.197	.188	.184	.199	.187	130
$S_2\sigma_1A_1$	$S_1\sigma_1$	.812	.874	.793	.752	.803	.742	.750	.742	.774	16
	$S_1\sigma_2$	.763	.826	.718	.752	.717	.727	.752	.757	.723	76
	$S_2\sigma_1$	.381	.140	.282	.237	.283	.303	.333	.368	.298	21
	$S_2\sigma_2$	.173	.075	.207	.237	.197	.188	.194	.159	.187	52
$S_2\sigma_1A_2$	$S_1\sigma_1$	.897	.874	.931	.839	.929	.897	.893	.880	.911	107
	$S_1\sigma_2$	.825	.826	.855	.839	.863	.842	.825	.824	.855	394
	$S_2\sigma_1$	.104	.140	.145	.085	.137	.118	.115	.101	.120	202
	$S_2\sigma_2$	.081	.075	.069	.085	.071	.058	.064	.065	.065	308
$S_2\sigma_2A_1$	$S_1\sigma_1$	.667	.874	.793	.752	.765	.742	.750	.741	.667	12
	$S_1\sigma_2$	.738	.826	.718	.752	.722	.727	.752	.714	.739	61
	$S_2\sigma_1$	.286	.140	.282	.237	.278	.303	.333	.279	.316	21
	$S_2\sigma_2$	.220	.075	.207	.237	.235	.188	.194	.199	.190	41
$S_2\sigma_2A_2$	$S_1\sigma_1$	.890	.874	.931	.839	.934	.897	.893	.905	.879	164
	$S_1\sigma_2$	.826	.826	.855	.839	.844	.842	.825	.849	.825	706
	$S_2\sigma_1$	.121	.140	.145	.085	.156	.118	.115	.125	.115	346
	$S_2\sigma_2$	.052	.075	.069	.085	.066	.058	.064	.055	.047	478
χ^2			150.38	45.60	62.11	42.73	20.78	18.37	13.66	12.00	
n			28	28	24	24	24	16	16	16	
P			$P < .001$	$P > .01$	$P < .001$	$P > .01$	$P > .60$	$P > .30$	$P > .60$	$P > .70$	

(7) $\qquad c(\delta_{ik}, j, i', j') = P(A_{1,n+1} \mid \sigma_{j',n+1} S_{i',n+1} A_{k,n} \sigma_{j,n} S_{i,n})$,

(8) $\qquad c(\gamma_{ijk}, i', j') = P(A_{1,n+1} \mid \sigma_{j',n+1} S_{i',n+1} A_{k,n} \sigma_{j,n} S_{i,n})$.

We now apply these eight models to the data for Group B.9.

3.5 Generalized Conditioning Models for Group B.9. The conditional observed proportions of A_1 responses and the predictions for the eight models are given in table 3. (The maximum likelihood estimates of the conditioning parameters for each model are easily derived by the methods given in [12, ch. 2].) The conditional proportions are given for the full sequence of events on trial n and $n + 1$ preceding the response on trial $n + 1$, and they are computed on the entire 320 trials of the experiment. Thus with 19 subjects in each group the tables are based on 6061 observations (these remarks apply as well to the tables given below for the other experimental groups). It would have been desirable to conditionalize the proportions of A_1 responses on trial $n - 1$ as well, but this would have yielded a matrix with 256 rows, which would have required an incredibly large number of observations for reliable analysis. The absolute frequencies of each row are shown in the last column of table 3 and it is apparent that some of them, with only 32 rows, are too small for the χ^2 tests we apply. However, collapsing those rows together with theoretical cell frequencies less than 10 does not appreciably affect any of our conclusions. It should also be emphasized that the goodness of fit of the models we consider is relative to the limited sequence of events given in the tables. The order tests reported above tend to support this cut-off point, but undoubtedly somewhat worse results would be obtained if data for still another trial back were included.

The three general questions we may ask for each experimental group are the following: (a) Is there a nontrivial model that accounts for the data (by "nontrivial" we mean a model that has less parameters than the number of degrees of freedom in the data)? (b) What is the minimum number of parameters needed to define such a model? (c) What kind of information is most effective in predicting responses—knowledge of the perceptual stimulus, the social stimulus, relations between these two stimuli, etc.?

The answer to the first question is provided by model (5). As shown at the bottom of table 3, the goodness-of-fit test yields a χ^2 of 20.78 with 24 df, which with $P > .60$ suggests acceptance of the null hypothesis. (For discussion of this χ^2 test, see [12, ch. 2].) Correspondingly, the answer to the second question is also provided by model (5); among the models we tested 8 is the minimum number of parameters needed to define a satisfactory model. However, there is one important methodological reservation to this conclusion (and this applies to later remarks about the other experimental groups as well). For a test based on over 6,000 observations it is unrealistic to hold Type I errors at the conventional significance level of .01 or .05. When this is done there is a strong asymmetry between Type I and Type II errors, for, with a large number of observations, the Type II error rapidly approaches zero. We have not made the detailed computations for this paper, but it may be shown that if a noncentral χ^2 test is used with model (2) as the null hypothesis, model (1) as the simple alternative and Type I and Type II errors equated, then model (2), with only 4 parameters, yields acceptable results. We shall not pursue this point in further detail, but the extreme sensitivity of χ^2 goodness-of-fit tests with 6,000 observations must be kept in mind.

We now turn to some detailed remarks about the comparison of relational and positional models for Group B.9. We note first that the poor fit of model (1) with parameters $c(i', j')$ eliminates the hypothesis of independence of the previous trial, which is a strikingly different result from that obtained by looking only at the sequence of response random variables. Secondly, of the two four-parameter models, model (2), the relational model, is very much better than model (1), a positional model, as has already been noted in the preceding paragraph. Also, model (3), which has 8 parameters and is a purely positional model, does not fit as well as model (2).

Model (4), a purely relational model with 8 parameters, has a χ^2 value that is not appreciably lower than that of model (2) with 4 parameters. The difference between the two models is that (4) takes account of the social stimulus on trial n (both take account of it on trial $n + 1$). Apparently this is not an important factor in conditioning for this experimental group.

The comparison of positional and relational models among these first four is unequivocally favorable to the relational models, which is consonant with the comparison we have reported in our earlier double-contingent study [14]. On the other hand, model (5), a mixed positional and relational model with 8 parameters, has a decisively smaller χ^2 than any of the four pure models. This model may be most directly compared with model (2). It improves on (2) by considering the actual perceptual and social stimuli on trial $n + 1$, rather than simply their agreement or disagreement.

We have delayed consideration of the third question raised above. We may begin by examining the influence of social information. In the first place we may infer from the poor fit of model (3) with parameters $c(i, k, i')$, which do not depend on the social stimulus, that the social information is important in determining the conditioning of subjects in this group.

On the other hand, there is some evidence from model (2) that social information is not as directly important in conditioning as response perseveration. The evidence is that $c(1, 0) > c(0, 1)$; i.e., the probability $c(1, 0) = .855$ of making a perceptually correct response on trial $n + 1$ when the social stimulus on trial $n + 1$ contradicted the perceptual one, is slightly greater than the probability $c(0, 1) = .793$ of making such a response when a perceptually incorrect response was made on trial n. The evidence of a similar effect in our earlier double-contingent study suggests that past responses play an important mediating role in conditioning. More detailed analysis of this role will depend on a deeper sequential analysis than we have been able to make here.

From the conditioning parameters of model (4) we may infer the perseveration of a similar conformity effect. If we examine pairs of parameters in model (4) defined for identical i, k, i', and j', and varying only on $\sigma_{j,n}$, we find that the probability of a conforming response's following a conforming response is always higher than the probability of its following a nonconforming response. Of course, these 16 inequalities for the pairs are not independent, but are determined by the 8 parameters. What is surprising is that when we ask the same question of the observed proportions in column 1 of table 3, the results are not all significant; 8 of the pairs have the inequality in one direction and the remaining 8 in the other.

Models (6)–(8) of table 3, each with 16 parameters, support a similar conclusion that the effects of the social stimulus are detectable, but are not large. Model (6), which does not take account of the social stimulus on trial n, has the worst fit of the three, but this is only comparatively, for in absolute terms its fit is quite good $(P > .30)$. It may also be noted that models (7) and (8) are mixed positional and relational models, whereas model (6) is a pure positional model.

Models (5)–(8) indicate that there is no simple answer, on the basis of our data, to the third general question we posed at the beginning of this discussion of Group B.9. The structure of the information to which subjects are conditioned in making their responses may be described in several ways. Model (5), which uses the relation between perceptual stimulus and response on trial n, and the actual perceptual and social stimuli on trial $n + 1$, gives one reasonably satisfactory answer $(P > .60)$. The relatively small net reduction of χ^2 value for model (6) over that for model (5), in spite of the addition of 8 parameters, indicates that the relational aspects on trial n are the essential thing rather than the actual perceptual stimulus and response. Models (7) and (8) show that if we add to the information of model (5) either the actual social stimulus on trial n or its relations to the perceptual stimulus and response, some gain in goodness of fit can be made.

More general comments we reserve until after analysis of the other three experimental groups.

3.6 Generalized Conditioning Models for Group A.9. The conditional observed proportions of A_1 responses and the predictions for the eight models tested for this group are given in table 4. It may be noticed immediately that the table for Group A.9 has 16 rows instead of the 32 in table 3. This is because the social stimulus occurred after rather than before the subject's response on trial $n + 1$, and consequently this event is deleted from the possible events occurring on trial $n + 1$ prior to the subject's response.

The eight models whose conditioning parameters and goodness of fit are tabulated in table 4 are defined in a manner similar to that used for defining the eight models tested on Group B.9. These definitions need not be repeated if two observations are made. First, i always refers to the perceptual stimulus on trial n and i' to the perceptual stimulus on trial $n + 1$; j refers to the social stimulus on trial n; and k to the response on trial n.

TABLE 4

GROUP A.9—EIGHT GENERALIZED CONDITIONING MODELS

n	$n+1$	A_1 obs.	(1) $c(i')$	(2) $d(\delta_{ik})$	(3) $d(\gamma_{ijk})$	(4) $d(\hat{i}, k)$	(5) $c(\gamma_{ike}')$	(6) $c(\gamma_{ijke}')$	(7) $c(\hat{i}, k, i')$	(8) $c(\gamma_{ike}', \hat{j})$	N
$S_1\sigma_1 A_1$	S_1	.916	.901	.912	.911	.915	.914	.911	.917	.916	275
	S_2	.083	.097	.088	.089	.085	.091	.088	.086	.097	264
	S_1	.806	.901	.810	.818	.798	.784	.802	.780	.785	31
	S_2	.125	.097	.190	.182	.202	.164	.167	.182	.103	24
$S_1\sigma_2 A_1$	S_1	.917	.901	.912	.912	.915	.914	.916	.917	.914	1079
	S_2	.087	.097	.088	.088	.085	.091	.092	.086	.088	1132
	S_1	.773	.901	.810	.804	.798	.784	.774	.780	.784	128
	S_2	.193	.097	.190	.196	.202	.164	.162	.182	.186	119
$S_2\sigma_1 A_1$	S_1	.907	.901	.810	.804	.822	.836	.838	.853	.897	54
	S_2	.226	.097	.190	.196	.178	.216	.226	.211	.215	62
	S_1	.896	.901	.912	.912	.908	.909	.908	.905	.903	541
	S_2	.084	.097	.088	.088	.192	.086	.084	.088	.084	523
$S_2\sigma_2 A_1$	S_1	.823	.901	.810	.818	.822	.836	.833	.853	.814	96
	S_2	.200	.097	.190	.182	.178	.216	.198	.211	.216	80
	S_1	.910	.901	.912	.911	.908	.909	.912	.905	.912	846
	S_2	.090	.097	.088	.089	.092	.086	.089	.088	.086	807
χ^2			64.29	8.19	7.92	6.90	5.30	4.62	3.82	1.85	
n			14	14	12	12	12	8	8	8	
P			$P<.001$	$P>.80$	$P>.70$	$P>.80$	$P>.90$	$P>.70$	$P>.80$	$P>.98$	

Secondly, the parameter $d(\ldots)$ used in models (2), (3) and (4) is defined as follows.

$$d = c\delta_{i'_1} + (1 - c)(1 - \delta_{i'_1}) .$$

The effect of this definition of d is to make the conditional probabilities in these three models depend on the perceptual stimulus on trial $n + 1$. We mean by this that if an S_1 occurs on trial $n + 1$ in the case, for instance, of model (2) then the conditional probability of an A_1 response is .912. If an S_2 occurs on trial $n + 1$ the conditional probability of an A_1 response is $1 - .912 = .088$.

Concerning the general questions raised at the beginning of the discussion of Group B.9, we may immediately answer the first two by referring to model (2) in table 4. We find that a model requiring only two parameters fits extremely well. What is surprising is that this relational model does not directly use any social information whatsoever, that is, the conditioning parameters of the model do not depend in any direct way on the preceding occurrence of a particular social stimulus σ_1 or σ_2.

From the comparison of model (1) and model (2) we may infer several significant facts. In the first place from the poor fit of model (1) it is clear that knowledge simply of the perceptual stimulus on trial $n + 1$ does not yield adequate predictions of responses on that trial. Secondly, model (1) is probably the simplest positional model with two parameters and model (2) the simplest relational model with two parameters. The relative comparison of fit for the two is completely favorable to the relational model.

Because of the excellent fit of model (2), which does not explicitly include the social stimulus, there is little hope of making a case for the explicit consideration of this stimulus. Model (3), which adds two additional parameters in taking account of the social stimulus on trial n, does have a slightly smaller χ^2 value than does model (2), but because of the increase in the number of parameters the actual significance level is lower, although the significance level of both models is too high to draw anything significant from this fact. In this respect the results for Group A.9 differ from those for Group B.9. As we saw in the above discussion of B.9, the direct inclusion of the social stimulus did improve the prediction of response on trial $n + 1$.

As would be expected from the excellent results shown in table 5 the consideration of additional parameters in models (6)-(8) given in table 4 is even better. The fit of the last of the three, model (8), is almost unbelievably good when one considers that the χ^2 of 1.85 is based on more than 6,000 observations. One can only conclude from results of this kind that the eight parameters of the model take account of *all* information of significance to the subjects in conditioning their responses. The detailed comparison of the conditioning parameters of this model and the observed proportions shown in the first column suggest that one can scarcely expect a model to fit data any better than does this one.

The relatively good fit of model (2) with only two parameters suggests that the answer to our third general question is that it is sufficient for Group A.9 to know the relation between the perceptual stimulus and response on trial n in order successfully to predict responses on trial $n + 1$, given that one adjusts the prediction to the occurrence of perceptual stimulus S_1 or S_2 on trial $n + 1$. This conclusion rules out any direct role for the social stimulus shown to the subject after his response on trial n.

Somewhat subtler conclusions can be obtained by moving from consideration of the goodness of fit of the models to the relative order of magnitude of the various conditioning parameters. The necessity for even these effects to be very small may be seen by comparing the observed proportions in A_1 for the pairs in which the only thing varied is the social stimulus on trial n. A very slight variation of response proportions on the members of these pairs is evident. For the two pairs having the largest number of observations, namely, the pair consisting of row 1 and row 5, the difference in observed proportions is .001 and for the other pair consisting of row 2 and row 6 the difference in observed proportions is .004. Clearly for these pairs change in the social information had no significant effect whatsoever.

This same conclusion about the relatively complete ineffectiveness of the social stimulus on trial n determining responses on trial $n + 1$ may be seen by examining the four conditioning parameters of model (3). The maximum likelihood estimates of these four parameters involve the entire 6061 observations and not simply the rows with the largest number of observations. The interesting thing to note about the four parameters of model (3) is that if the social stimulus has no effect whatsoever, then the model reduces effectively to the model with two parameters, and this is in fact very close to being the situation. When the social stimulus agrees with the perceptual stimulus and the response, the value of the parameter is .911; when the social stimulus disagrees with these two the value of the parameter is .912, a difference of only .001. When the perceptual stimulus and response disagree, if the social stimulus agrees with the perceptual stimulus, the value of the parameter is .818; when the social stimulus agrees with the response, on the other hand, the value of the parameter is .804, which is a larger difference than in the previous case but still only a matter of .014.

3.7 Generalized Conditioning Models for Group B.5. The conditional observed proportions of A_1 responses and the predictions for four models are given in table 5. The conditional proportions are given for the same sequence of events as for Group B.9 in table 3. However, only four models have been tested because the distinction between perceptual stimulus S_1 and S_2 is wholly arbitrary for group B.5. It will be recalled that experimentally this group corresponds to the condition of Sherif, since an objective perceptual discrimination is impossible.

We may begin by observing that because perceptual stimuli have no significance for this group, we would expect model (5) for B.9 to fit very poorly here although this model did very well on the data for B.9. That this is the case is evident from the data for the goodness of fit results for model (4) in table 5. The value of χ^2 is significant at the .001 level. The

TABLE 5

GROUP B.5—FOUR GENERALIZED CONDITIONING MODELS

n	$n+1$	A_1 obs.	(1) $c(k, j')$	(2) $c(\gamma_{jkj'})$	(3) $c(j, k, j')$	(4) $c(\delta_{ik}, i', j')$	N
$S_1\sigma_1 A_1$	$S_1\sigma_1$	.562	.639	.630	.642	.563	32
	$S_1\sigma_2$	.353	.446	.442	.396	.399	119
	$S_2\sigma_1$	.627	.639	.630	.642	.549	67
	$S_2\sigma_2$	.336	.446	.442	.396	.400	113
$S_1\sigma_1 A_2$	$S_1\sigma_1$	.517	.508	.519	.487	.577	29
	$S_1\sigma_2$	.490	.371	.364	.366	.425	96
	$S_2\sigma_1$	.389	.508	.519	.487	.576	54
	$S_2\sigma_2$	.391	.371	.364	.366	.393	69
$S_1\sigma_2 A_1$	$S_1\sigma_1$	.663	.639	.636	.637	.563	92
	$S_1\sigma_2$	.490	.446	.481	.475	.399	406
	$S_2\sigma_1$	.576	.639	.636	.637	.549	184
	$S_2\sigma_2$	.462	.446	.481	.475	.400	331
$S_1\sigma_2 A_2$	$S_1\sigma_1$	.507	.508	.558	.514	.577	136
	$S_1\sigma_2$	.378	.371	.370	.372	.425	596
	$S_2\sigma_1$	.520	.508	.558	.514	.576	296
	$S_2\sigma_2$	.360	.371	.370	.372	.393	417
$S_2\sigma_1 A_1$	$S_1\sigma_1$	.709	.639	.630	.642	.577	55
	$S_1\sigma_2$	.431	.446	.442	.396	.425	267
	$S_2\sigma_1$	.641	.639	.630	.642	.576	128
	$S_2\sigma_2$	.408	.446	.442	.396	.393	218
$S_2\sigma_1 A_2$	$S_1\sigma_1$	.462	.508	.519	.487	.563	52
	$S_1\sigma_2$	.327	.371	.364	.366	.399	217
	$S_2\sigma_1$	.544	.508	.519	.487˙	.549	103
	$S_2\sigma_2$	.331	.371	.364	.366	.400	145
$S_2\sigma_2 A_1$	$S_1\sigma_1$	.630	.639	.636	.637	.577	73
	$S_1\sigma_2$	.492	.446	.481	.475	.425	303
	$S_2\sigma_1$	.704	.639	.636	.637	.576	142
	$S_2\sigma_2$	.443	.446	.481	.475	.393	210
$S_2\sigma_2 A_2$	$S_1\sigma_1$	.527	.508	.558	.514	.563	110
	$S_1\sigma_2$	.364	.371	.370	.372	.399	453
	$S_2\sigma_1$	.502	.508	.558	.514	.549	209
	$S_2\sigma_2$	.389	.371	.370	.372	.400	339
	χ^2		33.77	35.89	27.50	91.05	
	n		28	28	24	24	
	P		$P > .20$	$P > .10$	$P > .20$	$P < .001$	

parameters of model (4) depend on both i and i', that is, on the two perceptual stimuli. The arbitrary assignment of values 1 or 2 to the same stimulus does not have any empirical significance, and this fact is reflected in the bad fit of the model for Group B.5.

Our second observation for this group is contrary to one we just made for group A.9. It is that model (2), a purely relational model, is somewhat inferior to model (1), a purely positional model. Both models have four parameters. The parameters of model (1) depend on the social stimulus on trial $n + 1$ and the response on trial n. The parameters of model (2) depend upon the agreement or disagreement among the social stimuli on trial n and $n + 1$, and the response on trial n. The slight difference in goodness of fit between models (1) and (2) is not interpreted as of great significance. The fact, however, that the difference is slightly in favor of the positional model is in contrast to the very sharp differential results in favor of the relational model in the case of Group A.9.

It may also be noted that model (3) yields a slight improvement over model (1), and this is indicative of the usefulness for predictive purposes of incorporating into the positional model the actual social stimulus on trial n as well as that on trial $n + 1$, which is the additional feature of model (3). In general, model (1) would seem to provide a satisfactory answer to the first two general questions we have been asking of each experimental group, namely, that it is a model with only four parameters which provides an adequate fit to the data of this experimental group.

We turn now to more detailed consideration of the role of social information for this experimental group, with particular emphasis on its relative importance. Prior to any detailed comments we would certainly expect the social stimuli to have a more important influence on responses of subjects for this group than in the two previous cases, because of the impossibility of any real perceptual discrimination for the $\delta = .5$ condition.

First, we may observe from the conditioning parameters of model (1) that the social stimulus on trial $n + 1$ is more important to the subject than the response he made on trial n, contrary to the evidence for Groups B.9 and A.9. In particular, we may note that when $k = 2$ and $j' = 1$ then the probability of an A_1 response on trial $n + 1$ is .508. In the contrary case, when $k = 1$ and $j' = 2$, that is, when response 1 is made on trial n and social stimulus 2 occurs on trial $n + 1$, then the probability of an A_1 response is .446.

The direct importance of the social stimulus on trial $n + 1$ immediately preceding the subject's response is also attested to by model (3). Examination of the conditioning parameters of this model shows that when we consider the two extreme cases of $\sigma_{1,n}A_{1,n}\sigma_{2,n+1}$ and $\sigma_{2,n}A_{2,n}\sigma_{1,n+1}$, in the first case the probability of an A_1 response is .396 and in the second case, the probability is .514. This would seem to show the clear dominance of the social stimulus on trial $n + 1$ over the preceding response or preceding social stimulus. This same fact is reflected in the relationally defined

parameters of model (2).   In the first place, there is small difference between the probability of an A_1 response in model (2) when, on the one
hand, the social stimulus on trial $n + 1$ and the response on trial n agree
with the social stimulus on trial n and when, on the other hand, these
first two events disagree with the social stimulus on trial n.   In the first
case, the probability of an A_1 response is .630 and in the second case,
.636.   The difference of .006 leaves little room for the effect of the social
stimulus on trial n to be evident.   The other two parameters also reflect the
importance of the social stimulus on trial $n + 1$.   When the response and
social stimulus on trial n are both 1 but the social stimulus is 2 on
trial $n + 1$, the probability of an A_1 response is then .442.   When the two
social stimuli are 1 on both trial n and $n + 1$ and the response on trial n
is 2 the probability of an A_1 response is .519, indicating again that the
social stimulus on $n + 1$ is more important than the response on trial n.

To summarize, the analysis of conditioning parameters for the three
models that fit reasonably well, that is, models (1)–(3), indicates that the
order of importance of information is as follows.   The most important information is the social stimulus on trial $n + 1$; the next most important
is the actual response made on trial n; and least important of the three is
the social stimulus on trial n.   Secondly, the relative goodness of fit of the
three models indicates that in this case the positional information is more
important than the relational information (in using the phrase "more important" we mean, of course, important for predicting correctly the probability of an A_1 response).

It should be remarked of model (3) that it actually tests only the goodness of our experimental design, for it takes account of all objectively
observable events occurring on trials n and $n + 1$ prior to a response on
trial $n + 1$.   This observation does not invalidate the importance of this
model for the analysis of the relative significance of social information
for the subjects, as reflected in its parameters.

3.8 Generalized Conditioning Models for Group A.5.   The conditional observed proportions of A_1 responses and the predictions for five models are
given in table 6.   The conditional proportions are given for the same
sequence of events as for Group A.9 in table 4.   But as in the case of
Group B.5, the first four models tested have not utilized the artificial distinction between perceptual stimuli S_1 and S_2.   Model (5), which does utilize
this distinction, has been included only for direct comparison with the results
for Group A.9.

As in the case of Group A.9 it is clear that the social stimulus' coming
after the subject's response does not have the importance that it has
for the two groups in which it comes prior to that response.   This is
clearly indicated by comparison of models (1) and (2) in table 6, both of
which are positional models.   Each has two parameters.   Model (1) takes
account of the social stimulus on trial n, and model (2) takes account of
the response on trial n.   Once again, we find the mediating role of the

TABLE 6

GROUP A.5—FIVE GENERALIZED CONDITIONING MODELS

n	$n+1$	A_1 obs.	(1) $c(j)$	(2) $c(k)$	(3) $c(\delta_{jk})$	(4) $c(j, k)$	(5) $c(\gamma_{ijki'})$	N
$S_1\sigma_1A_1$	S_1	.523	.491	.552	.522	.527	.541	149
	S_2	.470	.491	.552	.522	.527	.515	151
	S_1	.419	.491	.472	.441	.451	.437	124
	S_2	.461	.491	.472	.441	.451	.469	154
$S_1\sigma_2A_1$	S_1	.555	.522	.552	.559	.562	.544	607
	S_2	.559	.522	.552	.559	.562	.550	662
	S_1	.509	.522	.472	.478	.480	.479	625
	S_2	.472	.522	.472	.478	.480	.450	566
$S_2\sigma_1A_1$	S_1	.527	.491	.552	.522	.527	.531	315
	S_2	.556	.491	.552	.522	.527	.563	315
	S_1	.461	.491	.472	.441	.451	.485	280
	S_2	.450	.491	.472	.441	.451	.459	278
$S_2\sigma_2A_1$	S_1	.576	.522	.552	.559	.562	.550	460
	S_2	.563	.522	.552	.559	.562	.521	453
	S_1	.462	.522	.472	.478	.480	.450	478
	S_2	.471	.522	.472	.478	.480	.456	444
	χ^2		46.49	12.65	7.84	7.26	11.45	
	n		14	14	14	12	8	
	P		$P < .001$	$P > .50$	$P > .85$	$P > .80$	$P > .10$	

previous response to be an important and an excellent predictor of the next response. Model (1) is significant at beyond the .001 level, whereas the fit of model (2) is excellent ($P > .50$).

The fit of the positional model (2), however, is improved upon in a still significant manner by the purely relational model (3), which takes account of the agreement or disagreement between the social stimulus and response on trial n. The goodness of fit of model (3) could hardly be better ($P > .85$). In fact, model (4), which takes account of the actual social stimulus and response on trial n, and therefore has four parameters, does not fit any better. The actual value of the χ^2 shows only a very slight difference between models (3) and (4), and the addition of two more parameters to model (4) renders its significance level slightly worse than that of model (3). It may be noted that model (4), like model (3) in table 5, actually tests only the experimental design, for it takes account of all observable events occurring on trials n and $n + 1$.

Model (5) has been included because it fits the data of Group A.9 extremely well (it is model (6) in table 4). It is evident that it does not do nearly as well in the present case, for which the distinction between the perceptual stimuli is wholly artificial ($P > .10$ in comparison to $P > .70$ in the former case).

Model (2) with only two parameters provides an adequate answer to the two general questions raised at the beginning of our discussion of the experimental groups. Concerning the third question regarding the most important information, the remarks that have just been made about the various models outline the situation. Because of the importance of this question, we may describe our conclusions as follows. In the first place, knowledge of the social stimulus by itself does not provide adequate information to predict responses, even though the perceptual stimuli are actually wholly neutral. This is shown by the poor fit of model (1). Secondly, the social stimulus is decidedly less important in predicting responses than the actual preceding response. This is shown by the good fit of model (2). Thirdly, the social stimulus does have some effect when considered in relation with the actual response. This is shown by the excellent fit of model (3) and a consideration of the actual parameter values of this model. We note that when the past response and social stimulus both agree (and σ_1 occurred) the probability of an A_1 response is .522 whereas when they disagreed and σ_2 occurred the probability of an A_1 response is .559. The paradoxical thing, of course, about this result is that the probability of an A_1 response goes up when the preceding response was an A_1 and the preceding social stimulus was different, namely, σ_2. A difference of .037 in these two parameter values provides some evidence for a kind of negative recency effect for this experimental group. It would be interesting to know if this kind of negative recency effect could be shown to increase with consideration of longer sequences of past information. We have not analyzed our own data from this standpoint. The present effect does show that social conformity in the direct sense is not playing a major role at all in the responses of the subjects in this group. It can be claimed in terms of the conditioning parameters of model (3) that there is a slight tendency of the subjects to "anticonform."

3.9 General Conclusions. From the many detailed remarks about the four experimental groups, we extract four conclusions that we believe are of general importance. First, the information provided by the social stimulus is relevant for three of the groups, and is essentially irrelevant for one of the groups, namely, A.9. Second, the temporal position of the social stimulus is of crucial importance. The effect of the social stimulus is much greater when it precedes than when it follows a response. When the social stimulus follows the response its effect on the next trial's response is not as great as in those situations when it immediately precedes the response on the same trial. As far as we know, the present experiment is the first to establish this conclusion with a uniform treatment of both kinds of experimental groups. As we noted in the introduction, previous studies of social conformity have been made under one of these two conditions regarding the position of the social stimulus. Third, the difficulty of the perceptual judgment crucially affects the use of the social information. For the B Groups, this is shown for instance by the good fit for B.9 of the model with parameters $c(\delta_{ik}, i', j')$ and the bad fit of the same model for B.5. In the case of the A Groups, this is shown by the good fit for A.9 and bad fit for A.5 of the model with parameters $c(\delta_{ijki'})$. Fourth, the temporal position of the social stimulus is more important than the difficulty of the perceptual judgment in evaluating the role of social information. Perhaps the best evidence of this conclusion is the relatively unimportant role of the social stimulus for both of the A Groups as compared with the B Groups. The detailed analysis above of the efficacy of using the social information to predict responses substantiates this conclusion.

There is a meta-conclusion we want to mention as a postscript. Neither much of the detailed analysis for the various experimental groups nor the general conclusions given above follow from a consideration of the mean learning curves. Almost everything of significance we have inferred from the data has been obtained by use of detailed sequential analysis in terms of the generalized conditioning models. Because of their ability to identify the events affecting behavior, we believe that these models have a useful role to play in further studies of social interaction. Their application to more complicated conformity situations is reasonably straightforward. It would be particularly interesting to extend the present studies to conformity studies involving more than two persons with particular attention to the elaboration of various combinations of positions for the social information passing from one participant to another.

References

[1] Asch, S. E., Effects of group pressure upon the modification and distortion of judgments, chap. 12 in *Group Dynamics*, D. Cartwright and A. Zander, eds., London: Tavistock, 1953.

[2] Asch, S. E., Studies of independence and conformity. I. A minority of one against a unanimous majority, *Psychol. Monog.*, 1956, No. 9.

[3] Atkinson, R. C., and P. Suppes, An analysis of two-person game situations in terms of statistical learning theory, *J. Exptl. Psychol.*, 1958, **55**, 369-78.

[4] Cohen, B. P., A probability model for conformity, *Sociometry*, 1958, **21**, 69-81.

[5] Deutsch, M., and H. B. Gerard, A study of normative and informational social influences upon individual judgment, *J. Abnorm. Soc. Psychol.*, 1955, **51**, 629-36.

[6] Di Vesta, F. J., Effects of confidence and motivation on susceptibility to informational social influence, *J. Abnorm. Soc. Psychol.*, 1959, **59**(2), 204-9.

[7] Estes, W. K., Component and pattern models with Markovian interpretations, chap. 1 in *Studies in Mathematical Learning Theory*, R. R. Bush and W. K. Estes, eds., Stanford, Calif.: Stanford Univ. Press, 1959.

[8] Flament, C., Ambiguité du stimulus, incertitude de la réponse et processus d'influence sociale, *Année Psychol.*, 1959, **1**, 73-92.

[9] Flament, C., Modèle stratégique des processus d'influence sociale sur les jugements perceptifs, *Psychol. Française*, 1959, **2**, 91-101.

[10] JANIS, I. L., G. I. HOVLAND, and H. H. KELLEY, *Communication and Persuasion*, New Haven: Yale Univ. Press, 1953.

[11] SHERIF, M., A study of some social factors in perception, *Arch. Psychol.*, 1935, No. 187.

[12] SUPPES, P., and R. C. ATKINSON, *Markov Learning Models for Multiperson Interactions*, Stanford, Calif.: Stanford Univ. Press, 1960.

[13] SUPPES, P., and F. KRASNE, Application of stimulus sampling theory to situations involving social pressure, *Psychol. Rev.*, 1961, **68**(1), 46-49.

[14] SUPPES, P., and M. SCHLAG-REY, Test of some learning models for double contingent reinforcement, *Psychol. Reports*, 1962, **10**, 259-68.